Environmental Economics and Natural Resource Management in Developing Countries

Edited by Mohan Munasinghe

Compiled by Adelaida Schwab

Committee of International Development Institutions on the Environment (CIDIE)

Distributed for CIDIE
by
The World Bank
Washington, D.C.

Copyright © 1993
The International Bank for Reconstruction
and Development/The World Bank
1818 H Street, N.W.
Washington, D.C. 20433 U.S.A.

ISBN 0-8213-2670-8

Committee of International Development Institutions on the Environment (CIDIE)

CIDIE was established in 1980, and consists of 17 multinational organizations active in the field of economic development. The membership of each such institution is composed of governments rather than private or nongovernmental organizations.

CIDIE serves as an inter-institutional mechanism which promotes dialogue among members, helps them pool knowledge and information, facilitates discussion of common environmental issues and identification of cooperative strategies to address these issues, and improves communications with other interested agencies and organizations.

The current membership includes:

- African Development Bank (ADB)
- Arab Bank for Economic Development in Africa (BADEA)
- Asian Development Bank (AsDB)
- Caribbean Development Bank (CDB)
- Central American Bank for Economic Integration (CABEI)
- Commission of the European Communities (CEC)
- European Bank for Reconstruction & Development (EBRD)
- European Investment Bank (EIB)
- Food and Agriculture Organization of the UN (FAO)
- Inter-American Development Bank (IDB)
- International Fund for Agricultural Development (IFAD)
- Nordic Investment Bank (NIB)
- Organization of American States (OAS)
- United Nations Development Programme (UNDP)
- United Nations Environment Programme (UNEP)
- World Bank Group (WB)
- World Food Programme (WFP)

Contents

Foreword

The decade of the 1980s has witnessed a fundamental change in the way governments and development agencies think about the environment and development. The two are no longer regarded as mutually exclusive. It is now recognized that a healthy environment is essential to sustainable development and a healthy economy. Moreover, economists and planners are beginning to recognize that economic development which erodes natural capital is often not successful. In fact, development strategies and programs which do not take adequate account of the state of critical resources—forests, soils, grasslands, freshwater, coastal areas and fisheries—may degrade the resource base upon which future growth is dependent.

Since its inception in 1980, the Committee of International Development Institutions on the Environment (CIDIE), now up to 17 members, has played a key role in coordinating work and facilitating information exchange on the full range of sustainable development issues. This volume provides ample evidence of progress made by the group in the area of environmental economics—which is a vital prerequisite to help incorporate environmental concerns into development decisionmaking. I am sure that the results of the workshop presented here are a significant step forward in the search for sustainable development options and, therefore, will be most helpful to the work of all CIDIE member institutions, as well as others in the development community.

Mohamed T. El-Ashry
Chief Environmental Adviser
to the President and
Director of Environment
The World Bank

Introduction

At the CIDIE Annual Meeting of April 29-May 1, 1991 in Washington, D.C., a statement was issued on behalf of the heads of member organizations which endorsed the principles of CIDIE, called for a global partnership involving greater collaboration among CIDIE members and other organizations, and urged CIDIE members to promote an active collaborative program.

CIDIE Conference on Environmental Economics

As a response to this communique, CIDIE launched a series of cooperative activities, the first of which was the Conference on Environmental Economics and Natural Resource Management in Developing Countries, organized by the World Bank in January 1992. The contents of this volume are based on the conference deliberations (see Appendix for full list of participants).

This meeting proved to be most successful, not only as a means of exchanging the latest information on environmental economics among members, but also stimulating ideas for new initiatives. In view of the high priority accorded to the subject matter, and the need to disseminate the material as rapidly and widely as possible, the World Bank was requested to put together this monograph on behalf of CIDIE. A second follow-up meeting focused more on macroeconomic-environmental linkages was held in February 1993 in Washington, D.C.

Outline of volume

The first three papers in this volume are broad in scope, covering topics ranging from environmental economics, valuation and scope for application (as a step towards sustainable development), to poverty, population, and environment linkages.

The paper by Abaza (United Nations Environment Programme) examines the appraisal methodology for sustainable development projects. Background information is discussed, as well as the advantages and drawbacks of different kinds of analyses (technical, social, financial, institutional, environmental, and economic).

Munasinghe and Lutz (World Bank) describe the role of environmental economics in development decisionmaking. The paper briefly reviews the analytical background, including the concepts of economic valuation of environmental assets, as well as the practical techniques of determining such values. A number of case studies that illustrate the application of various valuation techniques in developing countries are described, and directions for future work are summarized.

The special invited paper by Dasgupta (Cambridge University) examines the linkage between family size and environmental degradation (for example, vanishing sources of water, and reducing sources of fodder and household fuel) for poor rural households. There are different motivations for parents to want many children; among the more common arguments are that children are desirable in themselves to carry on the family lineage and that they serve as security for old age. In poor countries, a third motivation may be that children are useful as income-earning assets. They are needed on a daily basis for the household to survive. If this third motivation is important, a different set of government policies may be needed in order to manage population growth.

The next four papers describe specific applications of economic valuation techniques in a variety of projects.

Darling, Gomez, and Niklitschek (Inter-American Development Bank) present a case study of a public sewage system on a Caribbean island, with the objective of evaluating the economic feasibility of the construction of such a system. The methodology used is contingent valuation, with risk analysis (through the calculation of ranges for all benefits). It is then possible to determine how sensitive the project is to different assumptions, and to estimate the expected costs of making the wrong decision.

The paper by Markandya and Muñoz (African Development Bank) addresses the experience of the African Development Bank in environmental economics and natural resource management. The role of cost-benefit analysis is examined, as well as different techniques for monetary valuation. Thereafter, they review the environmental issues in a number of African Development Bank projects and conclude by discussing means to expand the analysis of environmental aspects in project appraisals.

Ahmad (International Fund for Agricultural Development) carries out an economic valuation of environmental changes in the context of marginal areas, with a case study of a project in the day forest of Djibouti. Costs and benefits are quantified and valued, and risk and uncertainty are discussed, as well as the fiscal impact and income distribution effects of the project. The paper concludes with a discussion of the importance of extended time horizons, the applicability of valuation methods, fiscal obstacles to loan financing of environmentally focused projects, equity concerns, and constraints on data availability for projects in marginal areas.

Meier and Munasinghe (World Bank) present a case study describing attempts to incorporate environmental considerations into energy decisionmaking in Sri Lanka. Environmental impacts of both thermal and hydro power projects are valued and input into a power system planning model. Environmental impacts that cannot be valued are physically quantified and used in a multicriteria analysis that trades off environmental issues against other concerns (like economic costs). The results provide a basis for improving energy policymaking in Sri Lanka.

The last four papers in the book go beyond local project level to deal with environmental economic issues that are sectorwide, national, or global in scope.

Norse and Saigal (Food and Agriculture Organization) describe a method developed to assess the cost of soil erosion in Zimbabwe. The methodology is applied to data collected in the former southern Rhodesia in the 1950s and 1960s. The impact of erosion is quantified, and the cost of replacing lost nutrients is calculated. The methodology used is subject to a number of qualifications and assumptions, and the paper goes on to describe the limitations of the methodology and the options for refining it.

The paper by Recalde (Organization of American States) provides an economic analysis of the main national level environmental problems of Uruguay and proposes a set of specific economic measures to deal with them. Previously, environmental resources in Uruguay had been handled using a command and control approach. The paper discusses an economic strategy for environmental management and proposes its use as a complement to existing methods. The causes of the problems are identified, and economic measures are proposed to incorporate environmental objectives in the country's economic policy.

The van Tongeren, Schweinfest, Lutz, Luna, and Martin (UN Statistical Office and World Bank) paper contains a case study of integrated environmental and economic accounting for Mexico. The national accounts are expanded to include productive asset balances. Oil depletion, degradation of environmental assets, deforestation, and land use are integrated into the national accounts. Valuation approaches are discussed, and the environmental variables are then expressed in monetary terms. The depletion and degradation caused by different sectors are identified.

The paper by Munasinghe and King examines issues that arise in the case of a global environmental problem—ozone layer depletion. A framework for efficiently eliminating ozone depleting substances is discussed. Practical constraints that impede implementation of the Montreal Protocol are described and methods of overcoming them are presented.

Summary of principal issues and findings at the conference

The participants at the CIDIE Conference on Environmental Economics agreed that there is a growing awareness of the need to incorporate environmental concerns into projects. The vital role of environmental economics in the decisionmaking process has been accepted by

CIDIE member institutions. At the same time, the majority of participants felt the need to work toward a consensus among CIDIE member institutions (and other relevant international institutions) on the appropriate application of economic instruments for environmental management and protection. More specifically, based on practical applications and the experience gained, economic methodologies best suited to the valuation of environmental costs and benefits in developing countries should be identified, and guidelines devised that will establish a standardized methodological approach for the implementation of these techniques. A system of data gathering, updating, and analysis should be introduced and established to facilitate exchange of information and ideas among relevant institutions.

Development agencies should ensure that staff members are trained in environmental assessment techniques and applications of environmental economics in project analysis. Staff members should be encouraged to utilize these techniques when sufficient data is available.

Participants stressed the importance of identifying and evaluating the sectoral, economywide, and global impacts of development projects. Projects should be examined within the context of an integrated framework for sustainable development, in order to ensure adequate recognition and funding, and to achieve quantitatively specified environmental targets in a given sectoral and geographical area. Several participants called for more research into the integration of environmental economics at the sectoral level. Furthermore, in order to provide consistent guidance on structural adjustment policies and macroeconomic policy reform, the environmental impacts of such economywide policies should be examined.

Participants felt that the causal link between poverty and the environment merited further examination, and that the distributive aspects of a project were a key factor in the decisionmaking process. The importance of relating the achievement of environmental objectives to social and economic objectives was highlighted. It was suggested that a specific workshop to further explore this issue would be beneficial.

Environmental valuation techniques were considered a useful extension of standard cost-benefit analysis (CBA), despite the dearth of applications in the developing world, and problems of identifying environmental changes (particularly in the case of complex biological systems).

It was felt that the linkages between environmental impact assessment, traditional CBA, and environmental economics needed to be more clearly defined. The difficulties of applying direct valuation methods (contingency valuation method, travel cost method) in developing countries were discussed. However, participants were virtually unanimous in their belief that environmental valuation techniques should be immediately incorporated into project analysis, while recognizing the need for further development and refinement of these techniques. It was suggested that the multicriteria approach could be adopted in cases where environmental impacts were hard to quantify.

Participants recognized the need for a framework for determining and prioritizing information needs for developing countries including the identification of the type of data required, as well as the system of gathering, storage, analysis, harmonization, and coordination of data used by different ministries and government bodies. The framework should also help identify the type of technology to be used, as well as expertise and institutional mechanisms required to collect and analyze data.

Participants stressed the importance of information dissemination, both within CIDIE member institutions and other international agencies, and through public awareness campaigns and technical assistance. As an immediate follow-up, participants agreed to systematically exchange information on environmental economics, especially case studies of applications in developing countries. The World Bank was requested to: (a) prepare a monograph containing selected papers presented at the conference, as well as the principal findings; and (b) organize another conference on environmental economics in 1993, with the focus more on the links between the environment and policies at the sectoral and macroeconomic level.

Mohan Munasinghe
July 1993

Acknowledgments

The assistance provided by Noreen Beg, Annika Persson, and Luz Rivera, as well as Mary Louise Hollowell, Rebecca Kary, Timothy Kary, and Malissa Ngo Van Duc of Alpha-Omega Services., Inc., in the preparation of this volume is gratefully acknowledged.

Special thanks are owed also to the conference participants and paper authors for their valuable contributions and cooperation.

About the Contributors

Hussein M. Abaza is Assistant Policy Advisor to the Executive Director, United Nations Environment Programme.

Nessim J. Ahmad is a Resource Economist in the Technical Advisory Division, of the International Fund for Agricultural Development (IFAD).

Arthur H. Darling is Senior Research Economist, Project Advisor's Office, Inter-American Development Bank.

Partha Dasgupta is Professor of Economics, Cambridge University, and Chairman, Beijer International Institute of Ecological Economics, Stockholm.

Christian Gomez is Advisor, Office of the Executive Vice-President, Inter-American Development Bank.

Kenneth King is Senior Environmental Specialist in the Environment Department of the World Bank.

Maria Gomez Luna is Director of the National Accounts and Economic Statistics Department of the Instituto Nacional de Estadistica, Geografica y Informatica (INEGI) in Mexico.

Ernst Lutz is Senior Economist in the Environmental Policy and Research Division of the World Bank.

Anil Markandya, Harvard Institute for International Development, Harvard University, Cambridge, Mass., USA.

Francisco Guillen Martin is Sub-Director of the National Accounts and Economic Statistics Department of INEGI.

Peter Meier is Consultant to the World Bank, Environment Department, and Chief Economist, IDEA, Inc.

Mohan Munasinghe is Chief, Environmental Policy and Research Division, The World Bank.

Carlos Muñoz, Director, Environmental Economics Department, Ministry of Social Development, Mexico City, Mexico.

Mario Niklitschek is Economist, Sanitation and Urban Development Division, Inter-American Development Bank.

David Norse is Senior Research Fellow, Environmental Change Unit, University of Oxford, and Research Associate, ODI, London. He was formerly Senior Policy and Planning Coordinator, Agriculture Department, FAO.

Roberto Alfredo Recalde is a Development Economist in the Department of Regional Development and Environment, The Organization of American States.

Reshma Saigal is Consultant, Agriculture Department, FAO.

Stefan Schweinfest is Statistician in the National Accounts Section of UNSO.

Jan van Tongeren is Chief of the National Accounts and Classifications Branch in the United Nations Statistical Office (UNSO).

1

Appraisal Methodology for Sustainable Development Projects

Hussein Abaza

There has been increased awareness of the need to incorporate environmental considerations in the appraisal methodologies of projects. This paper reviews the various analyses, including information, technical, economic, financial, social, institutional and environmental analyses, which have to be made at the various stages of the project cycle in order to ensure that projects implemented are environmentally sound and sustainable. It highlights elements of environmental concerns which need to be considered for possible integration in the project cycle adopted by international development assistance organizations, and governmental and non-governmental institutions in order to ensure the development and implementation of environmentally sound projects.

Different terms have been used to describe the various stages of the project cycle. According to the World Bank (Baum and Tolbert 1987), the project cycle falls into the following main categories:

- *Identification.* During this phase the project ideas which represent a high priority use of the country's resources to achieve development needs are identified. These project ideas should meet a preliminary test of feasibility. This involves ensuring that institutional and technical solutions, with costs commensurate with the expected benefits, will be sought and appropriate policies adopted.

- *Preparation.* Once a project passes the identification phase, a refinement of the project in all its dimensions—technical, economic, environmental, financial, social, institutional—has to be made.

- *Appraisal.* This phase involves the assessment of the overall soundness of the project and justification for its implementation.

- *Implementation.* This stage covers the actual development of the project until it becomes operational, including monitoring and supervision of project activities.

- *Evaluation.* An ex post evaluation of the project is intended to determine the extent to which the project's objectives have been realized and to draw lessons from the experience gained in the implementation of the project for use in future projects.

Throughout the various stages of the project cycle several analyses have to be made—including information, technical, social, financial, institutional, economic, and environmental. This document attempts to highlight these analyses and the considerations to be taken into account in order to ensure that projects implemented are environmentally sound and sustainable. It provides elements of environmental concerns that need to be considered for their possible integration into the project cycle adopted by international development assistance organizations and by governmental and nongovernmental institutions.

It is intended that this document be revised and refined on a continuous basis as more experience and knowledge in the analysis of development and execution of projects are acquired.

The emphasis given to the various stages of the project cycle and to the various analyses will depend to a very large extent on the nature and type of project in question and the prevailing conditions and state of development in which the project is being implemented, as well as to the mandate of the international development institution supporting the project.

General Considerations For Project Design

Each project should be designed using a framework to ensure a logical relationship and hierarchy between the project's activities, outputs, and inputs. Project design should clearly identify the following:

- Problem(s) or issue(s) the project intends to address
- Long and short-term objectives of the project
- Target groups or main project beneficiaries
- Activities required to achieve the objectives
- Financial and human resources required to achieve the set objectives
- Management responsibility and structure
- Implementation modalities

The project should be designed to ensure replicability within the boundaries of the country or region in which it is being implemented and in countries with similar socioeconomic and environmental conditions. Replication could be in one of the following forms: technology, administrative setup (management), processes and styles, or experience.

The project should be designed to allow flexibility in the modification of its activities to attain its set objectives and in the modification

The author is most grateful to his colleagues at the United Nations Environmental Programme (UNEP) who have provided comments and contributions at the various stages of the preparation of this paper.

of those objectives to reflect the changes in government policies and in the priorities of the government and the local population (Harrison 1987). Flexibility is also required to allow for delays in the implementation of project activities that could be attributed to one or a number of the following: (a) withdrawal of one or more of the project collaborators; (b) delay in the delivery of imported components of equipment and material required for the project; (c) delay in the delivery of local inputs by the government implementing agency; (d) shortage of local material and equipment and spare parts needed for the implementation of project activities; (e) change in government leadership or structures; and (f) local commotions and disturbances.

The project should also be flexible enough to allow for adjustments and changes in its design to meet changing requirements or flaws in its design. The project design should provide for suspension if it becomes apparent that unforseen negative impacts and environmental damage are resulting from project implementation.

A mechanism should be built into the project for the recording of the experience gained during the process of implementation and results and outputs obtained. Provisions for the periodic review and evaluation of project activities involving all project collaborators should be conducted at least once a year or at shorter intervals as deemed necessary. The findings of the project reviews will be reflected in adjustments and modifications in project design. The project should also include provisions for ex post evaluation in order to learn more about its impact and the extent of its sustainability (UN Joint Inspection Unit 1989).

Information analysis

Preliminary background information

Relevant information on the country in which the project will be implemented should be gathered, to assist in the identification as well as the design of the project. Existing sources (such as national environmental profiles and conservation strategies) should be consulted to minimize the amount of time and effort devoted to gathering information. Certain types of information listed below will be more relevant depending on the nature of particular projects.

The analysis of background information is intended, among other things, to:

- Provide a preliminary understanding of the priorities given by the government to environmental concerns.

- Establish possible interlinkages between previous activities, and ongoing and planned activities being undertaken in the country concerned, whether by the government, nongovernmental organizations (NGOs), United Nations (UN) agencies, or donor countries.

- Show the relation of proposed projects to the broad national development, its replicability (similar areas, similar situations). Projects should provide experience that can be used in a broader context.

- Ensure complementarity of activities and avoid duplication.

- Enable the preliminary identification of potential project beneficiaries and collaborators.

- Identify possible funding agencies and organizations.

Information gathered should include the following:

- Data on the country in question, including demographic structure, economic situation of the country, national development plan, debt structure, and political system adopted.

- General environmental situation of the country, including climatic conditions, topography, the natural resource base, the dependence of development on this base, its degradation and depletion (for example, land degradation and soil erosion, deforestation), major environmental and resource constraints on development, environment-related activities being implemented, and existing government institutional structure(s) dealing with the environment.

- Related projects and activities undertaken or being implemented by international development assistance organizations, UN agencies, and governmental and nongovernmental organizations in the country in question. This should include types of projects, their duration and timing, amount and sources of funding, implementing institutions involved, outcome of projects or activities, extent of successes or failures, and lessons learned. (This information could be obtained either from the relevant agencies and United Nations Development Programme (UNDP) office located in the country or from their head offices.)

- For projects aiming to produce a marketable good or service, a market analysis to determine the effects of project outputs on the local and neighboring markets, various options or possibilities for the marketing of these outputs, income expected to be generated, distribution of generated income to project beneficiaries, and use of income to cover the project's running cost.

- For agricultural projects, existing land ownership, system of cultivation adopted, pricing of agricultural commodities, and accessibility of individual farmers or cooperatives to local markets.

The project should thus be designed on the basis of a realistic appraisal of existing local conditions including the socioeconomic and political environment existing in the country. Realities of developing countries such as lack of, or poor, infrastructure, recurrent financial problems, lack of foreign exchange, and technical and managerial skills should be fully taken into account in the project design (Harrison 1987).

Technical analysis

The technical issues relating to projects are interwoven with issues and cannot be examined in isolation. That is why project formulation missions should normally consist of multidisciplinary teams of expertise relevant to the main activities of projects. This step will ensure that the technical, environmental, socioeconomic, and institutional aspects are taken into account in project development (Baum and Tolbert 1987).

Many issues of technical design are specifically related to certain projects and have to be addressed in that context. However, there are certain broad issues relevant to most projects that can be identified, including size, location, timing and technology (Baum and Tolbert 1987).

Size

Project size and scope depend on a number of factors—including the market demand, the administrative capacity of the implementing agency, economies or diseconomies of scale, and financial considerations (Baum and Tolbert 1987). The physical limitations of the site and the natural resources to be used, the extent of their availability, and their consumption in a sustainable manner also determine the size of the project.

Location

Identification of the project area will be affected by the type of project and activities to be implemented. The criteria for the selection of a project area to implement agroforestry activities will differ from those intended to implement a pastoral management or a human settlement activity. The selection of a project site may involve a tradeoff among various considerations such as the proximity to sources of raw materials, markets, and infrastructure facilities, access to the labor market; and government premises.

The following should be considered in determining the project area:

- Surveys, studies, and information available on the geography of the country in question. This includes information on surface and underground water, land and soil conditions, and climate—including main seasons, precipitation, and seasonal winds.

- Socioeconomic development, environmental conditions, and related problems in the various regions of the country.

- Principal economic activities undertaken by the local population living in the main regions of the country, for example, agriculture, pastoralism, and industry.

- Location of areas with high conservation significance, for example, centers of biodiversity and endemism, mangroves, or important sites for migratory species.

- Priority given by the government to the various regions.
- Extent of security and social stability of the different regions.

Timing

Consideration of the duration and the most appropriate time to start a project has not always been given enough attention. Determining the right time to start a project, given the availability of the required financial resources, depends on the demand for a project's outputs, the availability of the right technology, the existing state of the environmental and natural resources, and the extent of the impacts that a project is likely to have on them. It is sometimes too late to implement a specific project that aims at rectifying a certain environmental issue. At other times, such a project may need to be redesigned for a different launch date (Baum and Tolbert 1987).

The project should also be realistic in the planning and scheduling of activities. A reasonable take-off or lead period at the beginning of a project should be provided for, during which all the essential elements would be assembled before project activities move into full swing (UN Joint Inspection Unit 1989).

Technology

Appropriate technologies should be used in the implementation of project activities. Such technologies normally would be described as suiting local conditions and the available skills and training, and being within the financial means of the population. The use of traditional technologies and material would reduce the dependence of a project on outside technologies that are usually expensive and require hard currencies in short supply in developing countries; destructive traditional technologies, however, should be replaced by environmentally sound alternatives. Ideally a combination of both modern and traditional technologies should be used, which leads to updating of the former by the latter.

Only fully tested new technologies that are acceptable to the local population and that are likely to function in the project area should be introduced. Moreover, the transfer of environmentally sound technologies should be made

available for use in projects implemented in developing countries.

For many developing countries, an appropriate technology would be one that makes full use of labor while minimizing the use of capital and advanced skills. In the selection of the right technology, therefore, inappropriate government policies such as overpricing of labor, underpricing of capital through subsidized interest rates, and undervaluing of exchange rates should be taken into account; otherwise the project might lead to the adoption of economically inefficient technologies (Baum and Tolbert 1987). Better still would be the pursuit of macroeconomic policies conducive to the adoption of a appropriate technology.

The project should allow for the proper maintenance of equipment and for onsite training for their use and maintenance. It is therefore often encouraged to use local equipment with which the local population will be more familiar, and local skills that would be available to provide training for personnel.

A major objective to be pursued in the selection of technology is that of overcoming shortages of human and institutional resources. In addition, governments should particularly focus on enhancing public awareness of the use of appropriate technologies, encouraging industry and the private sector to devote sufficient resources to technological research for the development and introduction of sound technologies (Baum and Tolbert 1987).

Social analysis

Social analysis of the project should begin at the outset of project identification and continue through the various stages of the project cycle. Projects that ignore the traditions, values, and social organization of the intended beneficiaries have little chance of success (Baum and Tolbert 1987).

Public participation

The various levels of authority in the government—the central government authority, and provincial and local authorities—as well as representatives of the local populations, in particular, the project beneficiaries, should be involved in all phases of project formulation and design, and in the various stages of the project cycle. This involvement would ensure that the needs and problems of the population concerned are addressed and that their support and participation in project activities are secured. It should be borne in mind, however, that there will be instances when community organizations will pursue narrow interests that would not be of much value in this process (Baum and Tolbert 1987).

The project design should ensure an increased role for the local population in project management and a gradual takeover once external project collaborators pull out. Through this process it is also anticipated that the capabilities of the grassroots population in organizing themselves for self-reliance will be improved.

Participation of the local population not only minimizes opposition, mobilizes support, and increases the impact and sustainability of projects, but it is also a means to gather relevant information for project design. Taking into consideration the social aspects in project design is needed not only to adapt project design to the traditions, and social and cultural norms of local populations, but also to organize and mobilize people to foster the process of social change (Baum and Tolbert 1987).

Contact with the concerned population should be organized by the local authorities through the central government or government implementing institution(s). The various segments of the local population should be contacted, to ensure that the interests of the different social, economic, and religious groups are accounted for. Communication with the local population in their local language should be made possible.

Contact with the local population is intended to establish the following:

- Main economic activities of the population

- Major ecological zones in the project area

- Size of the population in the project area and project beneficiaries or target groups

- Structure of the local community and existing leadership and extent of its influence on the population

- Local systems governing the access to and control of natural resources—for example,

land tenure system, water, forest, and pasture resources rights

- Gender roles in the local society, particularly with respect to resource management

- Basic infrastructure available in the area—for example, roads, schools, hospitals or clinics, and cooperative societies, and the extent to which the population is satisfied with available facilities and services provided

- Sociocultural and demographic characteristics of the project population including ethnic, tribal, and class composition

- Environmental and development problems facing the population and how they foresee the solution to them

- Epidemiological and demographic factors that are likely to affect the potential participation of the population

- Effective local groups in the area, their organizational setups, and types of activities in which they are involved.

This information should be used in formulating the project framework, modalities of implementation, and a strategy to secure the commitment of the project population throughout the project cycle. It will also assist in the selection of technologies to be adopted in the project implementation (including new and innovative technologies).

The project should include a public awareness component aimed at sensitizing the population to the positive effects of applying the environmentally sound approaches and technologies, as well as the detrimental effects on the environment, the population, and the economy of using inappropriate technologies.

Project beneficiaries

In any project, the beneficiaries must be clearly identified. While the cost of environmental management projects, such as the setting up of a national wildlife conservation area, may fall on the local community, benefits might accrue more to future generations and to the international community at large. Mechanisms for defraying the costs on the local community must therefore be worked out.

The project should aim, where possible, to benefit the poorest segments of the population

(Timberlake 1985). Aside from the issue of intragenerational equity, there is also an environmental argument for targeting the poorest of the poor. The poorest segments of the population are often trapped in a vicious cycle of poverty and environmental degradation. Helping them to break this cycle and lengthen their time horizon beyond a day-to-day existence may significantly ease the pressure on the resource base.

In identifying project beneficiaries, gender roles have often been neglected. Women's access to local resources (both natural and otherwise) is frequently markedly different from men's. This information must be incorporated into project design from the beginning to ensure that the effects of projects, particularly on resource use, are those intended. The role of women, as distinct from that of men, needs to be clearly identified in project implementation.

The project should be designed to lead to an equitable distribution of benefits among and within target groups and not to exacerbate any inequities among local populations.

Training

Since no project, program, or plan can be successfully implemented without skilled and trained manpower, the project should provide for an appropriate environment training component. The training of a locally available, skilled workforce will help ensure project sustainability and contribute to capacity building.

The project should be designed to allow for the training of the local population in introduced techniques whether these relate to the implementation of project activities, to the management and monitoring of project activities and their evaluation, or to the operation and maintenance of organizational systems established through projects. Where possible, this training can be integrated with technical training. Training provided should be part of, or linked to, training programs in the country in question.

Financial analysis

An integral part of every project is setting a financial plan that ensures the availability of funds for completing as well as operating and maintaining a project. The financial analysis of a project should determine the ideal recovery policy. This is normally a policy that secures maximum financial benefits to the economy from a project, taking into account its impact on the distribution of income and on the government fiscal policy (Baum and Tolbert 1987).

The financial profitability of a project can be measured by the internal financial rate of return. This is the discount rate that equalizes the present value of the streams of financial costs and benefits over the life of a project. The difference between the financial and the economic rate of return is that the latter adjusts various costs and prices to eliminate the impact of transfer payments such as subsidies, duties, taxes, and other distortions in the valuation of traded and nontraded goods by using shadow prices that reflect their true value to the economy. The main difference between the financial and economic analysis is that while the former deals with the costs and benefits from the point of view of the individual enterprise, the latter does so from the point of view of the economy as a whole (Baum and Tolbert 1987).

The following financial considerations should be taken into account in project design:

- The project should include the financial contribution of the local population. This could be in the form of land to be provided for the project site or activities, of labor to undertake some of the project activities, or of material and equipment. This contribution will ensure that the project reflects the interests and needs of local populations and will secure their commitment to the project. The project should clearly demonstrate that it will result in financial benefits to the population. For certain types of projects, it may also be necessary to consider the ability of the local population to participate in, and contribute to, the project (Baum and Tolbert 1987).

- The project should be designed to ensure that its activities and achievements will continue after financial support from donors and supporting agencies ceases. Funds required to cover the continued running and operating cost of a project should be made available whether through income generated by project activities or through community fund-raising initiatives. Project design should clearly identify who will cover these costs.

- Project costs should be kept to a minimum, particularly those related to forgone benefits. This strategy will facilitate the self-financing of the project as well as its adaptability and replicability (Harrison 1987).

- The use of imported components in projects should be avoided or kept to minimum—whether to financial resources, labor, management, skills and experience, or equipment and material (Timberlake 1985).

Institutional analysis

The institutional dimension in project analysis has until recently been receiving less attention from international development assistance institutions than the technical, economic, and financial ones. It has now become evident that the availability of the necessary institutional structures and arrangements is a primary means of ensuring the efficient implementation of sustainable development projects (Baum and Tolbert 1987).

Inadequate institutional arrangements in developing countries are characterized by a serious shortage of skilled manpower, and experienced staff, a lack of training and staff incentives, overloaded facilities, low salaries, and counterproductive government policies and legislation (Baum and Tolbert 1987).

Government policies have their repercussions on institutional arrangements necessary for the implementation of sustainable development projects. These policies include exchange rates, trade policies, pricing policies, taxes, and export duties. Such policies affect the economic performance of projects and the use of environmental goods and services involved. Moreover, inadequate policies can divert attention from the development functions of government institutions and undermine incentives, morale, and management capacities of the institutions themselves (Baum and Tolbert 1987).

Because the formulation of field projects requires the design of complex, interrelated activities that could probably extend over a

period of five to ten years, careful consideration and thought should be given in project design to all possible collaborators and beneficiaries. These include: (a) the ministry of environment or government agency responsible for the environment; (b) the ministry of planning or finance; (c) other relevant ministries or government institutions expected to be involved in a particular project; (d) donor country or agency providing funding for the project in question; (e) United Nations Development Programme (UNDP) office in the country; (f) relevant UN agencies represented in the country; (g) relevant NGOs.

Where possible, a preliminary field visit should be undertaken to expand on contacts with possible collaborators and beneficiaries. This visit is intended to complement the initial background information (see Information analysis section) by providing more detailed information through direct contacts and primary sources. The field visit will involve contacts with all the agencies and institutions listed in the preceding paragraph. The visit is intended to ascertain/identify:

- Main government implementing agency for the project and various collaborating ministries or departments

- Environmental goods and services provided by the project area and the likely impact of the project on them

- Major economic and environmental problems facing the country as identified by the government

- Government priorities and policies

- Region or project area

- Main sources of funding for the project

- Government counterpart contribution—whether in cash or in kind

- Actual collaborators of the project and the expected financial contribution of each

- Starting date of the project and its estimated duration

- Main projects or activities which the project activities could either be linked with or complement

- Role of UNDP (Office of Project Services) in the implementation of the project

- Role of NGOs

This preliminary field visit should also identify the people that are likely to be involved in, or affected by, the project, as well as their social and community organizations or other bodies that may be important in ensuring public participation in planning and implementation.

The ministry of planning or finance should be involved in the early stages of the project development in order to ensure that the project is a government priority; that the project is well integrated in the country's national plan; that project activities are coordinated with other on-going or planned activities; and that financial support can be allocated for the project, whether through government sources or through bilateral and multilateral channels. The involvement of the ministry of planning or finance will also acquaint officials of the country with the process of developing environmentally sound projects for future applications.

The nature and type of project determines the level of institutional structures and arrangements required for its implementation. Institutional arrangements for implementing infrastructure projects are familiar and can be specified closely with the required technology identified. In the case of environmental projects, these institutional arrangements are not always likely to be available.

Establishing and strengthening local institutions and capabilities for sustainable development involves a lengthy process of experiment and adaptation. It is a time consuming process since it involves economic and technical as well as social and cultural constraints. Fostering this process has been hampered by the shortage of required budgetary resources (Baum and Tolbert 1987).

Attempts should be made in project formulation to address the issues of institutional strengthening and capacity building. For projects with specific environmental components, consideration should be given to the integration of environmental considerations into development plans, the introduction of appropriate environmental legislation and modes of their application, and demonstration-type projects (for example, development and testing of new technology for energy conservation,

reduction of CO_2, stabilization of climate change, coastal area development, and new patterns in land use and settlements development).

Project management and administration

Institutional arrangements required for successful project implementation—and the role of each collaborating agency or body—should be clearly defined, with the timing of the delivery of specific outputs identified. Structures and capabilities of existing local institutions should be assessed. The upgrading of existing structures, skills, and adopted management and organizational systems by local institutions should be enhanced through their participation in projects.

To reduce the negative impact of the rapid turnover of counterpart staff, the project should be designed to be part of the existing government administrative setup (central, regional, or local) rather than operate through ad hoc project management, which generally relies on expatriates (UN Joint Inspection Unit 1989). Also, to reduce the administrative burden of the recipient government, decentralization of project support and monitoring functions from the central to the regional or district level should be encouraged (UN Joint Inspection Unit 1989).

Institutional arrangements in project design should include the costs and benefits of conservation and rehabilitation of the manmade, as well as the natural, capital stock. Institutional arrangements should thus be put in place to ensure the self-financing of projects.

Indigenous capabilities

Projects should be supportive of the creation and strengthening of indigenous institutions dealing with the assessment and development of environmentally sound models and technologies;

The participation of local institutions and entities such as farmers' associations, cooperative societies, nongovernmental organizations, and women's groups should be encouraged. They are usually the most organized local entities, possessing both the minimum organizational structures required to undertake specified set of activities and the knowledge of existing conditions as well as needs and requirements of the population.

Integration of project activities

The project should be fully integrated into the country's national development plans and well coordinated with other related activities being implemented by other government ministries and departments, UN organizations, donor agencies, and NGOs. This coordination could be achieved through the establishment of a coordinating committee in which the various government departments or ministries, as well as outside agencies concerned, are represented.

Project formulation may also entail an assessment of the policies and regulations adopted by a country and the extent to which such policies would need to be adjusted to take environmental considerations into account in the development process.

Environmental analysis

The issue addressed here is how environmental damage can be avoided or reduced to ensure that development initiatives and their benefits are sustainable. The objective of environmental management should be to achieve the greatest present benefit possible from the use of natural resources without reducing their potential to meet future needs and the carrying capacity of the environment (Baum and Tolbert 1987).

The traditional approach to environmental management of undertaking projects with primarily environmental objectives or ensuring that components of other projects include elements to mitigate negative environmental impacts, though important, is inadequate. A more comprehensive approach where environmental and natural resource management is integrated into economic and social policy should supplement the project-by-project approach (Schramm and Warford 1989).

Taking environmental considerations into account in development planning does not imply that the pace of socioeconomic progress will be slowed. According to the World Bank (Baum and Tolbert 1987), in almost every sector of the economy, projects have demonstrated that incorporating environmental safeguards

enhanced economic and social benefits or reduced economic and social costs when compared with the risk of irreversible damage or the cost of remedial action that could result.

Taking environmental considerations into account in the various phases of the project cycle must not be seen as placing undue constraints on the development options of a country. If a project is to be suspended on environmental grounds, alternative options that are environmentally sound must be provided to meet the country's development needs. Moreover, implications of environmental impacts assessed from the global standpoint cannot be insensitively translated into specific action in developing countries in the absence of concrete alternatives that would enable the poor countries to relate the short-term well-being of their populations to their long-term well-being and to that of the world.

For most projects, particularly those involving large public investment in areas such as infrastructure, an environmental impact assessment (EIA) should be carried out and linked with the cost-benefit analysis (CBA—see Economic analysis section). The objective of EIA is to ensure that environmental aspects are addressed and potential problems are foreseen at the appropriate stage of project design. The EIA should be envisaged as an integral part of the planning process, initiated at the project level from the start.

Various guides on EIA are available; the main steps are as follows (Ahmad and Sammy 1987):

- *Preliminary activities* include selecting a coordinator for the EIA and collecting background information. This action should be undertaken as soon as a project has been identified.

- *Impact identification* involves a coarse analysis of the impacts of project activities with a view to identifying those impacts that are worthy of a detailed study.

- *Baseline study* entails the collection of detailed information and data on the condition of the project area prior to its implementation.

- *Impact evaluation* should be done in quantitative terms, where possible, and should include the working out of potential mitigation measures. Impact evaluation cannot proceed until project alternatives have been defined but it should be completed early enough to permit decisions to be made in a timely fashion.

- *Assessment* involves combining environmental losses and gains with economic costs and benefits to produce a complete account of each project alternative. Cost-benefit analysis should include environmental impacts where these can be evaluated in monetary terms (see Economic analysis section).

- *Documentation* is prepared to describe the work done in the EIA. A working document is prepared to provide clearly stated and argued recommendations for immediate action. The document should contain a list of project options with comments on the environmental and economic impacts of each.

- *Decisionmaking* begins when the working document reaches the decisionmaker, who will either accept one of the project alternatives, request further study, or reject the proposed action altogether.

- *Post audits* are made to determine how close to reality the EIA predictions were.

Due to the negative impacts that many previous development initiatives have had on the environment, safe minimum standards with which projects have to comply have been increasingly introduced into project design. In addition, safeguards to prevent, minimize, or compensate for the negative impacts of projects on the environment are being incorporated into project design from the start (Baum and Tolbert 1987).

Pursuing sustainable development projects should be regarded as an essential process through which environmental considerations are integrated with economic planning and consequently with the national development plans of countries. The following are major criteria to be taken into account in the design and formulation of environmentally sound field projects.

Environmentally sound projects should:

- Be designed to meet the needs of the present generations without compromising the ability of future generations to meet their own needs. Projects should therefore emphasize intergenerational equity. Sustainable development projects should ensure that they do not result in a net capital loss for future generations. (Whereas some economists argue that sustainable development can be attained by ensuring that capital wealth, whether man-made or environmental, does not decline over time, others emphasize that a constant or increasing stock of environmental capital should be transferred to future generations (Pearce 1989).

- Ensure that their activities are compatible with sustainable environmental management and lead to development without destruction.

- Involve activities which at least leave the level of environmental quality intact, or which compensate for its loss in value terms. The project should lead to the maximization of net benefits of economic development provided that the value of services and quality of basic natural resources are being maintained (Barbier, Burgess, and Pearce 1989).

- Not disrupt ecological systems through over-exploitation of natural resources. Project activities should be designed to use natural resources in a rational way without hampering or denying future generations the use of such resources (Timberlake 1985). Activities leading to an irreversible loss of natural capital such as complex life-support systems, biological diversity, aesthetic functions, and climatic conditions are not compatible with sustainable development and therefore should be avoided.

- Where applicable, lead to the conservation of natural habitats, forests, and species; reverse deforestation; introduce sustainable water management schemes; reduce acidification and hazardous wastes; develop and introduce environmentally safe industrial processes; slow and eventually stabilize rapid population growth; establish patterns of consumption that respond to local needs and contribute to sustainable development.

- Incorporate the costs of rectifying any expected negative or detrimental environmental effects. This is referred to as the anticipatory approach and is preferable to the reactive one, which involves waiting until problems occur before taking any remedial action (Pearce 1989).

- Be designed to introduce or increase the understanding of the local population and their participation in activities leading to the conservation and protection of the environment, particularly those projects relating to efficient energy production and consumption.

- Restrict the use of chloroflourocarbons (CFCs), pesticides, chemical fertilizers with negative environmental effects, and material or components producing carbon emissions; and introduce and encourage the use of environmentally benign substitutes.

- Be supportive of and consistent with an acceptable environmental strategy or program adopted in the country as well as with global and regional environmental conventions and protocols (Montreal Protocol on Substances that Deplete the Ozone Layer, Vienna Convention for the Protection of Ozone Layer, Basel Convention on the Control of Transboundary Movements of Hazardous Wastes and their Disposal, Convention on Biological Diversity, and Convention on Climate Change).

Economic analysis

Sustainable development projects should be considered within the context of projects promoting development rather than growth in its strict sense. Development includes all factors that lead to increases in the well-being of the population concerned, with economic growth being one of the important sources of increases in welfare (Barbier, Burgess, and Pearce 1989).

Cost-benefit analysis

Economic analysis of projects usually takes place during the appraisal stage and attempts to measure the profitability of a project from the society's point of view through the application of cost-benefit analysis. CBA seeks to determine not only if a project can be expected to provide a satisfactory return to the economy, but also if there is an alternative way of achieving a project's objectives that would offer a higher return. This is done by comparing the costs and benefits of projects throughout their lifetimes (Baum and Tolbert 1987).

Because market prices of project inputs and outputs are distorted by taxes, subsidies, quotas and other government interventions, these prices may not reflect the true costs and benefits of a project to society. Shadow prices are therefore used to reflect the value of inputs and outputs. Shadow prices reflect the true willingness to pay by individuals to have access to certain goods and services whether these were marketed or not. It is the price which would prevail if all resources in the economy were optimally allocated (Barbier, Burgess, and Pearce 1989). Social CBA expands on this procedure by giving special weighting (in a systematic manner) to benefits and costs of a project that help promote the attainment of broader social goals, such as income redistribution (Baum and Tolbert 1987).

To measure a project's profitability, three methods are used: the net present value, the internal rate of return, and the benefit-cost ratio. The net present value of a project is the value of the benefits after deducting the costs both discounted at the opportunity cost of capital. For a project to be economically viable the present value of the net benefits must be zero or positive, and higher or at least as high as that of mutually exclusive project alternatives. The internal rate of return is the discount rate which results in a zero net present value for a project. A project can be justified if the discount rate equals or exceeds the opportunity cost of capital. This method should however be avoided in comparing mutually exclusive project alternatives. The benefit-cost ratio is a variant of the net present value in which both benefits and costs are defined in terms of their present value. If the net present value is positive or zero the benefit-cost ratio will exceed or equal unity (Baum and Tolbert 1987).

Costs to a project normally fall into three categories, those being direct cost, indirect costs, and opportunity costs. While indirect costs refer to external costs caused by a project, the opportunity cost of a resource used in a certain way refers to the value that would have been derived from its best possible alternative use. Opportunity cost plays a central role in cost-benefit analysis. It can be applied in market-oriented, centrally planned or mixed economies (Baum and Tolbert 1987).

Cost-benefit analysis and environmental considerations

The application of methodologies and evaluation criteria used in cost-benefit analysis to account for environmental considerations are, however, not straight forward, since the environmental costs and benefits often occur over a long period of time and are difficult to predict and quantify. Nevertheless, the extent to which environmental costs and benefits are incorporated into CBA, with values assigned to environmental services and damages, will serve to establish the fact that environmental services are not free and damages accruing from a project should be accounted for (Pearce 1989).

For environmental costs and benefits to be incorporated into CBA, the environmental impacts of a project must first be identified and quantified. Since natural systems are very complex and their reaction to exogenous impacts are characterized by uncertainty, a comprehensive environmental impact assessment (EIA) should be carried out (see Environmental analysis section). Apart from its own intrinsic value, an EIA serves to systematically identify and quantify the impacts of a project on the natural environment.

Risk assessment

In conjunction with environmental impact assessment and cost-benefit analysis, a third tool, environmental risk assessment, should also be used where appropriate to integrate environmental and development considerations. Risk assessment is the process by which the form, dimension, and characteristics of the risks that environmental problems pose for human health, ecosystems, the economic system or the quality of human life are estimated. Risk management is the process by which these risks are reduced. The concept of environmental risk

assessment allows many environmental problems to be measured and compared in common terms and different risk reduction options to be evaluated from a common basis.

Despite uncertainties and controversies associated with the evaluation of environmental hazards, comparative risk assessment serves as a tool for indicating the most promising road to follow, for the targeting of limited resources and for mobilizing and deploying expertise in an efficient and rational manner. Establishing environmental priorities on the basis of relative risks is fraught with contentiousness and difficulty. It requires a tolerance of uncertainty, a willingness to deal with error and to learn from mistakes, and the capacity to adapt to new information and changing circumstances.

The ranking of risks is, however, hampered by the gaps in key data sets and the uncertainty associated with existing data. Moreover, methodologies used to estimate the costs and benefits of risk reduction are also inadequate and therefore hinder the assessment and comparison of risk. An additional difficulty is that value judgements must always be made in comparing and ranking environmental risks. Further efforts are therefore needed in the area of risk assessment, particularly to bridge the gap that exists between the public's perception of environmental risks and what is considered most serious by the technical professionals charged with reducing such risks.

Valuation of environmental goods and services

Once the environmental impacts and risks of a project have been identified, the next task is to value these impacts and risks (Dixon et al. 1988). Man-made and human capital may be valued relatively easily by observing existing market systems. However, valuing environmental assets and their functions, such as the ozone layer, functions of tropical forests, wetlands, and the like, is difficult since the market system is unable to reflect the full contribution of these assets and functions to economic activity and human welfare. Because there exist market failures, such as the presence of monopoly and external costs and benefits, market mechanisms will not automatically secure an optimal allocation of resources. For example, the market prices of assets, such as water, neither reflect the environmental services they provide, nor the irreversible loss or damage of natural resources if environmental degradation exceeds a threshold level (Barbier, Burgess, and Pearce 1989).

In order to interpret sustainability in economic terms, the environment has to be looked at as providing three main functions, those being (a) source of raw materials and energy; (b) sink for assimilating emitted wastes; and (c) natural or environmental services (recreational benefits, health and life-support systems, preservation of genetic diversity, scientific and educational benefits) (Barbier, Burgess, and Pearce 1989).

Accordingly, evaluation of natural assets should not only focus on one function, that being the provision of material and energy, but should also include the other two functions those being waste assimilation and the provision of essential processes, life support functions, and amenities—even more so because while material and energy inputs could be substitutable, others are not.

One should thus seek to place economic values on all the environmental functions that may possibly be affected by a project. These values may be classified under the following types:

- *Direct use* values are derived from the economic uses made of the natural system's resources and services.

- *Indirect use* values are the indirect support and protection provided to economic activity and property by the resource system's natural functions or environmental services.

- *Nonuse or preservation* values are the values that are derived neither from current nor indirect use of the resource system (Barbier, Burgess, and Pearce 1989).

For example, while the direct uses of harvesting forest resources include the provision of timber and fuelwood, the indirect uses include, among others, the ecological functions of forests that support or protect economic activity. The nonuse value lies in the special attributes of the system as a whole, that is, its

cultural and heritage uniqueness (Barbier, Burgess, and Pearce 1989).

The price of natural resources should include extraction costs, environmental costs, and user costs. While market prices account for extraction costs, they do not account for either environmental costs or user costs. The environmental costs will reflect the loss of indirect values provided by the resource and its natural system. The user costs will reflect the value of foregone benefits from depleting or degrading a resource now as opposed to later—the nonuse values. Thus, various means have been developed to try to measure these other values, including the use of surrogate markets and experimental techniques (Barbier, Burgess, and Pearce 1989).

Further development of valuation techniques are still required for improving the quantitative valuation of social and environmental costs and benefits for inclusion in project analysis.

Problems with incorporating environmental considerations into cost-benefit analysis

A major problem with trying to incorporate environmental considerations into CBA arises from the difficulty of predicting all of a project's environmental effects. Natural systems are very complex, and knowledge of their dynamics and interrelationships is often very limited, inhibiting accurate predictions of their responses to external pressures. This problem is compounded by the lack of data in many developing countries, which makes the identification and quantification of environmental impacts of projects very difficult and sometimes impossible. The lack of data can also make it very difficult to reliably determine and measure people's preferences regarding environmental goods and services. In addition, the techniques for evaluating these preferences are complicated and not suitable for all circumstances. For all these reasons, it is usually impossible to place economic values on all of the functions provided by environmental and natural resources.

Moreover, undertaking project appraisals individually may not be able to capture the provision of environmental benefits and costs at a wider level, because the contribution of each project to the overall benefit or cost might be marginal (Barbier, Burgess, and Pearce 1989). A program may entail a significant environmental cost or benefit to society as a whole, while individual project appraisals may not account entirely for this benefit or cost.

Another serious problem in the application of cost-benefit analysis arises from the use of a discount factor to arrive at the net present value of future costs and benefits. The analysis is intended to relate future costs and benefits to their present value. Many of the important benefits of environmental management accrue, however, to future generations and become discernible only after the time at which standard cost-benefit analysis discounts future benefits to zero, thus discouraging investments in projects specifically designed to provide substantial environmental or conservation benefits far into the future (Baum and Tolbert 1987).

Suggestions for ensuring better accounting for the environment in project appraisal

No consensus exists on how CBA should be modified or supplemented to properly incorporate environmental considerations. The suggestions listed below are only preliminary attempts at putting into operation sustainable development in economic analysis, and they have not been brought into widespread use. The proponents of such modifications usually place them within the context of a whole package of reforms including:

- Adjusting the national accounts system to reflect the relation of changes in the environment to changes in the economy (environmental and natural resource accounting)

- Adjusting or correcting market prices (for example with the use of taxes) to reflect the full costs and benefits of using the environment

- Providing for the economic value of environmental impacts in project appraisals (Barbier, Burgess, and Pearce 1989)

Environmental and natural resource accounting has recently been recognized as one instrument that can be used to integrate environmental considerations into economic policy

at the national, regional, or sectoral level. Extensive efforts are underway to develop and promote these techniques. Various methodologies have been proposed for resource accounting that can fulfill one or more functions including, among others, the provision of an information system on environment-economy linkages and the calculation of revised national income figures. Such accounts could be used to reflect the effects of a project or a program on a country's corrected national income, particularly where a project, or set of projects, significantly affects the exploitation of the country's natural resources, as is often the case in large-scale development projects. Natural resource accounts have not yet been established by any developing country government and by only a few developed countries. It is hoped, however, that as prescriptions emerge from pilot studies and relevant experience in developed countries on the most useful and cost-effective methodologies for NRA, more countries will adopt this tool as an integral part of the decisionmaking process. Nevertheless, further research and development of analytical frameworks to integrate environmental considerations into macroeconomic policy analysis and formulation is required since many aspects of macroeconomic policy (for example, fiscal policy) can have significant effects on the use of environmental and natural resources (Muzondo, Miranda, and Bovenberg 1990).

Correcting market prices to reflect the full costs and benefits of using the environment involves internalizing environmental externalities. Once this is done, the users of environmental goods and services would then be forced to take into account the full costs and benefits of using the environment in their decisionmaking process.

Due to the problems arising from the use of a conventional discount rate, some observers and practitioners have advocated using lower (than usual) or even negative discount rates that place a higher value on future benefits and weigh future costs heavily. However, for several reasons—because money has a time value, because a low discount rate could admit projects with a low return, and because use of different discount rates for environmental and other projects could distort investment choices—using low or negative discount rates has not been widely recommended. The analysis therefore needs to be developed to combine, within the framework of CBA, a positive discount rate and a means of weighing the long-term benefits and costs of environmental components (Baum and Tolbert 1987).

One approach to better incorporate environmental considerations into project appraisal suggests that any environmental degradation resulting from a project should be rectified by the implementation of another project. These projects need not be accepted for implementation on the basis of their discounted economic values but on whether environmental benefits derived compensates environmental damages caused by other projects (Barbier, Burgess, and Pearce 1989).

A more conventional suggestion proposes that, in order to ensure sustainability, depletion of natural resources can only be acceptable if it leads to the creation of other forms of capital whether human or physical that can substitute for any of the environment's functions. In order to attain this objective, environmental losses, as well as investments for their substitutes, must be properly valued (Barbier, Burgess, and Pearce 1989).

A stricter sustainability criterion claims that a constant environment stock should be maintained over time. Thus, apart from passing the CBA test, a project should not result in a net reduction in the value of the stock of environmental capital. That means that if a project entails such negative effects on the environment, it would be necessary to include in the investment program measures to compensate for this environmental loss (Pearce 1989).

Bibliography

Ahmad, Y.J., and G.K. Sammy. 1987. *Guidelines to Environmental Impact Assessment in Developing Countries*. United Nations Environment Programme (UNEP) Regional Seas Reports and Studies, No. 85. Nairobi: UNEP.

Barbier, Edward, Joanne Burgess, and David Pearce. 1989. *The Environment and Sustainable Development: The Economic Contribution*.

Baum, Warren, and Stokes Tolbert. 1987. *Investing in Development: Lessons of World Bank Experience*. New York: Oxford University Press for the World Bank.

Dixon, et al. 1988. *Economic Analysis of the Environmental Impacts of Development Projects*. London: Earthscan Publications Ltd.

Harrison, Paul. 1987. *The Greening of Africa: Breaking Through in the Battle for Land and Food*. London: IIED Paladin.

Muzondo, Miranda, and Bovenberg. 1990. *Public Policy and the Environment: A Survey of the Literature*. International Monetary Fund (IMF) Working Paper. Washington, D.C.: IMF.

Pearce, David. 1989. *The Implications of Sustainable Development for Resource Accounting, Project Appraisal and Integrative Environmental Policy*.

Schramm, Gunter, and Jeremy Warford. 1989. *Environmental Management and Economic Development*. Washington, D.C.: World Bank.

Timberlake, Lloyd. 1985. *Africa in Crisis: The Causes, the Cures of Environmental Bankruptcy*. London: Earthscan Publications Ltd.

United Nations Joint Inspection Unit. 1989. *Evaluation of Rural Development Activities of the United Nations System in Three African Least Developed Countries*.

2

Environmental Economics and Valuation in Development Decisionmaking

Mohan Munasinghe
and
Ernst Lutz

One essential step towards achieving sustainable development is the economically efficient management of natural resources. This paper explains the key role of environmental economics in facilitating the more effective incorporation of environmental concerns into development decisionmaking. It also reviews concepts and techniques for valuation of environmental impacts that enable such environmental considerations to be explicitly considered in the conventional cost-benefit calculus used in economic decisionmaking. Key related aspects including environmental impacts of economywide policies, discount rate issues, and multicriteria analysis are reviewed. The process of internalizing environmental externalities may be facilitated by making even rough qualitative assessments early on in the project evaluation cycle. The advantages of such an approach include: (a) the early exclusion of options that are not sound environmentally; (b) more effective in-depth consideration of those alternatives that are preferable from the environmental viewpoint; and (c) better opportunities for redesigning projects and policies to achieve sustainable development goals.

A number of developing country case studies, which cover a wide range of practical valuation methods, are reviewed. We may conclude generally, that further application to practical problems in developing countries is required (rather than further theoretical development), of the environmental valuation concepts and techniques presented in the paper. Such case study work can be most effective when carried out as part of project preparation.

In recent times, the environment has emerged as a major worldwide concern. Pollution in particular is perceived as a serious threat in the industrialized countries, where the quality of life had hitherto been measured mainly in terms of growth in material output. Meanwhile, natural resource degradation is becoming a serious impediment to economic development and the alleviation of poverty in the developing world.

Mankind's relationship with the environment has gone through several stages, starting with primitive times in that human beings lived in a state of symbiosis with nature, followed by a period of increasing mastery over nature up to the industrial age, culminating in the rapid material-intensive growth pattern of the twentieth century that adversely affected natural resources in many ways. The initial reaction to such environmental damage was a reactive approach characterized by increased clean-up activities. In recent decades mankind's attitude towards the environment has evolved to encompass the more proactive design of projects and policies that help anticipate and avoid environmental degradation. The world is currently exploring the concept of sustainable development—an approach that will permit continuing improvements in the present quality of life and will lower the intensity of resource use, thereby leaving behind for future generations an undiminished or even enhanced stock of natural resources and other assets.[1]

Environmental assets that we seek to protect provide three main types of services to human society, and the consequences of their degradation must be incorporated into the decisionmaking process. First, the environment provides essential raw materials and inputs that support human activities. Second, it serves as a sink to absorb and recycle (normally at little or no cost to society) the waste products of economic activity. Finally, it provides irreplaceable life support functions (for example, the stratospheric ozone layer that filters out harmful ultraviolet rays).

This paper reviews how environmental economics facilitates the efficient use of natural resources (both mineral and biological), as well as manmade capital and human resources—an objective which is a vital prerequisite for sustainable development. Special attention is paid to the key role of environmental economics in helping value environmental and natural resources more precisely and in internalizing the costs and benefits of using such resources into the conventional calculus of economic decisionmaking. More generally, the identification of sustainable development options requires:

- Good understanding of the physical, biological and social impacts of human activities

- Improved estimates of the economic value of damage to the environment that improve the design of policies and projects and lead to environmentally sound investment decisions

- Development of policy tools and strengthening of human resources and institutions to implement viable strategies and manage natural resources on a sustainable basis

Linking economics and the environment

The role of environmental economics

Environmental economics plays a key role in identifying options for efficient natural resource management that facilitate sustainable development. It is an essential bridge between the traditional techniques of decisionmaking and the emerging more environmentally sensitive approach. Environmental economics helps us incorporate ecological concerns into the

The authors are grateful to Edward Barbier, Robin Bates, Noreen Beg, Jan Bojo, Wilfrido Cruz, John Dixon, John English, Gunnar Kohlin, Karl-Goran Maler, David Pearce, Adelaida Schwab, Jeremy Warford, and Dale Whittington for comments and contributions at various stages in the preparation of this paper. This work was supported in part by a grant from the Government of Norway.

[1] This broad definition is based on *Our Common Future* (World Commission on Environment and Development 1987). For a recent review of alternative definitions of sustainable development, see Pezzey 1992.

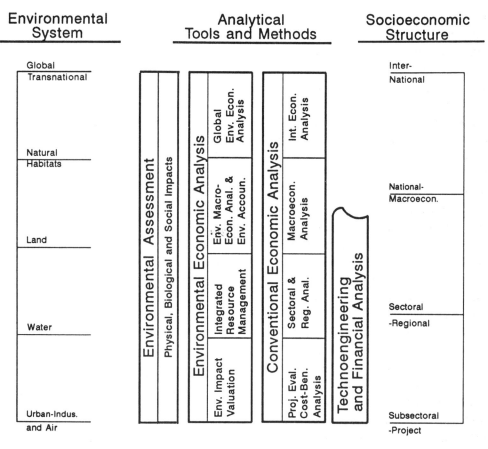

Figure 2-1: Incorporating Environmental Concerns into Decisionmaking

conventional framework of human society, as shown in Figure 2-1.

The right-hand side of the diagram indicates the hierarchical nature of modern society. The global and transnational level consists of sovereign nation states. In the next level are individual countries, each having a multisectoral macroeconomic structure. Various economic sectors (such as energy, industry, agriculture, transport, etc.) exist within each country. Finally, each sector consists of different subsectors, projects and local schemes.

Unfortunately, the analysis of the environment cannot be carried out readily using the above socioeconomic structuring. As shown on the left side of Figure 2-1, one convenient breakdown recognizes environmental issues that are (1) global and transnational (for example, climate change, ozone layer depletion); (2) natural habitat (for example, forests and other ecosystems); (3) land (for example, agricultural zone); (4) water resources (for example, river basin, aquifer, watershed); and (5) urban-industrial (for example, metropolitan area,

airshed). In each case, a holistic environmental analysis would seek to study a physical or ecological system in its entirety. Complications arise because such natural systems tend to cut across the decisionmaking structure of human society. For example, a forest ecosystem (like the Amazon) could span several countries, and also interact with many different economic sectors within each country.

The causes of environmental degradation arise from human activity (ignoring natural disasters and other events of nonhuman origin), and therefore, we begin on the right side of Figure 2-1. The physical (including biological and social) effects of socioeconomic decisions on the environment must then be traced through to the left side. The techniques of environmental assessment (EA) have been developed to facilitate this difficult analysis. For example, deforestation of a primary moist tropical forest may be caused by hydroelectric dams (energy sector policy), roads (transport sector policy), slash and burn farming (agriculture sector policy), mining of minerals (industrial sector policy), land clearing encouraged by land-tax incentives (fiscal policy), and so on. Disentangling and prioritizing these multiple causes (right side) and their impacts (left side) will involve a complex environmental assessment exercise.

Meanwhile, the usual decisionmaking process on the right side of Figure 2-1 relies on techno-engineering, financial and economic analyses of projects and policies. In particular, we note that conventional economic analysis has been well developed over the past several decades, and uses techniques including project evaluation/cost-benefit analysis (CBA), sectoral/regional studies, multisectoral macroeconomic analysis, and international economic analysis (finance, trade, etc.) at the various hierarchic levels.

Figure 2-1 also shows how environmental economics plays its bridging role, by mapping the EA results onto the framework of conventional economic analysis. Once again, a variety of environmental economic techniques including economic valuation of environmental impacts (at the local/project level), integrated resource management (at the sector/regional level), environmental macroeconomic analysis and environmental accounting (at the economy-wide, multisector level), and global/transnational environmental economic analysis (at the international level), facilitate this process of incorporating environmental issues into traditional decisionmaking. The analytical techniques described above overlap considerably, and therefore this conceptual categorization should not be interpreted too rigidly.

Once the foregoing steps are completed, projects and policies must be redesigned to reduce their environmental impacts and to shift the development process towards a more sustainable path. Clearly, the formulation and implementation of such policies is itself a difficult task. In the deforestation example described earlier, the decisionmakers who wish to protect this single ecosystem are likely to face problems in coordinating policies in a large number of disparate and (usually) non-cooperating ministries and line institutions (such as energy, transport, agriculture, industry, finance, and forestry).

Recent developments

Although the consolidation of environmental economic theory and its application to empirical issues spread throughout the developed world in the 1970s, the incorporation of environmental issues into development planning is a relatively recent phenomenon. A review of the literature in the field reveals the paucity of writings touching upon the environment. Academic development economics barely acknowledged the field until recently (Dasgupta and Maler 1990). Much of the literature on the environmental economics of developing countries has emerged since the mid-1980s. This is largely as a result of the increasing emphasis being placed on environmental issues by major aid-giving institutions.

The Brundtland Report recognized the role of economics in sustainable development—both in assessing costs of environmental degradation in developing countries, and in designing relevant incentives to limit such degradation (World Commission on Environment and Development 1987). The recent worldwide concern regarding the environment has strengthened the emphasis placed on environmental sustainability as an important criterion for sound natural resource management. Another facet of this concern is reflected in the increased attention paid to intergenerational equity and the role of discount rates in economic calculations.

In recent years most governments have adjusted their policy objectives to include the proper management of natural resources alongside economic growth and income distribution/poverty alleviation. These objectives may be somewhat complementary but it is accepted that trade-offs are required, at least in the short term. Given the existing scarcities of financial and human resources in developing countries and the emerging pressure on environmental resources, it is particularly important to use these limited resources in a way that can be sustained and that will have the maximum benefit in terms of the country's objectives. Sound economic analysis of projects and policies is an important means of making the allocation process more efficient, and thereby more sustainable. However, economic efficiency does not necessarily guarantee sustainability.

The growing attention to environmental issues in the work of the World Bank over the past decades culminated in November 1989 in the issuing of the mandatory environmental impact assessment required for all World Bank projects.[2] Thus environmental analysis has been elevated to the same level of importance as the three traditional aspects of project evaluation: financial, economic, and technical analyses. The valuation of environmental impacts takes on added urgency in this context, since it would permit environmental concerns to be incorporated effectively into the normal decisionmaking process in all World Bank operations.

Conventional project evaluation

The successful completion of a development project usually involves several well-defined steps. The systematic approach used by the World Bank in a typical project cycle includes identification, preparation, appraisal, negotiations and financing, implementation and supervision, and evaluation.

The project cycle

Project identification involves preliminary selection (by the borrowing country and the World Bank) of potential projects that appear to be feasible and conform to national and sectoral development goals. In the preparation phase which may last one year or more, the borrower studies the engineering-technical, environmental, institutional, economic and financial aspects of a proposed project. Project appraisal consists of a comprehensive and systematic review of all aspects of the project, culminating in an appraisal report that discusses the national and sectoral strategies as well as the engineering/technical, environmental, institutional, economic, and financial issues.

The appraisal report is the basis for justifying the investment, as well as the negotiations at which the borrower and financier (the World Bank) discuss the measures required to ensure the success of the project, and the conditions for funding. The resulting agreements are included in loan agreements which together with the appraisal report are considered and

accepted by the World Bank's Board of Executive Directors and the borrowing government. The borrower is responsible for implementing the project according to conditions mutually agreed on with the World Bank. Supervision of the implementation process is carried out by the World Bank through periodic field visits and progress reports from the borrower. Evaluation is the final stage of the project cycle, following disbursement of the loan. Project performance audits are carried out by an independent World Bank department, and where appropriate, involve review of previous project documents and field visits. This analysis yields valuable experience that helps improve the work at all stages of the project cycle.

Economic analysis and cost-benefit criteria

Cost-benefit analysis (CBA) is the key element in the appraisal stage of the project cycle. CBA seeks to assess project costs and benefits using a common yardstick. Benefits are defined relative to their effects on the improvements in human well-being. Costs are defined in terms of their opportunity costs, which is the benefit foregone by not using these resources in the best available alternative application.

In addition to this economic test, as previously mentioned, a number of other aspects (including technical, environmental, institutional, and financial criteria) also need to be considered in project appraisal. The *economic* analysis of projects differs from *financial* analysis. The latter focuses on the money profits accruing to the project enterprise or firm, based on market or financial costs. The economic analysis of a project, on the other hand, measures the effect on the *efficiency objectives* in relation to the whole economy. Rather than financial prices, shadow prices are used that reflect opportunity cost, including valuation of externalities wherever practical (as described below). Some of the criteria commonly used in the cost-benefit test of a project are described next, with the emphasis on economic rather than financial evaluation.

The most basic criterion for accepting a project compares costs and benefits to ensure that the net present value (NPV) of benefits is

---

[2] For details, see World Bank Operational Directive 4.01.

positive:

$$NPV = \sum_{t=0}^{T} (B_t - C_t)/(1 + r)^t$$

Where   Bt and Ct are the benefits and costs
in year t,
r is the discount rate, and
T is the time horizon.

Both benefits and costs are defined as the difference between what would occur *with and without* the project being implemented. In economic testing, as described later, B, C, and r are defined in economic terms and appropriately shadow priced using efficiency border prices (see the following discussion on discount rate). However, for the financial analysis of projects, B, C and r may be defined in financial terms.

If projects are to be compared or ranked, the one with the highest (and positive) NPV would be the preferred one, that is, if $NPV_I >$ NPV_{II} (where NPV_i = net present value for project i), then project I is preferred to project II, provided also that the scale of the alternatives is roughly the same. More accurately, the scale and scope of each of the projects under review must be altered so that, at the margin, the last increment of investment yields net benefits that are equal (and greater than zero) for all the projects. Complexities may arise in the analysis of interdependent projects.

The internal rate of return (IRR) is also used as a project criterion. It may be defined by:

$$\sum_{t=0}^{T} (B_t - C_t)/(1+IRR)^t = 0.$$

Thus, the IRR is the discount rate which reduces the NPV to zero. The project is acceptable if IRR > ARI (Accounting Rate of Interest), which in most normal cases implies NPV > 0 (ignoring cases in which multiple roots could occur, which may happen if the annual net benefit stream changes sign several times). Problems of interpretation occur if alternative projects have widely differing lifetimes, so that the discount rate plays a critical role.

Another frequently used criterion is the benefit-cost ratio (BCR):

$$BCR = [\sum_{t=0}^{T} B_t/(1+r)^t] / [\sum_{t=0}^{T} C_t/(1+r)_t].$$

If BCR > 1, then NPV > 0, and the project is acceptable.

Each of these criteria has its strengths and weaknesses, but NPV is probably the most useful. The NPV test may be used to derive the least-cost rule. In certain cases, the benefits of two alternative projects may be equal (that is, they both serve the same need or demand). Then the comparison of alternatives is simplified. Thus:

$$NPV_I - NPV_{II} = \sum_{t=0}^{T} [C_{II,t} - C_{I,t}]/(1+r)^t ,$$

since the benefit streams cancel out. Therefore, if

$$\sum_{t=0}^{T} C_{II,t}/(1+r)^t > \sum_{t=0}^{T} C_{I,t}/(1+r)^t ,$$

this implies that $NPV_I > NPV_{II}$.

In other words the project which has the lower present value of costs is preferred. This is called the least-cost alternative (when benefits are equal). However, even after selecting the least-cost alternative, it would still be necessary to ensure that this project would provide a positive NPV.

Shadow pricing

In the idealized world of perfect competition, the interaction of atomistic profit-maximizing producers and utility-maximizing consumers gives rise to a situation that is called Pareto-optimal.[3] In this state, prices reflect the true marginal social costs, scarce resources are efficiently allocated and, for a given income distribution, no one person can be made better off without making someone else worse off (Bator 1957).

---

[3] Further details concerning the summarized material in this section may be found in Dasgupta, Marglin, and Sen 1972; Little and Mirrlees 1974; Munasinghe 1990b; Ray 1984; and Squire and Van der Tak 1975.

However, conditions are likely to be far from ideal in the real world. Distortions due to monopoly practices, external economies and diseconomies (such as environmental impacts which are not internalized in the private market), interventions in the market process through taxes, import duties and subsidies, all result in market (or financial) prices for goods and services which may diverge substantially from their shadow prices or true economic values. Furthermore, the reliance on strict efficiency criteria for determining economic welfare implies the passive acceptance of the existing (skewed) income distribution—this may be socially and politically unacceptable, especially if there are large income disparities. Such considerations necessitate the use of appropriate shadow prices (instead of market prices) of project inputs and outputs, to determine the optimal investment decisions and policies, especially in the developing countries where market distortions are more prevalent than in the industrialized countries.

Consider a general equilibrium model of the economy in which the national goal is embodied in an acceptable objective function such as aggregate consumption. This consumption is to be maximized subject to constraints that might include limits on resource availabilities, distortions in the economy, and so on. Then, the shadow price of a given scarce economic resource represents the change in value of the objective function, caused by a marginal change in the availability of that resource. In the more specific context of a mathematical programming macroeconomic model, the optimal values of the dual variables (that correspond to the binding resource availability constraints in the primal problem) have dimensions of price, and could be interpreted as shadow prices (Luenberger 1973 and Sassone 1977). While the general equilibrium approach is conceptually important, it is too cumbersome and data-intensive to use in most cases. In practice, partial equilibrium techniques that evaluate the impact of the change in the availability of a given resource on a few key areas, rather than throughout the economy, may be used. (See the following sections on environmental accounting and environmental impacts of economywide policies.)

Two basic types of shadow prices exist. These involve whether or not society is indifferent to income distribution considerations. To illustrate this point, consider the simple national goal of maximizing the present value of aggregate consumption over a given time horizon. If the consumption of different individuals is added directly regardless of their income levels, then the shadow prices derived from such a model are termed efficiency prices because they reflect the pure efficiency of resource allocation. Alternatively, when increasing the consumption of the lower income groups becomes an important objective, this consideration is given a greater weight in evaluating aggregate consumption. Then, the resultant shadow prices are called social prices.

The goal of shadow pricing is, therefore, either efficiency or socially oriented. In brief, efficiency shadow prices try to establish the actual economic values of inputs and outputs, while socially oriented shadow prices take account of the fact that the income distribution between different societal groups or regions may be distorted in terms of overall national objectives. This may call for special adjustments—giving greater weight to benefits and costs accruing to the poor relative to the rich, for example. In practice, such formal weighting schemes are seldom used in project evaluation—instead, income distributional and other social issues are addressed through direct targeting of beneficiaries and similar ad hoc approaches. In our analysis, we will place primary emphasis on efficiency shadow pricing.

Nonpriced inputs and outputs must be shadow-priced to reflect their economic opportunity costs (see Annex 2A for details of border shadow prices and conversion factors). Major categories of such nonpriced inputs and outputs are public goods and externalities (especially environmental impacts). Public goods are defined as those goods and services that are free to all without payments once they have been made available, such as police protection and transportation and navigation facilities. Externalities are defined as beneficial or adverse effects imposed on others for which the originator of these effects cannot charge or be charged (as the case may be).

Unfortunately, many externalities are not only difficult to measure in physical terms but even more difficult to convert into monetary equivalents (that is, to measure the "willingness to pay" of the parties affected by the externalities). Quite often therefore, the approach taken is to impose regulations and standards, expressed in physical measurements only, that try to eliminate the perceived external damages. However, this approach may not be effective, because no attempt is made to compare the costs of compliance with the real benefits provided (that is, damages avoided). The basic concepts and techniques for economic valuation of environmental impacts are discussed later in the chapter.

Numeraire

To derive a consistent set of economic shadow prices for goods and services, a common yardstick or numeraire to measure value is necessary. The choice of the numeraire, like the choice of a currency unit, should not influence the economic criteria for decisionmaking, provided the same consistent framework and assumptions are used in the analysis.

The same nominal unit of currency may have a different value depending on the economic circumstances in which it is used. For example, a rupee-worth of a certain good purchased in a duty free shop is likely to be more than the physical quantity of the same good obtained for one rupee from a retail store, after import duties and taxes have been levied. Therefore, it is possible to distinguish intuitively between the border-priced rupee, which is used in international markets free of import tariffs, and a domestic-priced rupee, which is used in the domestic market subject to various distortions. A more sophisticated example of the value differences of a currency unit in various uses arises in countries where investment for future economic growth is considered inadequate. In these instances, a rupee-worth of savings that could be invested to increase the level of future consumption, may be considered more valuable than a rupee devoted to current consumption.

A most appropriate numeraire in many instances is a unit of uncommitted public income at border shadow prices (Little and Mirrlees 1974). Essentially, this unit is the same as freely disposable foreign exchange available to the government, but expressed in terms of units of local currency converted at the official exchange rate. Annex 2A contains a discussion of this particular yardstick of value. The border-priced numeraire is particularly relevant for the foreign exchange-scarce developing countries. It represents the set of opportunities available to a country to purchase goods and services on the international market.

National income accounts and macroeconomic performance

In order to accurately recognize and include environmental concerns in economic analyses, standard income accounting techniques must be re-examined. Performance is currently measured by the growth in gross domestic product (GDP), and policy reforms are justified routinely on the basis of their short-, medium-, or long-term contribution to such growth. While GDP measures market activity reasonably well, it has been criticized for its neglect of nonmarket value added. More importantly, since GDP does not consider depreciation of manmade capital and also leaves out the degradation of "natural capital," it is an inaccurate measure of true, sustainable income. In terms of the environment, there are three specific shortcomings in the current national accounting framework:

4. Natural and environmental resources are not included in balance sheets; therefore, national accounts represent limited indicators of national well-being, since they are a poor, or even "perverse," measure of changes in environmental and resource conditions.

5. Conventional national accounts fail to record the depreciation of natural capital, such as a nation's stock of water, soil, air, nonrenewable resources, and wilderness areas, which are essential for human existence. Dasgupta and Maler (1991) make the case that resource-based goods are underpriced in the market—the lower the value added, the larger is the extent of underpricing of the final product. It follows that countries that export primary products do so by subsidizing them, usually

with disproportionately large adverse impacts on the poorest members of society (who are less able to protect themselves)—the small cultivator, the forest dweller, the landless peasant, and so on. Currently, there are no estimates of such hidden costs or "subsidies." If there were, the GDP of many countries could well be significantly lower. In addition, natural resource depletion raises intergenerational equity issues to the extent that the productive assets available to future generations are unfairly diminished (see the discussion on discount rate in the next section).

6.   Cleanup costs (for example, expenditures incurred to restore environmental assets) are often included in national income, while environmental damages are not considered. For private firms, defensive environmental expenditures (that is, measures to reduce or avoid environmental damage) are netted out of final value added. In contrast, such cleanup costs are considered as productive contributions to national output if they are incurred by the public sector or by households. The calculation of GDP is distorted in two ways—undesirable outputs (for example, pollution) are overlooked while beneficial environment-related inputs related to environmental needs are often implicitly valued at zero.[4]

The deficiencies in the accounting techniques employed at present point to the need for a system of national accounts (SNA) which permits the computation of an environmentally-adjusted net domestic product (EDP) and an environmentally-adjusted net income (EDI). Such measures would help to better capture environmental services, account for the depreciation of both manmade and natural capital, exclude relevant categories of defensive environmental expenditures, and/or estimate damages as a result of economic activities. To the extent that national level decisionmakers and macroeconomic planners (typically, in a Ministry of Finance or National Planning) rely on the conventional SNA to formulate economic policies, a supplementary environmentally-adjusted

SNA and corresponding performance indicators would encourage policymakers to reassess the macroeconomic situation in light of environmental concerns and to trace the links between economywide policies and natural resource management (Muzondo et al. 1990).

Based on ongoing work since 1983, the World Bank has actively encouraged the consideration of environmental issues during the ongoing revision of the SNA by the United Nations. As an interim measure, it proposed that a satellite system for integrated environmental and economic accounting (SEAA) be created. This approach represents a compromise that does not change the core of the SNA, its production boundary, and the relevant time series—but at the same time, the satellite accounts will encourage the collection and compilation of relevant information on natural resources and the environment. The satellite accounts are an interim step that will permit further progress towards the computation of an EDP and an EDI. The World Bank, together with the UN Statistical Office (UNSO), has recently completed case studies in Mexico (van Tongeren et al. 1991) and Papua New Guinea (Bartelmus et al. 1992), to determine how such accounts can be prepared.

The "UNSO Framework" (Bartelmus, Stahmer, and van Tongeren 1989) was used as a basis for the above studies. This framework is a system for environmentally-adjusted economic accounts which represents one approach to deriving EDP and ENI. Its objective is to integrate environmental data sets with existing national accounts information, while maintaining SNA concepts and principles insofar as possible. Environmental costs, benefits, and natural resource assets, as well as expenditures for environmental protection, are presented in flow accounts and balance sheets in a consistent manner, while maintaining the accounting identities of the SNA.

On the basis of the UNSO framework, a draft Handbook for Environmental Accounting has been developed (UNSO 1990) which outlines in detail the possibilities for computing an EDP. Until the EDP concept becomes more

---

[4]   Dasgupta and Maler (1991) suggest that in order to avoid doublecounting, expenditures that enhance resource bases, such as forests, should not be included in national income computations, as they are already reflected in the value of changes in the resource stocks.

widely accepted and used, decisionmakers and policy analysts should keep in mind the limitations of current national accounts information. Ultimately, the most desirable policy reforms are the ones that would focus on increasing EDP rather than GDP, since EDP more accurately measures "sustainable" income (see also Peskin 1990, and Repetto et al. 1989, for related research).

Economywide policies and the environment

Economywide policies (both macroeconomic and sectoral) play a significant role in the rate of depletion of natural resources and the level of environmental degradation. Fiscal and monetary policies, structural adjustment programs, and stabilization measures all have an effect on the natural resource base. Unfortunately, interactions between the economy and the environment are complex and our understanding of them limited. Ideally one would wish to trace the effects of economywide policy reforms (both macroeconomic and sectoral) through the economic and ecological systems. Time and data limitations generally preclude the use of such comprehensive approaches in developing countries. Practical policy analysis is usually limited to a more "partial equilibrium" approach that involves an effort to trace the most important impacts of specific economywide policies, at least qualitatively, and wherever possible, quantitatively.

Macroeconomic policies

In the 1980s, debtor countries adopted emergency stabilization programs that necessitated currency devaluations, controls on capital, and interest rate increases. When income levels dropped, tax revenues decreased accordingly. As unemployment increased, governments fell back upon expansionary financing policies, which led to increases in consumer prices. The effect of such policies on the poorest population groups often drove them onto marginal lands, resulting in soil erosion and desertification. Fuel price increases and lowered incomes combined to cause deforestation and reductions in soil fertility, as the poor were forced to use fuelwood and animal dung for heating, lighting, and cooking.

Real currency devaluations have the effect of increasing international competitiveness, and raising production of internationally tradable goods (for example, forestry and agricultural products). If the agricultural response occurs through crop substitution, environmental impact would depend on whether the higher priced crop had environmental benefits (for example, tea, cocoa, and rubber) or was environmentally damaging (for example, tobacco, sugarcane, and corn). Environmental impacts would also depend on whether increased production led to farming on new land (which could result in increased deforestation) or resulted in more efficient use of existing farmland. By increasing the competitiveness of world exports, it has been demonstrated by Capistrano and Kiker (1990) that the opportunity cost of keeping timber unharvested increases as a result. This could lead to forest depletion that significantly exceeds natural regenerative capacity.

Overvaluation of the exchange rate results in negative terms of trade, encouraging the production of subsistence crops at the expense of internationally tradable products. If these subsistence crops are environmentally harmful, then currency overvaluation leads to environmental degradation. In addition, decreased competitiveness of products and lower farmgate prices push small cultivators onto marginal lands in an attempt to absorb the effects of the price changes.

In a recent review of the links between growth, trade policy, and the environment (Lopez 1991), the author argues that the output from a natural resource such as a forest or fishery (where production depends critically on the stock) also will be affected by other factors (for example, property rights). Thus, if trade policy increased the value of output (for example, timber or fish exports), then the degree of ownership would influence how production and resource stocks were managed. Reactions might range from more investment in and maintenance of assets (if environmental costs were internalized by owner-users) to rapid depletion (when the users had no stake in the resource stock).

Structural adjustment

The conditionality clause embodied in structural adjustment loans (SALs) implemented by the World Bank covers many of the elements discussed above: increases in agricultural prices, currency devaluations, and removal of agricultural subsidies (Sebastian and Alicbusan 1989). Export taxes are often one of the policies included. Such taxes, which are a means of generating public revenues, result in lower agricultural prices. Again, environmental impacts depend on the nature of the crops.

SALs often call for reductions in energy subsidies, to decrease pollution and encourage energy conservation. However, such policies may force poor consumers to substitute fuelwood and animal dung for liquid fuels, thereby increasing deforestation and decreasing soil fertility.

SALs usually entail the adoption of policies designed to (a) promote trade liberalization through removal of barriers to external trade, and encouragement of exports; and (b) implement institutional reform through privatization, encouragement of foreign investment, better training and marketing, and reform of land ownership.

The benefits and costs of such projects are highly country-specific. There is some concern that encouraging foreign investment and privatization might lead to the growth of "pollution havens," given the weakness of environmental regulations in most developing countries. Trade liberalization also could encourage the growth of energy-intensive and/or highly polluting industry. However, pollution caused by industrialization could be offset by afforestation (although this does not necessarily compensate residents of polluted areas), and limited by appropriate taxation policies that encouraged the use of pollution abatement technologies. In a recent review of the Latin American experience, Birdsall and Wheeler (1991) conclude that there is no evidence to show that open economies are more prone to pollution. They argue that the inflow of foreign technology and capital would tend to bring in better pollution standards. At the same time, it is the pollution-intensive heavy industries sector that has generally benefited from protective industrial and trade policies.

Public investment/expenditure reviews

Reductions in public expenditure are an integral part of many SALs, and usually emerge from recommendations on spending priorities made in Public Investment/Expenditure Reviews (PI/ERs). The main purpose of PI/ERs is to provide recommendations to governments on the size and composition of their spending programs and on ways to strengthen local institutions in ways that enhance country capabilities to design and implement such programs. They have also been used to carry out basic sector work and to identify projects appropriate for World Bank support. PI/ERs can form the heart of the World Bank's country dialogue, as expenditure decisions by the core planning and finance agencies are central to the key objectives of structural adjustment, poverty alleviation, and sound management of natural resources.

Public investment programs in most countries may not have given adequate weight to environmental objectives as compared to efficiency and poverty alleviation. The potential clearly exists for investment reviews to appropriately elevate environmental concerns and thereby help to avoid making investments that have serious long-term environmental consequences. The expenditure reviews are perhaps less crucial; nevertheless, these could be used to ensure, for example, that conservation-oriented agencies and extension programs get a fair share of current government expenditures.

Sectoral policies

Practical examples of the effects sectoral policies have on the environment have been described in several studies.[5] Some countries subsidize urban consumers by placing price ceilings on food. In such cases, the environmental consequences will be the same as for currency overvaluation, as both result in lowered incentives to increase production of internationally tradable crops.

---

[5] See for example: Binswanger 1989, Mahar 1989, Repetto 1988, Sebastian and Alicbusan 1989, and Lutz and Young 1990.

Lutz and Young (1990) traced the effects of agricultural policies on the natural resource base. They found that where the removal of a fertilizer or pesticide subsidy is being considered in an adjustment program, government expenditures will decrease, farmers' use of these inputs will decrease, and adverse environmental side effects will tend to diminish as well.

In the case of Brazil, Binswanger (1989) showed that general tax policies, special tax incentives, the rules of land allocation, and the agricultural credit system all accelerate deforestation in the Amazon. These policies also increase the size of landholdings and reduce the land available to the poor.

Mahar (1989) traced many of today's problems in the Amazon in Brazil to the decision in the mid-1960s to provide overland access to Amazonia. This decision was made before enough was known about the region's natural resource base and how to develop it in a sustainable manner. The initial error was compounded by subsequent decisions to provide generous incentives to investors willing to undertake environmentally questionable livestock projects, and more recently, smelting projects in the greater Carajas areas. Official settlement projects have also contributed to deforestation, although it would be wrong to place all of the blame on the settlers. Pushed by poverty and skewed land distribution in their regions of origin, the settlers have merely responded to incentives created by the government in the form of access roads, title to public lands, various public services, and, in the case of the Transamazon scheme, subsistence allowances.

Environmental cost-benefit analysis for economic decisionmaking

Recently, Little and Mirrlees (1990) noted that from the mid-1970s to 1990, there had been a "rise and decline of project appraisal in the World Bank and elsewhere", and they concluded that currently the incentives were inadequate for project analysts to undertake thorough, in-depth evaluations of projects.

Given the existing discrepancy between what ought to or could be done and what is actually being done in practice, the question arises whether it is realistic to expect a more thorough treatment of environmental issues. Our view is that even in situations where analysts have limited resources at their disposal, natural resource and environmental issues may be critical ones that can make a difference between success and failure of a project or policy. Therefore, depending on the nature of the project or policy reform package, a significant share of available resources should be devoted to environmentally oriented economic analysis, preferably early in the project cycle. Even in cases where the physical impact on the environment cannot be easily valued in economic terms, techniques of multiobjective analysis may be used to improve the quality of the investment decision.

The following section contains a summary of "best practice" that can be pursued to better integrate natural resource and environmental issues into economic analyses of projects and policies. Four key aspects are discussed: (a) determining the physical impacts and valuing the impacts in monetary terms; (b) multiobjective decisionmaking; (c) discounting; and (d) risk and uncertainty. The main emphasis is given to methods and approaches for valuing environmental effects.

Valuation of environmental costs and benefits

The first step in conducting environmentally sound economic analyses is to determine the environmental and natural resource impacts of the project or policies in question. These physical impacts (broadly defined to include also biological and social effects) are determined by comparing the "with project" and the "without project" scenarios. For determining such impacts, the economist will have to rely on the expertise of engineers, ecologists, agronomists, social scientists, and other experts. An important issue, outside the scope of this paper, is that such physical impacts are complex and often poorly understood.

The second step in considering environmental effects involves valuing the physical impacts and relationships. An environmental impact can result in a measurable change in production and/or change in environmental

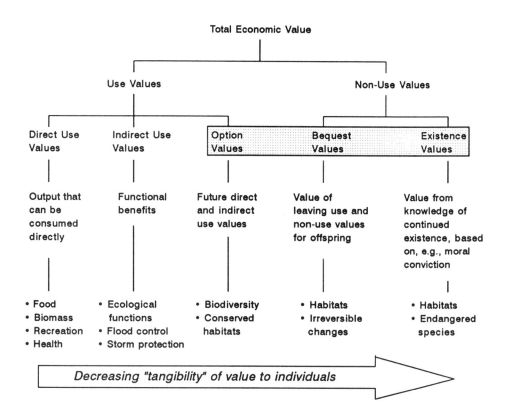

Total Economic Value

Use Values — Non-Use Values

| Direct Use Values | Indirect Use Values | Option Values | Bequest Values | Existence Values |

| Output that can be consumed directly | Functional benefits | Future direct and indirect use values | Value of leaving use and non-use values for offspring | Value from knowledge of continued existence, based on, e.g., moral conviction |

| • Food
• Biomass
• Recreation
• Health | • Ecological functions
• Flood control
• Storm protection | • Biodiversity
• Conserved habitats | • Habitats
• Irreversible changes | • Habitats
• Endangered species |

Decreasing "tangibility" of value to individuals

Figure 2-2: Categories of Economic Values Attributed to Environmental Assets

quality. A number of concepts of value, and practical valuation techniques have been developed to trace the welfare impacts of these changes.

Basic concepts of economic value

Conceptually, the *total economic value* (TEV) of a resource consists of its (a) use value (UV) and (b) nonuse value (NUV). *Use values* may be broken down further into the direct use value (DUV), the indirect use value (IUV), and the option value (OV) (potential use value). One needs to be careful not to double count both the value of indirect supporting functions *and* the value of the resulting direct use.[6] The categories of *nonuse value* are existence value (EV) and bequest value (BV).[7] Therefore, we may write:

TEV = UV + NUV or
TEV = [DUV + IUV + OV] + [EV + BV]

Figure 2-2 shows this disaggregation of TEV in schematic form. Below each valuation concept, a short description of its meaning and a few typical examples of the environmental resources underlying the perceived value, are provided. Option values, bequest values, and existence values are shaded to caution the analyst concerning some of the ambiguities associated with defining these concepts. As shown in the examples, they can spring from similar or identical resources, and their estimation could be interlinked as well. However, these concepts of value are generally quite distinct. *Option value* is based on how much individuals are willing to pay today for the option of

---

[6]   For a discussion and example of this, see Aylward and Barbier 1992.
[7]   The various terms in the equation for TEV may be grouped in somewhat different ways, for convenience. See, for example, Walsh, Loomis, and Gillman 1984. In order to measure willingness to pay for wilderness protection, they sought to separate (a future-oriented) preservation value from recreational use value (in current use). Accordingly, these authors defined preservation value (PV) as option value plus existence value plus bequest value, that is, PV = [OV + EV + BV].

Table 2-1: Taxonomy of Relevant Valuation Techniques

	Conventional market	*Implicit market*	*Constructed market*
Based on actual behavior	Change of productivity Loss of earnings Defensive expenditure	Travel cost Wage differences Property values	Artificial market
Based on potential behavior	Replacement cost Shadow project		Contingent valuation

preserving the asset for future (personal) direct and indirect use. *Bequest value*, while excluding individuals' own use values, is the value that people derive from knowing that others (perhaps their own offspring), will be able to benefit from the resource in the future. Finally, *existence value* is the perceived value of the environmental asset unrelated either to current or optional use, that is, simply because it exists.[8]

A variety of valuation techniques may be used to quantify the above concepts of value. The basic concept of economic valuation underlying all these techniques is the willingness to pay (WTP) of individuals for an environmental service or resource, i.e., the area under the compensated or Hicksian demand curve.[9] As shown in Table 2-1, valuation methods can be categorized, on the one hand, according to which type of market they rely on, and on the other hand, by considering how they make use of actual or potential behavior.

Next, we group the valuation techniques in Table 2-1 according to analytical method and provide some general comments, before discussing each technique in greater detail.

Under specific conditions, such as when the environmental impact leads to a marginal change in the supply of a good or service that is bought on a competitive market, the WTP can be estimated directly in terms of changes valued at prevailing market prices. If the market is not fully competitive, then the market valuation will be a partial measure, and shadow price corrections may need to be made. The

foregoing comments apply to change of productivity.

Often, the result of the impact cannot be directly related to a market activity. In some of these cases, the WTP could be estimated at conventional market value by using a closely related proxy. Care should be exercised on the following points: (a) the relevant attributes affected by the environmental impact might, in the case of the proxy measure, be mixed with other attributes, thereby affecting the value of proxy; and (b) if the proxy attributes are identical to the ones lost by the impact, then the value given by the proxy is only a lower bound for the true WTP. This approach applies to the following techniques: loss of earnings, defensive expenditure, replacement cost, and shadow project.

In certain cases the WTP can be estimated through derivation of a demand function for the environmental asset through analysis of actual behavior. Examples of this approach (also called surrogate market techniques) include travel cost, wage differential, and property valuation.

The WTP can also be elicited through a controlled experiment or direct interviews, using the artificial market and contingent valuation.

Direct effects valued on conventional markets

The primary feature of the methods considered in this section is that they are directly based on market prices or productivity. This is

---

[8] See for example Randall and Stoll 1983.
[9] For an up-to-date exposition, see Braden and Kolstad 1991.

possible where a change in environmental quality affects actual production or productive capability.

Change in productivity. Development projects can affect production and productivity positively or negatively. The incremental output can be valued by using standard economic prices. There are examples of this in the following case studies. In the study on soil conservation in Lesotho, the increased production from conserved land is estimated. In the valuation of 1 hectare of Peruvian rainforest, the values of different production schemes are compared. Other examples include impacts on tropical wetlands (Barbier et al. 1991) and the effects of sedimentation on coral diversity and ultimately on fish production (Hodgson and Dixon 1988).

Loss of earnings. Changes in environmental quality can have significant effects on human health. Ideally, the monetary value of health impacts should be determined by the willingness to pay, of individuals, for improved health. In practice, one may have to resort to "second best" techniques such as using foregone earnings in cases of premature death, sickness, or absenteeism (and increased medical expenditures, which can be considered a type of replacement cost). This approach may be relevant, for example, when considering road and industrial plant safety, and projects that affect air pollution in major cities of developing countries.

The "value-of-life" approach is often questioned on ethical grounds. It is argued that it dehumanizes life, which is considered to have infinite value. In practice, however, society implicitly places finite values on human life and health in policy and project decisions that affect environmental quality, workers' safety, or health. If this was not so, we would be justified in spending all of GDP on health improvements.

In the case of an increase or a reduction in the probability of numbers of deaths, an approximate estimate of value is the loss in estimated future earnings of the individuals

involved (also called the human capital approach) (see Fredriksson and Persson 1989).

Actual defensive or preventive expenditures. Individuals, firms, and governments undertake a variety of "defensive expenditures" in order to avoid or reduce unwanted environmental effects. Environmental damages are often difficult to assess, but information on defensive expenditures may be available or can be obtained at lesser cost than direct valuations of the environmental good in question. Such *actual* expenditures indicate that individuals, firms, or governments judge the resultant benefits to be greater than the costs. The defensive expenditures can then be interpreted as a minimum valuation of benefits.[10] However, caution is advisable with this approach, especially in cases where defensive expenditures are arbitrarily mandated by governments, with little or no consideration to market forces or free choices by informed economic agents.

Potential expenditure valued on conventional markets

Replacement cost. Under this approach, the costs that would have to be incurred in order to replace a damaged asset are estimated. The estimate is *not* a measure of benefit of avoiding the damage in the first place, since the damage costs may be higher or lower than the replacement cost. However, it *is* an appropriate technique if there is some compelling reason as to why the damage should be restored, or certainty that this will occur.

The replacement cost approach has been applied to protecting groundwater resources in the Philippines, by determining the cost of developing alternative water sources (Munasinghe 1990c). A second type of application involves estimating erosion prevention benefits by calculating the value of fertilizer needed to replace the nutrients lost through soil erosion. The method is only relevant if, in the absence of erosion control measures, the fertilizer would actually be applied. Another example would be the cost of an artificial fish

---

[10] As mentioned in the section on national income accounts, work is ongoing to identify defensive expenditures. Such expenditures by firms are treated in the current system of national accounts as intermediate costs and are therefore not part of value added or final output. Defensive expenditures by households and governments, on the other hand, are treated as final expenditures and included in GDP. Present research seeks to address this and other issues and inconsistencies in the SNA (see Lutz and Munasinghe 1991).

nursery to estimate the value of wetlands that might be impaired by a project. The same technique of estimating potential ex-post mitigation expenditures represented by the increased costs of health care, is used in the tobacco case study.

Shadow project. When evaluating projects that have negative environmental impacts, this approach involves the design and costing of one or more "shadow projects" that provide for substitute environmental services to compensate for the loss of environmental assets under the ongoing projects. This approach is essentially an institutional judgment of the replacement cost, and is increasingly being mentioned as a possible way of operationalizing the concept of sustainability at the project level. It assumes that maintaining environmental capital intact is a constraint. Its application, therefore, could be most relevant when "critical" environmental assets are at risk.

Valuation using implicit (or surrogate) markets

The methods and techniques described in this section use market information indirectly. The approaches discussed here include travel cost, property value, wage differential, and marketed goods as surrogates for nonmarketed goods. Each technique has its particular advantages and disadvantages as well as its specific requirements for data and resources. The task of the analyst is to determine which of the techniques might be applicable to a particular situation.

Travel cost. Most often connected with recreational analysis in industrial countries, the travel cost method measures the benefits produced by recreation sites (parks, lakes, forests, wilderness). A related method can also be used to value "travel time" in projects dealing with fuelwood and water collection.[11]

In this method, the area surrounding a site is divided into concentric zones of increasing distance. A survey of users, conducted at the site, determines the zone of origin, visitation rates, travel costs, and various socio-economic characteristics. Users close to the site would be expected to make more use of it, because its implicit price, as measured by travel costs, is lower than that for more distant users. Analysis of the questionnaires enables a demand curve to be constructed (based on the willingness to pay for entry to the site, costs of getting to the site, and foregone earnings or opportunity cost of time spent) and an associated consumers' surplus to be determined. This surplus represents an estimate of the value of the environmental good in question.

Two of the case studies summarized below use the travel cost method. In one study, the travel cost for *domestic* trips to a forest reserve in Costa Rica is used. In the other, a study on the value of elephants in Kenya, the travel cost of tourists from Europe and North America is used as one estimate of consumer surplus.

Property value. Also referred to as a "hedonic price" technique, the property value method is based on the general land value approach. The objective is to determine the implicit prices of certain characteristics of properties. In the environmental area, for instance, the aim of the method is to place a value on the benefits of environmental quality improvements, or to estimate the costs of a deterioration (for example, the effects of air pollution in certain areas).

The property value approach has been used to analyze the effects of air pollution in certain areas. Where pollution is localized, the method compares prices of houses in affected areas with houses of equal size and similar neighborhood characteristics elsewhere in the same metropolitan area. The approach is based on the assumption of a competitive real estate market, and its demands on information and statistical analysis are significant. Its applicability to developing countries is, therefore, limited.

Wage differential. This method is based on the theory that in a competitive market the demand for labor equals the value of the marginal product and that the supply of labor varies with working and living conditions in an area. A higher wage is therefore necessary to attract workers to locate in polluted areas or to undertake more risky occupations. Again, as in the case of property value, the wage differential can only be used if the labor market is very competitive (see earlier discussion on shadow pricing). Other considerations are that this

[11] For a recent example, see Hanley 1989.

method relies on private valuation of health risks, not necessarily social ones. In this context, the level of information concerning occupational hazards must be high in order for private individuals to make meaningful trade-offs between health risks and remuneration. Finally, the effects of all factors other than environment (for example, skill level, job responsibility, and so forth) that might influence wages must be eliminated, to isolate the impacts of environment.

Marketed goods as proxies for nonmarketed goods. In situations where environmental goods have close substitutes that are marketed, the value of the environmental good in question can be approximated by the observed market price of its substitutes. For example, the value of a nonmarketed fish variety can be valued at the price of the most similar fish being sold in local markets (Barbier et al. 1991).

Valuation using constructed markets

Contingent valuation. In the absence of people's preferences as revealed in markets, the contingent valuation method tries to obtain information on consumers' preferences by posing direct questions about willingness to pay. It basically asks people what they are willing to pay for a benefit, or what they are willing to accept by way of compensation to tolerate a cost (or both). This process of asking may be either through a direct questionnaire/survey, or by experimental techniques in which subjects respond to various stimuli in "laboratory" conditions. What is sought are personal valuations of the respondent for increases or decreases in the quantity of some good, contingent upon a hypothetical market. Willingness to pay is constrained by the income level of the respondent, whereas willingness to accept payment for a loss is not constrained. Estimates of willingness to accept tend to be significantly higher than willingness-to-pay estimates.

Pearce and Markandya (1989) compared the contingent valuation method with other, more market-based methods. In seven studies

done in industrial countries they found that the overlap of estimates is complete, if accuracy is expressed as plus or minus 60 percent of the estimates computed. This result provides some reassurance that a rigorously applied contingent valuation method, while not being very precise, nevertheless can produce valuations that are of the right order of magnitude and that may be sufficient to rule out certain alternative projects or favor others.

The contingent valuation method has certain shortcomings, including problems of designing, implementing, and interpreting questionnaires.[12] While its applicability may be limited, there is now considerable experience in applying this survey-based approach in developing countries, for example, to evaluate the quality of supply of potable water and electricity services.[13]

In certain circumstances, contingent valuation may be the only available technique for estimating benefits. It can be and has been applied to common property resources, amenity resources with scenic, ecological or other characteristics, and to other situations where market information is not available (Mitchell and Carson 1989). Caution should be exercised in seeking to pursue some of the more abstract benefits of environmental assets such as existence value (of an asset that may never be used, but promises psychic satisfaction merely because it exists)[14].

Two examples of contingent valuation surveys are given in the case studies. The use of the contingent valuation method for estimating the value of viewing elephants in Kenya shows that it is possible to achieve an understanding of the order of magnitude of the benefits with only small means. The study described below on willingness to pay for water services in southern Haiti tests the methodology for different biases, proving its reliability.

Artificial market. Such markets could be constructed for experimental purposes, to determine consumer willingness to pay for a good or service. For example, a home water purification kit might be marketed at various price

---

[12] See for example several papers appearing in The Energy Journal, December 1988.

[13] For examples of contingent valuation studies, see the case studies on Haiti and Kenya in this paper, and in Munasinghe 1990a.

[14] See for example Randall and Stoll 1983.

levels or access to a game reserve might be offered on the basis of different admission fees, thereby facilitating the estimation of the value placed by individuals on water purity or on the use of a recreational facility, respectively.

Multi-objective decisionmaking

The methods described above are used to estimate costs and benefits of a given project in monetary terms. When projects/policies and their impacts are to be embedded in a system of broader (national) objectives, some of which cannot be easily quantified in monetary terms, multi-objective decisionmaking offers an alternative approach.

Desirable objectives need to be specified. These often exhibit a hierarchical structure. The highest level represents the broad overall objectives (for example, improving the quality of life), often vaguely stated and, hence, not very operational. Some of these, however, can be broken down into more operational lower level objectives (for example, increase income) so that the extent to which the latter are met may be practically assessed. Sometimes only proxies are available (for example, if the objective is to enhance recreation opportunities, the attribute number of recreation days can be used). Although value judgements may be required in choosing the proper attribute (especially if proxies are involved) in contrast to the single-criterion methodologies used in economic cost-benefit analysis, measurement does not have to be in monetary terms. More explicit recognition is given to the fact that a variety of concerns may be associated with planning decisions.

An intuitive understanding of the fundamentals of multi-objective decisionmaking can be provided by a two-dimensional graphical exposition such as in Figure 2-3. Assume that a project has two non-commensurable and conflicting objectives, Z_1 and Z_2. Assume further that alternative projects or solutions to the problem (A, B, and C) have been identified. Clearly, point B is superior to (or dominates) A in terms of both Z_1 and Z_2. Thus, alternative A may be discarded. However, we cannot make such a simple choice between solutions B and C since the former is better than the latter with respect to objective Z_2 but worse with respect to Z_1. In general, more points (or solutions) such as B and C may be identified to define the set of all non-dominated feasible solution points that form a "non-inferior" curve (or curve of best options).

For an unconstrained problem, further ranking of alternatives cannot be conducted without the introduction of value judgements. Specific information has to be elicited from the decisionmaker to determine the most preferred solution. In its most complete form such information may be summarized by a family of equi-preference curves that indicate the way in which the decisionmaker trades off one objective against the other, as illustrated in Figure 2-3. The preferred alternative is that which results in the greatest utility—which occurs (for continuous decision variables as shown here) at the point of tangency D of the highest equi-preference curve, with the Pareto optimal curve. In this case, point E (on an even higher equi-preference curve) is not attainable.

Several multicriteria methods have been developed.[15] Which practical method in particular is suitable to determine the best alternative available depends upon the nature of the decision situation. For instance, interactive involvement of the decisionmaker has proved useful in the case of problems characterized by a large number of decision variables and complex causal interrelationships. Some objectives can be dealt with through direct optimization, while others require the satisfaction of a certain standard (for example, level of biological oxygen demand (BOD) not below 5 milligrams per liter).

The major accomplishment of multi-objective decision models is that they allow for more accurate representation of decision problems in the sense that several objectives can be accounted for. However, a key question concerns whose preferences are to be considered. The model only aids a single decisionmaker (or a homogeneous group). Various interested groups will often assign different priorities to

---

[15] For an introductory overview relevant to natural resource analysis, see Munasinghe 1992. An extensive survey including references to about 150 applications has been done by Romero and Rehman 1987. A shorter but more recent survey is by Petry 1990.

the respective objectives, and normally it may not be possible to determine a single best solution via the multi-objective model. Also, the mathematical framework imposes constraints upon the ability to effectively represent the planning problem. Nonlinear, stochastic, and dynamic formulations can assist in better defining the problem but impose costs in terms of complexity in formulation and solving the model (Cocklin 1989).

Nevertheless, in constructing the model the analyst communicates information about the nature of the problem. He specifies why factors are important and how they interact. Liebman (1976) observes that "modelling is thinking made public" and considers the transfer of knowledge as perhaps the most important contribution of modelling. With respect to the second point of criticism (that is, diverse preferences), Liebman suggests that there is value to be gained in constructing models from differing perspectives and comparing the results.

Discount rate

Discounting is the process by which costs and benefits that occur in different time periods may be compared. The discount rate to be used has been a general problem in cost-benefit analysis[16], but it is particularly important with regard to environmental issues, since at least some of the associated costs and benefits are long-term in nature.

In standard analysis, past costs and benefits are treated as "sunk" and are ignored in decisions about the present and future. Future costs and benefits are discounted to their equivalent present value and then compared. In theory the interest rate in a perfect market reflects both the subjective rate of time preference (of private individuals) and the rate of productivity of capital. These rates are equated at the margin by the market, so that the rate at which individuals are willing to trade present for future values is just equal at the margin to the rate at which they are able to transform present goods (in the form of foregone consumption), into future goods (through capital investment).

Often, the rate of time preference and the rate of capital productivity are not equal, because of imperfect financial markets and government distortions introduced by taxation. Also, individual decisions differ from social decisions in that individuals are relatively short-lived, whereas societies persist for much longer periods. Thus one strong reason for individual preference for the present—the certainty of death coupled with the uncertainty of when it will occur—is absent from the viewpoint of society. The community has reason to discount the future less than individuals.

The rate of capital productivity is often very high in developing countries, because of the scarcity of capital. In the poorer countries, the rate of time preference also is elevated in many cases, because of the urgency of satisfying immediate food needs rather than ensuring long-term food security (Pearce and Turner 1990).

Higher discount rates may discriminate against future generations. This is because projects with social costs occurring in the long term and net social benefits occurring in the near term, will be favored by higher discount rates. Projects with benefits accruing in the long run will be less likely to be undertaken under high discount rates. It is therefore a logical conclusion that future generations will suffer from market discount rates determined by high rates of current generation time preference and/or productivity of capital.

Based on the foregoing, it is often argued that discount rates should be lowered to reflect environmental concerns and issues of intergenerational equity. However, this would have the drawback that not only would ecologically sound activities pass the cost-benefit test more frequently, but also a larger number of projects would generally pass the test and the resulting increase in investment would lead to additional environmental stress. Norgaard (1991) argues that lowering discount rates can in fact worsen environmental degradation—lowering the cost of capital and thereby lowering the cost of production such that more is consumed in the near-term relative to the case where discount rates were higher.

---

[16] For more details, see Dasgupta 1972, Harberger 1976, Little and Mirrlees 1974, Marglin 1963, and Sen 1967.

Many environmentalists believe that a zero discount rate should be employed to protect future generations. However, employing a zero discount rate is inequitable, since it would imply a policy of total current sacrifice, which runs counter to the proposed aim of eliminating discrimination between time periods—especially when the present contained widespread poverty (Pearce 1991).

Norgaard makes the case that manipulating discount rates to reflect sustainability concerns results in an inefficient use of capital. Instead he suggests direct income transfers to compensate for environmental degradation. He utilizes a general equilibrium model to demonstrate that income transfers to future generations, through the efficient allocation of resources, results in new levels of savings and investment, a shift in the types of investments, and a different interest (or discount) rate. The rate of interest may increase or decrease, but this is irrelevant, since it merely serves as an equilibrating price.

In order to facilitate such intergenerational transfers, one alternative might be to impose a sustainability constraint, whereby current well-being is maximized without reducing the welfare of future generations below that of the current generation. In practice, this would entail monitoring and measurement of capital stocks (man-made, human, and natural) and an overarching investment policy that sought to ensure that compensating investments offset depreciation of existing assets (Pearce 1991). The aim would be to ensure that the overall stock of capital (broadly defined) is preserved or enhanced for future generations. Apart from the previously detailed attempts to include depreciation of natural resource stock in national income accounting, little has been accomplished in this area.

In the case of projects leading to irreversible damage (such as destruction of natural habitats, and so on), the benefits of preservation may be incorporated into standard cost-benefit methodology using the Krutilla-Fisher approach (Markandya and Pearce 1988). Benefits of preservation will grow over time as the supply of scarce environmental resources decreases, demand (fueled by population growth) increases, and, possibly, existence value increases. The Krutilla-Fisher approach incorporates these increasing benefits of preservation by including preservation benefits foregone within project costs. The benefits are shown to increase through time by the use of a rate of annual growth. While this approach has the same effect on the overall CBA as lowering discount rates, it avoids the problem of distorted resource allocations caused by arbitrarily manipulating discount rates.

In summary, the following conclusions may be reached, within the context of environmental cost-benefit analysis: (a) the standard opportunity cost of capital (for example, 6-12 percent) should be used as for NPV calculations, and as the comparator when the IRR is computed; (b) efforts should be made to ensure that compensating investments offset capital stock degradation within a framework of policy and project decisions; and (c) in the case of projects leading to irreversible damage, CBA should be adapted to the extent possible, to include a measurement of the foregone benefits of preservation in the computation of costs.

Risk and uncertainty

All projects and policies entail some element of risk and uncertainty. Risks are measured usually by the probabilities that can be assigned to the likelihood of occurrence of an undesirable event (for example, an industrial accident). Uncertainty describes a situation where little is known about future impacts. Therefore, no probabilities can be assigned to definite outcomes, or even the outcomes are so novel that they cannot be anticipated.

Risk can be treated probabilistically on the basis of known or estimated data, and therefore insured against and treated like any other project cost. However, uncertainty defies actuarial principles because of undefinable outcomes. For example, stratospheric ozone layer depletion was an unknown outcome of the introduction of chlorofluorocarbons (CFCs) and could not have been costed as a risk when they were first used. Uncertainty is especially important in environmental issues. As projects grow larger in scale and introduce new substances into the environment, the category of uncertainty looms much larger than risk. The proper response to risk is to count it as a cost in expected value computations. However, the use of a single number (or expected value of risk) does not indicate the degree of variability or the range of values that might be expected. Additionally, it does not allow for individual perceptions of risk. The proper response to uncertainty is to proceed with caution—if the future cannot be perceived clearly, then the speed of advance should be tailored to the distance over which the clarity of vision is acceptable.

In practice, the way risk and uncertainty are included in project appraisal work is through sensitivity analyses, which determine how the IRR is dependent on different variables. Using optimistic and pessimistic values for different variables can indicate which variables will have the most pronounced effects on benefits and costs. Although sensitivity analysis need not reflect the probability of occurrence of the upper or lower values, it is useful for determining which variables are most important to the success or failure of a project (Dixon et al. 1988). Much work has been done on the subject of risk and uncertainty in project appraisal (for a recent treatment, see Anderson and Quiggin 1990).

The issue of uncertainty plays an important role in environmental valuation and policy formulation. Option values and quasi-option values are based on the existence of uncertainty. Option value (OV) is essentially the premium that consumers are willing to pay to avoid the risk of not having something available in the future (see the study on valuation of elephants in Kenya). The sign of option value depends upon the presence of supply and/or demand uncertainty, and on whether the consumer is risk averse or risk loving.

Quasi-option value (QOV) is the value of preserving options for future use in the expectation that knowledge will grow over time. If a development takes place that causes irreversible environmental damage, the opportunity to expand knowledge through scientific study of flora and fauna is lost. Uncertainty about the benefits of preservation to be derived through future knowledge expansion (which is independent of development) leads to a positive QOV. This suggests that the development should be postponed until increased knowledge

facilitates a more informed decision. If information growth is contingent upon the development taking place, which is unlikely in an environmental context, then QOV is positive when the uncertainty regards the benefits of preservation, and negative when the uncertainty is about the benefits of the development.[17]

Environmental policy formulation is complicated by the presence of numerous forms of uncertainty. As an illustration, Bromley (1989) identified six different aspects of uncertainty in the case of air pollution resulting from acid deposition. They are (1) identification of the sources of particular pollutants; (2) ultimate destination of particular emissions; (3) actual physical impacts at the point of destination; (4) human valuation of the realized impacts at the point of destination of the emissions; (5) extent to which a particular policy response will have an impact on the abovementioned factors; and (6) actual cost level and incidence of those costs that are the result of policy choice.

Bromley suggests that the way in which policymakers address these uncertainties depends on their perception of the existing entitlement structure. The interests of the future are only protected by an entitlement structure that imposes a duty on current generations to consider the rights of future generations. He terms them "missing markets," noting that "future generations are unable to enter bids to protect their interests." In the absence of such a structure, decisionmakers may tend to follow a policy that ignores costs to future generations, and minimizes costs to current generations at the expense of the future. If the entitlement structure is adjusted, the policymaker can then examine three policy instruments to ensure that future generations are not made worse off: mandated pollution abatement; full compensation for future damages (for example, by taxation); and an annuity that will compensate the future for costs imposed in the present. In the face of uncertainty, the first option would appear to be the most efficient.

Other important sources of uncertainty linked with environmental issues include uncertainty about land tenure, which leads to deforestation and unsustainable agricultural practices, and uncertainty about resource

---

[17] See Pearce and Turner 1990, and Fisher and Hanemann 1987.

rights, which can accelerate the rate of depletion of a nonrenewable resource. Policymakers can address these issues by instituting land reforms, and by designing appropriate taxation policies that return rents to public sources rather than to private agents.

Case studies of valuation of environmental impacts

In this section, selected case studies from developing countries are briefly outlined to illustrate the implementation of some of the techniques of environmental impact valuation. Further details of these case studies are provided in Annex 2B. These illustrations apply primarily to the direct and indirect use value categories shown in Figure 2-1. Because developing country examples describing attempts to estimate option, existence, and bequest values are rare, several studies applied to the industrialized countries are also presented.

Change in productivity method

Cost-benefit analysis of land improvement in Lesotho

The Farm Improvement with Soil Conservation (FISC) project was initiated in Southern Lesotho in 1985, with the overriding aim of raising agricultural production among smallholder farming households through soil conservation measures, subsidized inputs, and afforestation.[18] In pursuit of this goal the project has rehabilitated old terrace structures, constructed new ones, and added other structures for conservation. It has promoted the use of hybrid maize and sorghum, the planting of fodder grasses, and tree planting. It has also promoted rotational grazing on communal rangeland. In this study, conservation is defined as the promotion of optimum use of land in accordance with its capability so as to assure its maintenance and improvement.

A financial analysis is carried out that compares a high input alternative (implying the use of commercial fertilizer and hybrid seed) with the traditional alternative (implying no use of fertilizer and locally saved seeds as opposed to hybrids). The calculation, which is valid for one year only, does not take into consideration the impacts on soil conservation. Calculations for maize and sorghum show a negative real marginal IRR of 21 and 30 percent, respectively.

An economic cost-benefit analysis is performed, distinguishing between productivity impacts due to increased use of commercial inputs, and impacts due to increased soil conservation. Costs are primarily labor and material input costs. Primary benefit categories include increased production of sorghum and maize (incremental yield due to conservation relative to future decline in yield due to erosion), fruit, fuelwood, and fodder. Given various assumptions regarding the rate of growth of project implementation factors (see case study in Annex 2B), the results of the base case are an NPV of -M 7.0 million at a discount rate of 10 percent and -M 5.6 million at 1 percent (Table 2B-2 demonstrates that conservation crop benefits are more significant at a lower discount rate, as they are slow to materialize).

The qualitative interpretation is that the project makes a loss that is significant in comparison to the resources invested. In terms of the overriding target of the project, to raise agricultural production among smallholder farming households, the project cannot be termed successful. However, the benefits of soil conservation may have been underestimated in the desire to improve crop yields (FISC has a production, as opposed to a preservation, orientation). Given (a) demand uncertainty arising from lack of information on future population, food habits, agricultural technology, and capacity to import food, and (b) supply uncertainty about the possibility of droughts leading to soil losses, it may be advisable to ascribe a positive option value to soil conservation efforts, to be incorporated into the stream of costs and benefits. Again, if long-term protection of the land base is assigned a higher priority relative to immediate productivity increases, there would be a basis for more substantial subsidization of cover crops such as fodder grasses at the expense of traditional cropping.

Aside from the debatable benefits of its production—as opposed to conservation

---

[18] This case study is derived from Bojo 1991.

—oriented approach, FISC serves as an important model in terms of its emphasis on consultation and community participation and of its reliance on low-cost, labor-intensive field techniques.

Valuation of an Amazonian rainforest

Most financial appraisals of tropical forests have focused exclusively on timber resources and have ignored the market benefits of non-wood products, thus providing a strong market incentive for destructive logging and widespread forest clearing.[19] In an effort to illustrate the values of nonwood forest products, the authors present data concerning inventory, production, and current market value for all the commercial tree species occurring in 1 hectare of Amazonian forest. They arrive at a combined NPV of US$6,820 for a fruit and latex production and selective cutting project, with logging contributing just 7 percent of the total. This compares favorably with an estimated NPV of US$3,184 for timber and pulpwood obtained from a 1-hectare plantation in Brazilian Amazonia, and an NPV of US$2,960 for fully stocked cattle pastures in Brazil.

In order to extrapolate the value of the project, which is based on the value of 1 hectare, it would be useful if attempts were made to incorporate elasticities of demand for the products. (This approach is being followed for a World Bank study of a similar nature in India.)

Another methodological concern is the use of returns per hectare as the unit of comparison between different uses. A recent World Bank study concludes that an appropriate analysis would compare returns per productive unit, including land, labor and capital valued at their opportunity cost. Since land in the Amazon is generally abundant relative to labor, an analysis based on the returns to labor would better predict the market outcome than one which focused on the returns to land. This deduction is confirmed by behavior in the market, where forest extractivism has tended to vanish wherever labor has had reasonable alternatives.[20]

Loss of earnings method

Economic analysis of a water supply and health program in Zimbabwe

Fredriksson and Persson (1989) evaluate the Manicaland Health, Water, and Sanitation Program in Zimbabwe using social cost benefit analysis. The objectives of the program are to improve living conditions in the communal areas of Manicaland through: (a) improving existing and constructing new water supplies that ensure an acceptable quantity and quality of water for domestic use and that are reliable and accessible to the community; (b) improving sanitation conditions by constructing latrines and consequently preventing flies from breeding and diseases from being transmitted; and (c) providing health education to improve hygienic practices and motivate behavioral changes.

The domestic price of labor is used as a numeraire. The shadow price of foreign exchange was estimated to be Z$ 1.75/US$1 in the analysis.

The shadow price of unskilled labor is set at zero in the dry season, due to unemployment in Zimbabwe. In the peak season, there is a shortage of labor. As uncertainty exists because of possible delays in the harvest, a sensitivity analysis is made in the evaluation, where the shadow wage of unskilled labor is set to 100 percent, 75 percent, and 50 percent of the market wage of Z$ 0.46 per hour. The opportunity value of children's labor is set to zero during the whole year. (This is a little surprising, given that children represent a significant labor force in many developing countries.) For skilled labor, the shadow wage is set at the market wage.

The social discount rate is assumed to be the rate of return in the private sector, which would mean a real social discount of 4.86 percent, since the commercial bank lending rate to the industrial sector at the end of 1987 was 14.75 percent and the inflation rate was 9.89 percent. A time horizon of 40 years was established, which was the duration time of benefits from the project. Materials supplied by the

---

[19] This case study is from Peters et al. 1989.
[20] World Bank 1992.

project were valued at market prices. Community input is valued at the opportunity cost of unskilled labor. The constructor is assumed to be paid the shadow price of skilled labor.

The change in consumer surplus is determined by calculating the average price for water collected in the wet season and dry season, both before and after the project. The price of water in the wet season is calculated using 75 peak period days with no energy savings but with a shadow wage greater than zero. In the remaining 105 days energy is saved and the shadow wage equals zero. Using this information, the change in consumer surplus is then calculated at shadow wages of 50 percent, 75 percent, and 100 percent.

Cost of illness estimates consist of treatment costs, costs of lost production, and costs for extra transportation. Since willingness to pay for healthier and longer lives was not estimated, the values used significantly underestimate the true values. For treatment costs, the costs for private treatment are used as the opportunity cost. A life saved would be valued very highly by the individual concerned and his or her family. From society's viewpoint, a lower bound or minimum estimate of the gain from a life saved is derived by the authors using future production and consumption. The weighted average of the wage adjusted for both unemployment and the income in communal lands is used as an estimate of a child's future production, and future consumption is estimated as final household expenditure per capita. The net present value of the difference between production and consumption is the net output gained by saving the child. The same measure is utilized to determine net present output produced by an adult's life if he is saved today. Sensitivity analyses were conducted for social discount rates of 2 percent, 4.86 percent, 7.24 percent, and 9 percent; disease reductions of 40 percent, 70 percent, and 100 percent; and wet season shadow wages for unskilled labor of 50 percent, 75 percent, and 100 percent of the market wage for casual workers on commercial farms in Manicaland.

In the base case, with an estimated social discount rate of 4.86 percent, shadow wage 100 percent of the market wage, and a 100

percent health improvement, the internal rate of return was greater than the social discount rate, and the net present value of the project was strongly positive. At a social discount rate of 7.24 percent, estimated in the alternative approach, the project is not found profitable even if a shadow wage of 100 percent and 100 percent disease reduction is achieved.

While most of the benefits come from disease reduction, it must be pointed out that benefits are probably underestimated through the use of a lower bound. This is because the value of a saved life has been underestimated, through the use of a lower bound. Secondly, the paper does not take into account other benefits such as local industry that would benefit from improved water supply. Third, as income distribution will probably improve as a result of the project, benefits could have been given a greater weight. The authors conclude that the project is probably a success from a societal point of view as the necessary increase in estimated lower bound value for a child's life (in the case of 40 percent disease reduction and a shadow wage of 50 percent of the market wage) is rather small.

Travel cost and contingent valuation methods

Domestic consumer surplus from visits to a rainforest reserve in Costa Rica

This study measures the value of ecotourism at a tropical rainforest site in Costa Rica using the travel cost method.[21] By observing travel behavior, the authors reveal that Costa Rican visitors are willing to pay US$35 per household to visit the site. The study finds that visitation is highly correlated with education (and therefore probably income), and that households in areas with high population densities make more trips.

The paper only considers domestic visits, although foreign visitors to the site outnumbered domestic visitors by four to one in 1988. Foreign visitation is likely to be worth far more than domestic, as foreign visitors have higher travel costs, and a greater value of travel time because of higher earnings. Additionally, they provide foreign exchange.

---

[21] This study is derived from Tobias and Mendelsohn 1991.

Nevertheless, if we use the same value of US$35 per visit for all visitors, this would result in an NPV of US$1,250 per hectare. This figure is one to two times the magnitude of the purchase price currently paid by the reserve for the acquisition of new lands.

It is unclear, however, whether the authors assess the cost (in foregone earnings) of time spent at site. It would have been useful to have a clearer definition of their term "cost of travel time." In addition, they use a linear demand function as opposed to the more popular semilog functional form, as visitation rates from many zones were zero. In a similar study, Willis and Garrod (1991) made the case for the superiority of the semilog functional form over the linear for the Clawson-Knetsch Zonal Travel Cost Method. They also found that the zonal travel cost method probably overestimated the consumer surplus for their sample of travel cost studies. The individual travel cost method comes closer to contingent valuation results.

As in the Costa Rican study, most travel cost studies look at single-purpose, single destination trips. A more general methodological problem is how to deal with multiple destination trips. In most cases of international tourism to developing countries the travel cost would need to be attributed to many activities at a number of sites. The problem then becomes to elicit the specific value given to a certain site. An ongoing World Bank study on environmental valuation of a forestry development and conservation project in Madagascar is attempting to do this.[22] Their model uses a household production framework in which the household examines cost functions for specific activities within the potential destination countries to compare the expected satisfaction and cost of trips of various bundles of activities. However, this demands much from the empirical data. A survey of tourists is being used to collect travel cost data as well as itinerary data that includes the distribution of time between activities for each individual, the costs of pursuing the activities, and the features of the various activities that lead to differences across individuals in their ability to undertake them.

Value of viewing elephants on safaris in Kenya

The travel cost method was used to estimate a demand function for safaris in Kenya.[23] The analysis is based on the 80 percent of tourists who come to Kenya from Europe and North America. Surveys of tour operators and visitors provided data for the estimation of land costs, air fare, and travel time costs. Travel time costs were weighted at 30 percent to reflect the fact that vacation time is valued at lower than the gross wage rate. A weighted average consumers' surplus of US$725 is estimated. This gives a total consumer surplus for those on safari in the range of US$182 million to US$218 million annually, depending on the assumed level of visitation.

To identify the contribution elephants make to the value of a safari, tourists were asked to allocate the pleasure and enjoyment of their trip over various categories of experience. Elephants represented 12.6 percent of total enjoyment. Therefore, the estimated economic value of a safari yields a viewing value for elephants of US$23 million to U$27 million per year.

In order to assess consumers' willingness to pay to maintain the elephant population at current levels through increased enforcement activity, a survey was designed, utilizing the contingent valuation approach. Attempts were made to adjust for biases. The average value was US$89 while the median was US$100. This yields an annual viewing value of US$22 million to US$27 million and US$25 to US$30 million, respectively, based on an estimate of 250,000 to 300,000 adult safaris per year. (This is an example of option value—the premium consumers are willing to pay to avoid the risk of supply uncertainty.)

Note that both methods produced annual viewing values for elephants of around US$25 million. Although these estimates are rough, they are a useful guide to the order of magnitude of value.

---

[22] Kramer et al. 1992.

[23] Derived from Brown and Henry 1989.

Willingness to pay for water services in Haiti

The contingent valuation method was used in this study to estimate consumers' willingness to pay for an improved water system in a village in southern Haiti.[24] The project was executed by CARE. The research team devised tests in an attempt to correct biases that could threaten the validity of the survey results, such as strategic bias, starting point bias, and hypothetical bias. The results of the survey, utilizing an ordered probit model as opposed to a linear model, demonstrated that willingness to pay for a new water system (whether for a public standpost or for a private connection) was positively correlated to income, the cost of obtaining water from existing sources, and the education of household members. It was negatively correlated with the individual's perception of the quality of water at the traditional source used before the construction of the improved water supply system. The sex of the respondent was statistically significant in the model for public standposts but not in the model for private connections.

The mean of WTP bids for public standposts represented 1.7 percent of household income, while the mean WTP bid for private connections was 2.1 percent of household incomes. These bids are significantly lower than the 5 percent rule-of-thumb often used in rural water supply planning as an estimate of maximum "ability to pay" for private connections. However, the bids are based on the assumption that the public standposts are already in place.

The results of this study show that it is possible to obtain reasonable, consistent answers in a contingent valuation survey conducted among a very poor, illiterate population. Contingent valuation has the potential to become a viable method in developing countries: both for collecting information on individuals' willingness to pay for a wide range of public infrastructure projects, and for environmental protection services (such as the treatment of industrial wastewater flowing through residential areas).

Contingent valuation method to estimate option, existence, and bequest values

Since hardly any developing country examples are available in this category, four U.S. examples are provided below. An ongoing World Bank study seeks to determine nonuse values of tropical forests in Madagascar (Kramer et al. 1992).

The following studies all used the contingent valuation approach to obtain actual measures for option, existence, and/or bequest values: The first was quite possibly the original survey that developed a methodology to attempt to determine existence value. Both the first and second studies, while revealing the significance of existence values, examine them as an adjunct to their main focus, which is recreational use value. The third is perhaps the first one that undertook to examine total preservation value in depth, broken down into its three separate components of option, existence, and bequest value. The last study is basically an attempt to measure the effects of information disclosure (endangered status and physical appearance) on existence values for endangered species.

Existence value of preserving visibility

The survey attempts to measure annual household willingness to pay (WTP) to preserve visibility in the Grand Canyon—both WTP if visibility preservation were to be extended to the entire southwestern parklands region and WTP to prevent plume blight seen from Grand Canyon National Park.[25] For the purpose of the study, only the major source of air pollution in the region, coal-fired power plants, was the focus. Over 600 households in Denver, Los Angeles, Albuquerque, and Chicago participated in the survey. One-third of the respondents were asked a pure user value question: How much would they be willing to pay in higher entrance fees per day for visibility protection at the Grand Canyon or other parks? The other two-thirds of the respondents were asked how much they would be willing to pay in higher electric power bills to preserve

---

[24] This case study is derived from Whittington et al. 1990.
[25] Derived from Schulze et al. 1983.

visibility in the parklands, a measurement of total preservation value (defined by the authors as the sum of existence plus user value). The authors interpreted existence value as the difference between total preservation value and user value.

The preservation value bids are substantially higher than the user value bids, apparently signifying that existence value is an important component of total economic value. The authors are careful to point out that visitation plans were not an overwhelming factor in determining preservation value bids, and that knowledge acquired through previous visits was also considered relatively unimportant in the determination of bids. Moreover, preservation bids did not decline with distance, which seems to indicate that nonuse value was an important component in the respondents' bids.

Option price and existence value of wildlife

This study measures the option price (option value plus expected consumer surplus) and existence value of grizzly bears and bighorn sheep in Wyoming—both of these species being endangered by human activity in the area.[26] A mail survey was sent out, with questions being directed towards hunters and nonhunters. Hunters were asked their WTP for a "stamp" allowing them to hunt in new hunting areas in either five or fifteen years for grizzly bear or bighorn sheep. Respondents were each confronted with only one time horizon. The probability of supply was variable. Nonhunters were asked to specify their WTP for the existence of the animals or for the opportunity to observe them in the future.

As expected, the overall option price increased as the probability of supply increased. Contrary to expectations, no systematic relationship could be determined showing that bids based on certain demand exceeded those based on uncertain demand. Existence values and observer option prices were significant. The mean bids for observer option prices were in the range of US$20 for both grizzly bear and bighorn sheep, regardless of the time element. This is on a par with option bids for hunters at high

levels of supply certainty. Existence values are high for grizzly bear (US$24 at 5 years, US$15.20 at 15 years), but are significantly lower for bighorn sheep (US$7.40 and $US6.90, respectively).

Option, existence, and bequest values of wilderness

The key question posed here is the amount of wilderness to be protected in Colorado. A sample of 218 resident Colorado households participated in a mail survey.[27] Respondents were asked to report their willingness to pay into a special fund to be used exclusively for the purpose of protecting wilderness. This payment vehicle is recognizable to Colorado residents, being similar to the state income tax form's checkoff for nongame wildlife preservation. Respondents were asked to write down the maximum amount of money they would be willing to pay annually for protection of current wilderness, and for hypothetical increases in wilderness depicted on four maps. Once this budget allocation was completed, respondents were asked to allocate the highest amount reported among four categories of value: recreational use, option, existence, and bequest demands. Total preservation benefits were estimated as the residual after recreation use benefits have been subtracted from total WTP for wilderness protection. Preservation values were estimated by developing an appropriate econometric model of willingness to pay by survey households, and by aggregating values across households in the state.

Results indicate that as the quantity of wilderness increases, annual household preservation values increase at a decreasing rate, except for bequest value, which is linear. Option value had a strong positive association with income. In-state wilderness users had a much higher option value than nonusers, indicating that recreational use is an important element in the determination of option value. Existence value was positively related to the importance of preservation of natural scenery, ecosystems, and genetic strains. Existence value increased with frequency of wilderness trips undertaken. All income groups valued existence of

---

[26] This study is derived from Brookshire 1983.

[27] Derived from Walsh et al. 1984.

wilderness about equally. Interestingly, a wide range of workers (skilled and unskilled) would pay US$1.50 more for existence demands than would persons in other occupations. Bequest value was not influenced by the number of children living at home with respondents. This seems to indicate that bequest value is correctly defined as the satisfaction from interpersonal transfers of wilderness to indefinite future generations rather than specifically to the children of the respondent. Retired persons were willing to pay US$6.15 more for bequest demand than were other respondents. All income groups valued bequest demands about equally.

The authors conclude that, even without taking into account the preservation estimates of nonresidents of the state, adding preservation value to the consumer surplus of recreational value had a substantial effect on the benefit value for wilderness.

Existence value of endangered species

This study tests the hypothesis that an individual's WTP to preserve a particular animal is significantly influenced by information provided about the animal's physical and behavioral characteristics and about its endangered status.[28] Public awareness about endangered species and preservation alternatives plays an important part in determining the replicability and usefulness of existence valuation results.

The experiment was conducted using isolated experimental and control groups of paid university-level student subjects in the United States. CVM was used to measure preservation bids for a humpback whale preservation fund. The experimental group was then provided with more information about the whales (through the screening of a film), and both groups were then questioned again. The experimental group increased their bids by 32 percent from their original values, and the control group increased their bids by 20 percent. This may be attributable to the fact that all respondents had more time to reconsider their bids, and perhaps demonstrates how preferences are learned through the interview process itself, even in the absence of new information.

Finally, all control and experimental subjects were asked to fully allocate a lump-sum

windfall gain of US$30 among preservation funds for three animal species, given four scenarios containing different levels of information about physical appearance and endangered status.

The effects of information disclosure on responses was more evident here. Faced with zero information distinguishing species, the subjects' willingness to pay to preserve each species was nearly equal. Given information on physical appearance, they allocated more to the monkeylike animal as compared with the rabbitlike or ratlike animal, reflecting a strong anthropomorphic tendency. Given information on endangered status, respondents allocated significantly more funds to the animal that was endangered but savable as compared with ubiquitous or extremely rare animals. When information was provided on both physical appearance and endangered status, the endangered but savable species received the highest allocation followed by the rare and abundant species. These results suggest that information about endangered status may be relatively more important to respondents than information about physical characteristics in formulating preservation bids.

In conclusion, it appears that information disclosure can influence perceived marginal efficiency of investment in a preservation fund and thereby result in changes of an individual's budget allocation strategy.

Conclusions

One essential step towards achieving economically efficient management of natural resources and formulating a practical strategy for sustainable development, is the effective incorporation of environmental concerns into decisionmaking. Traditionally, the economic analysis of projects and policies (including the techniques of shadow pricing), has been developed to help a country make more efficient use of scarce resources. "External effects," especially those arising from adverse environmental consequences, often have been neglected.

This report has reviewed concepts and techniques for valuation of environmental impacts that enable such environmental considerations to be explicitly considered in the

[28] This case study is derived from Samples et al. 1986.

conventional cost-benefit calculus used in economic decisionmaking. Even rough qualitative assessments early on in the project evaluation cycle may facilitate the process of internalizing these environmental externalities. The advantages include early exclusion of environmentally unsound alternatives, more effective in-depth consideration of environmentally preferable alternatives, and opportunities for redesigning projects and policies in order to achieve sustainable development goals.

Certain specific shortcomings and difficulties associated with the case studies were discussed earlier. More generally, greater application of the environmental valuation concepts and techniques to practical problems in a developing country is required rather than further theoretical development. Such case study work can be most effectively carried out as part of project preparation. A major purpose in this endeavor is not to provide fine-tuned numbers but to indicate orders of magnitude. Some alternatives can be ruled out and gross environmental errors avoided in this fashion.

Also, one can often identify the key environmental indicators to which the decision is sensitive and focus attention on them.

Some modest evidence exists that the valuation techniques for determining use values may be applied successfully in appropriate cases. However, examples involving the estimation of nonuse values are virtually nonexistent in the developing world, and rather scarce even in the industrialized nations. The use of multiobjective decision methods also needs to be explored, where valuation is not feasible.[29]

Nevertheless, developing countries are attempting increasingly to both improve and make use of economic techniques to value environmental assets. While the academic literature usually focuses mainly on the development of the techniques, there are also sector- or topic-related approaches.[30] For practitioners, the important concern is to keep up with and make use of the advances most relevant to their own areas of application. To facilitate this, a range of publications is included in the bibliography at the end of this paper.

---

[29] A recently completed World Bank case study, (Meier and Munasinghe 1992), involves energy and environmental issues in Sri Lanka and utilizes this approach.

[30] See for example Dixon et al. 1989, Sherman 1990, and Turner 1988.

Annex 2A: Using Shadow Prices

The estimation and use of shadow prices is facilitated by dividing economic resources into tradeable and nontradeable items. Tradeables and nontradeables are treated differently. The values of directly imported or exported goods and services are already known in border prices, that is their foreign exchange costs converted at the official exchange rate. Locally purchased items whose values are known only in terms of domestic market prices, however, must be converted to border prices by multiplying the former prices by appropriate conversion factors (CFs).

Border (Shadow) Price = Conversion Factor x Domestic (Market) Price

$$BP = CF \times DP$$

For those tradeables with infinite elasticities—of world supply for imports, and of world demand for exports—the cost, insurance, and freight (c.i.f.) border price for imports and the free-on-board (f.o.b.) border price for exports may be used (with a suitable adjustment for the marketing margin). If the relevant elasticities are finite, then the change in import costs or export revenues, as well as any shifts in other domestic consumption or production levels or in income transfers, should be considered. The free trade assumption is not required to justify the use of border prices since domestic price distortions are adjusted by netting out all taxes, duties, and subsidies.

A nontradeable is conventionally defined as a commodity whose domestic supply price lies between the f.o.b. export price and c.i.f. import price. Items that are not traded at the margin because of prohibitive trade barriers, such as bans or rigid quotas, are also included within this category. If the increased demand for a given nontradeable good or service is met by the expansion of domestic supply or imports, the associated border-priced marginal social cost (MSC) of this increased supply is the relevant resource cost. If the incremental demand for the nontradeable results in decreased consumption of other domestic or foreign users, the border-priced marginal social benefit (MSB) of this foregone domestic consumption or of reduced export earnings, would be a more appropriate measure of social costs.

The socially optimal level of total consumption for the given input (Q_{opt}) would lie at the point where the curves of MSC and MSB intersect. Price and nonprice distortions lead to nonoptimal levels of consumption $Q \ Q_{opt}$ characterized by differences between MSB and MSC. More generally, a weighted average of MSC and MSB should be used if both effects are present,. The MSB would tend to dominate in a short-run, supply constrained situation; the MSC would be more important in the longer run, when expansion of output is possible.

The MSC of nontradeable goods and services from many sectors can be determined through appropriate decomposition. For example, suppose one peso-worth of the output of the construction sector (valued in domestic prices) is broken down successively into components. This would include capital, labor, materials, and so on, which are valued at pesos $C_1, C_2, \ldots C_n$ in border prices. Since the conversion factor of any good is defined as the ratio of the border price to the domestic price, the construction conversion factor equals:

$$CCF = \sum_{i=1}^{n} C_i$$

The standard conversion factor (SCF) may be used with nontradeables that are not important enough to merit individual attention or that lack sufficient data. The SCF is equal to the official exchange rate (OER) divided by the more familiar shadow exchange rate (SER), appropriately defined. Using the SCF to convert domestic priced values into border price equivalents is conceptually the inverse of the traditional practice of multiplying foreign currency costs by the SER (instead of the OER) to convert foreign exchange to the domestic price equivalent. The standard conversion factor may be approximated by the ratio of the official exchange rate to the free trade exchange rate (FTER), when the country is moving toward a freer trade regime:

$$SCF = \frac{OER}{FTER} = \frac{eX + nM}{eX(1-t_x) + nM(1+t_m)}$$

where X = f.o.b. value of exports,
M = c.i.f. value of imports,
e = elasticity of domestic supply of exports,
n = elasticity of domestic demand for imports,
t_x = average tax rate on exports (negative for subsidy), and
t_m = average tax rate on imports.

Illustrative of important tradeable inputs used in many development projects are capital goods and petroleum-based fuels. Some countries may have other fuels available, such as natural gas or coal deposits. If no clear-cut export market exists for these indigenous energy resources, then they cannot be treated like tradeables. If there is no alternative use for such fuels, an appropriate economic value is the MSC of the production or extraction of gas or coal plus a markup for the discounted value of future consumption foregone (or "user cost"). If another high value use exists for these fuels, the opportunity costs of not using the resources in alternative uses should be considered as their economic value.

Two important nontradeable primary factor inputs are labor and land, the next subjects for discussion. The foregone output of workers used in the energy sector is the dominant component of the shadow wage rate (SWR). Consider a typical case of unskilled labor in a labor surplus country—for example, rural workers employed for dam construction. Complications arise in estimating the opportunity cost of labor, because the original rural income earned may not reflect the marginal product of agricultural labor. Furthermore, for every new job created, more than one rural worker may give up former employment. Allowance must also be made for seasonal activities such as harvesting, and overhead costs like transport expenses. Based on the foregoing, the efficiency shadow wage rate (ESWR) is given by:

$$ESWR = a.m + c.u$$

where m and u are the foregone marginal output and overhead costs of labor in domestic prices, and a and c are corresponding conversion factors to convert these values into border prices.

If we are interested only in efficiency pricing, then we may stop here. However, if social pricing is important, consider the effect of these changes on consumption patterns. Suppose a worker receives a wage W_n in a new job and that the income foregone is W_o, both in domestic prices. Note that W_n may not necessarily be equal to the marginal product foregone m. It could be assumed, quite plausibly, that low-income workers consume the entire increase in income $(W_n - W_o)$. Then this increase in consumption will result in a resource cost to the economy of $b(W_n - W_o)$. The increased consumption also provides a benefit given by $w(W_n - W_o)$, where w represents the MSB, in border prices, of increasing domestic-priced private sector consumption by one unit. Therefore,

$$SWR = a.m + c.u + (b - w)(W_n - W_o)$$

The symbol b represents the MSC to the economy, resulting from the use of the increased income. For example, if all the new income is consumed, then b is the relevant consumption conversion factor or resource cost (in units of the numeraire) of making available to consumers one unit worth (in domestic prices) of the marginal basket of n goods that they would purchase. In this case

$$b = \sum_{i=1}^{n} g_i.CF_i$$

where g_i is the proportion or share of the i th good in the marginal consumption basket, and CF_i is the corresponding conversion factor.

The corresponding MSB of increased consumption may be decomposed further; w = d/v, where l/v is the value (in units of the numeraire) of a one-unit increase in domestic-priced consumption accruing to someone at the average level of consumption (c_a). Therefore, v may be roughly thought of as the premium attached to public savings, compared to "average" private consumption. Under certain simplifying assumptions, b = 1/v. If MU(c) denotes the marginal utility of consumption at some level c, then d = $MU(c)/MU(c_a)$. Assuming that the marginal utility of consumption is diminishing, d would be greater than unity for "poor" consumers with c < c_a, and vice versa.

A simple form of marginal utility function could be

$$MU(c) = c^{-n}.$$

Thus, d = $MU(c)/MU(c_a)$ = $(c_a/c)n$.

Making the further assumption that the distribution parameter n = 1, gives

$$d = c_a/c = i_a/i$$

where i_a/i is the ratio of net incomes, which may be used as a proxy for the corresponding consumption ratio.

The consumption term (b-w) in the expression for SWR disappears if, at the margin (a) society is indifferent as to the distribution of income (or consumption), so that everyone's consumption has equivalent value (d=1), and (b) private consumption is considered to be as socially valuable as the uncommitted public savings (b=1/v).

The appropriate shadow value placed on land depends on its location. Usually, the market price of urban land is a useful indicator of its economic value in domestic prices, and the application of an appropriate conversion factor (such as the SCF) to this domestic price, will yield the border-priced cost of urban land inputs. Rural land that can be used in agriculture may be valued at its opportunity costs—the net benefit of foregone agricultural output. The marginal social cost of both urban and rural land should reflect the value of associated environmental assets (see main text). Examples might be the flooding of virgin jungle because of a hydroelectric dam that would involve the loss of valuable timber, or spoilage of a recreational area that has commercial potential.

The shadow price of capital is usually reflected in the discount rate or accounting rate of interest (ARI), which is defined as the rate of decline in the value of the numeraire over time. Although there has been much discussion concerning the choice of an appropriate discount rate, in practice the opportunity cost of capital (OCC) may be used as a proxy for the ARI, in the pure efficiency price regime. The OCC is defined as the expected value of the annual stream of consumption, in border prices net of replacement, which is yielded by the investment of one unit of public income at the margin.

A simple formula for the social-priced ARI, which also includes consumption effects, is given by

$$ARI = OCC [s + (1 - s)w/b]$$

where s is the fraction of the yield from the original investment that will be saved and reinvested.

Usually, the rigorous estimation of shadow prices is a long and complex task. Therefore, the energy sector analyst is best advised to use whatever shadow prices have already been calculated. Alternatively, the analyst would estimate a few important items such as the standard conversion factor, opportunity cost of capital, and shadow wage rate. When the data are not precise enough, sensitivity studies may be made over a range of values of such key national parameters.

Annex 2B: Summaries of Environmental Valuation Case Studies Change in Productivity Method

Land improvement in Lesotho

The Farm Improvement with Soil Conservation (FISC) project was initiated in 1985 in Mohale's Hoek district in southern Lesotho, and is gradually being expanded.[1] The project is now used as a model for a national training program in soil conservation. Other soil conservation projects are already using FISC as a model. The choice of the FISC project for study is further justified by its modern approach in dealing with land degradation: production orientation, labor-intensive techniques, and popular participation. Furthermore, information for research could be obtained at low cost. The project area is fairly typical for lowland Lesotho where most of the crop production takes place. With some adjustments the calculations could be used for other areas in Lesotho, or even for other areas with similar geographic and socio-economic features in other countries.

The overriding aim of the FISC project is to raise agricultural production. It has rehabilitated old terrace structures, constructed new ones, and added other structures for conservation; promoted hybrid maize, hybrid sorghum, and fodder grasses; and planted thousands of tree seedlings. It has also promoted rotational grazing on communal rangeland. The project area covers almost 26,000 hectares and reaches about 22,000 people.

Financial analysis

The financial analysis was done from a household perspective, using market prices.

Two management options for cultivation of maize and sorghum have been compared in financial terms. The high-input alternative implies the use of commercial fertilizer and hybrid seed. The "traditional" alternative implies no use of fertilizer and locally saved seeds instead of hybrids. The less immediate impact of soil conservation measures is left out of this calculation, which is valid for one year only.

Crop sampling was carried out in cooperation with the FISC staff during five seasons, 1986-1990. The results show that farmers using a high-input management do receive higher yields on average, but that very substantial variations of yields make this a risky investment.

Financial calculations for maize and sorghum show that the yield must increase by 125 percent and 144 percent, respectively, in order to achieve a real rate of return of 10 percent. The demands are significantly higher than the average achieved under high-input management as sampled, which give a negative real marginal IRR of 21 and 30 percent, respectively.

Maintained participation in the project appears limited after the initial boost when conservation efforts result in in-kind payments. Most likely, project sales are merely replacing alternative, less accessible sources of supply. There are no convincing signs of a major transformation of the crop management regime. The long-term impact of physical conservation works may be the only net impact as far as the major grain crops are concerned. Financial budgets for fruit and fuelwood trees show more

---

[1] This case study is derived from Bojo 1991.

promising returns, however, and have also met with greater interest among local people.

Possible explanations for the lack of farmer response to the promotion of high-input management are discussed, including, among other things, land tenure, credit for agricultural investments, and risk pertaining to agricultural investments. Most serious is the problem of risk. Crop yields are very unreliable in Lesotho. The farmers are quite aware of this and will (informally) calculate the chances of losing invested resources. Demands for yield increases for maize and sorghum have been shown to be considerable in order to reach an acceptable level of financial return (10 percent real rate). It is certainly not irrational of the farmer to adopt a careful approach in the face of these risks.

Economic analysis

Overall project performance has been recorded for the period March 1985 to December 1990. Current, firm plans for work until mid-1992 have been incorporated, and extrapolations have been made from past performance in relation to the availability of future financial means.

The analysis distinguishes between productivity impacts due to increased use of commercial inputs and to improved soil conservation. The distribution, sale, and use of commercial fertilizer and hybrid seed in the project areas has been monitored. In the short term, distribution of these inputs has increased somewhat as they are used as in-kind payments for conservation work on individually controlled land. Convincing signs are lacking, however, for a lasting impact in terms of commercial sales or their use. Farmers are known to save project-distributed inputs for several years, and the level of use in the project areas is not significantly different from use in nonproject areas. Therefore, the project cannot be credited with a rise in productivity due to increased use of inputs.

Identification of costs and benefits. Financial costs are identified through project and donor accounts. There are also costs of soil conservation works. These are borne by the farmers and have to be estimated separately. Financial costs have to be adjusted in several

ways to arrive at real economic costs, however. Potential benefits of the project include increasing production of:

- Maize, sorghum, and crop residues due to the use of fertilizer, hybrid seed and conservation of soil and nutrients
- Fruits (peaches and apples)
- Fuelwood from pine and other tree species
- Fodder grasses such as Eragrostis and Bana grass
- Vegetables from communal gardens sponsored by the project
- Livestock products by promoting improved grazing management.

Additional benefit items to consider are:

- Training of personnel, and the introduction of improved communal management, with potential extra-project impacts
- Off-site physical impacts, such as less siltation of dams, less maintenance costs for roads and bridges, improved water quality, etc.
- Secondary benefits for the community at large as a result of the increase in income from agriculture.

Quantification of costs and benefits. Not all costs are readily available in monetary terms. Examples are the temporary loss of soil from new, ungrassed terraces, "loss" of land to terraces and other structures, and increased maintenance for roads due to greater use. Labor cost for soil conservation is not included since it was reported to be negligible. This view is, however, controversial. Monetary cost data were taken from project accounts and complemented by the executing company's data for costs paid by the donor agency directly to the company.

The crop benefits due to hybrid seeds and fertilizer use is assumed to be negligible. Only small quantities of the inputs have been distributed through the project and the financial analysis showed their use to be questionable. For those that wanted the inputs they were available through other channels.

To determine the benefits from soil conservation a number of factors need to be considered. First is the issue of whether soil loss actually affects crop production at all in this particular area. Second, if it does, to what extent soil loss occurs, and third, how this rate affects productivity.

There is reason to believe that soil loss immediately affects the average crop production area since the average topsoil depth is estimated to be 25 centimeter, a level at which the water retention capacity is reduced. Research in the area indicates that the annual soil loss is roughly 15 tons per hectare on poorly managed soils and 5 tons per hectare for the areas under project-influenced conservation management. Through comparisons with other studies on loss of productivity due to soil loss, a 1 percent annual decline in yield on nonconserved land was assumed.

The impact of soil conservation on crop production can be expressed as

$$IQ_{it} = dY_{it} \times AYi \times \Sigma AC_t \times PI \times CS_i$$

where   IQ = incremental production (kilogram),

dY = relative crop decline avoided due to conservation,

AY = the base level of average (14-year) yield for the district (kilogram per hectare),

ΣAC = accumulated area under the conservation management (hectare),

PI = project impact: the share of AH affected by the project's actions (percent),

CS = the share of maize and sorghum respectively of the cultivated land (percent),

t = time index (year 1 ... T), and

i = crop index. The assumption here is that PI (project impact) equals 1, as conservation activities are assumed to be nil in the absence of the project.[2]

Up to 1992, more than 18,000 seedlings of apple and peach trees were to be delivered to farmers in the project area. The survival rate was estimated at 50 percent. The number of survived fuelwood trees by 1992 is estimated at roughly 130,000. The fodder benefits are rather small due to the small areas planted and the opportunity cost of the land used.

Road and bridge maintenance in the area will not be significantly affected by the improved land management and soil retention, and no major dams for hydropower or irrigation in the project areas will be affected.

Valuation in economic prices. The Loti (pl. Maloti) is fixed on a par with the internationally convertible South African Rand. There is no black market for Rands or Maloti. This indicates that the distorting impact of foreign exchange restrictions is not significant. The official exchange rates have therefore been used, based on International Monetary Fund data. In 1990 the exchange rate was set to roughly 3 Maloti per U.S. dollar.

Since there is a transfer of income to Lesotho of about 20 percent of the import value, inclusive of duties, the value of *imported* components is multiplied by a factor of 0.8 when going from financial to economic prices.

Skilled and semi-skilled labor has access to the large South African labor market and is priced at the financial wage. The project payment of M3.5 per day for unskilled labor is shadow priced at M2.5 which is the generally accepted local wage for daily laborers.

Local financial prices were used for the crops. Based on a comparison of the protein and energy content of maize residues as compared to five substitutes, the approximate price of M 60 per ton of maize crop residues was derived. The same figure will be applied to sorghum residues.

The value of fuelwood is based on the values and calorific content of its substitutes, displayed in Table 2B-1.

The actual substitution value will vary depending on the household's situation. A rough, weighted average could be calculated as follows:

- 25 percent will substitute dung (0.25 * M100.61)

- 75 percent will substitute brushwood (0.75 * M24.33)

- Weighted average: M43.40

As for the period after 1992, a number of assumptions have been made. The level of costs is assumed to remain as the average for 1985-92, but with all costs associated with

---

[2]   This is supported by observations during field work in the area before project initiation.

Table 2B-1: Economic Value of Fuelwood Substitutes per Cubic Meter

	Megajoules per kilogram	Equivalent kilograms	Maloti per kilogram (1987)	Maloti (1990)
Brushwood	16.0	550	0.03	24.33
Dung	12.9	682	0.10	100.61
Crop residues	14.0	629	0.02	18.54

Table 2B-2: Discounted Share of Total Benefit

	Benefit Shares	
Item	1 percent	10 percent
Sorghum	30	25
Maize	28	23
Fruit	29	38
Fuelwood	11	12
Fodder	1	2
Total	100	100

expatriate (nondomestic) services, such as consultant fees, back-stopping by the executing company, external evaluation missions, and so on, taken out. This implies a level of 54 percent of the previous average.

As for benefits, it is assumed that the project continues to add newly conserved crop land at a performance rate of 50 percent of the previous level. However, from the accumulated area under conservation management reached the previous year, a decline rate of 2 percent per year is applied. Another assumption is that there will be no lasting impact on the level of use of fertilizer and hybrid seed. Furthermore, it is assumed that distribution of fruit trees continues, but declines to a level of 50 percent of project maximum. For fuelwood it is assumed that tree planting declines to a level of 50 percent of project average achievement in 1986-91. For fodder grasses, the assumption in the base case will be that fodder growing stabilizes at 50 percent of the level achieved in 1986-91.

Results and sensitivity analyses

Given these assumptions, the results of the base case are an NPV of -M7.0 million at a discount rate of 10 percent and -M5.6 million at 1 percent. The internal rate of return is -0.8 percent.

The qualitative interpretation is that the project makes a loss that is significant in comparison to the resources invested. The present value of costs is only M9.9 million at 10 percent and M 33.6 million at 1 percent. In terms of the overriding target for the project as defined by the donor—to raise agricultural production among smallholder farming households—the project cannot be shown to be successful when the benefits are related to the costs. Table 2B-2 summarizes the benefit categories, which provide some overview of the relative importance of various benefit items. Each benefit category has been discounted by 1 and 10 percent respectively.

Table 2B-2 shows that fruit is a significant benefit item that deserves more thorough monitoring in the future. This, and conservation benefits, make up the bulk of benefits, and deserve closer scrutiny in terms of sensitivity testing.

The robustness of this base case result is tested using sensitivity analysis of alternative assumptions with regard to discount rate, post-1992 project performance, fruit income, erosion impact on crop yields, future grain prices, and distributional weights.

The qualitative impression of the sensitivity analysis is that, if the rate of 10 percent is used, the base case result remains robust, although the size of the deficit is changed. If the lower rate of 1 percent is considered acceptable as a standard, however, the base case result could be qualitatively altered by several factors, making the project perform better than expected. With the lower rate, the project could also be justified using a heavy distributional weight reflecting the higher marginal utilities of the recipients as a group as opposed to the donors as a group. This weight, however, should then be consistently applied to alternative projects.

Discussion

In the quantification of costs, the labor requirement for maintenance of conservation structures was omitted. However, if a higher cost estimate is accepted, the size of conservation benefits change drastically. It can be shown that the break-even point for maize is 15 person-days, given a time horizon of 50 years and a discount rate of 10 percent. Given a discount rate of 1 percent, the maximum labor input is raised to 34 days, before the net present value of conservation benefits approximate zero. Thus, it is possible that this benefit item has been considerably overestimated. Only empirical measurement in project areas could resolve this issue.

An additional point is option value. Lesotho is extremely dependent upon migrant labor remittances. A high price scenario is designed to build into the calculation the possibility of a substantial increase in relative prices as a proxy for the somewhat unlikely, but not impossible, event that a mass of migrant workers are forced to return to Lesotho. While the nominal price level in fact may not be changed

considerably due to the extent of the market, the real price would increase for Basotho farmers as incomes would fall. The value of the project is thus correlated to the size of the GNP of Lesotho. From both a macro and a micro perspective, the soil conservation program is an insurance against hard times. This leaves the decisionmakers with a partially quantified problem: is the present value of the options higher than the negative NPV of the stream of costs and benefits that have been valued?

However, soil conservation is not the only possible insurance against declines in migrant labor incomes. Lesotho needs *food security*, not necessarily more domestic production of grain. Establishing an economic capacity to buy grain on the world market through other development projects may be a more efficient alternative. Lesotho has a comparative advantage in inexpensive labor, not in good agricultural land and a beneficial climate. Screening available development project options for their profitability is therefore a useful exercise. Furthermore, the capacity to ensure food security is dependent on the *size* of the population, a neglected matter which needs urgent attention in Lesotho.

While nonagricultural investments may be more efficient from a macroeconomic point of view, the majority of the population, and the poorest part, live in the rural areas. If the primary value of a project like FISC is not so much to raise production immediately but rather to protect to a significant degree the land base in the long term, more substantial subsidization of cover crops such as fodder grasses at the expense of traditional cropping could be justified. Even if fodder could not be commercially sold, the grower would provide an insurance service while protecting the land for future potential uses. The economics of this option need to be worked out.

This study cannot conclusively provide an answer to the future value of the FISC approach, but has given some reasons why massive, full-scale replication involving a substantial number of expatriate personnel should be avoided. Continued efforts should be subject to close monitoring of their efficiency in order to justify any further funding. The original report also contains a discussion of the income distributional impacts of the project, which is not analyzed here due to lack of space and direct relevance to the topic of environmental valuation.

Valuation of an Amazonian rainforest

Most financial appraisals of tropical forests have focused exclusively on timber resources and have ignored the market benefits of nonwood products. This has given a strong incentive for destructive logging and widespread forest clearing.[3]

This valuation was based on a systematic botanical inventory of 1 hectare of Peruvian rainforest along the Rio Nanay near the small village of Mishana, 30 kilometers southwest of the city of Iquitos. Annual precipitation in the region averages 3,700 millimeters; soils are predominantly infertile white sands. The inhabitants of Mishana are detribalized indigenous people who make their living practicing shifting cultivation, fishing, and collecting a wide variety of forest products to sell in the Iquitos market.

Method and data

The inventory showed 50 families, 275 species, and 842 trees of at least 10.0 centimeters in diameter. Of the total number of trees on the site, 72 species (26.2 percent) and 350 individuals (41.6 percent) yield products with an actual market value in Iquitos. Annual production rates for fruit trees and palms were either measured from sub-samples or estimated from interviews with collectors. Latex yields were taken from the literature. The merchantable volume of each timber tree was calculated using published regression equations relating diameter to commercial height.

Average retail prices for forest fruits were collected in monthly market surveys. The officially controlled rubber prices were used. Four independent sawmill operators were interviewed to determine the mill price of each timber species. The labor investment associated with fruit collection and latex tapping was estimated in person days per year based on interviews and direct observation of local collecting techniques. The harvest cost was based on the

minimum wage rate, US$2.50 per day.[4] Based on earlier studies the transport cost for fruit and latex was estimated at 30 percent of total market value while extraction cost for timber was set at 40 percent of total value.

Results

The market value of the fruit production in the sample area was almost US$650 per year. Annual rubber yields amount to about US$50. Deducting collection and transportation costs gives net annual revenues from fruits and latex of US$400 and US$22, respectively. The net present value (NPV) of this production, at 5 percent discount rate and assuming that 25 percent of the fruit crop is left in the forest for regeneration, is estimated at US$6,330.

The hectare of forest also contains 93.8 cubic meters of merchantable timber. If liquidated in one felling, this sawtimber would generate a net revenue of US$1,000 on delivery to the sawmill. A logging operation of this intensity, however, would damage much of the residual stand and greatly reduce, if not eliminate, future revenues from fruit and latex trees. The net financial gains from timber extraction would be reduced to zero if as few as 18 trees were damaged by logging.

Periodic selective cutting would yield a maximum of about 30 cubic meters per hectare every 20 years. With a weighted average price of US$17.21 per cubic meter and deducting harvest and transport costs, the net revenue is about US$310 at each cutting cycle. The net present value would be US$490.

The combined NPV of fruit, latex and selective cutting would be about US$6,820, with logging contributing to about 7 percent of the total. Timber management appears to be a marginal financial option in this forest, especially considering the possible impact of logging on fruit and latex trees.

Comparisons

The NPV of this piece of rainforest compares well with other uses of rainforests. Using the same discount rate, 5 percent, the NPV of the timber and pulpwood obtained from a 1-hectare plantation of Gmelina arborea in

---

[3] This case study is derived from Peters et al. 1989.
[4] All prices given in 1987 U.S. dollars using an exchange rate of twenty intis to the dollar.

Brazilian Amazonia is estimated at US$3,184, or less than half that of the forest. Similarly, gross revenues from fully stocked cattle pastures in Brazil are reported to be US$148 per hectare per year. This gives a present value of US$2,960. Deducting the costs of weeding, fencing, and animal care would lower this figure significantly. Both these estimates are based on the optimistic assumption that plantation forestry and grazing lands are sustainable land-use practices in the tropics.

Tropical forests perform vital ecological services, they are the repository for an incredible diversity of germplasm, and their scientific value is immeasurable. The results from this study indicate that tropical forests can also generate substantial market benefits if the appropriate resources are exploited and properly managed.

Loss of earnings method—economic analysis of a water supply and health program in Zimbabwe[5]

The purpose of the paper is to evaluate the Manicaland Health, Water, and Sanitation program in Zimbabwe utilizing social cost-benefit analysis. Data was gathered on cost-benefit analysis, water and sanitation projects, and health statistics in Zimbabwe. Because the health statistics do not fully reflect the mortality and morbidity rates, benefits of the proposed water and sanitation program will be underestimated.

Only communal lands in rural Manicaland are studied. No consideration is given to resettlement areas or commercial farm areas. The study considers only two major benefits—health improvements and change in consumer surplus for water.

Background

The Manicaland Province, organized in seven districts, is situated in the east of Zimbabwe. It is characterized by a relatively high altitude and a diverse relief, implying varying patterns of rainfall, temperature, soils, and natural farming regions, and has the highest rainfall in the country. The province is agriculturally rich and produces forestry, fruit, maize, groundnuts, sunflower, tea, coffee, cotton,

dairy, and beef products. Approximately 90 percent of the provincial population of 1.2734 million (1987) live in rural areas, and 66 percent live in communal lands. Over 50 percent of the populations under 15 years of age. Over 65 percent of the economically active population in Manicaland are working in agriculture, either as subsistence farmers or as permanent or seasonal laborers on commercial farms.

The objectives of the program, within the framework of Swedish and Norwegian support to Zimbabwe's health sector, are to improve living conditions in the communal areas of Manicaland through:

- Improving existing and constructing new water supplies that ensure an acceptable quantity and quality of water for domestic use and that are reliable and accessible for the community,

- Improving sanitation conditions by constructing latrines, and

- Giving health education to improve hygienic practices and instigate behavioral changes.

Prices

Domestic prices were used as a numeraire. That is, local currency is expressed in Zimbabwean dollars (Z$) and foreign currency is expressed in U.S. dollars ($US).

Foreign exchange rate. Harberger's formula is utilized to calculate the shadow price of foreign exchange. Since Zimbabwe is a price taker, the supply and demand elasticities of foreign exchange can be replaced by the import demand and export supply elasticities. Assuming that the export supply elasticity is set to zero, and that no quantitative restrictions exist, the Harberger's formula reduces to

$$R' = \frac{n M (1 + T)R}{n M} = (1 + T) R$$

where   R' = the shadow price of foreign exchange and R the official exchange rate,
M = c.i.f. value of imports in terms of foreign currency,
T = import duties, and

[5] This case study is derived from Fredriksson and Persson 1989.

n = elasticity of demand for foreign exchange.

Given the assumption that the export supply elasticity equals zero, the Harberger's formula now approaches the standard United Nations Industrial Development Organization (UNIDO) guidelines approach. Using 1987 data, the authors determine that one extra unit of foreign exchange can buy goods worth 1.1799 units on the domestic market. Because of the existence of capital restrictions in the form of quotas in Zimbabwe, import duties are increased substantially so that the demand for foreign exchange equals the supply. Therefore a shadow price of foreign exchange of 1.75 is used.

Shadow price of labor. In the dry season, there is underemployment in the agricultural sector, so the shadow wage for labor is set at zero. Given that uncertainty exists in the peak harvest season, when there is a shortage of labor, the authors conduct a sensitivity analysis, where the shadow wage is set qt 100 percent, 75 percent, and 50 percent of the market wage of Z$ 0.46 per hour. For skilled laborers, it is assumed that the shadow wage meets the market wage. The opportunity cost of children's time is set at zero.

The social rate of discount. Using Helmer's approach (taking the rate of return in the private sector), one would derive a real social discount rate of 4.86 percent. If the World Bank discount rate of 10 percent were used, adjusted for foreign exchange rate changes, the real discount rate would be 7.24 percent. There is no official discount rates for government projects in Zimbabwe, so the authors conducted a sensitivity analysis with the social discount rate ranging from 2 percent to 4 percent.

Time horizon. A time horizon of 40 years is used in the analysis, given that benefits are expected to remain as a result of reinvestment.

Calculations

Costs. The materials supplied by the project are valued at market prices. Community input, except for the constructor's payment in case of latrines, is valued at the opportunity cost of labor. Since the shadow wage of unskilled labor has been set at zero during the dry season (when construction takes place), the costs of community input except for the

constructor's payments are zero. The constructor is paid the shadow price of skilled labor: $Z50 for a double latrine, and $Z250 for a multicompartment latrine.

Benefits

♦   Change in consumer surplus. The price of water is calculated by mean kCals of energy used in walking to and carrying water, the energy cost per $Z1, and the time cost with shadow wages set at 50 percent, 75 percent, and 100 percent. The change in consumer surplus per year is equal to

$$180[q_1(p_{w1} - p_{w2}) + \frac{(q_2 - q_1)}{2}(p_{w1} - p_{w2})]$$
$$+ 185[q_1(p_{d1} - p_{d2)} + \frac{(q_2 - q_1)}{2}(p_{d1} - p_{d2})]$$

where q_1 = quantity carried home in 1 day, before the project

q_2 = quantity carried home in 1 day, after the project

p_{w1} = price/1 in the wet season, before the project

p_{w2} = price/1 in the wet season, after the project

p_{d1} = price/1 in the dry season, before the project

p_{d2} = price/1 in the dry season, after the project

The change in consumer surplus per person, when full coverage is reached, is shown in Table 2B-3.

Table 2B-3. Change in consumer surplus per person, when full coverage is reached

Shadow wage (percent)		
50	75	100
0.99	1.18	1.37

♦   Health improvements. Cost of illness estimates consist of treatment costs, costs of lost production, and costs for extra transportation. The authors point out that as willingness to pay is not taken into account, the values arrived at may severely underestimate true values.

For treatment costs, the costs of private treatment are used as the opportunity cost. A consultation with a physician costs $Z10.80, and the cost of nursing is $Z3.00 per hour. The transportation cost used is $Z 0.50 per single journey for all inpatients. The lower bound of the total value per year of reduced morbidity when full reduction is reached, is shown in Table 2B-4.

Table 2B-4. Total value in $Z of health improvements per year after the year 2005 at a social discount rate of 4.86 percent with different disease reductions and shadow wages

Shadow wage (percent)	Disease reduction		
	40 percent	70 percent	100 percent
50	2,501,936	4,378,388	6,254,839
75	2,505,760	4,385,081	6,264,401
100	2,509,585	4,391,774	6,273,962

The value of a life saved would be very high to the individual concerned or his/her family. The authors attempt to establish a minimum value by adopting society's viewpoint to determine the net output gained by saving a life. They use the human capital approach—based on the stream of average income minus average consumption, discounted back to the time of avoided death.

The average household income in communal lands is $Z 550. If the household consists of 2 adults and 4.5 children on average, the income received by each adult is $Z275. The authors estimate that each child consumes $Z 64.71 per year, and that each adult living on communal lands consumes $Z 129.41.

Assuming an urban migration rate of 20 percent, and an unemployment rate of 20 percent, the authors use the weighted average of the wage adjusted for unemployment and the income in communal lands as an estimate of the child's future production: $Z 1307.21. Future consumption is estimated as final household expenditure per capita, $Z 795.13.

The net present value of output gained by preventing a child's death, taking into consideration only production and consumption aspects, is:

$$V_C = -64.71/(1 + i)^t + (1307.21 - 795.13)/(1 + i)^t$$

The corresponding net present value of output gained by society, for each adult saved, is:

$$V_A = (275.00 - 129.41)/)1 + i)^t$$

with i = social rate of discount.

In Table 2B-5, the values for different discount rates are shown as lower bound estimates.

Table 2B-5. Lower bound gain to society from a saved life in $Z at different discount rates (percent)

	Social discount rate (percent)			
	2	4.86	7.24	9
Child (<5 yrs)	8,441.91	2,813.77	1,094.56	934.35
Adult (>5 yrs)	1,307.77	1,131.89	1,011.31	489.04

In the base case, with an estimated social discount rate of 4.86 percent, shadow wage 100 percent of the market wage, and a 100 percent health improvement, the internal rate of return was greater than the social discount rate, and the net present value of the project was strongly positive. At a social discount rate of 7.24 percent, estimated in the alternative approach, the project is not found profitable even if a shadow wage of 100 percent and 100 percent disease reduction is achieved.

While most of the benefits come from disease reduction, it must be pointed out that benefits are probably underestimated because the value of a saved life has been understated—through the use of a lower bound. Secondly, the paper does not take into account other benefits such as local industry that would benefit from improved water supply. Third, as income distribution will probably improve as a result of the project, benefits could have been given a greater weight on social equity grounds. Therefore the authors conclude that the project is likely to be a success from a societal point of view.

Travel cost and contingent valuation methods

Domestic consumer surplus from visits to a rainforest reserve in Costa Rica. This study[6] measures the value of domestic ecotourism to the privately owned Monteverde Cloud Forest Biological Reserve (MCFR). The MCFR straddles the continental divide in Costa Rica and consists of 10,000 hectares of rugged terrain, the vast majority of which is virgin rainforest. Tourism to the reserve has increased markedly over the 18 years of its existence, both in terms of domestic and foreign visitation rates, despite the relatively remote locality and difficulty of accessing the site.

• Data, method, and results. In 1988, 755 out of approximately 3,000 domestic visitors left their addresses at the reserve for the opportunity to win wildlife photographs. The sample showed a similar geographical distribution as a control sample and is assumed to be representative of the true domestic visitor population.

Costa Rica is divided into 81 cantóns. Each cantón is treated as an observation. Visitation rates (number of visits per 100,000 residents) were calculated for each cantón by dividing observed numbers of trips by census populations. Populations, densities, and illiteracy rates for each cantón were taken from a 1986 census. Distances were measured along the most likely roads between the major population center of each cantón and MCFR. The travel cost was estimated at US$0.15 per kilometer. This includes out-of-pocket costs, a fraction of fixed costs, and the value of travel time.

The demand function for visits (VISITATION RATE) was assumed to be linear and to depend on the travel cost (DISTANCE), the population density (DENSITY) and the illiteracy rate (ILLITERACY).

$$VISITATION\ RATE = a_0 + a_1 DISTANCE + a_2 DENSITY + a_3 ILLITERACY + e$$

where e is an error term assumed to be independent and normally distributed. The model was estimated using multiple regressions. The semi-log functional form could not be used on this data because the visitation rate from many cantóns was zero. Two specifications were estimated; with and without illiteracy rates. The results are presented in Table 2B-6.

All coefficients have the expected sign. The coefficient on price is negative and statistically

significant. Higher population densities result in more trips, which is expected since people living in less dense cantóns probably have nearby rainforests to visit. The higher the illiteracy rate the lower the visitation rate, which indicates that visitation is positively correlated with education, and probably permanent income.

The visitation rates predicted in Table 2B-6 are lower than actual rates, since they only predict the visitation observed in the sample. Adjusting this for the whole sample (3000/755) yields an accurate per capita visitation rate. The linear demand functions estimated in Table 2B-6 suggest that visitation would drop to zero only at distances of 328 kilometers and 347 kilometers, respectively, for the two regressions. At the presumed US$0.15 per kilometer, this implies a maximum price per visit of US$49 and US$52, respectively.

The consumer surplus for each cantón is the integral under the demand function I between the actual price for this cantón and the maximum price. The results are summed across all cantóns, yielding an annual consumer surplus estimate of US$97,500 and US$116,200, respectively. Given that there are about 3,000 Costa Rican visitors per year, the site is worth about US$35 per domestic visit. Assuming the real value of this recreational flow remains the same over time and using a real interest rate of 4 percent, the present value of domestic recreation at this site is between US$2.4 million and US$2.9 million.

• Discussion. This consumer surplus estimate of about US$100,000 per year does not include foreign visitors. Foreign visitors outnumbered domestic visitors by four to one in 1988. Foreign visitation is likely to be worth far more than domestic since foreign tourists with higher incomes and lack of nearby substitutes probably value the site more than domestic visitors. The present value estimate is probably too low when considered that visitation has been growing at 15 percent a year for the last five years. Still, if we use the same US$35 for all visitors and also for the future, that would mean a net present value of US$1,250 per hectare. The price that the reserve currently pays to acquire new land is

6 This case study is derived from Tobias and Mendelsohn 1991.

Table 2B-6: Willingness-to-pay Bids for Public Standpost and Private Connections

Dependent variable: Probability that a household's WTP falls within a specified interval

Independent variables:	For a public standpost		For a private connection	
	Co-efficient	*t*-ratio	Co-efficient	*t*-ratio
Intercept	.841	1.350	-.896	-1.344
Household wealth index	.126	2.939	.217	4.166
Household with foreign income (1 if yes)	.064	.232	.046	.194
Occupation index (1 if farmer)	-.209	-.848	-.597	-2.541
Household education level	.157	2.113	.090	1.818
Distance from existing water source	.001	5.716	.000	1.949
Quality index of existing source	-.072	-2.163	-.099	-2.526
Sex of respondent (1 if male)	-.104	-5.41	-.045	-.207
Log-likelihood	-206.01		-173.56	
Restricted log-likelihood	-231.95		-202.48	
Chi-square (freedom=7)	51.88		57.83	
Adjusted likelihood ratio	.142		.177	
Degrees of freedom	137		120	

Table 2B-7: Land, Airfare, and Travel Time Costs (all monetary units US$)

Region	Land travel cost	Air fare	Travel time	Hourly wage	Weight	Time cost	Total price
North America	1,465	1,900	40 hrs	22.50	0.30%	270	3,635
Europe	957	1,300	18 hrs	22.50	0.30%	121	2,378

between US$30 and US$100 per hectare. This suggests expansion of protected areas near this reserve is a well-justified investment.

Finally, it should be noted that the recreational value of standing forests is but one of its potential benefits. The total value of the forest includes benefits from renewable harvests of many commodities, biological diversity, ecological services, and sites for scientific research.

Value of viewing elephants on safaris in Kenya

♦ Travel cost approach. The travel cost method can be used to estimate a demand function for going on safari in Kenya.[7] The consumer surplus (CS) is the difference between what people actually pay and the maximum they would be willing to pay. This net economic benefit from a safari does not show up in market observations but would be lost to the international society if safaris were prohibited.

The analysis is based on a survey taken from samples of the approximately 80 percent of the tourists to Kenya who came either from North America or Europe. The other 20 percent of the tourists were assumed to have the same average consumers' surplus as the sample.

In 1988 there were 63,000 visitors from North America and 350,000 from Europe. Normalizing for population differences gave 0.2316 and 0.9826 visitors per 1,000 population for North America and Europe, respectively.

The price of safari is defined as the sum of land travel costs, air fare, and travel time costs. These are summarized in Table 2B-7. Land costs were estimated by creating a quality weighted price index from the tour operators' surveys. The air fare and travel time were estimated from visitors' surveys.[8] Average annual income was US$45,000, which gives an estimated hourly wage of US$22.50, is weighted at 30 percent to reflect that vacation time is less valued than gross wage rate.

We now have the minimum requirement to estimate a demand curve—two observations of price-quantity. Expecting demand to be a linear function we have:

$$P = 4,023 - 1,674\, Q$$

where P is the sum of land and air travel time costs, and Q is holiday visits per 1,000 population. Note that we have yet to address the problem of the percentage of visitors on holiday to Kenya that actually goes on safari.

---

[7] This study is derived from Brown, Jr., and Henry 1989.

[8] The survey contained 17 questions and was distributed at some lodges and given to tourists during parts of May and June 1988. There were 53 respondents.

Question 10 in survey: Special Fees and Permits

Suppose that the current population of elephants can be maintained if additional foot, vehicle and aerial patrols are operated on a sustained and regular basis in the parks. If these patrols can be supported by a special 100 dollar annual permit (or included in each visitor's safari cost), are you willing to support this permit fee?

[18]   NO, I am not willing to pay $100 for this permit.

[34]   YES, I am willing to pay $100 for this permit.

[ ]   I am willing to pay a maximum of _____ for this permit.

Given a linear demand curve, where 4,023 dollars is the price at which demand is driven to zero, per person consumer surplus for North America is

$$C.S. = 0.5 * (4,023 - 3,635) = US\$194$$

For Europe it is

$$C.S. = 0.5 * (4,023 - 2,378) = US\$822.50$$

It seems reasonable that a safari, a once-in-a-lifetime adventure for most North Americans, most of whom had a very satisfactory experience, would be worth 5 percent more than it costs. It seems plausible that a similar experience at less cost would be worth 35 percent more than the cost for a European.

- Results from travel cost approach. The weighted average consumers' surplus is about US$725. Based on discussions with tour operators and with personnel in the economic section of the U.S. Embassy in Kenya, the number of adults going on safari each year was estimated at between 250,000 and 300,000. This gives a total consumer surplus for those on safari in the range of US$182-218 million annually, depending on the assumed level of visitation.

To identify the contribution elephants make to the value of a safari, tourists on safari were asked in the tourist survey to allocate the pleasure and enjoyment of their trip over four stipulated categories of experience. "Seeing,

photographing, and learning about the wildlife" made up 50 percent of the pleasure according to the answers. In a follow-up question concerning only the enjoyment of the wildlife, the interviewees attributed 25 percent of their wildlife pleasure to seeing African elephants. Applying the share of 12.6 percent, attributed by the visitors to elephants, to the estimated economic value of a safari yields a viewing value for elephants of 23 to 27 million dollars per year.

- Contingent valuation approach. The tourists' survey contains a series of contingent valuation questions. One of the questions (see box) asks people to pay in the form of a special annual permit (or increased safari cost) of 100 dollars which would maintain the elephant population at current levels through increased enforcement activity. Sixty-five percent of the respondents said they would pay 100 dollars. The average was 89 dollars while the median was 100 dollars.

Some respondents dislike translating important qualitative experiences into a dollar metric and respond with a zero response. There were a substantial number of zero responses. However, to maintain a short questionnaire, no follow-up questions were asked to distinguish "protesting" respondents from "genuine" zero respondents. To diminish the importance of the zeros, the median value, 100 dollars, has been used instead of the average.

Respondents could have a strategic bias to give large values if they thought the result would lead to policy decisions they like but would not have to pay for. Respondents may also put in large values if they regard the question as a sort of referendum in which they vote, as it were, for a broader, perhaps moral issue. However, the largest response to this question was 500 dollars, less than 1 percent of the respondent's income and about 3 percent of the cost of his safari. There was therefore no "trimming" of data.

Starting point bias was not tested for due to inadequate sample size. As to the credibility of the median value, 100 dollars, it seems modest inasmuch as it is 3 percent of the total cost of a safari. If one thinks introspectively about the value over and above the cost of a very satisfying moderately expensive experience, 100 dollars does not appear to be a suspiciously high number and some think it somewhat low.

◆ Results from contingent valuation method. Combining the median value of willingness-to-pay of 100 dollars with the estimate of 250,000 to 300,000 adult safaris per year yields an annual viewing value of elephants of between 25 to 30 million dollars. If the mean value of 89 dollars per person is accepted, the viewing value is decreased to between 22 million and 27 million dollars.

Note that both methods produce annual values of around 25 million dollars for viewing elephants. Although the estimates are rough, they are almost certainly a good guide to the order of magnitude of value. The viewing value of elephants is more likely 25 million dollars annually than 2.5 million or 250 million dollars. It does not seem prudent for Kenya's 1988 Wildlife Management and Conservation budget to be under 200,000 dollars when tens of millions of dollars in viewing value of elephants alone are at stake.

Willingness to pay for water services in southern Haiti. In rural areas, many of those who are in the service area of new water supply systems have chosen to continue with their traditional practices. If rural water projects are to be both sustainable and replicable, an improved planning methodology is required that includes a procedure for eliciting information

on the value placed on different levels of service, and tariffs must be designed so that at least operation and maintenance costs (and preferably capital costs) can be recovered. A key concept in such an improved planning methodology is that of "willingness to pay" (WTP).

Two basic theoretical approaches are available for making reliable estimates of households' WTP. The first, the "indirect" approach, uses data on observed water use behavior (such as quantities used, travel times to collection points, perceptions of water quality) to assess the response of consumers to different characteristics of an improved water system. The second, or "direct" approach, is simply to ask an individual how much he or she would be willing to pay for the improved water service. This survey approach is termed the "contingent valuation method" and is the focus of the case study.

◆ The study area. In August 1986 the research team conducted a contingent valuation survey and source observations in Laurent, a village in southern Haiti.[9] At the time, United States Agency for International Development (U.S. AID) was funding a rural water supply project designed to provide services to about 160,000 individuals in 40 towns and villages. The project was executed by the international agency CARE. The affiliation with CARE provided access to villages and justified the presence of the team to the local population.

Haiti, with two-thirds of the population at an annual per capita income of less than US$155 in 1980, provides a field setting similar to the situation in much of Africa and some parts of Asia. In such poor areas, an accurate understanding of the willingness of the population to pay for rural water services is likely to be particularly important for sound investment decisions.

The population of Laurent is about 1,500, predominantly small farmers with a few people having regular wage employment. Remittances from relatives and friends are common. More than 80 percent of the population is illiterate and malnourishment among children is widespread.

There are seven sources of fresh water within approximately 2 kilometers of most of

9 This case study is derived from Whittington et al. 1990.

the population: one protected well and six springs in dry river beds. The springs provide only modest amounts of water, and individuals often wait more than an hour to draw supplies. The average 3 kilometers round trip to a water source can sometimes take several hours. The preference for clean drinking water is strong, and people sometimes will walk considerable distances past alternative sources to collect drinking water that is considered pure.

♦   Research design. Economic theory suggests that an individual's demand for a good is a function of the price of the good, prices of substitute and complementary goods, the individual's income, and the individual's tastes. Maximum WTP for a new water system will vary from household to household and should be positively related to income, the cost of obtaining water from existing sources, and the education of household members, and negatively correlated with the individual's perception of the quality of water at the traditional source used before the construction of the improved water supply system. The authors hypothesize that the WTP bids of women respondents would be higher than those of men because women carry most of the water, but alternative interpretations are certainly possible.

The research design attempted to test whether WTP bids are systematically related to the variables suggested by economic theory. Different ways of posing the questions were tried. The bidding-game format worked better than direct, open-ended questions. The bidding-game was very familiar and easily understood because it was similar to the ordinary kind of bargaining that goes on in local markets of rural Haiti. Tests were also included for the existence and magnitude of several types of threats to the validity of the survey results, such as strategic bias, starting point bias, and hypothetical bias.

"Strategic bias" may arise when respondents believe they may influence an investment or policy decision by not answering the interviewer's questions truthfully. Such strategic behavior may influence answers in either of two ways. Suppose an individual is asked how much he would be willing to pay to have a public standpost near his house. If he or she thinks the water agency or donor will provide the service if the responses from the village are positive, but that someone else will ultimately pay for the service, there will be an incentive to overstate WTP. On the other hand, if the individual believes the water agency has already made the decision to install public standposts in the village and that the purpose of the survey is to determine the amount people will pay for the service (in order to assess charges), the individual will have an incentive to understate the true WTP.

An attempt to estimate the magnitude of the bias was made by dividing the study population into two groups. One group was read an opening statement intended to minimize strategic bias. The group was told that CARE had already decided to build the new system and that people would neither have to pay CARE for the system nor pay money at the public fountains. The second group was read another statement that was accurate but left more questions about the purpose of the study unanswered, especially concerning the role of the interview in designing a water fee.

The hypothesis was that if individuals acted strategically, then bids from the second group would be lower than bids from the first, because the former would fear that a high bid would result in a higher charge by the community water committee.

"Starting-point bias" exists if the initial price in a bidding-game affects the individual's final WTP. This could, for example, be the case if the respondent wanted to please the interviewer and interpreted the initial price as a clue to the "correct" bid. To test for starting-point bias, three different versions of the questionnaire were randomly distributed, each with different initial prices in the bidding game.

"Hypothetical bias" may arise for two kinds of reasons. First, the respondents may not understand or correctly perceive the characteristics of the good being described by the interviewer. This has been a particular problem when the contingent valuation method has been used to measure individuals' WTP for changes in environmental quality. For example, it may be difficult for people to perceive what a change in sulfur dioxide or dissolved oxygen means in terms of air or water quality. This bias is not likely in the present case. The respondents were familiar with public water fountains and private water connections and photos of public standposts built in nearby villages were shown during the interview.

The second source of hypothetical bias is the possibility that the respondents do not take the questions seriously and will respond by giving whatever answer first comes to mind. The test for this is the same as for the applicability of consumer demand theory: were bids systematically related to the variables suggested by economic theory?

◆   Field procedure. Fieldwork in the village consisted of two parts: household surveys and source observation. The majority of households in Laurent were interviewed (170 questionnaires completed out of approximately 225 households). The household interview consisted of four sections. The first dealt with basic occupational and demographic data on the family. The second consisted of a number of specific water-related questions. In the third section the enumerator read one of the statements used to test for strategic bias and showed the photographs of public standposts in other villages. The respondent was then asked to present bids per month for (a) public standposts (assuming no private connection) and (b) for a private connection (assuming public standposts were already installed). The fourth section was a series of questions on the health and education of family members and the household's assets (such as radios or kerosene lamps). The latter was used, along with observations about the quality of the house itself, as a substitute for expenditure questions, to form a household wealth index.

The second part of the fieldwork consisted of observing the quantities of water collected by individuals at all the sources used by the population of the village. The objective of these observations was to verify the information individuals provided in household interviews on the sources they used and the quantities of water collected. All sources were observed on the same day from sunrise to sunset. The analysis of the source observation data for Laurent increased the confidence in the quality of the water-use data obtained from the household interviews. Out of 119 observations of trips to water sources, the interview responses were

consistent with the source observation for 101 households (85 percent).

◆   Analysis of contingent valuation bids. Fourteen percent of the households answered an answer of "I don't know" in response to WTP question for public standposts; there was a 25 percent nonresponse rate for the WTP question for private connections. The mean for the bids for the standposts, 5.7 gourdes per month (US$1.14), seemed realistic.

The test for strategic bias showed the anticipated higher bids for those who had received the neutral statement, but the difference was not statistically significant (t-statistics of 1.1 and 0.5, respectively, for bids on standposts and private connections). On the basis of this test, the hypothesis that respondents were not acting strategically when they answered the WTP questions cannot be rejected.

The test for starting-point bias showed that the bids did not vary systematically with the starting-point. The null hypothesis that the three samples are from the same population cannot be rejected, although the confidence intervals are wide.

On the basis of these results, there was no reason to attempt to adjust the WTP bids for strategic or starting-point bias. The mean of WTP bids for the public standposts was 5.7 gourdes per household per month. Assuming an average annual income in Laurent of 4,000 gourdes (US$800), the mean bid is about 1.7 percent of household income and is significantly lower than the 5 percent rule of thumb often used in rural water supply planning for maximum "ability to pay" for public standposts. The mean of WTP bids for private connections, 7.1 gourdes, was not much higher (2.1 percent of household income), but these bids were based on the assumption that the public standposts were already in place.

The variations in the bids for public standposts and private connections were modeled as a function of the identified explanatory variables. The dependent variable obtained from the bidding game is probably not the maximum amount the household would be willing to pay but rather an interval within which the true willingness to pay falls. Linear regression is not an appropriate procedure for dealing with such an ordinal dependent variable because the assumptions regarding the specification of the error term in the linear model will be violated. An ordered probit model was instead used to explain the variations in WTP bids.

The results of the estimations can be seen in Table 2B-8. The coefficients for all the independent variables are in the direction expected. The *t*-statistics indicate that the variables for household wealth, household education, distance of the household from the existing water source, and water quality are all significant at the 0.05 level in both models. The sex of the respondent was statistically significant in the model for public standposts, but not in the model for private connections. The results clearly indicate that the WTP bids are not random numbers but are systematically related to the variables suggested by economic theory.

The ordered probit model can be used to predict the number of households in a community which will use a new source if various prices were charged. Such demand schedules are precisely the kind of information needed by planners and engineers to make sound investment decisions.

◆ Conclusions. The results of this study suggest that it is possible to do a contingent valuation survey among a very poor, illiterate population and obtain reasonable, consistent answers. The results strongly suggest that contingent valuation surveys are a feasible method for estimating individuals' willingness to pay for improved water services in rural Haiti. It may also prove to be a viable method for collecting information on individuals' willingness to pay for a wide range of public infrastructure projects and public services in developing countries.

Bibliography

Anderson, D. 1987. *The Economics of Afforestation - A Case Study in Africa.* World Bank Occasional Paper No. 1/New Series. Baltimore, Md: The Johns Hopkins University Press.

Attaviroj, P. 1990. "Soil Erosion and Land Degradation in the Northern Thai Uplands," in J.A. Dixon, D.E. James, and P.B. Sherman, eds., *Dryland Management: Economic Case Studies.* London: Earthscan Publications Ltd.

Aylward, B. 1991. *The Economic Value of Ecosystems: 3 - Biological Diversity,* LEEC Gatekeeper Series No. GK91-03, IIED/UCL London Environmental Economics Centre.

Aylward, B., and E.B. Barbier. 1992. "Valuing Environmental Functions in Developing Countries," in *Biodiversity and Conservation,* Vol.1, pp. 34-50.

Barbier, E.B. 1989. *The Economic Value of Ecosystems: 1 - Tropical Wetlands,* LEEC Gatekeeper Series No. GK89-02, IIED/UCL London Environmental Economics Centre.

_____. 1990. *The Economics of Controlling Degradation: Rehabilitating Gum Arabic Systems in Sudan,* LEEC Discussion Paper No. DP90-03, IIED/UCL London Environmental Economics Centre.

_____. 1991. *The Economic Value of Ecosystems: 2 - Tropical Forests,* LEEC Gatekeeper Series No. GK91001, IIED/UCL London Environmental Economics Centre.

Barbier, E.B., W.M. Adams, and K. Kimmage. 1991. *Economic Valuation of Wetland Benefits: The Hadejia-Jama'are Floodplain, Nigeria,* LEEC Discussion Paper No. DP91-01. IIED/UCL London Environmental Economics Centre.

Barde, J.P., and D.W. Pearce, eds. 1991. *Valuing the Environment: Six Case Studies.* London: Earthscan Publications Ltd.

_____. 1991. "A Note on the Economic Costs and Benefits of Bank Tobacco Projects." Dated 5/10/91.

Bartelmus, P., E. Lutz, and S. Schweinfest. 1992. "Integrated Environmental and Economic Accounting: A Case Study for Papua New Guinea", World Bank Environment Department Working Paper No. 54. Washington, D.C.

Bartelmus, P., C. Stahmer, and J. van Tongeren. 1989. "Integrated Environmental and Economic Accounting—Framework for an SNA Satellite System," *Review of Income and Wealth.*

Bator, F.J. 1957. "General Equilibrium, Welfare and Allocation," American Economic Review, March, pp. 22-59.

Binswanger, H. 1989. "Brazilian Policies that Encourage Deforestation in the Amazon," World Bank Environment Department Working Paper No. 16. Washington, D.C.

Birdsall, N., and D. Wheeler. 1991. "Openness Reduces Industrial Pollution in Latin

68

America: The Missing Pollution Haven Effect," paper presented at the Symposium on International Trade and the Environment, International Economics Department, World Bank. Washington, D.C. November.

Bojö, J. 1990. "Benefit-Cost Analysis of the Farm Improvement with Soil Conservation Project in Maphutseng, Mohale's Hoek District, Lesotho," in J.A. Dixon, D.E. James, and P.B. Sherman, eds., *Dryland Management: Economic Case Studies.* London: Earthscan Publications Ltd.

_____. 1990. *Economic Analysis of Agricultural Development Projects. A Case Study from Lesotho.* EFI Research Report, Stockholm School of Economics.

_____.1991. *The Economics of Land Degradation: Theory and Applications to Lesotho*, Dissertation for the Doctor's Degree in Economics, Stockholm School of Economics, pp. 259 - 350.

Braat, L.C., and J.B. Opschoor. 1990. "Risks in the Botswana Range-Cattle System," in J.A. Dixon, D.E. James, and P.B. Sherman, eds., *Dryland Management: Economic Case Studies.* London: Earthscan Publications Ltd.

Braden, J.B., and C.D. Kolstad, eds. 1991. *Measuring the Demand for Environmental Quality.* New York: Elsevier, chapter 2.

Bromley, D.W. 1989. "Entitlements, Missing Markets, and Environmental Uncertainty," *Journal of Environmental Economics and Management,* Vol. 17, 1181-194.

Brookshire, D.S., L.S. Eubanks, and A. Randall. 1983. "Estimating Option Prices and Existence Values for Wildlife Resources," *Land Economics*, Vol. 59, No. 1.

Brown, G., Jr., and W. Henry. 1989. *The Economic Value of Elephants*, Discussion Paper 89-12, London Environmental Economics Centre.

Capistrano, D., and C.F. Kiker. 1990. "Global Economic Influences on Tropical Closed Broadleaved Forest Depletion, 1967-1985," paper presented at the International Society for Ecological Economics Conference, World Bank. Washington, D.C.

Cocklin, C. 1989. "Mathematical Programming and Resources Planning I: The Limitations of Traditional Optimization," *Journal of Environmental Management,* Vol. 28, pp. 127-141.

Dasgupta, P., and K.G. Maler. 1990. "The Environment and Emerging Development Issues," Conference Proceedings of the Annual Conference on Development Economics, World Bank. Washington, D.C.

Dasgupta, P., S. Marglin, and A.K. Sen. 1972. *Guidelines for Project Evaluation,* New York: United Nations Industrial Development Organization (UNIDO).

Dixon, J.A., R. Carpenter, L. Fallon, P. Sherman, and S. Manipomoke. 1988. *Economic Analysis of the Environmental Impacts of Development Projects.* London: Earthscan Publications Ltd., in association with the Asian Development Bank.

Dixon, J.A., and M.M. Hufschmidt, eds. 1986. *Economic Valuation Techniques for the Environment: A Case Study Workbook.* Baltimore, MD: Johns Hopkins University Press.

Dixon, J.A., D.E. James, and P.B. Sherman. 1989. *The Economics of Dryland Management.* London: Earthscan Publications Ltd.

_____, eds. 1990. *Dryland Management: Economic Case Studies.* London: Earthscan Publications Ltd.

Dixon, J.A., and P.B. Sherman. 1990. *Economics of Protected Areas.* Washington, D.C.: Island Press.

Durojaiye, B.O., and A.E. Ikpi. 1988. "The Monetary Value of Recreational Facilities in a Developing Economy: A Case Study of Three Centers in Nigeria," *Natural Resources Journal,* 28(2):315-328.

Energy Journal. December 1988. Special Issue on Electricity Reliability, Vol. 9.

Finney, C.E., and S. Western. 1986. "An Economic Analysis of Environmental Protection and Management: An Example from the Philippines," *The Environmentalist,* Vol. 6, No. 1.

Fisher, A.C., and M. Hanemann. 1987. "Quasi Option Value: Some Misconceptions Dispelled," *Journal of Environmental Economics and Management,* 14, pp. 183-190.

Fleming, W.M. 1983. "Phewa Tal Catchment Management Programme: Benefits and Costs of Forestry and Soil Conservation in Napal," in L.S. Hamilton, ed., *Forest and Watershed Development and Conservation in Asia and the Pacific.* Boulder, CO: Westview Press.

Fredriksson, P., and A. Persson. 1989. *The Manicaland Health, Water, and Sanitation Program in Zimbabwe—A Social Cost*

Benefit Analysis. Department of International Economics and Geography, Stockholm School of Economics.

Gigengack, A.R. et al. 1990. "Global Modelling of Dryland Degradation," in J.A. Dixon, D.E. James, and P.B. Sherman, eds., op. cit.

Gilbert, A. 1990. "Natural Resource Accounting: A Case Study of Botswana," in J.A. Dixon, D.E. James, and P.B. Sherman, eds., op. cit.

Grandstaff, S., and J.A. Dixon. 1986. "Evaluation of Lumpinee Park in Bangkok, Thailand," in J.A. Dixon and M.M. Hufschmidt, eds., op. cit.

Hanley, N.D. 1989. "Valuing Rural Recreation Benefits: An Empirical Comparison of Two Approaches," *Journal of Agricultural Economics*, Vol. 40(3), pp. 361-374.

Harberger, A.C. 1976. *Project Evaluation: Collected Papers.* Chicago: University of Chicago Press.

Hartunian, N.S., C.N. Smart, and M.S. Thompson. 1981. *The Incidence and Economic Costs of Major Health Impairments.* Lexington, MA: D.C. Heath.

Hodgson, G., and J.A. Dixon. 1988. *Logging Versus Fisheries and Tourism in Palawan,* Paper No. 7, East West Center, Honolulu, HI.

Holmberg, G. 1990. "An Economic Evaluation of Soil Conservation in Kitui District, Kenya," in J.A. Dixon, D.E. James, and P.B. Sherman, eds., op. cit.

Kim, S., and J.A. Dixon. 1986. "Economic Valuation of Environmental Quality Aspects of Upland Agricultural Projects in Korea," in J.A. Dixon and M.M. Hufschmidt, eds., op. cit.

Kramer, R.A., M. Munasinghe, N. Sharma, E. Mercer, and P. Shyamsundar. 1992. "Valuing and Protecting Tropical Forests: A Case Study of Madagascar," paper presented at the IUCN World Parks Congress, Caracas, February.

Liebman, J. 1976. "Some Simple-Minded Observations on the Role of Optimization in Public Systems Decisionmaking," *Interfaces*, Vol. 6, pp. 102-108.

Little, I.M.D., and J.A. Mirrlees. 1974. *Project Appraisal and Planning for Developing Countries,* New York: Basic Books.

_____. 1990. "Project Appraisal and Planning Twenty Years On," paper presented at the Annual Conference on Development Economics, World Bank, April 26 and 27.

Lopez, R. 1991. "The Environment as a Factor of Production: The Economic Growth and Trade Policy Linkage," mimeograph, Economics Department, University of Maryland. College Park, MD. December.

Luenberger, D. 1973. *Introduction to Linear and Non-linear Programming.* Reading, MA: Addison-Wesley.

Lutz, E., and M. Munasinghe. 1991. "Accounting for the Environment," *Finance and Development*, Vol. 28, March, pp. 19-21.

Lutz, E., and M. Young. 1990. "Agricultural Policies in Industrial Countries and Their Environmental Impacts: Applicability to and Comparisons with Developing Nations," World Bank Environment Department Working Paper No. 25. Washington, D.C.

MacRae, D., Jr., and D. Whittington. 1988. "Assessing Preferences in Cost-Benefit Analysis: Reflections on Rural Water Supply Evaluation in Haiti," *Journal of Policy Analysis and Management*, 7(2):246-263.

Mahar, D. 1989. "Government Policies and Deforestation in Brazil's Amazon Region," a World Bank publication in cooperation with the World Wildlife Fund and the Conservation Foundation. Washington, D.C.

Markandya, A., and D.W. Pearce. 1988. "Environmental Considerations and the Choice of the Discount Rate in Developing Countries," World Bank Environment Department Working Paper No. 3. Washington, D.C. May.

_____. 1989. "Social Costs of Tobacco Smoking," *British Journal of Addiction*, Vol. 84, No. 10, pp. 1139-1150.

McConnell, K.E., and J.H. Ducci. 1989. Valuing Environmental Quality in Developing Countries: Two Case Studies. Prepared for session on "Contingent Valuation Surveys in Developing Countries," AEA/AERE Annual Meetings, Atlanta, Georgia.

Meier, P., and M. Munasinghe. 1992. "Incorporating Environmental Concerns into Energy Sector Decisionmaking," World Bank Environment Department. Washington, D.C. January.

Mitchell, R.C., and R.T. Carson. 1989. *Using Surveys to Value Public Goods: The Contingent Valuation Method.* Washington, D.C.: Resources for the Future.

Munasinghe, M. 1990a. *Electric Power Economics*. London: Butterworths Press.

_____. 1990b. *Energy Analysis and Policy*. London: Butterworths Press.

_____. 1990c. "Managing Water Resources to Avoid Environmental Degradation," World Bank Environment Department Working Paper No. 41. Washington, D.C.

_____. 1992. *Water Supply and Environmental Management*, Boulder, CO: Westview Press.

Munasinghe, M., and E. Lutz. 1991. "Environmental-Economic Analysis of Projects and Policies for Sustainable Development," World Bank Environment Department Working Paper No. 42. Washington, D.C.

Muzondo, T.R., K.M. Miranda, and A.L. Borenberg. 1990. "Public Policy and the Environment," International Monetary Fund (IMF) Working Paper. Washington, D.C.

Norgaard, R.B. 1991. "Sustainability as Intergenerational Equity: The Challenge to Economic Thought and Practice," internal discussion paper, Asia Regional Series, Report No. IDP 97, World Bank. Washington, D.C.

Pearce, D.W. *An Economic Approach to Saving the Tropical Forest*, LEEC Paper 90-06. London Environmental Economics Centre.

_____. 1991. "Economic Valuation and the Natural World," draft submitted for inclusion in *World Development Report 1992: Development and the Natural World*. Washington, D.C.: World Bank.

Pearce, D.W., E.B. Barbier, A. Markandya, S. Barrett, R.K. Turner, and T. Swanson. 1991. *Blueprint 2: Greening the World Economy*. London: Earthscan Publications Ltd.

Pearce, D.W., and A. Markandya. 1989. *Environmental Policy Benefits: Monetary Valuation*. Paris: Organization for Economic Co-operation and Development. (OECD).

Pearce, D.W., and K. Turner. 1990. *Economics of Natural Resources and the Environment*. Harvester Wheatsheaf.

Peskin, H.M., with E. Lutz. 1990. "A Survey of Resource and Environmental Accounting in Industrialized Countries," World Bank Environment Department Working Paper No. 37. Washington, D.C.

Peters, C.M., A.H. Gentry, and R.O. Mendelsohn. 1989. "Valuation of an Amazonian Rain- forest," *Nature*, Vol. 339, 29 June, pp. 655-656.

Petry, F. 1990. "Who Is Afraid of Choices? A Proposal for Multi-Criteria Analysis as a Tool for Decisionmaking Support in Development Planning," *Journal of International Development*, Vol. 2, pp. 209-231.

Pezzey, J. 1992. *Sustainable Development Concepts: An Economic Analysis*. World Bank Environment Paper No. 2. Washington, D.C.

Phantumvanit, D. 1982. "A Case Study of Water Quality Management in Thailand," in Y.J. Ahmad, ed., *Analyzing the Options*, United Nations Environment Programme (UNEP) Studies, 5. Oxford, England: Pergamon Press Ltd.

Phelps, C.E. 1988. "Death and Taxes: An Opportunity for Substitution," *Journal of Health Economics*, Vol. 7, pp. 1-24.

Randall, A., and J.R. Stoll. 1982. "Existence Value in a Total Valuation Framework," *Managing Air Quality and Scenic Resources at National Parks and Wilderness Areas*. Boulder, CO: Westview Press.

Ray, A. 1984. *Cost Benefit Analysis*. Baltimore, MD: Johns Hopkins University Press.

Repetto, R. May 1988. "Economic Policy Reform for Natural Resource Conservation," World Bank Environment Department Working Paper No. 4. Washington, D.C.

Repetto, R., W. Magrath, M. Wells, C. Beer, and F. Rossini. 1989. *Wasting Assets: Natural Resources in the National Income Accounts*. Washington, D.C.: World Resources Institute.

Romero, C., and T. Rehman. 1987. "Natural Resource Management and the Use of Multiple Criteria Decisionmaking Techniques: A Review," *European Journal of Agricultural Economics*, Vol. 14, pp. 61-89.

Samples, K.C., J.A. Dixon, and M.M. Gowen. 1986. "Information Disclosure and Endangered Species Valuation," *Land Economics*, Vol. 62, No. 3, August.

Sassone, P.G. 1977. "Shadow Pricing in CBA: Mathematical Programming and Economic Theory," *The Engineering Economist*, Vol. 22, Spring, pp. 219-33.

Schulze, W.D., D.S. Brookshire, E.G. Walther, K. Kelley MacFarland, M.A. Thayer, R.L. Whitworth, S. Ben-David, W. Malm, and J. Molenar. 1983. "The Economic Benefits of Preserving Visibility in the

National Parklands of the Southwest," *Natural Resources Journal*, Vol. 23, January.

Sebastian, I., and A. Alicbusan. 1989. "Sustainable Development: Issues in Adjustment Lending Policies," World Bank Environment Department Working Paper No. 6. Washington, D.C.

Society for Promotion of Wastelands Development. 1990a. "Economic and Social Change in a Small Rural Community in the Degraded Lower Shivalik Hill Range in North India," in J.A. Dixon, D.E. James, and P.B. Sherman, eds., op. cit.

_____. 1990b. "Dryland Management Options in Wastelands Development: Jawaja Block, Rajasthan (India)," in J.A. Dixon, D.E. James, and P.B. Sherman, eds., op. cit.

Squire, L., and H. van der Tak. 1975. *Economic Analysis of Projects*. Baltimore, MD: Johns Hopkins University Press.

Thomas, V. 1987. "Evaluating Pollution Control: The Case of Sao Paulo," in G.S. Tolley and V. Thomas, eds., *The Economics of Urbanization and Urban Policies in Developing Countries*. Washington, D.C.: World Bank.

Tobias, D., and R. Mendelsohn. 1991. "Valuing Ecotourism in a Tropical Rain-Forest Reserve," *Ambio*, Vol. 20, No. 2, April.

Turner, R.K. 1988. "Wetland Conservation: Economics and Ethics," in D. Collard, D.W. Pearce, and D. Ulph, eds., *Economics, Growth and Sustainable Environments: Essays in Memory of Richard Lecomber*. London: Macmillan.

United Nations Statistical Office (UNSO). 1990. *SNA Handbook on Integrated Environmental and Economic Accounting*, preliminary draft, October.

van Tongeren, J., S. Schweinfest, E. Lutz, M. Gomez Luna, and F. Guillen Martin. 1991. "Integrated Environmental and Economic Accounting: A Case Study for Mexico," World Bank Environment Department Working Paper No. 50. Washington, D.C.

Walsh, R.G., J.B. Loomis, and R.A. Gillman. 1984. "Valuing Option, Existence and Bequest Demands for Wilderness," *Land Economics*, Vol. 60, No. 1, February.

Wang, G., W. Wu, and F. Li. 1990. "Economic Evaluation of Land Levelling in Weibei Dry Upland," Shaanxi, China, in J.A. Dixon, D.E. James, and P.B. Sherman, eds., op. cit.

Wang, G., and L. Han. 1990. "Economic Evaluation of Dryland Peanut Growing with Perforated Plastic Mulch," in J.A. Dixon, D.E. James, and P.B. Sherman, eds., op. cit.

Whittington, D., J. Briscoe, X. Mu, and W. Barron. 1990. "Estimating the Willingness to Pay for Water Services in Developing Countries: A Case Study of the Use of Contingent Valuation Surveys in Southern Haiti," *Economic Development and Cultural Change*, Vol. 38, No. 2, January.

Whittington, D., A. Okorafor, A. Okore, and A. McPhail. 1989. "Strategy for Cost Recovery in the Rural Water Sector: A Case Study of Nsukka District, Anambra State, Nigeria." Draft. World Bank Infrastructure and Urban Development Department. Washington, D.C.

Willis, K.G., and G.D. Garrod. 1991. "An Individual Travel-Cost Method of Evaluating Forest Recreation," *Journal of Agricultural Economics*, Vol. 42, No. 1, pp. 33-42, January.

World Commission on Environment and Development. 1987. *Our Common Future*. Oxford, England: Oxford University Press.

World Bank. 1992. "Brazil: An Analysis of Environmental Problems in the Amazon," Report No. 9104-DR, Vol. 2, Annex 5. Washington, D.C.

3

Poverty, Resources, and Fertility:
The Household as a Reproductive Partnership

Partha Dasgupta

This article applies the theory of resource allocation to rural households in poor countries to see what one may mean by a "population problem". It is argued by an appeal to evidence that there is a serious population problem in these parts, and that it is related synergistically to poverty, and possibly also to an erosion of the local environmental-resource base. One aspect of the problem lies in that very high fertility rates are experienced by women bearing risks of death that should now be unacceptable. An argument is sketched to show how the cycle of poverty and high fertility rates can perpetuate within a dynasty. The one general policy conclusion which may be novel is that a population policy in these parts would not only contain such measures as family planning programmes and increased female education and outside-work opportunities, but also measures directed at the alleviation of poverty, such as improved credit and savings markets, and a ready availability of basic household needs, such as water and fuel.

Income, fertility, and food: the environmentalist's argument[1]

Excepting for sub-Saharan Africa over the past 25 years or so, gross income *per head* has grown in nearly all poor regions since the end of the Second World War. Moreover, growth in world *food* production since 1960 has exceeded the world's population growth rate; by an annual 0.8 percent during 1960-70, by an annual 0.5 percent during 1970-80, and by an annual 0.4 percent during 1980-1987. (See World Bank 1984, Table 5.6; FAO 1989, Annex, Table 2.) This has been associated with increases in the value of a number of indicators of well-being, such as the infant survival rate, life expectancy at birth, and literacy. All this has occurred in a regime of population growth rates substantially higher than in the past. Excepting for parts of East and South East Asia, modern-day declines in mortality rates haven't been matched by reductions in fertility. Moreover, in a number of places which did experience a decline in total fertility rates for a while (for example, Costa Rica, Thailand, Indonesia and India), they have stabilized at levels well above the *population replacement rate* (the fertility rate at which population would be expected to stabilize in the long run; a figure a bit over 2.1). Table 3-1 presents total fertility rates in several countries (and groups of countries). In the late 1980s, total fertility rate in the World Bank's list of low income countries (excluding China and India) was 5.6. The figures for China and India were 2.3 and 4.2, respectively.[2]

Table 3-1. Fertility Rates in the Late 1980s

	Total fertility rate
India	4.2
China	2.3
Sub-Saharan Africa	6-8
Japan, and Western industrial democracies	1.5-1.9

Source: World Bank (1990).

Cross-sectional curve-fitting on data from 98 so-called developing countries displays a declining relationship between the fertility rate and national income per head (see Figure 3-1). China, Sri Lanka, Thailand and South Korea are outliers, with fertility rates much lower at their levels of income than would be predicted by the statistical relationship. So are most nations of sub-Saharan Africa outliers, but they all lie on the other side of the curve. Nevertheless, cet. par. There would appear to be a link between income and fertility. A regional breakdown of even the Chinese experience displays the general pattern: fertility is lower in higher-income regions. (See Birdsall and Jamison 1983.) With the notable exception of China and Sri Lanka, poor countries are a long way from the so-called demographic transition, that is, transition to a regime of low fertility and low mortality rates.

Both time series and, as we have just observed, cross-section data are suggestive of a broad "inverse" (more accurately, declining) relationship between fertility (and mortality) rates and national income per head. That mortality rates would decline with increasing income is something to be expected. Rising income usually carries with it more education, improved diet, better health-care and sanitation.[3] However, a decline in the fertility rate

---

[1] This article has been adapted from Chapter 12 of the author's book: An Enquiry into Well-Being and Destitution (Oxford: Clarendon Press), forthcoming, 1993. In writing this article the author has gained much from members of the Environmental Studies Forum at the Institute for International Studies, and of the Workshop on Population and Environment at the Morrison Institute for Population and Resources, both at Stanford University, and most especially from discussions with Paul Ehrlich and Marc Feldman. For their comments on the earlier version he is grateful to Kenneth Arrow, Tony Atkinson, Tommy Bengtsson, Justin Yifu Lin, Karl-Göran Mäler, James Mirrlees, Sheilagh Ogilvie, Rolf Ohlsson, and Agner Sandmo.

[2] *Total fertility rate* is the number of live births a woman would expect to give were she to live through her child-bearing years and to bear children at each age in accordance with the prevailing age-specific fertility rates. The measure pertains to the number of live births, not pregnancies. To place international figures in perspective, we should observe that in western industrial countries today, total fertility rates lie between 1.5 and 1.9.

[3] Preston and Nelson (1974) and Preston (1980, 1986) are illuminating dissections of the evidence bearing on the causes of the decline in mortality rates during the 20th century. (See Preston, Keyfitz and Schoen 1972, for world tables.) To me their most striking finding from international data has been that reductions in respiratory diseases (e.g. influenza,

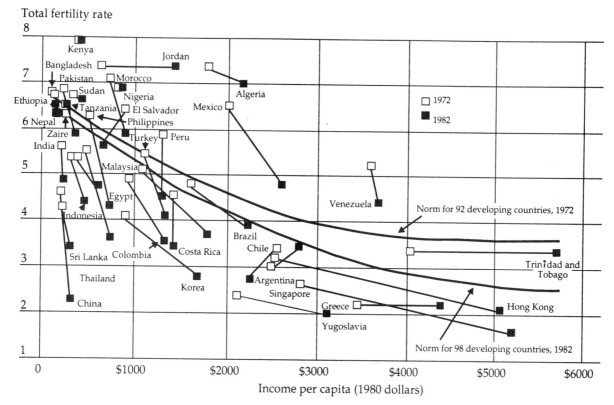

Source: World Bank (1984), Figure 4.4.

Figure 3-1: Fertility in relation to income in developing countries, 1972 and 1982

isn't self-evident. And to understand why it has occurred in many societies, and why at the same time the decline has been so sluggish in so many other societies (even while the mortality rate has been falling, as in modern sub-Saharan Africa), requires theory. One of my purposes in this article is to develop the theory a bit.

What we have been talking about are commodity production, not the commodity basis of production. Now, statistics concerning past movements of income and agricultural production per head can lull us into neglecting the environmental-resource basis of human well-being. They can even encourage the thought that human ingenuity can be guaranteed to solve the problems resource stress poses for growing populations (see Simon 1981; Simon and Kahn, eds. 1984). It may even explain why environmental resources have been so

confidentially neglected in the economics of poor countries. But gross income and its attendent benefits do not capture future consumption possibilities. So they don't quite bear on the confluence of concerns people have about population growth and the environmental-resource basis of human well-being, both of which are in large measure directed at the future.

While economists by and large have neglected these themes, demographers and ecologists haven't. Much of this discussion has been conducted at an aggregate plane. (See e.g., Ehrlich, Ehrlich and Holdren 1977; Birdsall 1988; Kelley 1988; Brown, et al. 1991.) Thus, in the literature on the environment it is a commonplace to read estimates of declining land-man ratios and of dwindling natural-resource bases associated with increases in the size of populations at both the global and regional

---

pneumonia and bronchitis) and infectious and parasatic diseases (e.g. tuberculosis, the diarrheas, whooping cough, malaria, cholera, diptheria, measles and typhoid) have contributed equally (about 25%-30%) to this decline. (There are exceptions, of course, such as Sri Lanka.) See Dasgupta (1992b, Chapter 4) for further discussion of the epidemiological transition.

levels. That rising numbers in the face of a finite environmental-resource base will have catastrophic effects has been argued eloquently by Ehrlich and Ehrlich (1990), among others. The assertion here is that beyond a point there are no substitution possibilities between environmental resources (e.g., genetic diversity, fresh water, breathable air, and so forth) and manufactured goods. Now policy-makers often aren't sensitive to ecological processes, which in any case are for the most part ill-understood.[4] Moreover, urban decisionmakers can be relied upon to underestimate the dangers of environmental degradation. The social value of additional knowledge about ecological processes is therefore large, certainly larger than its private value, and possibly a good deal larger than is officially acknowledged. This calls for greater expenditure on the acquisition and dissemination of such knowledge. Moreover, as long as uncertainty about the value of environmental resources is large and environmental destruction is at least partially irreversible, there is a case for awarding special weight to keeping our future options open. In the present context this means we ought to pursue what one could call a "conservationist" approach to environmental policy: we should preserve more than what standard cost-benefit analysis of the use of environmental resources will warrant. (See Arrow and Fisher 1974; Henry 1974.) This is at the intellectual heart of the ecological movement. It is a convincing chain of arguments.

The problem

Such estimates as are currently on offer about population and resources at the aggregate level are valuable. They alert us to problems. But on their own they aren't a guide to action. The reason is that neither the rate of population growth nor the intensity of environmental-resource use is given from outside. They are determined jointly by a complex combination of opportunities, human motivation, ecological possibilities, and chance factors. To identify and affect population

policy one needs to peer into the locus of decisionmaking over fertility matters. As human society is currently organized, this locus is in large measure the household.[5] I conclude that it is the household we must study. Formal accounts of fertility behaviour haven't placed the household explicitly in the context of rural poverty, and it is poor rural populations that are growing the fastest. Nor has the household been analysed in the context of environmental-resource use. We will see that the context matters.

In this article I shall put resource allocation theory to work on findings in applied demography so as to identify what we could today call *the population problem* in the poorest regions of the world, namely, the Indian subcontinent and sub-Saharan Africa. Both theory and evidence indicate that current rates of population growth in these regions are overly high, and we will try and identify the directions in which public policy needs to be put into effect. In addition to the ecologist's concerns, the population problem in these parts displays itself starkly in the form of unacceptable risks of maternal death for poor, illiterate women, and new lives doomed to extreme poverty. This identification has the air of banality about it, but it needs doing. I have not found in the literature an exploration of household behaviour which yields anything like the population problem we will uncover here. For example, even in the influential and informative report on population and development by the World Bank (see World Bank 1984) there are only 3 pages (pp. 54-56) devoted to the question why households may be producing too many children. Moreover, the answer it provides to the question is rough and limiting: the report says that households can get locked in a Prisoners' Dilemma game over fertility decisions, and that poor folk are typically ignorant of family planning measures.

More generally, in their search for the population problem demographers have in great part attempted to locate varieties of *externalities* in household reproductive activities (see

---

[4] It is remarkable how little even ecologists know about ecological matters of importance. I am grateful to Professor Paul Ehrlich for re-iterating this to me. See Ehrlich and Ehrlich (1991) for an account of the value of biological diversity.

[5] However, we will see below that for fertility analysis in sub-Saharan Africa and the Caribbean, the household isn't a very useful category.

e.g., Lee and Miller 1991). However, as we have just noted, the kinds of externalities they have mostly studied are those which yield the Prisoners' Dilemma. This has been limiting, because there are forms of reproductive externalities which do not lead to the Prisoners' Dilemma (see Annex 3A). They have been much neglected. In any event, we will find that there is a lot more to the population problem than run-of-the-mill externalities, the Prisoners' Dilemma, and ignorance (or fear) of birth control techniques. Thus, consider as an example gender-differences in the costs of reproduction. Assume that each successful birth involves a year and a quarter of pregnancy and breastfeeding. (It can be longer if really extended breastfeeding is practiced, as in sub-Saharan Africa.) On making the obvious corrections, we can then conclude that in a society where female life expectancy at birth is 50 years, and where the total fertility rate is 7 (this is approximately the average figure in sub-Saharan Africa today), well over a third of a woman's expected adult life would be spent either carrying a child in her womb, or in breastfeeding it. And we haven't allowed for unsuccessful pregnancies.[6] Now this assumes she survives all deliveries. In most poor countries maternal mortality is the largest single cause of death among women in their reproductive years, nutritional anaemia playing a central role in this. In parts of sub-Saharan Africa (e.g., Ethiopia), 1 woman dies for every 50 births.[7] We may conclude that, at a total fertility rate of 7 and over, the chance a typical woman entering her reproductive years will not make it through them is about 1 in 6. The reproductive cycle in a woman's life there involves her playing the Russian Roulette. This is one manifestation of the population problem. It is unacceptable.

I shall argue that *wrong* relative prices of household goods and services is as much a source of the population problem as are externalities. Among other things, we will find that for poor rural households environmental

degradation (e.g., vanishing sources of water, receding sources of fodder and household fuel) is likely to be both a cause and an effect of an increase in the net reproductive rate. To the best of my knowledge, this last has not been given any attention in the applied demographic literature.[8] But for a weak empirical substantiation in World Bank (1991), I have not been able to locate any empirical work which tests the thesis. It isn't known how powerful the mutual feedback is in rural communities we know. Should it prove important, the policies governments will be urged to pursue for bringing down fertility rates will be of a different nature from the ones usually espoused (see below). It would also go some way towards explaining the fact that fertility rates in sub-Saharan Africa have not responded to a decline in infant mortality rates. The theory deserves investigation, and it explains why I shall lay stress on it.

The household

In the standard theory of resource allocation the household for the most part is treated as a unit of analysis. This obviously makes sense for a single-membered household, it doesn't necessarily make sense otherwise. The standard theory interprets a household's utility function to be a numerical representation of the ranking of options on the basis of which its choice is actually made. This makes for a perfectly consistent analysis, but it puts strain on the normative significance of household choice. Choice may reflect a ranking which systematically favours some members (for example, males), and it may discriminate against others (for example, higher-birth order girls and elderly relatives). Household choice assumes strong normative significance only when the underlying ranking of options is based upon a defendable aggregate of each member's well-being. But this may not be common; at least not when the family is impoverished, and the stresses and strains of hunger, illness and physical weakness make themselves felt.

---

[6] In Bangladesh about 60 percent of a woman's reproductive life is spent in pregnancy or lactation. The corresponding figure in Pakistan is 50 percent. See McGuire and Popkin (1989).

[7] By way of contrast, we should note that the maternal mortality rate in Scandinavia today is 1 per 20,000 (see World Bank 1988).

[8] For example, Johnson and Lee eds. (1987) has nothing on it. Exceptions are Dasgupta and Mäler (1991) and Nerlove and Meyer (1991), which have explored the thesis analytically.

The matter is a delicate one. For the State to interfere with household choice and probe its inner workings systematically can have catastrophic consequences, if recent evidence in a number of poor countries is any guide. Nevertheless, there are indirect levers the State can pull which do not amount to direct interference with what happens inside the household, but which protect vulnerable members and enable them to reach a stronger strategic position. In this article I shall be much concerned with identifying such levers. But modelling household fertility decisions isn't for the faint-hearted: the motivations of the two central parties to a decision may well be quite different. Fortunately, I will lose nothing qualitatively in what follows by not specifying the household model in any sharp detail. I want to avoid doing the latter in any case. These are early days yet in our understanding of the exact springs of household behaviour, even in poor countries. So it is better to squeeze as much out of a partially unspecified model than to start with a precise model and work through its implications.[9] In any event, this is how I will proceed.

The current debate on how best to model the household isn't about the reasonableness of viewing it as an "optimizing agent". All current constructs of the household are optimization models. They nevertheless differ. One class of models sees some household agent consciously optimizing; for example, by taking reasonable account of the claims of all household members (Gary Becker's "altruistic dictator"; see Becker 1960, 1981; Mirrlees 1972; Cain 1981; Nerlove, Razin and Sadka 1987a,b; Becker and Barro 1988; Lee and Miller 1991), while another interprets household choice in terms of an "as if" optimization (as in the axiomatic theory of bargaining invoked by Manser and Brown 1980; McElroy and Horney 1981; Sundstrom and David 1988; Haddad and Kanbur 1989; McElroy 1990). Given this commonality, all the formal apparatus of optimization theory can be brought to bear on analyses of household decisions; for example, household fertility responses at various prices and income

levels. This is what I shall be involved with here.

At least two parties are involved in a fertility decision. So we may to begin with think of the household as comprising two members who may have concern for each other, but whose motivations aren't the same. As we are studying household decisions, we can ignore children from our analysis. Parents will be taken to act on their behalf, to a greater or lesser extent, and for better or worse. As household resources are inevitably scarce, individual well-being interests can never be entirely congruent. However, it is the members' motivations with which we are concerned here; and the pair's utility functions over allocations of goods, services, and responsibilities could in principle be the same.[10] When they are, the household can be regarded as a *team*, in the sense of Marschak and Radner (1972). What then remains to be analysed is the coordination of their tasks when the two know different things.

At the other extreme is a household composed of two with totally opposed orderings over allocations. That they remain together should be a cause for concern, but we may be unable to do anything about it. If they are forced to stay together, the couple is involved in something akin to a zero-sum game. There is no scope for cooperation here.

Neither model is of any relevance. Interest lies rather in those situations where both parties perceive that they add something by acting together (there are gains in forming a household and cooperating), where the pair can break up should either party be placed under undue stress (there is an outside option for each party), and where the parties' motivations aren't the same. This is not to say that an individual's ranking of household allocations may not reflect interpersonal comparisons of well-being, or interest or advantage. Mutual care and concern will not be absent, but we would expect identification to be only partial. This is the most common type of situation analysed in the theory of games, of which the two-person version has traditionally been called

---

[9] Singh, Squire and Strauss eds. (1986) have pursued this route to good effect. But they were not concerned with fertility decisions.

[10] The figures we have just studied about differences in reproductive costs between men and women inform us, however, that they aren't identical.

bargaining theory, the right basis upon which to build models of households.

To appreciate why bargaining theory is relevant, consider the costs of bearing and rearing children. Pregnancy involves foregone work-capacity for women and, as we have seen, it can involve a considerable addition to the risk of dying. After birth the offspring have to be fed, clothed, taught and cared for. Each of these tasks involves time and material resources. Reproductive costs differ enormously between men and women. Conflicts of interest between the genders arising from this is therefore a key ingredient of the population problem. We will also see that in some regions (e.g., sub-Saharan Africa) the cost of rearing children is shared among kith and kin. This can lead to reproductive free-riding, most especially by men. Understanding and modelling the cost side of reproduction doesn't pose any serious intellectual challenge.[11]

Formal accounts of fertility behaviour haven't placed the household explicitly in the context of rural poverty, and it is poor rural populations that are growing the fastest. Nor has the household been analysed in the context of environmental-resource use. We will see that the context matters.

Population externalities: household versus societal reasoning

That many parts of the globe are even now experiencing severe resource scarcity is widely recognized. This doesn't mean individual households are making irrational or abnormal choices. In an otherwise most illuminating essay Bauer (1981, pp. 61, 64) goes farther. Arguing that it would be wrong of us to think large families in poor countries necessarily pose a problem, he writes: "The comparatively high fertility and large families in many ldcs (less developed countries) should not be regarded as irrational, abnormal, incomprehensible or unexpected. They accord with the tradition of most cultures and with the precepts of religious and political leaders... Allegations or apprehensions of adverse or even disastrous results of population growth are unfounded. They rest on seriously defective analysis of the

determinants of economic performance; they misconceive the conduct of the peoples of ldcs; and they employ criteria of welfare so inappropriate that they register as deterioration changes which are in fact improvements in the conditions of people."

This is not convincing. Even when men and women at the household level rationally prefer large numbers of children to small numbers, it doesn't follow there is no population problem, a problem they themselves may acknowledge were they to be asked about it. As in every other field of individual choice we need here to ask as well if a collection of reasoned decisions at the individual level may be sub-optimal at the collective level. Putting it in a slightly different way, we need to ask if there can be a "resource allocation" failure here.

There are two broad reasons for a possible dissonance between household and societal levels of decisionmaking in the field of procreation. The first is that the relative prices of various goods and services that households face may simply be "wrong", for whatever reason. The second is provided by the ubiquitous phenomenon of externalities. In this section and in Annex 3A we will study the latter. We will identify the former in the sections "Children as consumption and insurance goods" and "Environmental degradation and children as producer goods".

Two sources of externalities suggest themselves. The first is simple enough, it has to do with the finiteness of space. Increased population size implies greater crowding, and we do not typically expect households, acting on their own, to "internalize" crowding externalities. This isn't a precious argument. The human epidemiological environment becomes more and more precarious as communication and population densities rise. Packed centres of population provide a fertile ground for the spread of viruses, and there are always new strains in the making. That environmental resources are usually common property is also cited as a harbinger of externalities. The point here is that because households have access to common property resources, parents don't fully bear the cost of rearing children, and so they produce

---

[11] This isn't to say that estimating the cost of having children isn't formidable. See Lindert (1980, 1983) and Lee and Bulatao (1983) for useful discussions of this.

too many. Admittedly, local common property resources in poor countries have in recent studies been found to be a good deal less of a source for free-riding than it has traditionally been taken to be (see Dasgupta and Heal 1979; Dasgupta and Mäler 1991); nevertheless, the static misallocation, however small, can cumulatively have a large effect on population, as we will see presently.

The second source of externality lies elsewhere, and is more subtle. Procreation is not only a private matter, it is a *social* activity as well. By this I mean that household decisions about procreation are influenced by the cultural milieu. In many societies there are norms encouraging high fertility rates which no household desires unilaterally to break. These norms may well have had a rationale in the past, when mortality rates were high, rural population densities were low, the threat of extermination from outside attack was high, and mobility was restricted. But norms often survive even when their purpose has disappeared. It can then be that so long as all others obey the norm no household on its own wishes to deviate from it; even though were all other households to restrict their fertility rates, each would desire to do so. Thus, there can be multiple social equilibria, and a society can get stuck at one which, while it may have had a collective rationale in the past, does not have one any more.

This doesn't mean society will be stuck with it forever. As always, people differ in the extent of their absorption of social norms, their readiness to digest new information, and to act upon new information. There are inevitably those who, for one reason or another, experiment and take risks. They are the norm-breakers, they often lead the way. In the context of fertility, educated women are among the first to make the move towards smaller families. (See, e.g., Farooq, Ekanem and Ojelade 1987.) Female education is therefore a potent force in creating norm-breakers, as are employment opportunities for women. (See the section "Birth control and female education".) Special costs are inevitably borne during transitional periods, when established modes of operation are in the process of disintegration without

being replaced immediately by new institutions to soften the costs. Demographic transition is potentially a prime example of this. When this is the situation, only a concerted effort (through a massive literacy drive and through improvements in employment opportunities for women) can dislodge the economy from the rapacious hold of high fertility rates. In Annex 3A we will study a formal account of it.

There is an additional force operating in rural communities of poor countries which encourages high fertility rates. It has to do with the relative prices of alternative sources of a number of vital household needs, which are nowhere in line with what they ought to be if human well-being is to increase there. From the household's perspective, the local environmental-resource base offers the relatively cheap sources of such needs. We will see that this can encourage high fertility rates and unsustainable resource-use. But in order to develop the argument we need to study the determinants of fertility. So we do this first.

Birth control and female education

All societies practice some form of birth control. Fertility is below the maximum possible in all societies. Even in poor countries, fertility is not unresponsive to the relative resource costs households face.[12] Extended breastfeeding and postpartum female sexual abstinence have been a common practice in Africa. In a noted study on Kung San foragers in the Kalahari region, Lee (1972) observed that among them the nomadic, bush-dwelling women had an inter-birth interval of nearly 4 years, while those settled at cattle-posts gave birth to children at much shorter intervals. From the perspective of the individual nomadic Kung San woman, it is significant that the social custom is for mothers to nurse their children on demand, and to carry them during their day-long trips in search of wild food through the children's fourth year of life. Anything less than a four-year birth interval would therefore increase mothers' carrying loads enormously, impose a threat on their own capacity to survive, and reduce their children's prospects of survival. In contrast, cattle-post women are

---

[12] See Coale and Trussell (1974) for an attempt at constructing a measure of the extent members of a society consciously control their fertility.

sedentary, and are able to wean their children earlier.[13]

Excepting under conditions of extreme nutritional stress, nutritional status does not appear to affect fecundity. (See Bongaarts 1980; Menken, Trussell and Watkins 1981.) During the 1974 famine in Bangladesh the rural population lost over 1.5 million additional children. The stock was replenished within a year. (See Bongaarts and Cain 1981.) Of course, undernourishment can still have an effect on sexual reproduction, through its implications on the frequency of still-births, maternal and infant mortality, and on possible reductions in the frequency of sexual intercourse. The central questions in economic demography are then these: what determines fertility, and what grounds are there for our thinking that there is a population problem? In the following section and in Annex 3A we will look at the latter question. The remainder of the body of this article studies the two together.[14]

The first and most obvious determinant is the nature of the available technology of fertility control. (Bongaarts 1984, and World Bank 1984, contain good discussions.) Traditional methods have consisted of abortion, abstinence or rhythm, prolonged breastfeeding, and coitus interruptus. These options are often inhumane, and usually ineffectual and unsafe. Contraceptives are superior on all three counts. Nevertheless, their use has been uneven within poor countries. In East Asia over 65 percent of married women in the age range 15-49 years use contraceptives as against somewhat under 10 percent in sub-Saharan Africa. In South Asia as a whole the figure in the early 1980s was about 25 percent, but in Sri Lanka it was a high 55 percent. (See World Bank 1984, Table

7.1.) These large variations across regions not only reflect a divergence in the public provision of family planning and health-care services, they reflect variations in demand as well. Surveys indicate that women themselves perceive an unmet need for access to methods for reducing their fertility. However, the extent of this felt need varies across regions substantially. (See World Bank 1984; Chomitz and Birdsall 1991; Hill 1992.) Successful family planning programmes have proved more difficult to institute than could have been thought possible at first. At one extreme (South-East Asia, Sri Lanka, and the state of Kerala in India), household demand and State commitment to family planning programmes and public-health services have merged in a successful way. China in particular has pursued an active policy of limiting family size. Total fertility rate was brought down, though not monotonically, to a remarkable 2.3 by 1978 from a high 5.9 in 1960.[15] In many places there has been a paucity of demand. In Thailand, for example, the population growth rate has fallen from an average of 3.1 percent per year during the decade 1960-70 to 1.9 percent during the decade 1980-90, but now shows signs of having stabilized there. At another extreme (sub-Saharan Africa), there has been next to nothing done at the State level in the way of a supply of such services. The population growth rate has increased in these decades from about 2.5 percent per year to something like 2.9 percent per year. We will see below that the absence of conjugal bond (in particular the practice of polygyny) as a norm in sub-Saharan Africa has something to do with such high rates, although it has little to do with the fact that fertility rates haven't declined there.[16]

---

[13] See also Blurton Jones and Sibly (1978) and Lee (1980). Child-spacing in sub-Saharan Africa is the subject of empirical inquiry in Page and Lesthaeghe eds. (1981).

[14] For illuminating empirical analyses of the determinants of fertility, see Leibenstein (1974), Easterlin (1975, 1978), Birdsall (1977, 1988), Bongaarts (1978), Preston ed. (1978), Cochrane (1979), Freedman (1979), Easterlin ed. (1980), Cain (1981, 1982, 1984), Bongaarts and Potter (1983), Bulatao and Lee eds. (1983), and Easterlin and Crimmins (1985).

[15] See World Bank (1980, 1988). However, rather draconian measures would appear to have been in use, and the cost has not been negligible. Hull (1990) has collated data reflecting the growing increase in the male/female sex ratio at birth in China. The 1987 One Percent Survey in China shows in addition dramatic patterns of high sex ratios for second and higher-order births. There are three possible explanations for this, all of which may be presumed to be operating: female infanticide, gender-specific abortions, and concealments of births. Tomich, Kilby and Johnston (1991) provide a fine discussion of the possibilities.

[16] The current tragedy over the rapid spread of AIDS in sub-Saharan Africa is also in part a consequence of this. See Caldwell (1991). See also a periodic feature article, titled "A Continent's Agony", in the New York Times (especially

We should not be surprised that in those regions where family-planning programmes have had an impact, it has occurred mostly in the initial stages. Couples would be expected to adopt new methods of birth control to satisfy unmet needs. However, over time it is the net demand for children which would be expected to dominate household decisions. Here is a substantiation: Starting in 1977, 70 "treatment" villages were serviced by a programme of birth control in the famous experiment in Matlab Thana in Bangladesh, while 79 "control" villages were offered no such special service. The contraceptive prevalence in the treatment villages increased from 7 percent to 33 percent within 18 months, and then more gradually to a level of 45 percent in 1985. The prevalence also increased in the control villages, but only to 16 percent in 1985. The difference in total fertility rates between the two groups reached a figure of 1.5. (See Phillips et al. 1988; Hill 1992.)

Even in the initial stages, however, family-planning programmes on their own do not do: it matters greatly if women have a measure of education and autonomy. This has been a central conclusion of a large number of empirical studies. Indeed, the beneficial effects of parents' education, particularly mothers' education, have been observed more generally on the well-being of their children. For the most part, the studies have explored the effect of some 6 to 7 years of schooling, no more. Where they have differed is over the measurement of well-being. Some have looked at the "input" side: for example, household consumption of nutrients (Behrman and Wolfe 1984a,b) and the use of contraceptives (Cochrane 1979; Satahr and Chigambaram 1984). Others have looked at the "output" side, for example, at child health in general (Cochrane et al. 1980; Cochrane, Leslie and O'Hara 1982; Wolfe and Behrman 1982, 1987; Strauss 1990), at infant and child survival rates (Caldwell 1979, 1986; Hobcraft, McDonald and Rutstein 1984; Mosley 1985; Mensch, Lentzner and Preston 1986; Victoria

et al. 1986; Bourne and Walker Jr. 1991; Thomas, Strauss and Henriques 1991), and children's height (Christian et al. 1988; Strauss 1990; Thomas, Strauss and Henriques 1990, 1991).[17] These studies confirm that education helps mothers to process information more effectively, and enable them to use the various social and community services which may be on offer more intensively. Among other things, education appears to impart a degree of self-confidence on one, to avail oneself of whatever new facilities that may be on offer. This is invaluable for rural populations living through changing circumstances.[18]

The links between female education, especially secondary education, and reproductive behaviour are varied. (Cochrane 1983, is an illuminating study.) The acquisition of education delays the age of marriage, and this would be expected to reduce fertility. Moreover, literacy and receptiveness to new ideas complement the efforts of family planning programmes. Furthermore, education increases women's opportunities for work and so their opportunity cost of time. (The cost of child-rearing is higher for educated mothers.) And finally, educated mothers would be expected to value education for their children more highly, so they are more likely to make a conscious tradeoff between the quality and number of their children. (See below.)

Set against these is an effect on fertility which runs the other way. Taboos against postpartum female sexual activity, where they exist, may well be weakened through education. In sub-Saharan Africa, where polygamy is widely practiced, postpartum female sexual abstinence can last up to 3 years after birth. It is also not uncommon for women to practice total abstinence once they have become grandmothers. The evidence is curious: in Latin America and Asia, increased female enrollment in secondary education has had the effect of lowering fertility rates, while in parts of sub-Saharan Africa there is evidence that the effect has been the opposite.[19]

16-19 September, and 19 and 28 October 1990).

[17] However, not all the studies I have cited here are methodologically immune to criticism. Indeed, in a few studies endogenous variables are treated as though are exogenous. Strauss (1990) has a good discussion of such failings.

[18] Here is an indication of orders of magnitude. The infant mortality rate in households in Thailand where the mother has had no education (resp. has had primary and secondary education) was found to be 122 per 1000 (resp. 39 and 19 per 1000). See Jamison and Mosley (1990).

There is then a strong complementarity between family planning programmes, and literacy and numeracy taken together. At a more general level, social and community services and female autonomy are complementary factors. Neither on its own will do. In the remainder of this chapter I shall take this for granted and try and identify the motivations for having children. Understanding household motivation is a key to locating desirable population policies.

Children as consumption and insurance goods

Two broad types of reproductive motivations have figured prominently in analyses of population growth in poor countries. The first stems from a regard for children as children. Not only are children desirable in themselves, they carry on the family line or lineage, and they are the clearest avenue open to what one may call *self-transcendence* (see Dasgupta 1992b, Chapter 13; Heyd 1992.) We are genetically programmed to want and to value them. In short: children are *durable consumption goods*.[20] This provides the broadest type of motivation. It comprises a disparate set, ranging from the desire to have children because they are playful and enjoyable, to the dictates of injunctions emanating from the cult of the ancestor, which sees religion as essentially the reproduction of the lineage. This latter motivation has been emphasized by Caldwell and Caldwell (1987, 1989) in explaining why sub-Saharan Africa has for the most part proved so resistant to fertility reduction. But it isn't a good argument. It explains why fertility rates there are high, it doesn't explain why they haven't responded to declining mortality rates. The cult of the ancestor may prescribe reproduction of the lineage, it does not stipulate an invariant fertility rate. Even in sub-Saharan Africa total fertility rates have been less than the maximum feasible rates.

The second kind of motivation stems from the *old-age security* children can provide in an economic environment where capital, or annuity, markets are next to non-existent. One way of formalizing this is to assume that parents are interested in some form of household welfare subject, however, to the condition that the chance of there being an offspring to care for them in old-age (i.e., providing sustenance, time and attention) is no less than some small amount. In many societies this translates itself to a requirement that the chance of there being a *son* alive when the parents are old is no less than some small amount. As a numerical example, we may consider the simulation study by May and Heer (1968), who estimated that an average Indian couple in the 1960s needed to have 6.3 children in order to be 95 percent sure of having a surviving son when the father reaches the age of 65 years. This is a high figure, about the same as the total fertility rate in India during the decade of the 1950s. This "safety first" model of fertility decision has recently been much explored in a series of articles by Cain (1981, 1982, 1983, 1984).[21] Here we should note that a preference for sons leads parents to discriminate against higher-birth order girl children, a not-infrequent practice in China and in the northern parts of the Indian subcontinent (see, e.g., Dasgupta 1992b, Chapter 11). In much of sub-Saharan

---

[19]   How powerful this countervailing force has proved in sub-Saharan Africa is a controversial matter, and it is possible that the increased fertility response to increased education seen in some of the data reflect aggregation biases. But see Hess (1988) for a time series analysis which attests to there being such an effect in parts of sub-Saharan Africa. See also Barro (1991), who analyses data from over 100 countries to show that during 1960-85 countries with higher a human capital base (as evidenced by school enrollment figures) had lower fertility rates.

[20]   Models with this general motivation have been explored in Becker (1960, 1981), Dasgupta (1969, 1974), Mirrlees (1972), Becker and Lewis (1973), Willis (1973, 1987), Becker and Tomes (1976), Behrman, Pollak and Taubman (1982), Caldwell and Caldwell (1987, 1989), Nerlove, Razin and Sadka (1987a), Barro and Becker (1989), Cigno (1991), Lee and Miller (1991), and in a powerful philosophical essay by Heyd (1991).
   Note that in evolutionary biology phenotypic costs and benefits of reproduction are important only to the extent that they are correlated with reproductive measures. Offspring in this theory are valued in terms of the end of increasing fitness. This isn't the point of view in economic demography, where instead children are valued as means, as durable consumption goods, or as producer and investment goods (see below).

[21]   Preston ed. (1978) is a useful collection of essays on the effect that have been observed on fertility rates of reductions in rates of infant mortality.

Africa even today, rural women lose something like a third of their offspring by the end of their reproductive years. This provides a strong reason for pro-natalism.[22]

Old-age security as a motivation for having children in poor countries is intuitively appealing. The question remains if there is anything to it in the world as we know it. In a significant study Nugent and Gillaspy (1983) used Mexican evidence to show that old-age pension and social security do act as a substitute for children. This doesn't mean fertility rates must inevitably decline when fully-functioning capital markets are introduced. They may well rise if parents display a mixed motivation for having children: viewing them both as investment and durable consumer goods. (See Nerlove, Razin and Sadka 1987a, b.)

Old-age security provides a potentially strong motive. In 1980 people aged 65-and-over in South Asia formed about 4 percent of the total population. The sex composition among the aged is far from even, being of the order of 80-85 men for every 100 women among the elderly. In South and South East Asia female life expectancy at birth is 59 years, while that of males is about 54 years. At age 60, however, they are approximately 15 years and 14 years, not much less than life expectancy at age 60 in advanced industrial countries. (See Trease and Logue 1986.) In the Indian subcontinent the proportion of the elderly who live with their children (for the most part, sons) is of the order of 80 percent or more. (In the United States the corresponding figure is about 15 percent.) Sons are an absolute necessity in these circumstances. A poor widow with no sons in northern parts of the Indian subcontinent is faced with a near-certain prospect of destitution.

Environmental degradation and children as producer goods

In poor countries children are also useful as income-earning assets; that is, as *producer goods*. This provides households in these parts with a third kind of motivation for having children. It has important consequences. There

are exceptions of course (e.g., Mueller 1976), but on the whole this motivation has been neglected in the demographic literature.

Poor countries for the most part are biomass-based subsistence economies. Rural folk there eke out a living from products obtained directly from plants and animals. Production throughput is low. Households there do not have access to the sources of domestic energy available to households in advanced industrial countries. Nor do they have water on tap. (In the semi-arid and arid regions water supply isn't even close at hand.) This means that the relative prices of alternative sources of energy and water faced by rural households in poor countries are quite different from those faced by households elsewhere. Indirect sources (e.g., tap water nearby) are often prohibitively expensive for the household. As we will see presently, this provides a link between high fertility, degradation of the environmental-resource base of a rural community, and an accentuation of hardship among its members.

From about the age of 6 years children in poor households in poor countries mind their siblings and domestic animals, fetch water, and collect fuelwood, dung and fodder. These are complementary to other household activities. They are needed on a daily basis if the household is to survive. As many as 5 hours a day may be required for obtaining the bare-essential firewood, dung and fodder. (One should contrast this with the direct time spent by households in acquiring water and fuel in advanced industrial economies, which is nil.)

All this may be expected to relate to the high fertility and low literacy rates in rural areas of most poor countries. Poverty, the thinness of markets, and an absence of basic amenities make it essential for households to engage in a number of complementary production activities: cultivation, cattle grazing, fetching water, collecting fodder and fuelwood, cooking food, and producing simple marketable products. Each is time consuming. Labour productivity is low not only because capital is scarce, but also because environmental resources are scarce too.[23] Children are then

---

[22] Leibenstein (1957) is an early exploration of the old-age security hypothesis regarding fertility behaviour. See also Neher (1971), Schultz (1974), Willis (1980), Sundstrom and David (1988), and Cremer and Pestieau (1991). Nugent (1985) provides an assessment of the then existing literature on the subject.

continually needed as workers by their parents, even when parents are in their prime. A small household simply won't do. Each household needs many hands, and it can be that the overall usefulness of each additional hand increases with declining resource availability.[24] In their study of work allocation among rural households in the foothills of the Himalayas, C.S.E (1989) recorded that children in the age range 10-15 years work 1½ times the number of hours adult males do, their tasks consisting of fuelwood, dung, and fodder collection, grazing domestic animals, household chores, and marketing. Now, a high rate of fertility and population growth further damages the environmental resource base (to the extent they are unprotected common-property), which in turn in a wide range of circumstances provides further (private) incentives for large families, which in turn further damages the resource base,..., and so on; until some countervailing set of factors (whether public policy, or some form of Malthusian checks) stops the spiralling process. But by the time this happens millions of lives have usually suffered.[25] Such an explosive process can be set off by any number of factors. Government or private usurpation of resources to which rural communities have had historical access is a potential source of the problem. So is the breakdown of collective agreements among users of common property resources a triggering mechanism. Indeed, even a marginal decline in compliance can trigger the process of cumulative causation. The static efficiency loss associated with minor violations is, to be sure, small; but over time the effect can be large.

As workers, children add to household income. They are often costless to rear by the time they are adolescents. This line of argument has been emphasized by Mueller (1976) and Lindert (1980, 1983). Cain (1977) has studied data from the village Char Gopalpur in Bangladesh. He showed that male children become net producers at as early an age as 12 years, and work as many hours a day as an adult. Using a zero (calorie) rate of interest, he estimated that male children compensate for their own cumulative consumption by the age of 15. This may not be typical in Bangladesh. I cite it, nevertheless, to show the vast difference in the motivation for having children between households in rich countries and poor households in poor countries.

It appears then that the transfer of *material* resources over a life cycle in poor households in poor countries is from offspring in the aggregate to their parents. The qualification is important. I have seen no study which includes in the calculation of resource transfers the value of time foregone in the rearing of children, nor the risks borne by the mother during the process of reproduction. These amount to resource transfers: from parents to their children. There is nevertheless a sense in which children are more valuable to parents as producers of income within poor households in poor countries than they are in rich communities. So I shall take it that the flow of resources there is from the offspring to their parents. However, it isn't mere poverty which leads to this directional flow. If mobility on the part of young children is routine matter (and this was the case in early 19th Century England), poor parents are not able to affect this transfer readily. In these circumstances much of the motivation for having children is absent, and even a poor society may display a move towards the *demographic transition*, that is, the transition from high to low fertility.[26] But this isn't so in the Indian subcontinent and sub-Saharan Africa, and it makes for a strong parental motivation for having large families.

In many societies (e.g., in the Indian subcontinent) daughters are a net drain on parental resources (dowries can be bankrupting), and this goes some way towards explaining the preference parents show for sons there. (Sopher ed. 1980.) It also helps explain why daughters in their childhood are expected to work relatively harder for their parents. All this

---

[23] Cooking in a poor household is a vertically-integrated activity: nothing is processed to begin with. It is time-intensive.

[24] This can happen especially if households discount the future at a high rate.

[25] For an account of this kind of spiralling process, see Nerlove and Meyer (1991) and Dasgupta and Mäler (1991). In an important empirical document, World Bank (1991) has provided partial confirmation of the thesis in the context of sub-Saharan Africa.

[26] I am grateful to Sheilagh Ogilvie for this point.

is in sharp contrast with advanced industrial nations, where material resources are transfered on average from the adult to the young. In a long sequence of writings, Professor Caldwell (see e.g., Caldwell 1976, 1977a, b, 1981, 1982) has argued that whether a society has made the demographic transition is related to the direction of the intergenerational flow of resources.

The motivation for fertility we have been emphasizing in this and the previous section springs from a general absence of certain basic needs in rural parts of poor countries: public-health services, old-age security, water, and sources of fuel. Children are born in poverty, and they are raised in poverty. A large proportion suffer from undernourishment. They remain illiterate, and are often both stunted and wasted. Undernourishment retards their cognitive (and often motor) development (see, e.g., Dasgupta 1992b, Chapter 14). Labour productivity is dismally low also because of a lack of infrastructure, such as roads. In this background it is hard to make sense of the oft-expressed suggestion (e.g., Simon 1977, 1981) that there are increasing-returns-to-scale in population size even in poor countries; that human beings are a valuable resource. They are potentially valuable as doers of things and originators of ideas, but for this they require inputs of the means for development. Historical evidence on the way pressure of population led to changes in the organization of production, property rights, and in ways of doing things, which is what Boserup (1965, 1981) studied in her far-reaching work, also does not seem to speak to the population problem as it exists in sub-Saharan Africa and the Indian subcontinent today. Admittedly, the central message one reads in these writings is that the spectre of the Malthusian trap is not to be taken seriously. But we should be permitted to ask of these modern writers what policy flows from their visions. The Boserup-Simon thesis implies that households confer an external benefit to the community when they reproduce. This means

fertility ought to be subsidized. I have not seen this implication advocated by its proponents.

Some special features of sub-Saharan Africa

Even among poor regions, sub-Saharan Africa is a special case on fertility matters, and it is worth asking why.[27] To be sure, sub-Saharan Africa is not a homogeneous social entity. There are regional differences in the ethos within this large land-mass (see Cochrane 1991). But for our purposes we will lose little by thinking in aggregate terms. There are central tendencies in any broad cultural group, and a number of features within sub-Saharan Africa would seem to be pertinent when we seek to locate them. When we have identified a few, we will contrast them with those prevailing in the Indian subcontinent, another region experiencing a population problem.

Unlike the Indian subcontinent, the "household" is not a very meaningful organizing unit for production, consumption and fertility decisions in Africa. (See e.g., Dow 1971; Caldwell ed. 1975; Cain 1984; Bleek 1987; Caldwell and Caldwell 1987, 1989; Kamarck 1988; Goody 1990.) Often, there is no common budget for a man and wife. Polygamy is widely practised. In the late 1950s some 35 percent of all married men in sub-Saharan Africa were polygamists (see Goody 1976). In rural areas matters would not appear to have changed much (see Farooq, Ekanem and Ojelade 1987). By "polygamy" we really mean "polygyny" here: it is the men who have more than one spouse. Women in sub-Saharan Africa, just as women among non-caste Hindus in India, often have more than one relationship at any given time. But they are extra-marital relationships, not marriages.[28] Recall also that the dowry system is virtually non-existent in sub-Saharan Africa. It is for the most part men who have to accumulate wealth to obtain a bride. This affords a reason why the median age difference between spouses in Africa is large; a fact of considerable importance, since it enables

---

[27] Caldwell and Caldwell (1992) contains a good account of fertility trends in sub-Saharan Africa.

[28] Among some non-caste Hindus in India extra-marital relationships offer a means of fertility-control. Abortion of a foetus resulting from a marital union is frowned upon, whereas the abortion of a foetus resulting from an extra-marital relationship is pretty much mandatory. I am grateful to Paul Seabright for this observation concerning norms of behaviour in rural South India.

women to have spouses despite the prevalence of polygyny: women on average become widows at an early age, and widow-remarriages are not only permissible, they are a commonplace.

The sexual division of labour is powerful, but it assumes a different form from the Indian subcontinent. Even though women do not inherit land, the primary responsibility for raising subsistence crops for the household usually rests with women, who as a consequence have greater power and control over food distribution than their counterparts in the Indian subcontinent. Some 40 percent of rural households are headed by women. (This goes a little way towards explaining why the dowry system is absent.) Women are as a consequence much more independent of their husbands than they are in the Indian subcontinent. Nevertheless, women's sexuality and labour power are firmly under control by the husband's lineage. Among other things it is the extent of kinship control of women which differentiates societies in sub-Saharan Africa from those in the Indian subcontinent. Until relatively recently, the fallow land was communally owned within kinship groups. All this makes for a considerable difference in the resource implications of having offspring. Children aren't raised by their parents in the way they are in the Indian subcontinent. Rather, this responsibility is more diffuse within the kinship group, affording a form of insurance protection to be expected in semi-arid regions. In much of West Africa about 1/3 of the children have been found to live with

their kin at any given time. Nephews and nieces have the same rights of accomodation and support as biological offspring. Sub-Saharan Africa has often been characterized by strong descent lineage and by weak conjugal bond. For the most part, as in much of the Indian subcontinent, descent is patrilineal and residence is patrilocal. (An important exception are the Akan people of Ghana.)

Modelling fertility decisions

Household fertility and savings decisions are interrelated. Indeed, children as old-age security identifies the two. Nevertheless, it will proves useful to consider them separately. It makes for expositional ease.

Earlier, we identified three different motives behind procreation. Hybrid models of fertility decision contain all of them in varying strengths. They enable us to analyse the matter in a unified way. The thing to do is to consider the "reduced form" of household utility as a function of, among other things, the number of children they have. Should the child mortality rate decline, the fertility rate would be expected to follow suit among households averse to facing risks in the number of children who survive. But even when mortality rates decline, it takes time for households to recognize this. Demographic transitions in the past have displayed sharp declines in fertility rates following only some time after steep declines in mortality rates.[29]

The effect on fertility of changes in income and the cost of rearing and bearing children is

---

[29] I am assuming that the cost of rearing children remains approximately the same despite falling mortality rates. Thus, let n be the number of children produced, and $\pi(N,n,\alpha)$ the probability that N will survive; where $0 \leq N \geq n$ and where α is an underlying parameter of the distribution. Now no matter what is the motivation for having children, we can always represent the reduced form of ex post parental utility (net of the ex post cost of child rearing) as V(N). For vividness, we may suppose that V(N) is increasing in N for low values of N and decreasing in N for high values of N. If the von Neumann-Morgenstern axioms are satisfied, ex ante parental utility is $U(n,\alpha) = \sum \pi(N,n\alpha)V(N)$. Parents choose n. Suppose, to take a sharp example, $\pi(.)$ is the binomial distribution, with α representing the probability that any one child will survive. This means that $\pi(n,N,\alpha) = {}^{n}C_{N}\alpha^{N}(1-\alpha)^{n-N}$. It can then be shown that if V(N) is concave in N, an increase in leads to a decline in the utility-maximizing choice of n. The argument generalizes to the case where there are child-bearing costs, provided they are increasing and convex in n; and it generalizes to the case where reproductive decisions are sequential. See Sah (1990).

The critical assumption is the concavity of V(N). Since V(N) is a reduced form (what we may call indirect utility) we should ideally derive it from postulates on primitives, and not merely stipulate it. Preston ed. (1978) contains valuable empirical evidence on the matter. It offers a varied picture. See in particular the essays by Ben-Porath and by Chowdhury, Khan and Chen. In the former study (based on Israeli data) child replacement is shown to be a significant phenomenon, and it occurs quickly. In the latter study (based on data from Bangladesh and Pakistan) the influence of child mortality on subsequent fertility was found to be of no great significance. But see Bongaarts and Cain (1981), who record substantial replacement through increased fertility following the Bangladesh famine of 1974; and Caldwell (1991) on sub-Saharan Africa.

more complex. (The pioneering work here is that of Becker 1960.) Letting c denote current parental consumption, n the number of children, and z an index of the quality of each child, we may assume household utility, U, to be a function of these three variables. So we write $U(c,n,z)$. It is appropriate to assume that U is an increasing function of both c and z.[30] We should view $U(.)$ as a "reduced form" of household utility, in that in those circumstances where children are seen at least partially as investment goods, z would in part reflect future parental consumption.

The quality of a child depends on the amount of time and resources devoted to him; it depends as well on the time and effort devoted by the child in acquiring education and skills. In a hybrid model, z itself would be an aggregate of different characteristics. The problem is that parents are faced with a tradeoff between c and z, and between n and z. Moreover, c is itself up to a point an increasing function of n in poor households, since children are valuable as producer-goods. This accentuates the tradeoff parents face between n and z.[31]

Earlier we observed that improvements in education appears to have a salutary effect on household circumstances. It is also useful to study the effect of an increase in parental income on fertility. (This leads us back to the aggregate data we studied in the first section, "Income, fertility, and food: the environmentalist's argument".) To begin with, we may trace the increase in parental income to a rise in their labour productivity; as a consequence for example, of rural investment, or more generally, better employment opportunities for men and women in the labour market. Now a rise in women's labour-productivity implies an increase in the opportunity cost of rearing children. At the same time, with increasing parental income children are needed less as producer goods, and possibly less also as investment goods, since one would imagine that

rising income brings in its wake greater access to the capital market. (For an empirical exploration of this last link, see Rosenzweig and Evenson 1977.)

Improvements in labour productivity are often associated with urbanization. This accentuates the directional changes we have already identified. Urbanization tends to disintegrate households into "nuclear" units. This raises the cost parents have to bear in rearing their children. (The contribution of grandparents, aunts and other kin is in this situation greatly reduced.) Growing urbanization in a growing economy also offers children better employment prospects, which improve their bargaining strength relative to their parents. This in turn lowers the gross return on children as investment goods, since children become less dependable as a source of income to their parents in their old age. (Sundstrum and David 1988, deploy this argument in the context of antebellum United States.) Moreover, State legislation on elementary schooling (for example, making it compulsory) and increased private returns to education (arising from general industrialization) make children relatively speaking less useful as producer goods. Compounding all these considerations enables us to have a glimpse of those forces at work which relate fertility to household income. The broad "inverse" relationship between income and fertility does not require of us to postulate that children are "inferior goods", in the sense made familiar in consumer-demand theory. Increased parental income, especially maternal income, raises the cost of children: children become more expensive relative to other goods. The causal chain is therefore more complex and somewhat reinforcing, and the "inverse" relationship between household income and the desired family size holds for a wide class of household utility functions.[32]

Both the costs and benefits of having children are experienced in different proportions by

---

[30] Children are taken to be identical, and are assumed to be identically treated. I do this simply in order to pose the problem in its pristine form. We will also ignore the externalities which social norms create.

[31] Increased life expectancy increases the return on children's education, and so human capital formation could be expected to assume a larger share of total investment. The Indian data conforms to this expectation. See Ram and Schultz (1979), who in addition estimated that during the 1970s human capital accumulation in India was of the order of 55 percent of physical capital accumulation.

[32] A formal model along the lines sketched in the text can easily be constructed. A simplified version of this is in Becker (1960, 1981), Nerlove, Razin and Sadka (1987a), and Cigno (1991). See also Easterlin, Pollak and Wachter (1980).

the parents. The cost of bearing and nursing a child is inevitably borne by the mother, but the cost of rearing children is culturally conditioned. In some cultures, as in much of sub-Saharan Africa, these costs are diffused across the kinship. (That women are vigorously engaged in agriculture presumably has something to do with this.) When this is so, there is an allocation failure, in that neither parent bears the full cost of their decision. In societies characterized by weak conjugal bond (as in much of sub-Saharan Africa and the Caribbean) male parents often bear little of the cost of rearing children. Here, then, we would expect to see another source of asymmetry in parental motivations over reproductive decisions. Men's desire for children would on balance be expected to exceed that of women by far, and this would brings in its wake all the attendant implications we observe in the data. Patriarchy, a weak conjugal bond, and a strong kinship support system of children taken together are a broad characteristic of sub-Saharan Africa. It provides a powerful stimulus to fertility.

That kinship support of one's children provides the basis of a free-rider problem (yet another externality), leading to too many children being born, has been noted in the demographic literature (see e.g., Cain 1984, for references.) But I have not seen it being recognized that this is only so if the benefits of having children are not equally diffused across the kinship. An excessive number of children is the outcome only when parents appropriate a greater proportion of the benefits their children provide than the proportion they incur of the cost of rearing them. Professor John Caldwell has told me that this would appear to be the normal case in sub-Saharan Africa.[33]

Matters are different in societies where the conjugal bond is powerful. This is the case in most of Asia. Parents together bear the bulk of the cost of raising their children, even though the sexes typically do so unevenly. The extent of economic dependency of women on men now assumes a central role. This dependency is enormous in the Indian subcontinent, most especially the North. In these types of patriarchal societies women rightly perceive sons as having especially high value as insurance against personal calamities, such as widowhood and abandonment. But sons can't be guaranteed. So one has to keep trying. In East and South East Asia (and also southern India and Sri Lanka) women's economic dependency is less. Among those that were the world's poorest countries in the early 1970s, fertility rates have fallen most dramatically in this part of the world. In a wide-ranging essay on the old-age security hypothesis, Cain (1984) used the median age difference between spouses as an index of female economic dependence in patriarchal societies to demonstrate a remarkably high correlation between this and the total fertility rate in a cross-section study of nations.

There are thus forces at work which move the fertility goals of women relative to men in opposite directions. In poor societies marked by gender-based asymmetry in employment opportunities and power, women's reproductive goals don't differ noticeably from those of men. (See Mason and Taj 1987.) But professed desires are sensitive to the extent to which women are educated: educated women tend to desire smaller families than illiterate ones. A preference for sons is nearly universal in the Indian subcontinent. In sub-Saharan Africa this isn't so. (See Williamson 1976.) Indeed, in parts of Africa for which data on uterine sibling groups have been obtained, there is no evidence of stopping rules which would reveal an

---

[33] To see that there is no distortion were the proportions the same, suppose c is the cost of rearing a child and N the number of couples within a kinship. For simplicity let us assume that each child makes available y units of output (this is the norm) to the entire kinship, which is then shared equally among all couples, say in their old age. Suppose also that the cost of rearing each child is shared equally by all couples. Let n* be the number of children each couple other than the one under study chooses to have. (We will presently endogenize this.) If n were to be the number of children this couple produces, it would incur the resource cost C=[nc+(N-1)n*c]/N, and it eventually would receive an income from the next generation equalling Y=[ny+(N-1)n*y]/N. Denote the couple's aggregate utility function by the form U(Y)-K(C), where both U(.) and K(.) are increasing and strictly concave functions. Letting n be a continuous variable for simplicity, it is easy to confirm that the couple in question will choose the value of n at which yU'(Y)=cK'(C). The choice sustains a social equilibrium when n=n*. (This is the symmetric non-cooperative Nash equilibrium of the social system.) It is easy to check that this is also the condition which is met in a society where there is no reproductive free-riding.

implicit sex-preference. (See Goody et al. 1981a, b.)[34]

Allocation Failure and Public Policy

A good bit of the motivation underlying analytical work on fertility behaviour has been in identifying circumstances where there is no allocation failure; that is, situations in which individual household decisions unencumbered by any public population policy yield Pareto-efficient outcomes.[35] The literature is a picture of economists busily burying any "distortion" they can imagine, and heaving a sigh of relief when they have fashioned a world in which none is visible. In this article we have identified reasons for rejecting this point of view. Nevertheless, for the moment let us leave aside social externalities. Let us leave aside as well the fact that a person's utility function doesn't necessarily correspond to the function which reflects her well-being. I want to argue that even then there is a need for public policy. Public policy does not end when well-being efficiency is in sight. The distribution of benefits and burdens can be unjust. We have noted the importance of children as producer and insurance goods in poor households. The availability of household infrastructure in the form of cheap fuel and potable water makes children less important as income earning assets. By a similar token, availability of credit and access to the capital market lowers the importance of children as insurance goods. Children as producer goods and children as old-age security yield somewhat different implications for public policy.

But they both entail public policy. The provision of such patterns of household infrastructure as we have identified requires resources, and standard resource allocation theory informs us why it is the State's obligation in poor countries to make attempts at ensuring their supply. The aim should not be to force people to change their reproductive behaviour.[36] Rather, it should be to identify policies which would so change the options men and women face that their reasoned choices would involve a lowering of their fertility rates to replacement levels. The evidence, some of which I have put together here, tells us that poor parents in poor countries *do* calculate when making such decisions as those which bear on household size and assets, even though what emerges at the end is a greater number of yet another cohort of poor, illiterate people. It would certainly be unjust of governments to insist on parents sending their children to schools for so many years if this requirement further impoverishes poor households. But it would not be unjust were the complementary household production inputs made available through the provision of family-planning and public-health service, and infrastructural investment, and for governments to then make free school attendance compulsory.[37] Reasoned choice at the household level would be expected to respond to this through an alteration in fertility goals.

Taxes required for the provision of such household infrastructure and family-planning and public-health service as we are discussing here can only be obtained from households that are better off. In the absence of such public provisions the dynamics of a social system can be horrifying. For reasons we have identified, the bulk of the very poor in poor countries have

---

[34] Stopping rules based on sex preference provide a different type of information regarding sex preference than sex ratios within a population. The reason is that in a steady state stopping rules have no effect on the sex ratio. To see this, suppose that in a society where sons are preferred, parents continue to have children until a son is born, at which point they stop. Assume for simplicity that at each try there is a 50 percent chance of a son being conceived. Now imagine a large population of parents, all starting from scratch. In the first round 50 percent of the parents will have sons and 50 percent will have daughters. The first group will now stop and the second group will try again. Of this second group, 50 percent will have sons and 50 percent will have daughters. The first sub-group will now stop and the second sub-group will have another try. And so on. But at each round the number of boys born equals the number of girls. The sex ratio is 1.

[35] See for example Becker and Barro (1986), Nerlove, Razin and Zadka (1987a), and Willis (1987). For a critique of this, see David (1986).

[36] The draconian measures employed in India during the Emergency period 1975-77 as regards sterilization are an example of the kinds of activities governments must avoid.

[37] The school-year in rural United States until the beginning of this century was shorter than in urban areas, and it took account of seasonal labour requirements. I am grateful to Professor Gary Becker for giving me an account of this.

continually to aim at large household sizes, making it in turn much more difficult for them to lift themselves out of the grip of poverty: household labour productivity remains abysmally low, investment credit is for the most part unavailable to them, and the avenue of savings is consequently that much constrained for them. The matter is different for those with a greater access to resources. They are, as always, in a position to limit their household size and increase the chance of propelling themselves into still-higher income levels. I have not been able to locate published data on the matter, but my impression is that among the urban middle classes in India, the demographic transition has already been achieved. This doesn't mean there is an inexorable "vicious circle of poverty". People from the poorest of backgrounds have been known to lift themselves out of the mire. Nevertheless, there are forces at work which pull rich and poor groups away from one another in terms of the quality of life. The Matthew Effect ("For unto everyone that hath shall be given, and he shall have abundance; but from him that hath not shall be taken away even that which he hath") works relentlessly in poor countries.

I am putting matters in stark terms so as only to focus on the idea that parents would have a different set of fertility goals were the relative prices of environmental and infrastructure goods different, and were the economic dependency of women on men less. As regards the latter, female education is now widely recognized to be a key propellent. But so are increased employment opportunities for females a route to greater autonomy.

There are, of course, other measures which should be thought about in parallel. Compulsory schooling, for example, makes children prohibitively expensive as assets for generating current income, so it reduces their attractiveness as a commodity. Making available alternative sources of basic household needs improve the well-being of poor households via an altered set of fertility goals.

Let us sum up. We have identified three broad categories of policies for alleviating the population problem: (i) increasing the costs of having children, (ii) reducing the benefits of reproduction, and (iii) improving the information base concerning the technology of reproduction, and affecting the locus of household decisionmaking. Now (i) and (iii) have found much expression in the demographic literature; unhappily, at the neglect of (ii). It is (ii) which raises the most interesting economic issues; it tells us that among the most potent avenues open for easing the population problem are those which involve social coordination (see Annex 3A), the provision of infra-structural goods, and measures of social security. But these services are desirable in themselves, and commend themselves even when we don't have the population problem in mind. It seems to me, this consonance among desirable social policies is a most agreeable fact.

Admittedly, in saying all this we are looking at matters wholly from the perspective of the parents. This is limiting.[38] But identifying the right basis for population policies is extremely difficult. (See Meade 1955; Narveson 1967; Dasgupta 1974, 1988, 1989, 1992b; Heyd 1992.) What I have tried to argue in this article is that there is much we can establish even were we to leave such conceptual difficulties aside. Population policy involves a good deal more than making family planning centres available to the rural poor. It also involves more than a recognition that poverty is a root cause of high fertility rates in a number of societies. The problem is deeper, but it is identifiable.

---

[38] Enke (1966) is a notable exploration in the value of prevented births when the worth of additional lives is based entirely on their effect on the current generation. As a simplification, he took the value of a prevented birth to be the discounted sum of the differences between an additional person's consumption and output over the person's lifetime.

Annex 3A: Strategic Complementarities in Fertility Decisions

In the section "Population externalities: household versus societal reasoning", we identified the social milieu as something which influences fertility decisions. It is a source of externality. We will call it an *atmospheric externality* (see Meade 1952). Here we will formalize a simple version of the idea. But it is as well to note that the formulation has wide applicability, and it isn't restricted to fertility behaviour. Our purpose here will be to demonstrate that social externalities often lead to multiple Nash equilibria. This means that history matters, and that societies which are similar in terms of technology and utility functions may gravitate in the long term to quite dissimilar states of affairs.

There is a wide variety of actions we all are regularly engaged in which are numerical; that is, they are scalar in dimension. (The analysis can be generalized to the case where decision variables are vectors.) They also share the feature that any given individual's goal-maximizing choice of action is an increasing function of the choice of action of *any* other individual. This isn't quite the primitive one wants (choice is to be explained, not assumed), and we look for properties of utility functions which will yield this. So, supposing there are M people ($k, n = 1, \ldots, M$), let x_k (a real number) be individual k's action. Assume too that k's utility function is of the form $U_k(x_1, \ldots, x_M)$; which we also write as $U_k(x_k, \underline{x}_{-k})$.[1] The primitive which will do the job is that k's marginal utility of her *own* action is an increasing function of the choice of action by any other person. Formally, this means:

$$\partial^2 U_k(x_k, \underline{x}_{-k})/\partial x_k \partial x_n > 0, \text{ for all } k \neq n. \quad (1)$$

When individual utility functions satisfy condition (1), we will say that the social system involves *strategic complementarities* among individuals' motivations. (See Cooper and John 1988.) In game theory it would be to say that payoff functions are *supermodular*. (See e.g., Milgrom and Roberts 1989, 1990).[2]

We will find it useful to appeal to a specification which is somewhat sharper than condition (1). It will be assumed that a person's utility is a function of her own action and of the *average* action of all others (hence the term atmospheric externality); and that the marginal utility of her own action is an increasing function of the average action of all others.

Examples abound. They include how hard we work at our's tasks, what wage rate we accept as reasonable, how much we spend on a particular type of consumer-durable (through, for example, what Duesenbery 1949, christened the "demonstration effect", or through what in modern industrial organization literature are called "network externalities", see Farrell and Saloner 1986), how much education we allow our daughters to attain, at what age they get married, how many children we aim for (albeit this only allows for non-integer values), and so forth. In sociological parlance these examples reflect peer-group emulation and norm-guided behaviour, and in economics they are often called *atmospheric external economies*.[3]

Earlier, we discussed household reproductive decisions, and the concomitant private

---

[1] $\underline{x}_{-k} = (x_1, \ldots, x_{k-1}, x_{k+1}, \ldots, x_M)$.

[2]   This isn't strictly correct. The inequality in (1) is taken to be weak in the definition of supermodularity. We lose nothing here by assuming strict inequality.

[3]   It is also on occasion called Marshallian external economies. The idea has a long and distinguished pedigree (see Rosenstein-Rodin 1943; Scitovsky 1954), and it has found rich expression in recent years (see e.g. Schelling 1978; David 1985, 1987; Stiglitz 1987; Cooper and John 1988; Hahn 1990). An underlying idea is to find a general condition

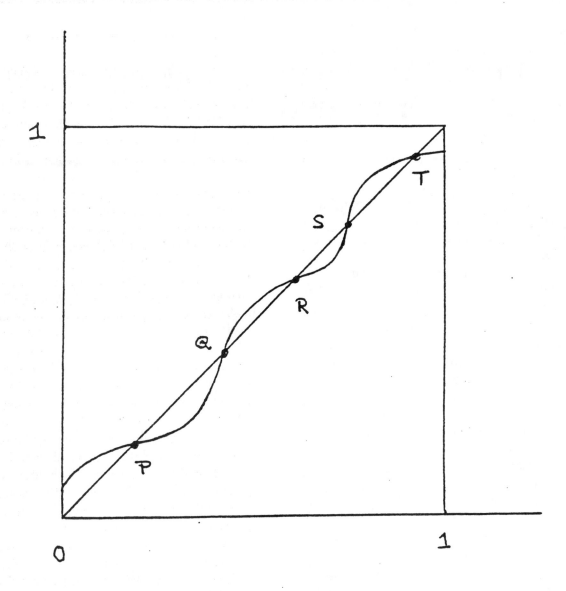

Figure 3A-1

costs and benefits of having children. These decisions are also influenced by aspects of shared values within a community. A woman on her own will not find it desirable to break out and assert her autonomy when no one else is doing so. (Among other things, the psychic costs may be too high.) But she may find it permissible do so if all others (or at least most others) are doing so as well. Both are self-enforcing situations, and they sustain quite different personal norms of behaviour. We often refer to this as a society's *custom*, (e.g., "The custom in rural India is to have many children"). Of course, there may well be several self-enforcing levels

of activity, not just two; which is to say, there may be several (non-cooperative) Nash equilibria, with their associated norms of behaviour. That we find ourselves at one equilibrium reflecting a particular custom is no reason for insisting there isn't another equilibrium (reflecting a different custom) at which individual well-being would be higher.

To see this, imagine a number of identical households, each of whose strategy (say, the level of some activity) is, without loss of generality, a number between 0 and 1. (See Figure 3A-1.) I denote the representative household's activity level by z, and the average value of the

(e.g. condition (1)) under which a social system can possess several non-cooperative (Nash) equilibria, at least two of which can be ranked on the basis of the Pareto criterion.

activity level chosen by all other households by Z. Let U(z,Z) denote the typical household's utility function, net of costs of choosing z. For each possible value of Z there is a corresponding value of z, say z*, at which U(.) is maximized. (We ignore multiple household optima for simplicity.) We write this as z*(Z). It is the household's *reaction curve*. We are assuming that $\partial^2 U(z,Z)/zZ \; \partial > \partial \; 0$. This means z*(Z) is upward-sloping, as shown in Figure 3A-1.

Since households are identical, the household whose reaction curve we have drawn is a representative one. We now simplify for expositional ease and pick a representative household from all the remaining households. This would be anchored most firmly were we to assume that when the average choice of all other households is Z, it is a consequence of each of them having chosen this average. So we do so. We are now interested in points at which z*(Z) intersects with the 45° line. Each intersection is a non-cooperative Nash equilibrium point of the social system. Each household's level of activity at an intersection is utility-maximizing on the assumption that all other households choose this same level. The intersections are social equilibrium points. In Figure 3A-1, there are 5 equilibrium points, P, Q, R, S and T. Notice that we have not assumed utility functions to be concave. Equilibrium is guaranteed by virtue of the assumption of strategic complementarities.

Because households behave identically at equilibria, the latter can be ranked by the Pareto criterion. Equilibria can also be ranked in terms of household well-being. So there is a best and a worst equilibrium, and there are ones of intermediate goodness.

The question arises as to which equilibrium point gets selected. The answer depends on the relative importance of a number of things, all of which can be succinctly captured by two notions: that of the *expectations* individuals have about one another (they have on occasion been called "eductive" considerations), and that of the *history* of the social system (they have frequently been called "evolutive" considerations). The former is the stuff of the pure theory of

games, the latter is the material of social sciences.[4]

To illustrate their differences, it is simplest to think of a situation where the activity level has to be chosen each period (day, week, year, or whatever). Imagine that decisions are costlessly reversible from period to period, so that everything starts afresh each period. If in any period each household expects every other household to choose a particular equilibrium action, each household will find it in its interest to choose this action as well. Expectations are not only self-fulfilling, it is expectations which do all the work. Under an eductive mode a Nash equilibrium is held up by its own bootstraps, so to speak. (A charismatic leader may come along and persuade people to change their expectations to a set of self-fulfilling ones.) There is no analytical reason why expectations must necessarily be based on historical experience. When they are not so based, history has no role to play in the determination of the final outcome, although of course, it is special contingencies (e.g., the emergence of a charismatic leader) which do the picking from the set of equilibria. On the other hand, expectations are typically influenced by history. In this case history has a strong role to play even under an eductive mode.[5]

An extreme alternative has history assuming the dominant role. Suppose, for example, in each period households base their expectations of what others will do on what was done on average in the previous period. This is sometimes called the Marshallian *tatonnement*. Its rationale is provided by substantial sunk costs incurred in each period's decisions, so that from period to period only marginal changes in individual decisions are undertaken, if they are undertaken at all. Consider the simplest form of this: each household in each period expects the average level of activity to be equal to the average level of activity during the previous period. It is now an easy matter to check that under the dynamics generated by such adjustments in behaviour, P, R and T are stable equilibrium points, while Q and S are unstable.

---

[4]   See Binmore and Dasgupta (1986) for an elaboration of this distinction.

[5]   Note that individuals in the society we are studying in the text are not locked in a Prisoners' Dilemma. There are multiple equilibria here, and no dominant strategy for any household.

To illustrate, imagine that through a sequence of chance events households find themselves at R (where, say, the average age of marriage for girls is low) and that household well-being would be greater at P (where the average age of marriage for girls is somewhat higher). There is then a precise sense in which households are engaged in an excessive level of activity at R (i.e., a rapid turnover of daughters in households). It is possible each household knows this. But no household on its own has an incentive to deviate from its chosen pattern of behaviour. This is a social dilemma, and only a coordinated policy can overcome it.

This is an extreme example. By this I don't mean the example's technical features, for example that households are identical. (This can be relaxed easily without our losing anything other than simplicity.) I mean something else. In the world as we know it norms over time are internalized, and so breaking out of established patterns of behaviour even when others are doing so can prove hard for an individual. This gives a certain additional stickiness to established equilibrium behaviour. Social equilibria are yet more history-dependent. Our present example has not reckoned with this additional reason why history matters. It has been designed only to explore the possible multiplicity of Nash equilibria.

Bibliography

Arrow, K.J. and A. Fisher (1974): "Preservation, Uncertainty and Irreversibility", *Quarterly Journal of Economics*, 88.

Barro, R. (1991): "Economic Growth in a Cross Section of Countries", *Quarterly Journal of Economics*, 106.

Barro, R. and G. Becker (1989): "Fertility Choice in a Model of Economic Growth", *Econometrica*, 57.

Bauer, P.T. (1981): *Equality, the Third World and Economic Delusion* (London: Weidenfeld and Nicolson).

Becker, G. (1960): "An Economic Analysis of Fertility", in G. Becker ed., *Demographic and Economic Change in Developed Countries* (Princeton, NJ: Princeton University Press).

Becker, G. (1981): *A Treatise on the Family* (Cambridge, MA: Harvard University Press).

Becker, G. and R. Barro (1986): "Altruism and the Economic Theory of Fertility", *population and Development Review* (Supplement), 12.

Becker, G. and R. Barro (1988): "A Reformulation of the Economic Theory of Fertility", *Quarterly Journal of Economics*, 103.

Becker, G. and H.G. Lewis (1973): "Interaction between Quantity and Quality of Children", *Journal of Political Economy*, 81.

Becker, G. and N. Tomes (1976): "Child Endowments and the Quantity and Quality of Children", *Journal of Political Economy* (Supplement), 84.

Behrman, J., R.A. Pollak and P. Taubman (1982): "Parental Preferences and Provision for Progeny", *Journal of Political Economy*, 90.

Behrman, J., and B.L. Wolfe (1984a): "The Socioeconomic Impact of Schooling in a Developing Country", *Review of Economics and Statistics*, 66.

Behrman, J. and B.L. Wolfe (1984b): "More Evidence on Nutrition Demand: Income Seems Overrated and Women's Schooling Underemphasized", *Journal of Development Economics*, 14.

Binmore, K. and P. Dasgupta (1986): "Game Theory: A Survey", in K. Binmore and P. Dasgupta eds.: *Economic Organizations as Games* (Oxford: Basil Blackwell).

Birdsall, N. (1977): "Analytical Approaches to the Relationship of Population Growth and Development", *Population and Development Review*, 3.

Birdsall, N. (1988): "Economic Approaches to Population Growth", in H. Chenery and T.N. Srinivasan eds., *Handbook of Development Economics*, Vol. 1 (Amsterdam: North Holland).

Birdsall, N. and D. Jamison (1983): "Income and Other Factors Influencing Fertility in China", *Population and Development Review*, 9.

Bleek, W. (1987): "Family and Family Planning in Southern Ghana", in C. Oppong ed. (1987).

Blurton Jones, N.G. and R.M. Sibly (1978): "Testing Adaptiveness of Culturally Determined Behaviour: Do Bushmen Women Maximize their Reproductive Success by Spacing Births Widely and Foraging Seldom?", in N.G. Blurton Jones and V.

Reynolds eds., *Human Behaviour and Adaptations* (London: Taylor and Francis).

Bongaarts, J. (1978): "A Framework for Analyzing the Proximate Determinants of Fertility", *Population and Development Review*, 4.

Bongaarts, J. (1980): "Does Malnutrition Affect Fecundity? A Summary of the Evidence", *Science*, 208.

Bongaarts, J. and M. Cain (1981): *Demographic Responses to Famine* (New York: Population Council).

Bongaarts, J. and R.G. Potter (1983): *Fertility, Biology and Behavior: An Analysis of the Proximate Determinants* (New York: Academic Press).

Boserup, E. (1965): *The Conditions of Agricultural Growth* (London: George Allen & Unwin).

Boserup, E. (1981): *Population Growth and Technological Change* (Chicago: Chicago University Press).

Bourne, K.C. and G.M. Walker Jr. (1991): "The Differential Effect of Mothers' Education on Mortality of Boys and Girls in India", *Population Studies*, 45.

Brown, L.R. et al. (1991): *State of the World* (New York: W.W. Norton).

Bulatao, R.A. and R.D. Lee eds. (1983): *Determinants of Fertility in Developing Countries*, 2 volumes (New York: Academic Press).

Cain, M. (1977): "The Economic Activities of Children in a Village in Bangladesh", *Population and Development Review*, 3.

Cain, M. (1981): "Risk and Insurance: Perspectives on Fertility and Agrarian Change in India and Bangladesh", *Population and Development Review*, 7.

Cain, M. (1982); "Perspectives on Family and Fertility in Developing Countries", *Population Studies*, 36.

Cain, M. (1983): "Fertility as an Adjustment to Risk", *Population and Development Review*, 9.

Cain, M. (1984): "Women's Status and Fertility in Developing Countries: Son Preference and Economic Security", World Bank Staff Working Paper No. 682.

Caldwell, J.C. ed. (1975): *Population Growth and Socioeconomic Change in West Africa* (New York: Columbia University Press).

Caldwell, J.C. (1976): "Toward a Restatement of Demographic Theory", *Population and Development Review*, 2.

Caldwell, J.C. (1977a): "The Economic Rationality of High Fertility: An Investigation Illustrated with Nigerian Data", *Population Studies*, 31.

Caldwell, J.C. (1977b): *The Persistence of High Fertility: Population Prospects in the Third World* (Canberra: Australian National University Press).

Caldwell, J.C. (1979): "Education as a Factor in Mortality Decline: An Examination of Nigerian Data", *Population Studies*, 33.

Caldwell, J.C. (1981): "The Mechanisms of Demographic Change in Historical Perspective", *Population Studies*, 35.

Caldwell, J.C. (1982): *Theory of Fertility Decline* (New York: Academic Press).

Caldwell, J.C. (1991): "The Soft Underbelly of Development: Demographic Transition in Conditions of Limited Economic Change", *Proceedings of the World Bank Annual Conference on Development Economics 1990*.

Caldwell, J.C. and P. Caldwell (1987): "The Cultural Context of High Fertility in sub-Saharan Africa", *Population and Development Review*, 13.

Caldwell, J.C. and P. Caldwell (1990): "High Fertility in Sub-Saharan Africa", *Scientific American*, 262 (May).

Caldwell, J.C. and P. Caldwell (1992): "Population Growth, Physical Resources, and Human Resources in sub-Saharan Africa", in P. Dasgupta and K.-G. Mäler eds. (1992).

Chomitz, K.M. and N. Birdsall (1991): "Incentives for Small Families: Concepts and Issues", *Proceedings of the World Bank Annual Conference on Development Economics 1990*.

Christian, P. et al. (1988): "The Role of Maternal Literacy and Nutrition Knowledge in Determining Children's Nutritional Status", *Food and Nutrition Bulletin*, 10.

Cigno, A. (1991): *Economics of the Family* (Oxford: Clarendon Press).

Coale, A.J. and J.T. Trussell (1974): "Model Fertility Schedules: Variations in the Age Structure of Childbearing in Human Populations", *Population Index*, 40.

Cochrane, S.H. (1979). *"Fertility and Education: What Do We Really Know?"* (Baltimore: Johns Hopkins University Press).

Cochrane, S.H. (1991): "Comment", *Proceedings of the World Bank Annual Conference on Development Economics 1990*.

Cochrane, S.H. (1983): "Effects of Education and Urbanization on Fertility", in R.A. Bulatao and R.D. Lee eds. (1983), Vol. 2.

Cochrane, S.H. et al. (1980): "Effects of Education on Health", World Bank Staff Working Paper No. 405 (Washington, D.C.).

Cochrane, S.H., J. Leslie and D. O'Hara (1982): "Parental Education and Health: Intracountry Evidence", *Health Policy and Education*, 2.

Cooper, R. and A. John (1988): "Coordinating Coordination Failures in Keynesian Models", *Quarterly Journal of Economics*, 103.

Cremer, J. and P. Pestieau (1991): "Bequests, Filial Attention and Fertility", *Economica*, 58.

C.S.E. (1990): *Human-Nature Interactions in a Central Himalayan Village: A Case Study of Village Bemru* (New Delhi: Centre for Science and Environment).

Dasgupta, P. (1969): "On the Concept of Optimum Population", *Review of Economic Studies*, 36.

Dasgupta, P. (1974): "On Optimum Population Size", in A. Mitra ed.: *Economic Theory and Planning: Essays in Honour of A.K. Dasgupta* (New Delhi: Oxford University Press).

Dasgupta, P. (1988): "Lives and Well-Being", *Social Choice and Welfare*, 5.

Dasgupta, P. (1989): "Population Size and the Quality of Life", *Proceedings of the Aristotelian Society* (Supplementary Volume LXIII).

Dasgupta, P. (1992a): "Population, Resources and Poverty", *Ambio*, 21.

Dasgupta, P. (1992b): *An Enquiry into Well-Being and Destitution* (Oxford: Clarendon Press), forthcoming.

Dasgupta, P. and G. Heal (1979): *Economic Theory and Exhaustible Resources* (Cambridge: Cambridge University Press).

Dasgupta, P. and K.-G. Mäler (1991): "The Environment and Emerging Development Issues", *Proceedings of the World Bank Annual Conference on Development Economics 1990*.

Dasgupta, P. and K.-G. Mäler eds. (1992): *The Economics of Transnational Commons* (Oxford: Clarendon Press), forthcoming.

Dasgupta, P. and P. Stoneman eds. (1987): *Economic Policy and Technological Performance* (Cambridge: Cambridge University Press).

David, P.A. (1985): "Cleo and the Economics of QWERTY", *American Economic Review*, Papers and Proceedings, 75.

David, P.A. (1986): "Comment", *Population and Development Review* (Supplement), 12.

David, P.A. (1987): "Some New Standards for the Economics of Standardization in the Information Age", in P. Dasgupta and P. Stoneman eds. (1987).

Dow, T. (1971): "Fertility and Family Planning in Africa", *Journal of Modern Studies*, 8.

Duesenbery, J.S. (1949): *Income, Savings and the Theory of Consumer Behaviour* (Cambridge, MA: Harvard University Press).

Easterlin, R.A. (1975): "An Economic Framework for Fertility Analysis", *Studies in Family Planning*, 6.

Easterlin, R.A. (1978): "The Economics and Sociology of Fertility: A Synthesis", in C. Tilley ed., *Historical Studies of Changing Fertility* (Princeton: Princeton University Press).

Easterlin, R.A. ed. (1980): *Population and Economic Change in Developing Countries* (Chicago: Chicago University Press).

Easterlin, R.A. and E. Crimmins (1985): *The Fertility Revolution: A Supply-Demand Analysis* (Chicago: University of Chicago Press).

Easterlin, R.A., R.A. Pollak and M.L. Wachter (1980): "Toward a More General Model of Fertility Determination: Endogenous Preferences and Natural Fertility", in R.A. Easterlin ed., *Population and Economic Change in Developing Countries* (Chicago: Chicago University Press).

Ehrlich, P. and A. Ehrlich (1990): *The Population Explosion* (New York: Simon and Schuster).

Ehrlich, P. and A. Ehrlich (1992): "The Value of Bio-Diversity", in P. Dasgupta and K.-G. Mäler eds., (1992).

Ehrlich, P., A. Ehrlich and J. Holdren (1977): *Ecoscience: Population, Resources and the Environment* (San Francisco: W.H. Freeman).

Enke, S. (1966): "The Economic Aspects of Slowing Population Growth", *Economic Journal*, 76.

FAO (1989): *The State of Food and Agriculture* (Rome: Food and Agricultural Organization).

Farooq, G.M., I.I. Ekanem and S. Ojelade (1987): "Family Size Preferences and Fertility in

South-Western Nigeria", in C. Oppong ed. (1987).

Farrell, J. and G. Saloner (1986): "Installed Base and Compatibility: Innovation, Product Preannouncements and Predation", *American Economic Review*, 76.

Freedman, R. (1979): "Theories of Fertility Decline: A Reappraisal", *Social Forces*, 58.

Goody, J. (1976): *Production and Reproduction: A Comparative Study of the Domestic Terrain* (Cambridge: Cambridge University Press).

Goody, J. (1990): "Futures of the Family in Rural Africa", *Population and Development Review* (Supplement), 16.

Goody, J. et al. (1981a): "On the Absence of Implicit Sex-Preference in Ghana", *Journal of Biosocial Sciences*, 13.

Goody, J. et al. (1981b): "Implicit Sex Preference: A Comparative Study", *Journal of Biosocial Sciences*, 13.

Haddad, L. and R. Kanbur (1989): "Are Better Off Households More Unequal or Less Unequal? A Bargaining Theoretic Approach to "Kuznets Effects" at the Micro Level", mimeo. World Bank, Washington, DC.

Henry, C. (1974): "Investment Decisions under Uncertainty: the Irreversibility Effect", *American Economic Review*, 64.

Hess, P.N. (1988): *Population Growth and Socioeconomic Progress in Less Developed Countries* (New York: Praeger).

Heyd, D. (1991): *Genethics: The Morality of Procreation* (Los Angeles: University of California Press).

Hill, K. (1992): "Fertility and Mortality Trends in the Developing World", *Ambio*, 21.

Hobcraft, J.N., J.W. McDonald and S.O. Rutstein (1984): "Socio-Economic Factors in Infant and Child Mortality: A Cross-National Comparison", *Population Studies*, 38.

Hull, T.H. (1990): "Recent Trends in Sex Ratios in China", *Population and Development Review*, 16.

Jamison, D.T. and W.H. Mosley (1990): "Selecting Disease Control Priorities in Developing Countries", in D.T. Jamison and W.H. Mosley eds., *Evolving Health Priorities in Developing Countries* (Washington, DC: World Bank).

Johnson, D. Gale and R. Lee, eds. (1987): *Population Growth and Economic Development: Issues and Evidence* (Madison: University of Wisconsin Press).

Kamarck, A.M. (1988): "The Special Case of Africa", in D.E. Bell and M.R. Reich eds.: *Health, Nutrition and Economic Crises* (Dover, MA: Auburn House).

Kelley, A.C. (1988): "Economic Consequences of Population Change in the Third World", *Journal of Economic Literature*, 26.

Lee, R.B. (1972): "Population Growth and the Beginnings of Sedentary Life among the !Kung Bushmen", in B. Spooner ed.: *Population Growth: Anthropological Implications* (Cambridge, MA: MIT Press).

Lee, R.B. (1980): "Lactation, Ovolution, Infanticide, and Women's Work: A Study of Hunter-Gatherer Population Regulation", in M.N. Cohen, R.S. Malpass and H.G. Klein eds.: *Biosocial Mechanisms of Population Regulations* (New Haven: Yale University Press).

Lee, R.D. and R.A. Bulatao (1983): "The Demand for Children: A Critical Essay", in R.A. Bulatao and R.D. Lee eds. (1983), Vol. 1.

Lee, R.D. and T. Miller (1991): "Population Growth, Externalities to Childbearing, and Fertility Policy in Developing Countries", *Proceedings of the World Bank Annual Conference on Development Economics 1990*.

Leibenstein, H. (1957): *Economic Backwardness and Economic Growth* (New York: John Wiley).

Leibenstein, H. (1974): "An Interpretation of the Economic Theory of Fertility: Promising Path or Blind Alley?", *Journal of Economic Literature*, 12.

Lindert, P. (1980): "Child Costs and Economic Development", in R.A. Easterlin ed. (1980).

Lindert, P. (1983): "The Changing Economic Costs and Benefits of Having Children", in R.A. Bulatao and R.D. Lee eds. (1983).

Manser, M. and M. Brown (1980): "Marriage and Household Decisionmaking: A Bargaining Analysis", *International Economic Review*, 21.

Marschak, J. and R. Radner (1972): *Economic Theory of Teams* (New Haven, Conn: Yale University Press).

Mason, K.O. and A.M. Taj (1987): "Differences between Women's and Men's Reproductive Goals in Developing Countries", *Population and Development Review*, 13.

May, D.A. and D.M. Heer (1968): "Son Survivorship Motivation and Family Size in India: A Computer Simulation", *Population Studies*, 22.

McElroy, M.B. (1990): "The Empirical Content of Nash-Bargained Household Behaviour", *Journal of Human Resources*, 25.

McElroy, M.B. and M.J. Horney (1981): "Nash Bargained Household Decisions: Toward a Generalization of the Theory of Demand", *International Economic Review*, 22.

McGuire, J. and B.M. Popkin (1989): "Beating the Zero-Sum Game: Women and Nutrition in the Third World: Part 1", *Food and Nutrition Bulletin*, 11.

Meade, J.E. (1952): "External Economies and Diseconomies in a Competitive Situation", *Economic Journal*, 62.

Meade, J.E. (1955): *Trade and Welfare* (Oxford: Oxford University Press).

Menken, J., J. Trussell and S. Watkins (1981): "The Nutrition Fertility Link: An Evaluation of the Evidence", *Journal of Interdisciplinary History*, 11.

Mensch, B., H. Lentzner and S. Preston (1986): *Socio-economic Differentials in Child Mortality in Developing Countries* (New York: United Nations).

Milgrom, P. and J. Roberts (1990): "The Economics of Modern Manufacturing: Technology, Strategy and Organization", *American Economic Review*, 80.

Mirrlees, J.A. (1972): "Population Policy and the Taxation of Family Size", *Journal of Public Economics*, 1.

Mosley, W.H. (1985): "Will Primary Health Care Reduce Infant and Child Mortality? A Critique of Some Current Strategies, with Special Reference to Africa and Asia", in J. Vallin and A.D. Lopez eds., *Health Policy, Social Policy and Mortality Prospects* (Paris: Institut National d'Etudes Demographiques).

Mueller, E. (1976): "The Economic Value of Children in Peasant Agriculture", in R.G. Ridker ed.: *Population and Development: The Search for Selective Interventions* (Baltimore: Johns Hopkins University Press).

Narveson, J. (1967): "Utilitarianism and New Generations", *Mind*, 76.

Neher, P. (1971): "Peasants, Procreation and Pensions", *American Economic Review*, 61.

Nerlove, M. and A. Meyer (1992): "Endogenous Fertility and the Environment: A Parable of Firewood", in P. Dasgupta and K.-G. Mäler eds., *The Environment and Emerging Development Issues* (Oxford: Clarendon Press), forthcoming.

Nerlove, M., A. Razin and E. Sadka (1987a): *Household and Economy: Welfare Economics of Endogenous Fertility* (New York: Academic Press).

Nerlove, M., A. Razin and E. Sadka (1987b): *Population Policy and Individual Choice: A Theoretical Investigation*, Research Report 60 (Washington, DC: International Food Policy Research Institute).

Nugent, J. (1985): "The Old-Age Security Motive for Fertility", *Population and Development Review*, 11.

Nugent, J. and T. Gillaspy (1983): "Old Age Pension and Fertility in Rural Areas of Less Developed Countries: Some Evidence from Mexico", *Economic Development and Cultural Change*, 31.

Oppong, C. ed. (1987): *Sex Roles, Population and Development in West Africa* (Portsmouth, NH: Heinemann).

Page, H.J. and R. Lesthaeghe eds. (1981): *Child-Spacing in Tropical Africa: Tradition and Change* (London: Academic Press).

Phillips, J. et al. (1988): "Determinants of Reproductive Change in a Traditional Society: Evidence from Matlab, Bangladesh", *Studies in Family Planning*, 19.

Preston, S.H. (1980): "Causes and Consequences of Mortality Declines in Less Developed Countries During the Twentieth Century", in R.A. Easterlin ed. (1980).

Preston, S.H. (1986): "The Decline of Fertility in Non-European Industrialized Countries", *Population and Development Review* (Supplement), 12.

Preston, S.H. ed. (1978): *The Effects of Infant and Child Mortality on Fertility* (New York: Academic Press).

Preston, S.H., N. Keyfitz and R. Schoen (1972): *Causes of Death: Life Tables for National Populations* (New York: Seminar Press).

Preston, S.H. and V.E. Nelson (1974): "Structure and Change in Causes of Death: An International Summary", *Population Studies*, 28.

Ram, R. and T. Schultz (1979): "Life Span, Health, Savings and Productivity", *Economic Development and Cultural Change*, 27.

Rosenstein-Rodan, P. (1943): "Problems of Industrialization in Eastern and Southeastern Europe", *Economic Journal*, 53.

Rosenzweig, M.R. and R. Evenson (1977): "Fertility, Schooling and the Economic Contribution of Children in Rural India:

An Econometric Analysis", *Econometrica*, 45.

Sah, R.K. (1990): "The Effects of Mortality Changes on Fertility Choice and Parental Welfare", *Journal of Political Economy*, 99.

Satahr, Z. and V. Chigambaram (1984): "Differentials in Contraceptive Use", *World Fertility Survey Studies*, 36.

Schelling, T. (1978): *Micromotives and Macrobehaviour* (New York: W.W. Norton).

Schultz, T.W. (1974): *Economics of the Family: Marriage, Children and Human Capital* (Chicago: University of Chicago Press).

Scitovsky, T. (1954): "Two Concepts of External Economies", *Journal of Political Economy*, 52.

Simon, J.L (1977): *The Economics of Population Growth* (Princeton: Princeton University Press).

Simon, J.L. (1981): *The Ultimate Resource* (Princeton: Princeton University Press).

Simon, J.L. and H. Kahn eds.: *The Resourceful Earth: A Response to Global 2000* (New York: Basil Blackwell).

Singh, I., L. Squire and J. Strauss eds. (1986): *Agricultural Household Models: Extensions, Applications and Policy* (Baltimore: Johns Hopkins University Press).

Sopher, D.E. ed. (1980): *An Exploration of India: Geographical Perspectives on Society and Culture* (Ithaca, NY: Cornell University Press).

Stiglitz, J.E. (1987): "Learning to Learn, Localized Learning and Technological Progress", in P. Dasgupta and P. Stoneman eds. (1987).

Strauss, J. (1990): "Households, Communities, and Preschool Children's Nutrition Outcomes: Evidence from Rural Cote d'Ivoire", *Economic Development and Cultural Change*, 38.

Sundstrom, W.A. and P.A. David (1988): "Old Age Security Motives, Labor Markets and Farm Family Fertility in Antebellum America", *Explorations in Economic History*, 25.

Thomas, D., J. Strauss and M.-H, Henriques (1990): "Child Survival, Height for Age, and Household Characteristics in Brazil", *Journal of Development Economics*, 33.

Thomas, D., J. Strauss and M.-H. Henriques (1991): "How Does Mother's Education Affect Child Height?", *Journal of Human Resources*, 26.

Tomich, T.P., P. Kilby and B.F. Johnston (1991): *Agriculture and Structural Transformation: Opportunities Seized, Opportunities Missed*, (Washington, DC: World Bank).

Trease, J. and B. Logue (1986): "Economic Development and the Older Population", *Population and Development Review*, 12.

Victoria, C.G. et al. (1986): "Risk Factors for Malnutrition in Brazilian Children: The Role of Social and Environmental Variables", *Bulletin WHO*, 64.

Williamson, N.E. (1976): *Sons or Daughters? A Cross-cultural Survey of Parental Preferences* (Beverly Hills, CA: Sage Publications).

Willis, R. (1973): "A New Approach to the Economic Theory of Fertility", *Journal of Political Economy* (Supplement), 81.

Willis, R. (1980): "The Old-Age Security Hypothesis and Population Growth", in T. Burch ed., *Demographic Behaviour: Interdisciplinary Perspectives on Decisionmaking* (Boulder, CO: Westview Press).

Willis, R. (1987): "Externalities and Population", in D. Gale Johnson and R.D. Lee eds. (1987).

Wolfe, B.L. and J.R. Behrman (1982): "Determinants of Child Mortality, Health and Nutrition in a Developing Country", *Journal of Development Economics*, 11.

Wolfe, B.L. and J. R. Behrman (1987): "How Does Mother's Schooling Affect Family Health, Nutrition, Medical Care Usage and Household Sanitation?", *Journal of Econometrics*, 16.

World Bank (1980, 1984, 1988, 1990): *World Development Report* (New York: Oxford University Pres).

World Bank (1991): *The Population, Agriculture and Environment Nexus in Sub-Saharan Africa* (Washington, DC: World Bank), mimeo.

4

The Question of a Public Sewerage System in a Caribbean Country: A Case Study

Arthur H. Darling, Christian Gomez, and Mario E. Niklitschek

*The objective of this study was to evaluate the economic feasibility of the construction of a public sewerage system. This paper focusses on two techniques: **contingent valuation** to estimate the value of preventing the deterioration of coastal water to the point that it becomes unswimmable, and **risk analysis** to reflect the possible margin of error in the estimates of benefits and to assess the robustness of the conclusion.*

In the contingent valuation study, people were directly asked what they would be willing to pay for specific improvements provided by a project. In risk analysis, the paper analyzes the implications of the likely error in the benefit estimates.

The results of the risk analysis are used in a number of ways. First, they give a general impression of whether or not the project is feasible with the range of assumptions used. Second, they permit an estimate of the expected loss of making the wrong decision, i.e., building the project when perfect information would have shown that it was not economically feasible, or alternatively, not building when perfect information would have shown that it was feasible. Third, they identify which information is most important to the decision to undertake the project, and permit the design of the terms of reference for cost-effective feasibility studies.

The public sewerage project under analysis is designed to run parallel to a densely populated beach area on a Caribbean island whose primary foreign exchange earnings are from tourism services. The service area includes commercial (including hotels), residential, and institutional users. At present, the island's citizens provide their own sanitary services. The majority have wells that allow excreta to filter slowly through the limestone formation to the sea. There are some septic systems and a few package treatment plants.

In general, the population of the potential service area is fairly satisfied with the existing system. The government fears, however, that the filtration of excreta into the coastal waters may be having serious consequences. It is believed that filtration of sewage may be damaging the fringing reefs: (a) which are important to the food chain of the fishing industry and (b) which help protect against beach erosion. More importantly, the government fears that continued filtration of sewage will make the waters unsafe for swimming by nationals and will cause tourism to decline.

Despite the implications of these concerns, the technical studies that accompanied the project did not make it easy to estimate project benefits. The studies did not analyze a number of other sources of pollution (including agricultural run-off, storm run-off, and filtration from solid waste dumps) that could be affecting the fringing reefs. It also was not clear that the decline that had been observed in commercial fishing would be solved by the project, since at least part of the problem was caused by overfishing and pesticides in the food chain. Finally, at least some of the erosion problem was caused by man-made civil works that had changed the ocean currents. In short, no technical data were given to show the relative role of the sewage in the context of the more general problem.

The technical study of water quality also made it difficult to know what benefits to at-tribute to the project. The consultant had taken a total of forty samples at ten beaches. The samples indicated that the coastal waters complied with U.S. Environmental Protection Agency (EPA) mean and extreme standards for class A waters. The study projected that contamination water would not exceed the mean standard in the foreseeable future and that it would not exceed the extreme standard until the year 2000. Unfortunately, the sample was not large enough to be definitive, so it was not certain that coastal waters met the standard.

Issue Studied

The objective of the study was to evaluate the economic feasibility of the construction of a public sewerage system. The results of a previous sewerage project in the country suggested that willingness to pay of private users was not sufficient to cover the costs of the project. In that previous case, potential users preferred to continue to use their own facilities rather than pay the connection fee and the costs to adapt their plumbing to use the public system. There was reason to believe, however, that significant benefits might be received by people who would not be connected to the system, and that it was worth analyzing the project.

The additional benefits were difficult to measure with precision, and the information provided was incomplete. The analysis presented here developed complementary information on the value of preventing the beaches from becoming unswimmable, and structured the analysis to reflect the imprecision of the estimates.

Methodology Used

This paper focuses on two techniques, one—the contingent valuation method *CVM*—to estimate the value of preventing the deterioration of coastal water to the point that it becomes unswimmable, the other—risk analysis—to reflect the possible margin of

The authors are economists at the Inter-American Development Bank (IADB). Jorge Ducci, now Director of Planning at the Ministry of Public Works in Chile, was the IADB economist who worked on the contingent valuation study, and Professor K.E. McConnell, of the University of Maryland, was primarily responsible for the execution of the subcontract.

error in the estimates of benefits and to assess the robustness of the conclusion.

Contingent Valuation

To determine the value of maintaining coastal waters in "swimmable condition," the analysis uses the direct questioning technique (contingent valuation[CV]).[1] The method estimates a price that reflects the value of cleaner beaches despite the fact that there is no market to reveal a price for cleaner beaches or better sewerage systems. It does this by presenting consumers with a hypothetical market in which they make the decision of whether to buy the good in question.

People were directly asked what they would be willing to pay for specific improvements provided by a project. The value that people gave depended (was *contingent*) upon the description of the good, its provision, and the way it would be paid for. Hence, the name "contingent valuation."

The typical interview contained three parts (see Annex 4A):

1. A detailed description of the good being valued and the hypothetical circumstance under which it would be made available to the respondent

2. Questions which elicited the respondent's willingness to pay for the good

3. Questions about the respondent's characteristics, preferences, and uses of the goods being valued

The economic literature suggests that the CVM can give skewed or invalid results if the willingness-to-pay question is incorrectly phrased or if respondents can guess the pattern of questions. To reduce the potential for these biases (called hypothetical and strategic biases[2]), the valuation questions were asked in a dichotomous (yes/no) format—for example, Would you be willing to pay $15 more on your water bill each quarter to have public sewerage or would you prefer to pay what you are now

paying and go without the public sewerage system?

Risk Analysis

Every survey has a margin of error, and CV survey estimates are no exception. The CV estimates, however, are only one area of uncertainty in the decision whether to undertake the project. Because of the absence of technical studies on the impact of sewage on fishery yields, beach erosion, and the tourism industry, the estimates of other benefits are rough. The analysis had to take into account this imprecision and reflect how certain the country could be that a large investment in public sewerage was worth undertaking.

To do this, we worked with ranges. We estimated the range for each benefit in a way that makes it unlikely that the true benefit is outside the range. To make systematic use of this information, we used risk analysis.[3] This method describes the range of each cost and benefit as a probability distribution. A computer is programmed to select one estimate from the probability distribution that describes each assumption about benefits and costs and use the set of selected assumptions to calculate one internal rate of return. Having finished one economic calculation, the computer selects a second set of assumptions and repeats the calculations. The computer calculates 500 results, each one based on the relative likelihood of the assumptions. The probability distribution of the results characterizes the range and relative likelihood of different results.

This information can be used in a number of ways. First, it gives a general impression of whether or not the project is feasible under most sets of assumptions. Second, it gives an estimate of the expected loss of making the wrong decision, that is, building the project when perfect information would have shown that it was not economically feasible or, alternatively, not building when perfect information would have shown that it was feasible. Third, it

---

[1] This method was chosen in preference to the travel cost method (an indirect approach based on observed behavior) because there was very little variation in travel distances from the residences to the beaches.

[2] Hypothetical bias refers to the possible difference in behavior when a consumer confronts a hypothetical, rather than a real, market. Strategic bias occurs when a respondent tries to answer a survey question to influence the project decision rather than to reveal his personal valuation of the services provided by the project.

[3] We used the PROPLAN project analysis and Monte Carlo simulation computer program written by Information for Information Decisions (IID) of Washington, D.C.

identifies which information is most important to the decision to undertake the project.

Description of the Study

Contingent Valuation

The first step in contingent valuation is the design and testing of the questions to be asked. It is well known that the form, wording, order, and context of a questionnaire can affect the answers received in unexpected ways. We therefore pretested the concepts and questions investigated with focus groups[4] and a pilot survey.

One of the issues explored in focus groups and the pilot survey was the likely upper bound of willingness to pay. As the questionnaire was designed to ask only one price on a take-it-or-leave-it basis, it was important that high prices were included so that benefits were not underestimated, but it was also important that the prices were not so high that a large percentage of respondents would indicate they were not willing to pay the price proposed. If this were the case, the size of the sample would have to be very large and the survey would be more expensive.

The final CV survey covered 277 households that would be connected to the sewerage system and 433 households that lived outside the area to be connected to the sewerage system but used the beaches that would be affected by the project. The total population of these two areas was 3,268 and 53,041 households, respectively.

A different questionnaire was used in each area. Households who lived outside the sewer district were asked only about the environmental benefits of the sewer system. They were offered two choices: pay a certain dollar amount in their quarterly water bill for the construction and maintenance of the sewer system, or not pay and not receive the corresponding services.

The specific dollar amounts that a respondent was asked about were assigned to the questionnaires on a random basis. For the households located in the area to be connected to the sewer system, the proposed method of payment was a sewerage charge that would cover both the services of the public sewerage system and cleaner beaches.

In each case, the interviewer read a preamble to the contingent valuation question that focused the respondent's attention on the issues that were relevant for the economic valuation. Households were told the potential impact of disposing of wastewater into the ground, and the potential for avoiding beach pollution and damaged reefs by construction of the sewer system. The interviewer also used an illustration (see Annex 4A) to reinforce the differences between the situation with and without the project.

The use of closed-end questions ("yes or no" to a specific dollar amount) made it impossible to determine directly the willingness-to-pay. Therefore, the willingness-to-pay responses had to be transformed into benefit estimates. To do this, we exercised the standard practice of using an econometric model to relate the probability of a "yes" response to the amount of payment and household characteristics to obtain mean values for the sample's willingness to pay.[5] The exogenous variables used were: whether the respondent used the beaches, the respondent's age, whether the respondent saw the television coverage about beach pollution, and the amount of the randomly assigned sewer charge. All of the coefficients estimated were significant at the 95 percent level. The estimates of mean willingness-to-pay were US$178 and US$11 per year for households inside and outside the area to be connected, respectively. The larger mean benefit derived for the catchment households captured

---

[4] Focus groups are discussion groups comprised of people selected from the population of potential beneficiaries and led by someone familiar with market research and social psychology. Their objective is to learn how respondents conceptualize and talk about the topics being investigated. Focus groups are used to explore hypotheses and to formulate specific questions for quantitative research. Often the vocabulary used in the discussion is adopted to phrase the questionnaire.

[5] The econometric estimation is set up as a logit function.

$$F(\delta) = \frac{1}{1+\exp(-\delta)} \text{ (probability of saying yes to the purchasing question)}$$

Furthermore, $\delta = f(P, x_i)$

where: P = price and x_i = exogenous variables

Maximum willingness to pay is derived by setting $\delta = 0$ and solving for P.

both the private and public benefit while the smaller mean benefits derived for the outside catchment households measured only environmental or public benefits.

Risk Analysis

In the feasibility analysis, we assigned probability distributions to all cost and benefit flows. This paper will focus on a few. For the investment and operating costs, we used normal probability distributions, with a mean equal to the engineer's estimate plus contingency allowance and an 80 percent confidence interval defined by a range 15 percent above and 15 percent below the engineer's estimate.

The benefits of particular interest were (a) the contingent valuation estimates, (b) the fishery benefits, (c) the coastal erosion benefits, and (d) the tourism benefits lost if a health crisis occurred.

Contingent Valuation Benefits

Instead of using the statistical confidence interval around the contingent valuation estimate, we used a normal distribution that assumed that the 80 percent confidence interval was within plus or minus 40 percent of the estimate. We used this wide estimate because we believed that the errors possible in contingent valuation include more than just sampling variation. This potential problem is treated in more detail in the section on assessment of the methodology.

Fishery Benefits

The data on fisheries were poor. There was a historical series indicating a significant decline in kilograms landed since 1980. Hearsay evidence suggested that this process had started long before 1980. There was no information to indicate what a maximum sustainable yield might be in perfect conditions, and no information on other factors that might be contributing to the decline (for example, pesticides, overfishing, agricultural and storm run-off). After consultation with a local university research center, we assumed that, without the project, the fishery yield would decline to zero in a period of ten years, but that with the project, the

yields would increase to 1980 levels in the ten years after project completion. We valued the fish catch at the cost of importing fish, and we assumed that the costs of fishing were half the value of the fish. Most of these assumptions have no empirical basis, and appeared—if anything—to be generous. To reflect the invented nature of the assumptions, we posited a uniform distribution—any estimate within the range equally likely—and a margin of error of 50 percent.[6]

Coastal Erosion

The value of preventing beach erosion was difficult to conceptualize. We used the cost of beach replacement ("beach nourishment") as the measure. This cost comprises the costs of obtaining sand by dredging or quarrying, transporting it to site, and dumping it. The process is a continuous one. A consultant estimated the likely frequency and volume of replacements with and without the project. The estimates themselves were far from precise: "without the project you will have to nourish beaches every five to ten years, with the project every ten to twenty years." To use this information, we established the extreme ranges: No difference with or without the project (that is, every ten years in any case) and a reduction from once every five years to once every twenty years. We annualized the costs associated with this range and assigned a uniform probability distribution to it.

Avoiding a Decline in Tourism

The government's concern that the absence of public sewerage might cause tourism to decline was based on two problems. First, it seemed that when hotels had problems with their package treatment plants or with delays in septage collection, they pumped septage into the ocean late at night. This action often produced odors or visual evidence the next day. In addition, it was believed that some septage tank cleaning companies were dumping their loads illegally rather than hauling them to the treatment plant. While the public sewerage project would solve these problems, it seemed that other, more cost effective measures, could be

---

6 The risk analysis program did not afford the possibility of making the decline and recovery periods stochastic, that is, shorter or longer than ten years.

taken.[7] Second, the system of letting excreta filter through the limestone formation and flow to the ocean could raise the level of pathogens to a level that could cause an outbreak of disease. Any such outbreak, traceable to the water on the beaches, would have an impact on tourism.

Although the problem was clear, it was not easy to estimate the probability that there would be a health problem or how large the impact would be if there were one. The consulting study that supported the project had attempted to deal with the problem. The consultants sent the statistics on the mean and extreme coliform readings to experts in public health and asked them to estimate the probability that fifty people (arbitrarily assumed to be the critical level that would trigger a crisis) would get sick. When we reviewed the question that had been asked the public health experts, we concluded that there was no basis for them to provide an accurate answer. First, the data on contamination did not specify the frequency with which coliforms exceeded safe levels. The mean coliform was within the norm and, while the extreme exceeded the norm, no frequency was associated with it. Second, the question did not specify how many people had contact with the water. Because of these problems, we had to reject the estimate and try to make our own.

The amount of "tourism benefits" that might be saved by the project depends on a number of factors. They are: (a) the probability that water has reached a critical level of contamination, (b) the probability that enough swimmers get sick to make contamination a perceived problem, (c) the number of tourists that stay away once the problem is perceived, and d) the economic value of each tourist lost. There is no basis to make a rigorous statistical estimate for these factors, so we used a range of estimates that appear reasonable. Because the assumptions and the evidence behind them are critical to the decision, they are presented in detail.

The U.S. EPA requires that the geometric mean for fecal coliforms be less than 200 per 100 milliliters, and that a ratio of 400 fecal coliforms per 100 milliliters in any 30-day period be exceeded no more than ten percent of the time. The feasibility study found that the mean was within EPA standards. The study had samples that exceeded 400 per 100 milliliters but there were not enough to conclude that the 10 percent of the samples exceeded the standard for a 30-day period. The feasibility study predicts that coastal waters will not exceed the standard for the mean in the foreseeable future and will not exceed the extreme standard until the year 2000.

Unfortunately, the study is not definitive. The level of coliforms found in the coastal waters is a function of three things: (a) rainfall (rain flushes out sewage wells and bacteriological run-off), (b) time of day (bright sunlight rapidly kills coliforms), and (c) tidal conditions (incoming tides keep coliform near shore). The consultant's sample did not control for these factors. The sample was small—four observations at each of ten beaches. This number of observations can not adequately characterize the contamination of coastal waters. Four of the consultant's six extreme readings were collected on the same day, and it is not known whether they were after a rain fall, at high tide, on a cloudy day, or all three; it is also not known whether the other readings were taken at high noon or at low tide. It is impossible to conclude whether the sample is representative. The sample seems to suggests that there is no problem at present, but we cannot be certain. If there is, it is probably not too serious yet.

To assess the probability of a health problem given the level of contamination, we examined the epidemiological literature. The literature indicates that, although a number of infectious diseases can be contracted by swimming in sewage polluted water,[8] research has only been able to establish a quantitative relationship for gastroenteritis, the most common of the diseases.[9] The present EPA standard is

---

[7] Such measures could have included greater supervision and fines for violation, investment in back-up truck facilities for emergencies; and changes in the structure of incentives to drivers, paying them for loads delivered to the treatment plant rather than for loads picked up.

[8] The diseases include hepatitis A, gastroenteritis, typhoid, shigellosis, and cholera.

[9] Epidemiological research reported several outbreaks of shigellosis from swimming in contaminated waters (Rosenberg, et al. 1976). These cases were reported in fresh water, and in one case the mean coliform count was 17,500 fecal coli-

Table 4-1: The Probability and Cumulative Probability Distributions of a Perceived Health Problem Resulting from Contaminated Ocean Water

Year	Probability of a crisis in this year (percent)	Cumulative probability of at least one crisis by this year (percent)
1	5	5.0
2	6	10.7
3	7	16.9
4	8	23.6
5	9	30.5
6	10	44.3
7	11	51.0
8	12	57.4

set consistent with the risk that 19 of 1,000 swimmers will contract gastroenteritis. If the standard (mean fecal coliforms 200 per 100 milliliters) were increased four times to 800 fecal coliforms per 100 milliliters, the incidence of gastroenteritis would increase 1.8 times.[10] In the consultant's sample the mean was well below 200, and there was only one observation above 800.

The coliform data for the country suggests that the probability of a health crisis is not high, but that it could grow over time as the sewage load increases. We assumed that if a crisis occurred, tourism would decline until the sanitation problem was fixed. The probability of this type of event is well described by the cumulative probability distribution that results from a binomial. A binomial distribution has two conditions: (a) crisis, and (b) no crisis. The data suggest that in any given year the probability of "no crisis" (p) is relatively large. The probability of at least one crisis can be

written (1 - p). The probability of no crisis in either the first or the second year is p*p or p^2, and the probability of at least one crisis in either the first or the second year is $1-p^2$. The cumulative probability of a crisis increases each year, as the probability of not having a crisis in any of the first, second, third, fourth, etc. decreases: p*p*p*p... The probability of a crisis in a specific year can increase over time if the sewage load increases. Thus the probability of not having a crisis in any of the first, second, third, fourth year can be written $p_1*p_2*p_3*p_4...$

We arbitrarily assumed that there was a 95 percent chance of no crisis in the first year of analysis, that is, $p_1=.95$. We assumed that each year, as the sewage load increased, the probability of no crisis would decline by one percentage point, that is, $p_2=.94$ in year two and $p_3=.93$ in year three. Table 4-1 shows the resulting assumptions with respect to the probability of a crisis having occurred by a specified year.[11]

forms per 100 milliliters.

[10] Even very high levels of readings do not appear to have dramatic effects. A study of Hong Kong beaches with contaminations ranging from 411 to 3,200 fecal coliform per 100 milliliters showed an illness rate of 22 per thousand to 12 per thousand on beaches under 400 coliforms per 100 milliliters (Holmes 1990).

[11] The economists who worked on this project believe that these probability estimates overestimate the risk of a crisis,

The probabilities imply that there is a 51 percent chance that a health crisis will have already occurred by the year the consultant projects that coastal waters exceed EPA's extreme standard. We assumed that once the project is completed, the probability of a crisis is reduced to zero.

The second factor that is impossible to predict with certainty is the amount of decline that will take place once a problem is perceived. We assumed that, in the absence of problems, tourist visitor days would grow between 0.2 percent and 2 percent per year. If a problem should occur, we assumed that these tourist days would decline *forever*[12] by somewhere between 0 and 50 percent. We assumed a large decline was extremely unlikely, because the type of health problems that are likely to result from the contamination now occurs at other international resort areas. We believed that it would take a true crisis (typhoid or cholera) to provoke anything larger than a 20 percent decline, and we assumed that there was only a 15 percent probability of this. More probable (85 percent) are declines of 20 percent or less.

The third factor not known with certainty is the value of expenditure lost. Based on studies of tourist expenditures, the import component, and the shadow price of labor, we estimated the net foreign exchange value of tourist expenditure at between US$30 and $40 million per year. The economic benefit of the project is computed as the difference between net expenditures (valued in economic terms) with and without the project.

Results of the Study

Figure 4-1 shows the range and probability distribution of the results simulated. The rates of return range from a low of 0.8 percent to a high of 26.8 percent. The use of risk analysis indicates that, with the range of estimates that we believe reasonable, the project could be either feasible or not feasible. The best estimate of the project's rate of return is 8.2 percent.[13] The expected net present value of the project is -US$11.7 million.

If the country is risk neutral, it should not undertake the project. If it does, it can expect to lose US$11.7 million. This is not the end of the story, however. Risk analysis allows us to look at the extremes. If the country carries out the project, the worst loss it could face would be $45 million (a little less than the capital cost of the project). If it does not carry out the project, the worst loss it might face is $127 million. A country that is risk averse might decide that it is worth taking a probable loss by building a project that is not needed currently, to avoid the possibility of a very large loss if a crisis should occur. In this sense the project would be viewed as an insurance policy.

It does not make a lot of sense to look only at the extremes. The probability of either of these extreme losses is 1 in 500 or 0.2 percent. It is better to take a more detailed look at the probability of losses and gains, their range, and the expectation (average to be expected). Risk analysis allows us to do this.

Table 4-2 indicates that the probability of gains (that is, the probability that the project is feasible) is small—only 21.2 percent. This is the same as saying the probability of large losses, if the country does not undertake the project, is small. Even a risk-averse country might not want to pay a large insurance premium to insure against losses with remote chances of occurring. Another way of looking at this is to calculate the cost of making the wrong decision: building the project when it

---

since the mean—on which all epidemiological calculations are based—will still be far below 200 fecal coliforms per 100 milliliters in the years shown. This specific estimate was the result of a negotiation within the Inter-American Development Bank that considered the inadequacy of the sample and the reluctance to run the risk of rejecting a project when it should be accepted.

12 It should also be noted that it is highly improbable that a significant crisis would go on forever, as has been assumed. If a significant decline in tourism occurred, hoteliers would take measures and the government would regulate the dumping of waste. The government could also carry out the project. Thus, the true upper bound benefit that should be assigned is the sum of four elements: (a) the cost of the project, (b) the lost expenditure from the beginning of the crisis to the end of the construction period, (c) the cost of advertising and promotion to bring tourism up to the level it would have attained without this crisis, and (d) the lost expenditure during the recovery period. This analysis does not truncate the benefit so *the extreme rate of return calculations are substantial overestimates, and the average results are pulled up by these extremes.*

13 This corresponds to the median rate of return (fiftieth percentile).

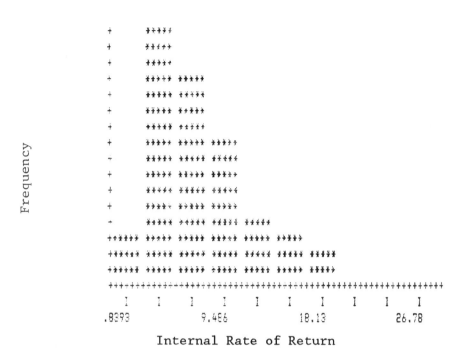

Figure 4-1: Frequency Distribution of Simulated Rates of Return

turns out not to be feasible, or not building it when it turns out to be feasible. The cost of either error is called the *expected opportunity loss*. Table 4-3 shows that the expected opportunity loss of building the project when it should not be built is three times greater than not building the project when it should be built.

The information on which the calculations have been based is flimsy at best. Under some assumptions believed possible, the project is feasible. The *cost of uncertainty*, because of imperfect information, is the expected opportunity loss the country incurs when it takes the best decision: in this case to reject the project. If the country could buy perfect information, the most it would rationally pay is $5.8 million, which is the loss it could expect to avoid if it had perfect information. The risk analysis technique makes it possible to identify what information could make us change our conclusion, that is, might lead us to conclude

that the project is feasible. The analysis indicates that the most important variables are those that have to do with (a) a decline in the tourist industry (the probability of the outbreak of disease, the amount of decline in tourism, the amount of net benefits from tourist expenditures), and (b) the contingent valuation estimates. The estimates of benefits from the recovery of the fishing industry and slowing the erosion of beaches are not important sources of error. Fishing and erosion benefits could be three and four times higher and our conclusions about feasibility would not change. It is not worth spending any money getting data on them.

Both the tourism estimates and the contingent valuation estimates are related to the bacteriological quality of the water. If the water were perceived as risky, nationals' willingness to pay and tourists' adverse reactions would probably be much greater. There was no

Table 4-2: Probability of Losses and Gains if the Project is Undertaken
(dollar amounts are present values)

Possible loss (US$ millions)	Probability (percent)
0-9	9.8
9-18	15.0
18-27	26.4
27-36	23.4
36-45	4.2
Probability project not feasible	78.8

Possible gains (US$ millions)	Probability (percent)
0-25	11.4
25-51	7.4
51-76	1.2
76-102	0.8
102-127	0.4
Probability project feasible	21.2

evidence that people, in fact, thought there was anything wrong with the coastal waters, and the limited sample that was carried out confirmed that people were correct in their perceptions.

Although a country that was highly risk averse might still want to carry out the project proposed, the Bank—in view of the existing information—did not want to encourage the country to do so. The Inter-American Development Bank concluded from the risk analysis that it was critical to be sure that there was not, in fact, a bacteriological problem. It recommended a statistical study to test the null hypothesis that coastal water quality at each beach complied with EPA standards. The cost

of the study was less than US$100,000 (much less than the cost of uncertainty) and should reduce much of the uncertainty. The study is being carried out beach by beach because Bank staff think that there may be more limited solutions to a specific problem that could postpone the need to invest in a large public system.

Assessment of the Methodology and Lessons

We are generally satisfied that the results from the contingent valuation study are believable and that the risk analysis method produced results sufficiently robust to justify the decision that was made (that is, not to go forward with

Table 4-3: Expected Opportunity Loss of a Wrong Decision
(dollar amounts are present values)

	Expected opportunity loss (US$ millions)
Build project when project is not feasible	17.5
Not build project when project is feasible	5.8
Cost of uncertainty	5.8

the project without clear statistical evidence that a violation of standards exists).

Our first conclusion, however, is that risk analysis is not a substitute for information. The terms of reference for future studies should carefully specify the environmental relations that the analyst will subsequently need to do his work. The study that supported the project in question did not deal with reefs, fish, beach erosion, or willingness to pay. Its primary concern was the quality of receiving water for sewerage discharge, not the quality of coastal waters where people swam. Increasing emphasis on environmental effects of projects and the increasing number of projects whose primary objective is to improve the environment will require a broader approach that must be built in from the beginning. The risk analysis method does, however, help identify what information is worth collecting (that is, could affect the decision), and it can be useful to do risk analysis even with very preliminary data, in order to design a cost-effective study.

Our second conclusion is that more attention should have been paid to the way the contingent scenario was conceived. With the benefit of hindsight some improvements could have been made: The question to people who were to receive sanitary services really comprised two elements. One had to do with the value of keeping coastal waters clean; the other had to do with the quality and cost of service of

the present system compared with that which would be provided by a public system. There was only one valuation question, and no obvious way to separate these two elements. This posed a problem because the consultants had made a separate estimate of the cost savings to prospective customers, and using both the CV estimate and the cost savings would have probably involved a double count. Although a group outside the service area was asked only about keeping coastal water usable, the means of the two samples could not merely be subtracted, because the choice of a residence proximate to the beach may indicate that these residents valued water and its quality more highly, and the groups may have been systematically different.

A second problem with the CV question was that it did not specify when the water would become unswimmable. It merely specified that it would eventually become unfit for swimming. In addition, there was no information on the views of the respondents on how contaminated the waters were or what their implicit time frame was. Clearly the perceived immediacy of the problem should have some impact on the amount people would be willing to pay to solve it.

The problem of urgency and consequences raises a more general problem with the method. The problem is how to express the implications of the problem. If the interviewers had stressed the immediacy of the problem or dramatized the possible consequences, they may have started a panic—which could have set off the tourist crisis that the project was to help avoid. If the interviewers had put the question in a low key way, the respondents might have assumed that the problem was remote and not worth spending much money on.

Because the results of the contingent valuation were ultimately used in Monte Carlo simulation, it would have been useful to have had the information necessary to simulate the confidence interval around the willingness-to-pay estimates. It is probably worth noting that the true margin of error is probably greater than that which would have been estimated from the statistical results.

Bibliography

Feachem, Richard G., David J. Bradley, Henda Garelick, and D. Duncan Mara. 1983. *Sanitation and Disease Aspects of Excreta and Waste Water Management*. New York: John Wiley and Sons.

Holmes, Paul. 1990. "Bathing Beach Pollution, Research and Control in Hong Kong," *U.K. Journal Institute of Water and Environmental Management*. London.

Kassalow, Jennifer, and Diane Cameron. 1991. "Testing the Waters, A Study of Beach Closings in Ten Coastal States." Natural Resources Defense Council, New York.

Mitchell, Robert, and Richard T. Carson. 1989. *Using Surveys to Value Public Goods: the Contingent Valuation Method*. Washington, D.C.: Resources for the Future.

Rosenberg, M.L., K.K. Hazlet, J. Schaefer, J.G. Wells, and P.C. Pruneda. 1976. "Shigellosis from Swimming," *Journal of the American Medical Association*, 230 (16), pp. 1849-52. Annex A.

Annex 4A: Questionnaire Survey For Household Connections

PREAMBLE

Good morning/afternoon. The Department of Health is conducting a survey on the feasibility of installing a public sewer system in this community. The interview will take just a few minutes, and your views are important for the study. Your answers are confidential. Before I start, may I ask how long you have lived in this house?

_____ Years/Months

1. **DENTIFICATION OF RESIDENCE**
   1.1 Address
   _____
   1.2 What is the tenancy of your residence?
      1. The dwelling is
      2. owned ( )
      3. rented/leased ( )
      4. other ( )
   1.3 The land is
      1. owned ( )
      2. rented/leased ( )
      3. other ( )
   1.4 Type of residence
      1. chattel ( )
      2. blockwall ( )
      3. wood and wall ( )
   1.5 Number of rooms _____
2. **RESPONDENT CHARACTERISTICS**
   2.1 Sex
      1. male ( )
      2. female ( )
   2.2 Age _____
   2.3 Does your work or that of members of your household depend directly on business from tourists? Examples: taxis, restaurants, hotels.
      1. yes ( )
      2. no ( )

2.4 How many people live in your house?
   _____
2.5 How many people 18 or over? _____
2.6 And what number best describes the total income of all persons in the household for 1990?_____ number
   1. Less than $3,000
   2. 3,001 to 5,000
   3. 5,001 to 7,500
   4. 7,501 to 10,000
   5. 10,001 to 15,000
   6. 15,001 to 25,000
   7. 25,001 to 35,000
   8. 35,001 to 50,000
   9. 50,001 to 75,000
   10. More than 75,000
   11. No response or don't know
2.7 Have you seen the recent TV coverage on the potential for marine pollution here on the island?
   1. yes ( )
   2. no ( )
3. **CONDITIONS OF HOUSE**
   3.1 Is your water piped into your house?
      1. yes ( )
      2. no ( )
      If yes, skip to 3.3.
   3.2 Into your yard?
      1. yes ( )
      2. no ( )
   3.3 Where does your sink and bath water drain (water from kitchen sink, laundry, and shower/bath)?
      1. sewage well ( )
      2. septic tank ( )
      3. garden ( )
      4. street ( )
      5. pit ( )
      6. public drain ( )
   3.4 Where does the sewage from the toilet drain?

1. sewage well ( )
2. septic tank ( )
3. pit toilet ( )

3.5 Do you share toilet facilities with other households?
   1. yes ( )
   2. no ( )

3.6 How long has the septic tank (pit or sewage) been in use?
   1. 0 to 5 years ( )
   2. 6 to 10 years ( )
   3. more than 10 years ( )

3.7 Have you had any problems with your sewage system in the last three years?

Problem	Yes	No
1.		
2. Overflow	( )	( )
3. Flooding	( )	( )
4. Blocked	( )	( )
5. Other	( )	( )

3.8 Do you think you will have to replace your septic tank (pit or sewage) within the next year?
   1. yes ( )
   2. no ( )

   If no. Within the next five years?
   3. yes ( )
   4. no ( )

3.9 How much have you spent in the last year for operation and maintenance or repair of your sewage system?

PREAMBLE TO CV QUESTION
Currently much of the community's waste water goes into the ground. This water drains through the ground into the ocean. The wastes in this water will eventually contaminate the beach water, making it unfit for swimming. This contaminated or polluted beach water might also discourage tourism to our island. There is also a possibility that polluted ocean water can damage some of the coral reefs.

3.10 How important are clean beaches to you?
   1. very important ( )
   2. important ( )
   3. not important ( )

3.11 Do you or members of your household visit beaches?
   1. never ( )

2. 1 to 15 times per year ( )
3. more than 15 times per year ( )

In order to keep beach water clean for swimming and to eliminate the potential threat to coral reefs, we need to build a central sewerage system. This system would collect waste and sewage water from households and establishment, carry it though a pipe to a sewage treatment plant where it would be treated to remove damaging pollutants. It could then be discharged safely into the ocean far from the shore. However, this is expensive. Substantial construction is required. One way to pay for part of the system is with a quarterly sewerage charge covering hookup and continuing operating costs.

3.12 Which of the following would you choose?
   1. Pay a quarterly sewer charge of $____ for public sewage disposal and clean beaches. ( )
   2. Not pay the $____ quarterly sewer charge and continue with the current system. ( )

   If yes, skip to 3.14.

3.13 What was the main reason you said NO or would not answer? (Ask and then categorize yourself)
   1. Does not use public beaches ( )
   2. Does not want a higher water bill ( )
   3. Can't afford it ( )
   4. Wants to pay another way ( )

5. Not enough information ( )
6. Does not understand question ( )
7. Cannot decide ( )
8. Other ( )

3.14 If the government installed the house connection on your property during construction of the sewer system, would you be prepared to meet the cost of connecting by a long-term, low-interest loan?
   1. yes ( )
   2. no ( )

3.15 By installments added to your quarterly sewer rate?
   1. yes ( )
   2. no ( )

3.16 If the public sewer system is constructed would you
   1. connect with the system immediately ( )
   2. connect eventually ( )
   3. not connect to the system ( )

5

Environmental Economics and Natural Resource Management: The African Development Bank Experience

Anil Markandya and Carlos Muñoz

This paper reviews the environmental issues of greatest importance on the continent of Africa, and examines how projects carried out by the African Development Bank have tried to address them. Methods of evaluation are discussed and several projects reviewed retrospectively. These include direct investment projects, as well as some sectoral loans. The paper concludes that more can be done to value environmental impacts systematically, and that such valuation needs to be extended, especially to cases where there are environmental damages and to sectoral loans.

The environmental crises of Africa are among the gravest in the world. The continent is suffering from population growth of 3 percent per year, which is creating pressures on its natural resources and resulting in them being used in an unsustainable way. Forests are being lost, primarily to agricultural encroachment, at the rate of 3.6 million hectares a year, or 0.6 percent of the stock. Soils in some regions are being degraded to an extent that is alarming and lands unsuitable for cultivation are being farmed from the sheer need to expand output under declining soil productivity and increasing population. The problem is particularly severe in the drylands of the Sudano-Sahelian region. Biodiversity from its terrestrial and marine resources is being irreversibly lost.

This dismal environmental picture is not brightened when one looks at the economic development of the region as a whole. Economic growth has barely kept pace with population growth, so that living standards, even as conventionally measured, are not rising. If one were to construct a measure of sustainable income (that is, the consumption level that the combination of natural physical and human capital that the continent can support in perpetuity), it is certain that the figure would have been declining over the last twenty years. So it is not the case that the environmental degradation is 'buying' economic development through the creation of other forms of capital.

In the face of this monumental challenge, the African Development Bank (ADB) has been making a serious attempt to arrest the losses and to contribute to the move to a more sustainable development process for the continent. To some extent, its main focus of activity (agriculture) has always been involved in the promotion of agricultural practices that would result in sustainable increases in living standards. In recent years, along with the rest of the development community, it has become even more aware of the complex ties that link activities in one sector with the use of resources in another; and with the need to allow for these linkages when planning its involvement at the project or sectoral level.

This paper looks at the integration of environmental concerns in the methods of project appraisal and sectoral planning, as carried out by the African Development Bank. The focus is on the economic valuation and planning, and the interface between that and the environment.

The paper first reviews the ADB's formal environmental policy. Next, it elaborates on the problems integrating the economic and environmental dimensions of projects; it lays out the basic questions that arise with regard to national and sectoral macroeconomic policy and its implications, both for the success of individual projects, and for policy relevance to the design of sectoral lending programs. The paper reviews twelve of the ADB's projects in which there was a significant environmental dimension. Some are still at the planning stages, and others are in the process of being implemented. They concentrate on land-based activities (as opposed to industrial projects, where different issues arise). Projects covered include a dam project, rural road construction projects, agricultural expansion, a resource conservation project, and rangelands improvement projects. This paper then reviews ADB's activities that are more sectoral in nature, and lastly, it provides some overall conclusions and recommendations.

Environmental Policy Paper

In June 1990, the ADB presented an Environmental Policy paper (ADB 1991a) that:

- Assessed the state of the environment in Africa.

- Outlined policies for its main areas of lending that addressed the environmental concerns described above.

- Presented a set of procedures for the conduct of projects that took proper account of environmental concerns.

- Discussed ways in which regional member countries (RMCs) could be assisted in implementing environmentally sound policies, and in setting up legislative frameworks that improved the management of natural resources in their respective countries.

That document includes many recommendations regarding policies that need to be followed for a sustainable use of resources in each of the sectors. Broadly speaking, the recommendations can be divided into those dealing with projects and those dealing with sectoral and economywide policies. Each is considered in turn below.

Project Appraisal and Environmental Issues

The ADB environmental policy document is primarily concerned to ensure that projects undertaken by the ADB are not environmentally damaging. It is proposed that projects be classified into four categories,[1] namely:

- Category I—projects that may have significant environmental impacts and that will require a detailed Environmental Impact Analysis (EIA).

- Category II—projects with limited environmental impacts or impacts that can be mitigated through routine measures and changes in project design.

- Category III—projects for which environmental impacts are not expected and that should not need a detailed environmental analysis.

- Category IV—projects that have an environmental sustainable development as a focus and for which "separate environmental analysis may not be required" (ADB 1991b).

A similar classification has been established by other development banks, such as the Inter-American Development Bank (IDB), and serves a useful purpose in screening projects so that the most important ones are allocated the scarce professional resources at the bank's disposal.

However, it is clear that, in arriving at the allocation, the emphasis is on the avoidance of negative environmental impacts, rather than on the active canvassing and development of projects with environmentally positive aspects. The allocation of projects concerned with the conservation of resources to category IV means that they will not have to run the gauntlet of environmental scrutiny that projects in category I will have to. Yet they may be precisely the ones that need careful examination, to see how they can best be designed to maximize environmental benefits. This is a point that emerges from a detailed review of some of the projects that the ADB has recently undertaken.

The ADB, in its attempt to achieve maximum benefit from its resources, needs to address both negative and positive impacts, and to integrate the analysis of the environmental and economic impacts. This is not an easy task, but tools for the monetary quantification of environmental costs and benefits are available and could be more exploited. Recent projects have started to do this but there is scope for more integration of the two areas.

The underlying philosophy behind the present approach is that where there are "unacceptable" environmental benefits, they should be mitigated and the costs of mitigation included as part of the costs of the project. If, after allowing for these impacts, the project meets the rate of return and other criteria, it may go ahead. However, this strategy has three important implications. First, it imposes a requirement on projects that may raise their costs to such an extent that they will become unviable. (This cannot always be discerned by looking at project reports, because ADB managers tend to select for consideration only those projects where there is a strong *prima facie* case that the project will meet the required rate of return.) It is reasonable to ask, are the mitigation requirements always justified in terms of the damage avoided? Or should one impose a lower level of mitigation requirement? This is not merely an academic issue. Many project managers can recount cases where, in their opinion, projects have had to be abandoned because the mitigation costs are too high. How should one decide on what level of mitigation to demand? This can be answered partly by recourse to the quantification of the value of the damage avoided. But such monetary quantification is not always possible or, if possible, gives answers that are too uncertain to be useful. In such cases one is obliged to use rules for deciding on mitigation, but these rules need to be set out more formally, within a framework of a set of sustainability criteria. Both these are

---

[1] Subsequently, the ADB has decided to merge categories II and III into one, with all projects under either category now not requiring detailed environmental analysis, but requiring attention to project design on environmental grounds, and an environmental mitigation plan.

discussed further in the next section of this paper.

The second difficulty with the present approach is the opposite—that is, that where mitigation is not required, or not possible, the project may still be acceptable, but may cause considerable environmental damage. In other words, the "residual" environmental damage may be quite high. For example, a project that involves the clearing of forest land with many indigenous species may be "mitigated" by the planting of a single species of equal land area elsewhere. One is not a replacement for the other, however, and some damage remains. Unless there are ways of accounting for it, the present approach could lead to poor choices and unsustainable practices.

Third, the point made earlier about the current emphasis on negative impacts needs to be repeated. Where one is seeking to justify environmentally positive projects, such as resource conservation, or dune protection, it is hard to quantify the benefits. Choices are then made on the basis of a limited quantification of benefits, which in turn means that there is much more arbitrariness in the decisions made, or that the project is justified only on the basis of the measurable benefits, which would result in an under-allocation of resources to such projects.

The essential messages from this discussion are: (a) there is a need to extend environmental cost and benefit estimation and (b) where this is not possible there is a need to formalize the use of sustainability criteria to establish guidelines for mitigation action and for resource conservation projects. These are issues that all development banks and bilateral donor agencies are grappling with and the African Development Bank is not alone in facing them. Arguably, however, its needs in coming up with solutions are as great, if not greater, than those of any other agency involved in international lending.

Macroeconomic Policy and the Environment

As important as a proper framework for the analysis of projects is the issue of how the ADB can encourage macroeconomic polices that are consistent with the goals of sustainable development. The links between macroeconomic and sectoral policies and these goals are only beginning to be understood but from what knowledge is available, they can be extremely important.[2] The ADB environmental policy document rightly alludes to the importance of policies in the areas of pricing of forestry resources, agricultural pricing, roads and rural development, and others where the economic strategies chosen have an impact on the environment in ways that are not always obvious or direct. It also mentions the importance of proper accounting of environmental assets as important for the sustainable use of natural assets.

Macroeconomic policy has to be formulated in the areas of:

- Pricing of natural resources (water, forests, land, energy).

- Pricing and subsidization of agricultural inputs and outputs.

- Exchange rates and trade controls.

- Government taxes.

- Government expenditure between urban and rural areas.

- Taxes on pollutants.

This policy must be designed in ways that recognize the impacts that such polices have on the environment. This needs information about the linkages at a quantitative level, that is by and large missing for most countries. Thus it must be a priority to assist RMCs in the collection of the relevant information on which to base sound polices for sustainable development. However some indications have emerged of the importance of certain areas.

Work by the World Resources Institute, and others (Repetto 1988, Panayotou 1989, and Markandya 1990) has shown that often it is the underpricing of key commodities that is resulting in their excessive use. This applies to water, timber and fuelwood (with low stumpage charges), fertilizer and pesticides, and food and energy subsidies to urban consumers. If such polices are in place, there will be a continuing pressure on certain resources that will remain even if new projects are initiated to increase forest area, or supply more water for

---

[2] For a survey of the issues involved, see Markandya and Richardson (1990).

irrigation etc. Resolving them however, runs into several political and social conflicts, created by vested interests. Sometimes underpricing is justified on the grounds of income support for the poor, but this is rarely proven. Even where this is a valid reason, alternatives that are less damaging environmentally need to be considered.

It is not just macroeconomic policy that is of importance but also the sociolegal context in which it is carried out. Where traditional systems of resource management are breaking down, and new ones not replacing them, there is the continuing danger that any attempt to conserve existing resources or to expand those that lie in disputed ownership, will fail. It is not easy to address this issue that has bedeviled many projects, particularly those concerned with reafforestation and rangelands improvement. However, a failure to take a realistic view of what can be achieved may result in resources being wasted in projects that do not achieve their desired goals.

Integrating Economic and Environmental Concerns

Role of Benefit Cost Analysis

As was explained in the last section, the monetary valuation of environmental impacts is important for the rational allocation of resources to the environment. In recent years many techniques, which are described later, have been developed for such a valuation. However, the results from the application of these techniques have to be credible and acceptable if they are to be adopted. Some of the issues and doubts that arise from the monetary valuation of environmental benefits and costs are as follows:

- Specifying the dimensions of the problem.
- Separability of the environmental problem.
- Discounting of costs and benefits.
- Sensitivity analysis and the environment.
- Acceptability of the monetary values.

Specifying the Dimensions of the Problem

One concern expressed by environmentalists about the use of benefit cost analysis

(BCA) is that it does not specify the dimension of the problem in a sufficiently wide manner to encompass all the environmental ramifications. Projects such as penetration roads or hydrodams could change the use of land and the nature of economic activities in an entire region, with secondary and indirect effects that swamp the direct ones. A benefit cost analysis, or even a cost effectiveness analysis, based on a narrow interpretation of the costs and benefits would be misleading in such a situation. In broad terms this concern is correct but what it points to is not a rejection of BCA as such, but a call for the use of a wider and more effective BCA. Indeed, one of the criticisms of many of the traditional applications of BCA that are made in the next section are precisely along these lines—that is, that the analysis does not look at the implications of the project widely and deeply enough. The fact that development programs and investments have many indirect impacts makes decisions regarding them more complex, and may even require the use of general equilibrium methods or macroeconomic models to obtain reasonable solutions. In these circumstances it would appear even more important to document and value the environmental impacts, so that they can be assessed along with the other changes.

Separability of the Environmental Dimension

When carrying out a BCA, it is normal to require that each independent component of the project satisfy the net present value (NPV) or internal rate of return (IRR) test. Some environmentalists argue that this is unreasonable when applied to environmental components of projects, essentially because the benefits are not properly measured. An example would be the sugar plantation projects where the environmental components are water and soil conservation measures and replanting of some lost forest.

Where the environmental component is separable in a technical sense, it makes sense to treat it separately if the benefits and costs associated with it are adequately and fully measured. If that is so, there is no reason why the environmental component should not be subject to the same rules as the other components.

However, the component is not always separable, and if separable, measurability is frequently not possible. Therefore, it is necessary to use some alternative rule to evaluating the component. One rule could be based on the notion of sustainability. This has been referred to earlier and is based on the concept that, if development is to be sustainable in the long term, *key environmental resources need to be protected irrespective of their current value* which, in any event cannot be properly assessed in many cases. Examples would be critical zones, such as wetlands, which provide a multitude of ecological functions. For such resources the separability assumption in project valuation is inappropriate. This does not resolve the issue of the *timing* of the investment, or the difficult problem of deciding which resources come under this category. However, there is an urgent need to define some sustainability criteria so that decisions on what environmental components should be required components of a project can be defined. It may well be the case that the sustainability criteria should not apply at the project level at all, but rather at the sectoral or regional level. The issues involved need to be clarified further, but some recent thinking on this subject has stressed the need to meet the sustainability criteria at least cost (see Pearce, Markandya, and Barbier 1990). This will probably require some rationalization of "compensating projects" so that costs are kept to a minimum.

Discounting Costs and Benefits

To many individuals concerned with the environment, the fact that projects are selected using an NPV criterion with a discount rate of 12 percent in real terms (as is the case at the ADB), or using an IRR criterion with a similar required rate, is a reason why the environment is inadequately protected by such processes. They argue that the high discount rates do not give enough value to future environmental benefits or costs and that the emphasis of such allocation rules is to go for short term projects, without paying enough attention to the long term implications. This issue has to be taken seriously, but it is more complex than this argument would suggest. It has received some attention in the economic literature in the

environment (see Markandya and Pearce 1991), where the thrust of the argument is that (a) it would be better if a lower discount rate could be used for *all* projects, but (b) it is likely to result in more problems and resource misallocation if, as some environmentalists have suggested, a lower rate is used for "environmental" projects and components.

In fact, the rate of return on environmental projects need not be so low. The ADB's recent projects, many of which have a major environmental component, manage to meet the IRR standard. The key to this lies in quantifying as many of the benefits as possible.

Sensitivity Analysis and the Environment

Conservationists have argued that the use of sensitivity analysis is an inadequate substitute for a proper treatment of risk, especially where environmental dangers are concerned. For example, a project may involve dumping hazardous waste in a site. One possibility is that the dumping may generate groundwater contamination, leading to many deaths and serious illnesses. This risk may be reduced by project design but cannot be eliminated. In the event that the leakage occurs, the project would obviously have a massively negative net value, but how is one to give that eventuality due weight? Even a full risk analysis using an expected utility criterion, or a standard decision rule such as risk benefit analysis or the maximin rule (see Pearce and Markandya 1989), would not resolve the dilemma, in the sense that the resulting choice regarding the desirability of the project would command universal agreement (for example, it might still be the case that the above "project" would be considered acceptable). Although the process of arriving at a judgment can be better informed and improved by using decision analysis methods when possible, there is, unfortunately, no serious alternative to a judgmental evaluation of the risks of a project, whether they are environmental risks or any other risks.

Acceptability and Confidence of the Monetary Values of Environmental Benefits

Although the methods for deriving the costs and benefits of environmental impacts described in the next section are relatively established in developed countries (most have been in use for around twenty years), they are less familiar to decisionmakers in developing countries. This raises the problem that the figures derived may not have the credibility and confidence they need to have to be acceptable. There is no simple answer to this; time and extensive use of a technique are needed for it to be considered acceptable. In Europe and North America, environmental benefit estimation has not been equally effective in all situations, nor have all the methods found equal acceptability, but the technique is becoming accepted as part of the decisionmaking process. Furthermore, the techniques described below are now beginning to be used in project appraisal in developing countries (see below).

Techniques for Monetary Valuation

This is not intended to be a survey of valuation techniques for environmental costs and benefits, but rather an indication of areas where particular techniques may be used successfully and where there is scope for their extension in the ADB's appraisal activities.

The approaches to the economic measurement of environmental benefits can be broadly classified as *direct* and *indirect* techniques. The former considers environmental gains—an improved level of output in agriculture, better levels of air quality or water quality, and so forth—and seeks directly to measure the money value of those gains. This may be done by looking for a *surrogate market* or by using *experimental* techniques.

The surrogate market approach looks for a market in which goods or factors of production (especially labor services) are bought and sold, and observes that environmental benefits or costs are frequently attributes of those goods or factors. Thus, piped water is an attribute or feature of a house, a risky environment may be a feature of certain jobs, and so on. The experimental approach simulates a market by placing respondents in a position in which they can express their hypothetical valuations of real improvements in specific environments. The aim is to make the hypothetical valuations as real as possible.

Indirect procedures for benefit estimation do not constitute a method of finding willingness to pay (WTP) for the environmental benefit—or the willingness to accept (WTA) compensation for environmental damage suffered. What they do is to estimate the relationship between the "dose" (pollution, for example) and the nonmonetary effect (health impairment, for example), and only then is some measure of preference for that effect applied. Although they have this obvious weakness, they are, nevertheless, frequently used in valuing environment changes, *especially in developing countries*, where the information available often only permits the use of such methods or where data for the calculation of preference based estimates is limited.

Direct Valuation: The Hedonic Price Approach

The value of a piece of land is related to the stream of benefits, but to be derived from that land. Agricultural output and shelter are the most obvious of such benefits, but the environmental quality of the neighborhood in which the land is located is also important. The property value approach to the measurement of benefit estimation is based on this simple underlying assumption. Given that different locations have varied environmental attributes, such variations will result in differences in property values. With the use of appropriate statistical techniques, the hedonic approach attempts to (a) *identify* how much of a property differential is due to a particular environmental difference between properties and (b) *infer* how much people are willing to pay for an improvement in the environmental quality that they face and what the social value of the improvement is.

The identification of a property price effect due to a difference in pollution levels is usually done by means of a *multiple regression* or similar technique in which data are taken either on a small number of similar properties or pieces of land over a period of years (time series), or on a larger number of diverse properties at a point in time (cross section), or on both (pooled data). In practice almost all property value studies have used cross section data, as controlling for other influences over time is much more difficult.

Hedonic price techniques have been successfully used in estimating the costs of air and noise pollution, and of changes in amenities, in developed countries. Their use in developing countries has been more limited, although the World Bank and the Inter-American Development Bank have used them for the valuation of improvements in sites and services (sewerage, potable water). There is a considerable body of literature on the issues arising in the application of these techniques (see Markandya 1991).

The question that is at the center of this discussion is, are hedonic price valuations reliable and accurate? The difficulty, of course is there is no absolutely correct yardstick against which to measure the reliability. If there were it would not be necessary to engage in hedonic price approaches! It is thus in the *nature* of non-market valuation that accuracy and reliability have to be tested by other means. The main tests are:

- Consistency of results in similar contexts.

- Consistency of results with other benefit estimation techniques.

- Consistency of results with "real market" experience.

On the basis of these tests, considerable evidence exists to show that hedonic price valuation, properly executed, provides reasonably reliable benefit estimates in areas where there are well-functioning land and property markets.

Direct Valuation: Contingent Valuation

The contingent valuation method (CVM) uses a direct approach—it asks people what they are willing to pay for a benefit, or what they are willing to receive by way of compensation to tolerate a cost, or both. What is sought are the personal valuations of the respondent for increases or decreases in the quantity of some good, contingent upon an hypothetical market. Respondents say what they would be willing to pay or willing to accept *if* a market existed for the good in question. A contingent market is taken to include not just the good itself (an improved view, better water quality, and so forth), but also the institutional

context in which it would be provided, and the way in which it would be financed.

One major attraction of CVM is that it should, technically, be applicable to all circumstances. Its aim is to elicit valuations—or bids—that are close to those that would be revealed if an actual market existed. The hypothetical market—the questioner, questionnaire, and respondent—must therefore be as close as possible to a real market. The respondent must, for example, be familiar with the good in question. If the good is improved scenic visibility, this might be achieved by showing the respondent photographs of the view with and without particular levels of pollution. The respondent must also be familiar with the hypothetical means of payment—for example, a local tax or direct entry charge—known as the payment vehicle.

The questioner suggests the first bid (the starting point bid [price]) and the respondent agrees or denies that he or she would be willing to pay it. An iterative procedure follows: the starting point price is increased to see if the respondent would still be willing to pay it, and so on until the respondent declares that he or she is not willing to pay the extra increment in the bid. The last accepted bid, then, is the maximum willingness to pay (MWTP). The process works in reverse if the aim is to elicit willingness to accept (WTA): bids are systematically lowered until the respondent's minimum WTA is reached.

A very large part of the literature on CVM is taken up with discussion about the accuracy of CVM. Accuracy is not easy to define. But since the basic aim of CVM is to elicit "real" values, a bid will be accurate if it coincides (within reason) with one that would result if an actual market existed. But since actual markets do not exist (otherwise there would be no reason to use the technique), accuracy must be tested by seeing that:

- The resulting bid is similar to that achieved by other techniques based on surrogate markets (house price approach, wage studies, and so forth).

- The resulting bid is similar to one achieved by introducing the kinds of incentives that exist in real markets to reveal preference.

One significant feature of the CVM literature has been its use to elicit the different kinds of valuation that people place on environmental goods. In particular, CVM has suggested that existence values may be very important.

CVM has been used extensively to elicit values of improvements in water quality, the benefits of less air pollution, and the option and existence values of species and sites. Until recently, the direct use of such techniques in developing countries was believed to be very difficult, if not impossible, due to the sophistication of the "as if" experiments involved. However, some recent work carried out through the World Bank on the valuation of water benefits in Pakistan and Nigeria, and the experience of the IDB on water projects, on tourism valuation, and on sites and services has shown that the technique can indeed be effectively employed in valuing the benefits of alternative water supply systems. Views on the relevance of this method are therefore changing fast and it is quite likely that their use will extend to the valuation of environmental impacts in agricultural areas.

Direct Valuation: Travel Cost

Travel cost models are based on an extension of the theory of consumer demand, in which special attention is paid to the value of time. In the developing countries, some models are being used to estimate benefits from tourism development in countries with game parks (such as Kenya), or special trekking areas (such as Nepal). Another area of applications has been to value benefits of fuelwood supply (or the supply of replacements such as kerosene), where households "pay" for the fuelwood by spending time collecting it (see Boyo, Maler, and Unemo 1990). Finally the World Bank and the IDB have also been supporting the use of travel cost data as part of the valuation of water benefits referred to above as well as of recreational benefits from improvements in beaches. Thus, travel cost models have a role to play in benefit estimation in developing countries and, moreover, a role that should increase in the future.

Indirect Valuation: Dose-Response

The procedures for valuing the use of environmental resources thus far have been based on individual preferences. However, other methods exist that do not seek to measure such preferences explicitly. Instead they calculate a "dose-response" relationship between pollution and some effect, and then they apply a measure of preference to that effect. Such methods are referred to as *indirect methods*. Examples of dose-response relationships include the effect of pollution on health, the effect of pollution on aquatic ecosystems, and the effect of soil erosion on agricultural productivity and the values of tropical forests. For example, there are now several fairly detailed studies valuing by this method the damage done by soil erosion.[3]

The dose-response tends to be used particularly for two situations. The first is when it is thought that people are unaware of the effects that pollution causes. The second is when eliciting preferences by any one of the direct methods is not possible for reasons of data, or lack of "market sophistication" in the population, or both. The second situation applies especially in developing countries, where price and expenditure data are generally poor and where, at least until now, the use of contingent valuation techniques has been limited because it is believed that the answers would suffer from strategic, hypothetical and operational biases.

Where environmental benefit estimation has been undertaken in developing countries, it has been mainly through the direct application of the dose-response function method. Some points to note about the use of this technique in the agricultural sector (which is a particular focus of ADB project activity) are the following:

* Environmental costs and benefits are estimated mainly for changes in agricultural output following land use and land management programs. However, the dose- response relationships on which these are based are frequently quite crude, with no allowance being made for the fact that individuals adapt to changes in their environment. Thus, for example, as soil conditions

---

[3] See, for example, the paper on "National Economic Cost of Soil Erosion in Zimbabwe," by David Norse and Resma Saigal, in this volume.

change, different inputs will be used and different crops grown. Not allowing for that would result in an underestimate of the benefits of such changes.

- Many environmental impacts are not valued in these exercises. The reasons range from a lack of data to an unwillingness to use the appropriate techniques. The former include benefits such as increased crop residues and the spillover effects of projects. The latter include benefits of conservation per se.

- Where environmental costs are involved, the impact is often dealt with through a requirement that certain standards be met and certain levels of protection be achieved. In these cases no cost or benefit estimation is carried out. The use of such methods is sometimes referred to as "gated responses." In these cases, the costs of meeting the standard are considered as part of the costs of the project and often are equated with the "environmental costs." However, the latter is a fallacy, as the costs of mitigation may or may not be equal to the costs of the environmental damage. Nevertheless, the use of gated responses can be important in project appraisal, particularly in connection with the criteria of sustainability. How they should be designed and carried out is discussed in the next section.

- In other instances, the issue of environmental benefit or cost estimation is avoided by comparing different means of achieving a given goal. The goal has environmental benefits that are assumed to be desirable. The analysis only concerns itself with the way of achieving this goal at least cost.

Conclusions on Methods for Valuing the Environment

There is considerable scope for the use of some of *direct* techniques in the valuation of environmental benefits in developing countries, and in their rural sectors, but this strategy has yet to be substantially exploited. Particular promise holds for contingent valuation methods and travel cost approaches. However, it is essential to note that such models really only

provide "orders of magnitude" to the size of the benefits, and that some inaccuracy is inherent in the nature of the task being attempted. Nevertheless, the values obtained are useful in reaching rational decisions with regard to investments involving such benefits.

Although there would appear to be little direct relevance of nonuser values to ADB projects and policies, such an impression is misleading. Nonuser values such as option and existence value can, for some natural resources, be so large as to influence conservation decisions. These in turn can have a major impact on sustainable development.

Sectoral and Macroeconomic Policy Formulation and the Environment

Both developing country governments and donors are becoming increasingly aware of the links between macroeconomic polices pursued for stabilization and growth, and the environment. As stated in the previous section, these links are imperfectly understood but they are important and need to be accounted for in both in project planning and sectoral lending. Broadly, the polices that affect the environment can be divided into the short-term stabilization policies and the long-term structural adjustment policies. Each is considered below.

The short-term policies seeking fiscal and monetary balance can affect the environment by cutting government programs that are concerned with environmental protection. In times of crises, it is often the environmental budget, small as it is, that gets cut. The same pressures, however, can be used to cut expenditures that are being environmentally damaging. For example, the need to cut subsidies, or the need to raise charges for water, will be greater. These can be environmentally beneficial. Recent reviews of government spending, taxation, and public enterprise pricing point to the importance of addressing government policy failures in these areas if environmental damage is to be reduced (Panayotou 1989; Bishop, Markandya, and Richardson 1991). Other policies, such as changes in import and export taxes, exchange rates, and direct and indirect taxation, can have ambiguous effects, although one recent survey has shown that the impact of World Bank sectoral lending and the polices that it has supported have not been particularly damaging (Sebastian and Alicbusan 1989).

In the longer term, the more fundamental question of what constitutes a sustainable development path has to be faced. There is a recognition that some environmental damage may be tolerated if the economic benefits are large and if the damage is not irreversible. In later years, when the country has more resources, it can start to tackle these less urgent environmental issues. This notion of an environmental Kuznets Curve is being examined by a number of environmental economists (Bishop, Markandya, and Richardson 1991). It suggests that policy makers need to distinguish between environmental damage that can be tolerated in the interests of general economic development and damage that cannot. At present, however, no guidelines exist on how one might distinguish between the two.

If the ADB is to design its sectoral and project lending to be more conscious of the macroeconomic framework, it will need to face these questions, and to collect information on what the links between the environment and macroeconomic policy are. On a piecemeal basis this information is beginning to be available. In the review of projects and programs that follows, where issues of macroeconomic policy are relevant they are highlighted, so that one can see when they matter most.

Analysis of Projects: Recent Experience

The object of this section is to analyze the way in which environmental issues are being integrated into the economic valuation of projects receiving consideration for funding from the African Development Bank (ADB) and the African Development Fund (ADF). A group of twelve projects was selected, for which the Appraisal Reports were examined. All but one of the projects were initiated in 1990 or 1991, and many are still under consideration. Hence this review would be useful in commenting on current ADB practices, but not of much use in understanding how these practices have evolved over the recent past.

Environmental impacts of projects may be divided into positive and negative ones. As far as the positive impacts are concerned, these are never quantified in monetary terms. Some quantification in physical terms is carried out but even this is quite limited. The most frequent approach is to evaluate the project by estimating its rate of return in the absence of the environmental impacts, and then to say that the latter are "additional unmeasurable benefits." This is the way, for example, that reforestation benefits associated with dam construction, sugar plantations, and so on, are evaluated. Alternatively, a project may have many components, including "environmental" ones, and the appraisal is carried out for the package as a whole and not for the specific contribution of the environmental component. This is done for rangelands projects, and for resource conservation projects.

Where projects have negative impacts, there is a tendency to underplay these; and in some cases a detailed environmental impact analysis would provide some much needed information of the wider environmental effects of a particular project. Where a negative impact is acknowledged, there is an attempt to include an element for mitigation. In no case is the potential environmental damage valued in money terms.

All projects reviewed were judged on the basis of a 12 percent real discount rate. In general, the authors take the view that this rate should not be adjusted for projects with a significant environmental dimension. However, if the benefits cannot be quantified, it may be necessary to do so. Otherwise it will be difficult to get such projects accepted.

The twelve projects reviewed here cover a wide range of activities, from projects that potentially could have a major negative impact on the quality of the environment, like dams or roads, to projects whose aim is precisely the opposite—to protect or recover the natural resources. Table 5-1 gives the country, the activity, and the main characteristics of the projects reviewed.

1. SUDAN: Kenana Sugar Plantation Expansion

Description of the project

Kenana Sugar Estate began working in 1975, and has been a successful enterprise. It

Table 5-1

	COUNTRY	TYPE OF PROJECT	ENVIRONMENTAL FEATURES
1	Sudan	Sugar Plantation	Reforestation, Soil and Water Conservation.
2	Malawi	Smallholder Sugar Cane	Sugar Cane Production & Its Possible Environmental Impacts.
3	Malawi	Rural Development	Expansion of Agriculture Combined with Forest Protection.
4	Tanzania	Irrigation and Rice	Reforestation, Soil and Water Conservation.
5	Burkina Faso	Irrigation	Reduced Water Loss.
6	Ghana	Forestry and Paper Mill	Substitution of Natural Forest With Commercial Species.
7	Morocco	Rangelands Improvement	Soil Preparation, Sowing, Small Dams, Dune Fixation. Improved Management of Commons.
8	Ethiopia	Rangelands Improvement	Resource Restoration. Improved Management of Commons.
9	Mozambique	Family Livestock	Potential Forest and Rangelands Impacts.
10	Morocco	Dam Construction	Flooding of Land, Resettlement, Water Deviation, Reforestation of Catchment Area.
11	Tanzania	Road Rehabilitation	Opening New Areas to Cultivation. Subsidence. Disposal of Spoil.
12	Morocco	Natural Resource Conservation	Reforestation Program, Forest Management. Sustainable Use of Forest Products.

covers 35,000 hectares, and processes all its production. The expansion project has six objectives:

4. Plant 3,000 additional hectares with sugar cane

5. Raise productivity and yields

6. Create an enterprise that uses byproducts to produce charcoal fuel

7. Increase power generating capacity by 10 megawatts with thermoelectricity

8. Reforest 1,800 hectares

9. Carry out soil and water conservation measures

The report was submitted to the ADB Board in October 1990, the starting date for the project was April 1991, and the project is expected to be completed by March 1996. The total costs are 39.4 million FUA[4] and it has an economic internal rate of return of 15.6 percent.

The rate of return was calculated by looking at the expected increase in yields of sugar over time and comparing them with the direct costs. No environmental benefits were included for items 5 and 6 above. Hence the marginal benefits of these components are not estimated. In fact, the project was appraised as a single entity and no attempt was made to look at the additional costs of the components parts. This may be justified on the grounds:

• Either that the outputs are genuinely "joint products" and if the soil and water conservation measures were not carried out, the other benefits would not be realized.

---

[4] The Fund Unit of Account (FUA) is the unit of account used by the ADB Group for its projects. 1 FUA US$1.2. It allows for changing exchange rates between the donor currencies.

- Or that it is a requirement for the sustainable use of resources that if new land is brought under cultivation, some degraded land should be conserved, so that in net terms there is limited loss of forest cover.

Similar reasoning would be used to justify the charcoal fuel production unit.

Environmental Issues

A number of environmental issues arise in connection with this project. One is the issue of water valuation. Although water is available for the project, its value will depend on its opportunity cost, which could be higher than the official price. There is no discussion of the shadow price of water resources used in the project.

A second issue is that of the environmental and other benefits lost from the land that is converted into sugar production. The benefits of the project are the difference between the two. It is possible that there are few benefits to be lost from existing uses, but it would be useful to know what they were. No information is given on what kind of vegetation or cultivation it is displacing.

Third, the project makes some passing reference to possible negative impacts, particularly increased breeding grounds for parasites and vectors from the increased irrigation, and the depletion of soil fertility if insufficient phosphates are applied, as is currently the case. For both these impacts, the project team has made some suggestions of mitigation. It is not clear, however, whether these measures will be carried out, and what the consequences are of them not being carried out.

The project has two environmental components, both of which are stand-alone items, but neither is quantified. One is the afforestation component, which will produce fuelwood and protect the soil from erosion. It will be done on land not suited for cane, and will provide a new wind barrier. This component is justified on the need to comply with the new regulation in Sudan, which makes it compulsory to have at least 5 percent of the estates with forest. Hence, no separate analysis is required of its costs and benefits. The same does not apply, however, to the production of charcoal fuel. The private benefits of this component are

included in the overall benefits, but they are not compared with the direct costs. Furthermore if, as is argued, the project would reduce deforestation by reducing the demand for fuelwood, the latter should be quantified and included as a component. It might, for example, suggest that this component be expanded.

2. MALAWI: Study for Expansion of Smallholder Sugar Cane Production

Description of the project

The Smallholder Sugar Authority in Malawi is responsible for coordinating sugar cane production in smallholder plots. A study on the feasibility of the expansion of its activities is proposed. It will look at land productivity in the prospect areas, the availability of processing facilities and the situation of markets. The possibility of introducing irrigation is also being considered. The study will design a full integrated program, including livestock production. No estimates of the costs and benefits of the project are available at this stage, but the ADB has allocated around 1.3 million FUA to a detailed study, including an environmental impact assessment (EIA).

Environmental Issues

As stated above, part of the preparation of the project will involve an EIA of the sugar cane production expansion. In the project's design, the consultants are asked to bear in mind the likely effects of recommended technological packages. They should suggest ways to avoid environmental damage. Reference must be made to the use of pesticides, the disposal of waste, and other kinds of air and water contamination. Thus the approach is to put together a mitigation package but without reference to the potential benefits of that package or to its costs. It would be useful if guidelines as to what is acceptable for these impacts were made available. They could then be reviewed from time to time, as more information about potential damages becomes available.

More importantly, the project needs to look at the implications of this expansion for the use of unpriced (or inadequately priced) resources, such as water. The increased demands may involve a shift away from other uses, and these should be taken into account. The project's terms of reference do indicate that the issue of water will be examined, but it is the efficient use that is difficult to plan for in this context.

3. MALAWI: Rural Development Project, Mwanza

Description of the project

Mwanza is a resource-rich district in southern Malawi. Having a low population density, the area is now receiving new settlers from neighboring districts. The aim of the project is to improve agricultural and livestock production and to help manage land resources effectively in the region. It covers a wide range of activities: extension, training, rural credits, and the construction and repairing of rural roads and water supplies.

The date of the report is July 1991, and the proposed starting date is February 1992. The project would be conducted by the Ministry of Agriculture (Blantayre Development Division). It's costs are 10.87 million FUA and the economic internal rate of return, supposing 27 percent of the farmers adopt the new practices and use the credits, is estimated around 33 percent.

Environmental Issues

To avoid the transformation of part of the forested areas into new agricultural and livestock ranching land, one of the prerequisites for the loan is that the government of Malawi must designate, gazette, and maintain the forest reserves in the Mwanza area. At present they are vulnerable to encroachment (although whether this is taking place is not known).

Another component of the project deals with the land not suited for agriculture. Some such land has in fact been used in this way. The project will suggest nonagricultural alternatives to the farmers. Other land that is still forest, but that will not be protected as reserves, will belong to the traditional authorities who will be advised on how best to allocate it most efficiently.

The report states that the project will have other positive environmental effects. The improved agricultural practices and the use of mineral fertilizers will avoid soil depletion.

Also, the cattle fattening program is said to avoid overgrazing.

None of the external environmental benefits (for example, the protection of forest reserves, the reductions in soil depletion, and the reductions in overgrazing) is measured in monetary terms. Again, as with other projects, all components are treated as a unified whole, and no attempt is made to appraise the parts: the effect of internalized environmental investments, like the soil and water conservation techniques, is not separated from the effect of the rest of the investments. Furthermore, many of the supposed benefits depend on changing farmer behavior, and on many previous occasions projects have been overoptimistic about such changes. A better appreciation of their perceptions of their self-interests is required of project planners.

The potential negative impacts of the project are underplayed (for example, the expansion on nonprotected forest land). The loss of forest land and its ongoing uses and values needs to be taken into account.

4. TANZANIA: Study for the Irrigation Project, DAKAWA II

Description of the project

Dakawa I was a project that began in the late 1970s. It cleared 2,110 hectares of land in the Morogoro region, devoting 2,000 of them to rice production on irrigated land. The project also built a rice mill complex, roads, and several functional and residential buildings. The project's performance has fallen short of expectations. The current proposal is to conduct a study that identifies past errors, proposes corrective measures, and designs an expansion of the project area (Dakawa II) to another 2,000 hectares.

Environmental issues

When Dakawa I began, there was no requirement to produce an environmental impact assessment. The current study's main aim in the environmental area is to assess the actual state of resources. The proposed ex post economic valuation of Dakawa I, however, does not include an ex post *environmental valuation*, which would be useful to gain experience for Dakawa II.

It is laudable that project preparation for Dakawa II will include an environmental impact analysis of "health hazards, pollution, ecology, etc." Such information can help in designing a better project. However, it would be useful to provide the team carrying out the EIA, with an indication of what alternative project designs are considered. In other words, the environmental analysis can both serve as a guide to the mitigation measures and assist in the design of the project itself. The project itself is rather vague as to what policies will be implemented to achieve the improved management of the natural resource base.

There are several suggestions about "compensating projects" for reforestation, energy from agricultural waste, and water and soil conservation. These need to be appraised individually, and with more monetary quantification than is indicated from the project document. Such quantification is possible, given resources.

If these environmental costs and benefits are not integrated into the analysis, a situation could be created where mitigation subprojects are carried on even if they are not cost effective, or, worse, where the whole project is carried on just because it "manages the resources well," even if residual environmental damage makes it unjustifiable.

5. BURKINA FASO: Institutional Support for Irrigation Management

Description of the project

There is a great pressure over natural resources in Burkina Faso. The irrigated sector comprises 13,000 hectares and it faces a continuous mismanagement and poor maintenance. The project is aimed to give institutional support to the government agencies dealing with irrigation. The costs are estimated at 2.76 million FUA. The project is due to begin in 1991 and the appraisal report was completed in August 1990.

Environmental issues

The report states two positive effects of the project. In the first place, good management leads to better use of water. In the second place, rising productivity reduces pressure on marginal land, so helping to avoid an unsustainable development path. No calculation or valuation of the probable benefits in those two issues is given.

The question here is whether it is possible to evaluate such a project in any more quantitative a manner. Clearly, one can set certain targets for the project to achieve, and ask whether the proposed measures will achieve those targets. This provides a discipline that can act both to help identify the linkages between the management changes and the targets, and to serve as a goal for the agencies involved. Targets have not been identified in this project, which could make it less effective as well as more difficult to evaluate ex post.

6. GHANA: Industrial Plantation Project, SUBRI

Description of the project

The appraisal report for this project dates from 1984, when the expected starting date was 1985. The project consisted of the conversion of 4,000 hectares of natural forest inside the Subri River Forest Reserve, into a *Gmelina arborea* (fast-growing tree) plantation. A plantation of 1,000 hectares was already existing at the time of the project.

While the plantation was young, an agro-silvicultural project would be developed, supplying food for labor and local sales. The timber would be directed to a pulp and paper mill in Daboase, seven kilometers away, a project started in parallel. The plantation project would be managed by a parastatal formed for that purpose. The costs were estimated at 40.45 million FUA, and the benefits would give an economic internal rate of return of 26 percent.

Environmental Issues

The appraisal report states that because only 69,000 of the 1.7 million hectares covered by forests in Ghana had been deforested by that time, and the plantation would convert only 8.3 of the Subri River Forest Reserve, the effects of the project would be "not alarming from the environmental point of view." However, no environmental impact assessment or valuation of the forgone forest benefits was made. Thus the rate of return is certain to be an overestimate. The loss of a small land area, such as that described here, however, can be associated with major losses in ecological and environmental terms; it depends on the sensitivity of the ecosystem to loss of forest. This is not to say that the project was necessarily a bad decision, but simply that a more careful evaluation of the selected project would in general be a desirable feature of an environmentally sensitive forestry policy. Incidentally, a post evaluation of this project would be interesting, to see what, if any, real impacts have been felt from the forest loss (including any secondary effects from the opening up of an area that lies within a forest reserve).

7. MOROCCO: Pastoral and Livestock Development in the Eastern Region

Description of the Project

The main activity in the Eastern region of Morocco is sheep farming. It is a region severely affected by drought and overgrazing, but it has still some forests. The land is mainly in communal ownership, with some private and state land existing alongside. The state land is mainly in forest areas.

The project seeks to restore the physical milieu of the region. The existing rangelands would be improved by soil preparation, sowing, dune fixation, and the building of small dams. Agricultural plots would receive incentives to produce fodder crops. Cooperatives would be organized and receive the rights to manage the pastoral areas; training and veterinary services would be provided to these cooperatives.

The project's total costs are 41.28 million FUA. The benefits are calculated using a dose-response model and valuing the yield increases at average current prices. The estimates show that in eight years the internal economic rate of return would be 15 percent. The project report was submitted in April 1990.

Environmental Issues

Most of the expected effects of this project on the environment are positive, and the notion of a regional development project encompassing many related agricultural and environmental impacts is a good one. The project clearly identifies two major issues: one is that the resource degradation is coming from the environmental stress caused by droughts, and the other is that there is a problem of the management of the commons.

It is not clear, however, how successful the proposed management of the rangelands commons, which is critical for the sustainable use of rangelands, will be. The effectiveness of governments in "organizing" communities to manage such commons has never been convincing and one might doubt its success in this case.

Although the project is rightly concerned with the management of the rangelands, it does not devote the same attention to the management of open access forests. The project takes the view that the mere process of increasing forest resources through reafforestation should reduce the depletion from existing forests. With open access, however, that may not be the case.

This project is one where the benefits of the environmental components have been quantified using dose-response relationships. The benefits are measured as the revenues from the increased production of marketed goods and the shadow price of self-consumption food. Thus the project offers an example of how such techniques can be used to value environmental benefits.

8. ETHIOPIA: South-East Rangelands Project

Description of the Project

This project is similar to the Moroccan one considered above, with the difference that there is less of an issue of forest management here. The southeast of Ethiopia is one of the poorest and driest regions in the country. The droughts have affected it heavily and, combined with the overgrazing, the natural resource base is being degraded at a fast pace. The project includes a series of actions to restore and upgrade the rangelands capacity to sustain livestock.

One of the components is the construction of infrastructure: the creation of stock routes, access roads, grain stores, and new water ponds. The project aims also to develop Pastoral Associations. They would be responsible for the management of communal lands and the would receive veterinary and agricultural extension, training, and assistance. A commercial effort would be to set up a marketing intelligence service and new infrastructure.

The project's total costs are 31.98 million FUA. The project report was submitted in July 1989 and the project was expected to begin in January 1990. The benefits are calculated using a dose-response model. The prices of the expected increase in skin, meat, and milk production of the different species are based on the 1990 averages. In a period of twenty years, the project reaches an economic rate of return of 18 percent. The sensitivity analysis, simulating draughts every seven years and rising costs, yields a minimum rate of return of 14 percent, so the project is considered a solid one.

Environmental Issues

Most of the expected effects on the environment are positive and the quantification of the environmental benefits provides a useful guide to the desirability of the project. Similar issues arise here, however, as with the Moroccan project. The key to the success of the project is the effective management of the rangelands. Even when the new roads and water availability expand their carrying capacity, the element that confers sustainability is the management of common property that the Pastoral Associations are expected to provide.

9. MOZAMBIQUE: Rehabilitation of Family Farming Livestock

Description of the Project

Expecting that the civil war can be settled and peace can be achieved in the near future, the government of Mozambique wanted to set the basis for quick economic recovery. This program is intended to support the family farming livestock sector in that recovery. It will concentrate in the ten safest rural districts and hopes to reach 150,000 families.

The project will build water points, provide veterinary services, and carry out extension programs. One of the main elements is the

import of cattle from other countries to sell them to the family farm sector. Also, research on resource use, marketing, and other areas will be conducted.

The report was submitted in May 1990 and the project's starting date was set for January 1991, with a proposed duration of five years. The total costs are 16.64 million FUA and, although there are some data problems, the best estimate of the economic internal rate of return is around 20 percent. The latter is based on much less data regarding the dose-response relationships than are the Moroccan and Ethiopian estimates.

Environmental Issues

The war has brought down the number of livestock, so the report states that the current situation is one of underutilization of pastures and water resources to well below carrying capacity. With the most optimistic results the program would enlarge the current stock just to prewar levels. Because at that time there was no evidence of overgrazing, deforestation to increase grazing lands, a lowering of the water table, or other environmental problems, this time the government is not expecting any. Changes in management regimes have occurred in the intervening years, however, and the assumptions of no effects may be overoptimistic.

Part of the research will develop technologies to ensure soil conservation and make optimal use of resources. Those results will be incorporated into the extension services. No estimate of the project's benefits (if adopted by the farmers) is incorporated into its valuation, although there is frequent mention of the notion of sustainability. Indeed, it is a commonly repeated idea in many of the projects that certain conservation measures do not need to be valued, because they will confer sustainability to the rest of the project.

10. MOROCCO: El Hachef Dam

Description of the Project

This dam will store the waters from the seasonal river El Hachef, to satisfy the growing requirements of Tangier, Asilah, and surrounding centers up to the year 2015. An area of 2,000 hectares will be deforested and flooded for that purpose. The land will be subject to compulsory purchase and the inhabitants resettled upstream. The project includes a development program for the catchment area (including the new settlements) that consists of technical support for agriculture in flat private land, development of fruit plantations in steep private land, and reafforestation of all public lands.

The economic analysis of the project is more sophisticated than that of many other ADB projects: The estimated cost of the project is 81.2 million African Development Bank's Units of Account (BUA). The cost includes the price paid in the compulsory purchase of land, the building and operation costs of the dam, and a measure of the forgone agricultural products in the flooded area. The benefits are calculated as the revenues from water sales at 1991 nominal prices and the value of the fruit produced by the development project in the catchment area. The balance gives a rate of return of 15 percent. The best alternative, a dam in the Maharauf area, would have a rate of return of less than 11 percent.

Environmental Issues

There appears to be a double counting of some of the costs of the project and no counting of other costs. Double counting occurs when the compulsory purchase price of land is added to the forgone benefits of that land: the former is in part at least based on the latter. If the compulsory purchase price were equal to the market value, which in turn fully reflected the commercial value of the land, then the project is exactly double counting the costs. However, there is no certainty that the price paid for land in the compulsory purchase is the price the market would give. Therefore the extent of the error in taking both figures is unknown and it would be better to take only the estimated forgone benefits. On the other side, the project errs in not including many of the environmental costs. The existence or nonexistence of original ecosystems or wildlife in the area to be flooded is not reported. Also, deviation of water would surely alter original ecosystems and economic activities downstream. The only mention of this issue is that the damage of seasonal flooding would be stopped; the loss of positive benefits is not mentioned.

The appraisal report does not mention if the whole 2,000 hectares to be flooded are private farm land. If some of there were public forest land, the loss of value would be ignored, as no value is attached to such land.

The project mainly considers the environmental problems that could affect the performance of the dam, not the effects that the dam can cause on the surrounding region. Thus, special works on the catchment area are considered as an environmental "investment" for the long-term viability of the dam. These include "sound agricultural practices," the plantation of fruit trees, and the fixing of river beds. It would be desirable to decide on the *extent* of such environmentally positive measures by looking at all their benefits, so that a larger budget may be allocated to such items.

Finally, the project has a component for the reafforestation of an area equal in size to the area that is being inundated. This is intended as a compensation in environmental terms—a putting into practice of the notion of sustainability. It is not clear, however, how good a compensation this is. It may be perfectly adequate, but more information is needed about the ecology and economic values, both of the lost forest and of the reforested areas.

11. TANZANIA: Road Rehabilitation Project

Description of the Project

The project seeks to rehabilitate and upgrade 389 kilometers of roads linking Chalize, Segera, Tanga, and Arusha, in the rich Chalize-Arusha corridor, and those linking Mutukula, Bukoba, and Lusahunga in the Lake Victoria Circuit. After fifteen years of neglect, they are in a very poor condition and are increasingly becoming a bottleneck to development efforts in the region.

The report was submitted in April 1990, and the starting date of the project was April 1991. The cost of the project is 45.01 million FUA. The benefits are calculated using a model which simulates the economic activity in the region over the next fifty years. The main benefits come from savings in time, vehicle operating costs, and reduced road accidents. Also, some effects on the economic activities carried in the influence zone of the roads are taken into account—for example, "high quality fruits and vegetables can be grown on the slopes of the Kilimanjaro and Usambara" (page 56). A high economic rate of return is expected. It varies between 24.5 percent and 28.5 percent, depending on the sensibility analysis.

Environmental Issues

In general, the project report looks carefully at the direct environmental consequences of the road. Issues such as effects of the road works themselves, potential land erosion, and damage at the material extraction sites are all properly addressed. Land erosion would be curbed by improved drainage of the roads, and material extraction sites would be restored. However, it is the *indirect* impacts of such a rehabilitation scheme that need to be examined. Although the appraisal report states that a consultant would be asked to conduct an EIA, which should look at some of these issues, the final decision does not seem to depend on its outcome. The Report argues that no significant environmental degradation would occur in the surrounding areas because the project just rehabilitates existing roads, it does not build new ones. Such an argument ignores the significant negative environmental changes that will result from the development of the region, as the overall costs of access to the areas affected are reduced. The transformation of surrounding uncultivated areas, with their attendant ecological functions, into agricultural land, could have some important consequences. These need to be looked at. This does not mean that the scheme is necessarily undesirable; it is merely part of a prudent strategy in any development program.

12. MOROCCO: Natural Resource Conservation

Description of the Project

This is a general project, acting widespread in the country and in several different ways. It's main features are: reafforestation, forest management, silvopastoral management, protection of water catchment areas, strengthening of government forestry services, and ecological studies.

The appraisal report dates from March 1990, and its expected starting date was June 1990. Different government agencies would be involved. The costs are 26.93 million FUA, and the project's economic rate of return is calculated at 18 percent.

The benefits come mainly from marketed forest products: timber, fuelwood, and fodder. By law, the recipients of the benefits are the communes. This creates problems of cost recovery, because the government does the investment, managing, and works. There are problems of continuing the project once the period of the loan runs out, because even when the law states that 20 percent of the forest earnings must be reinvested the communes actually reinvest around 10 percent.

Environmental Issues

As with the other project in Morocco reviewed in this report (see project number 7 above), there is an implicit assumption here that the very process of reafforestation will reduce man's pressure on forests. But if incentives to deforest are established, and these incentives remain in force, reafforestation would only delay depletion. In fact, the report recognizes that poor coordination in the management of common land hinders the efforts of getting back to a sustainable path. Such poor coordination may well result in the project not achieving its aims.

Nevertheless, it is encouraging to see that a project such as this, with many diverse environmental benefits, can be justified from the marketable benefits alone, assuming that the institutional issues can be resolved. The project manages to achieve an internal rate of return of 18 percent—without considering in quantitative terms such benefits as the protection of wildlife, the reduced siltation of dams, and the prevention of desertification and soil erosion. As the document rightly recognizes, these unmeasured impacts are the "most important part" of the project. Including such benefits could justify a higher level of spending in the sector. The constraint may well be the inability of the government to recover the costs of the initial investments; doing so would require a program of fiscal change that would be part of a drive to a more sustainable use of resources.

Conclusions on the Review of Projects

ADB projects in recent years have taken the environment seriously, as can be seen from these reviews. However, there is considerable room to extend and integrate the environmental analysis into the economic analysis. The monetary estimation of environmental benefits and costs are confined to a few cases where a dose-response model has been used. These have yielded useful results of benefits in the areas of conservation and should be extended. In addition, there is scope to apply other techniques referred to in here in ADB project appraisal; particularly, as mentioned at the beginning of this report, the treatment of positive benefits needs to be strengthened.

Where mitigation programs are recommended, a need exists, in some cases, to look at the wider impacts of the project, so that its indirect consequences can be allowed for. This is particularly the case where the ADB's involvement is going to change significantly the land use patterns in a region.

Finally, the success of many of the projects is dependent on institutional changes and alterations in land management systems, where experience would indicate that there is a real possibility of failure. There is not much that the analyst can do about this, except to scale down the expectations of the changes in yields, and so forth, that the project will result in, and to assist in setting the policy context for its activities. In the next section the relation between these policies and environmental impacts are discussed.

Environmental Issues in Sectoral Bank Activities

As indicated in the beginning of this paper, (a) the African Development Bank rightly recognizes the importance of the broader policy context in formulating its lending program, but (b) there is a great need to gather the relevant information on the linkages between government policy parameters and environmental degradation, and to establish a better understanding of the linkages. In this section, three sectoral projects with some potential environmental implications are reviewed: the Somalia Agricultural Sector Adjustment Program, the Ghana Health Service Rehabilitation Program, and the Malawi Study on the Social Aspects of Adjustment.

1. SOMALIA: Financing Agricultural Sector Adjustment Programme

Description of the Project

The Agricultural Sector Adjustment Programme (ASAP) is a medium-term adjustment program. The reviewed loan proposal is for its second phase. The report dates from November 1989 and it was expected to be effective from January to December 1990.

The project seeks to liberalize controls and institutional bottlenecks throughout the sector. Privatizing or closing parastatals, eliminating state monopolies on commodities trade, and liberating inputs and outputs from price control are some of its measures. The effects of these measures, combined with good climate, have resulted in a fast recovery. The loans will be used to import inputs to develop agriculture, livestock, fisheries, and forestry.

Environmental Issues

One of the stated objectives of the Agricultural Development Policies is to preserve the environment at a sustainable level. Somalia's fragile ecology makes this goal difficult to achieve. Because this is a sectoral program, few details are given on the specific projects to be carried out. The only information in the report on environmental matters concerns the use of fertilizers, pesticides, and herbicides for which Somalia has one of the lowest use rates in Africa. To encourage their adoption by farmers, these inputs are currently provided with credit and price subsidy. Five dangerous pesticides are banned from imports. On the livestock sector, the current rising stock is said to be causing overgrazing and rangelands degradation.

The main issues here are the linkages between changes in agricultural prices and land use. How will the revised prices affect the supply of fruits, the growth of wheat and sorghum, and the holding of livestock? That there are strong relationships through price elasticities has been established (Gammage 1990). However, the linkage backwards from the changed supply to changes in land use is less clear. The program should have access to a set of studies that would allow it to predict the environmental consequences of the macroeconomic policy changes it is proposing. At present this cannot be done and it would be too much for one program to undertake the research.

Related to this is the need to introduce additional measures specifically to reduce land degradation and misuse. For example, a program which raises the prices paid to farmers for annual export crops could increase the pressure to bring land into cultivation for this purpose, land that is not suited for this purpose. But the fact that such pressure exists does not mean that the original measure is invalid; rather it points to the need to introduce proper incentives for sustainable land use and management.

2. GHANA: Health Service Rehabilitation

Description of the Project

The project seeks to rehabilitate the health service in the whole country, strengthening hospital maintenance and management. Support is also to be given for primary health care. The report was submitted on December 1989. The total cost amounted to 18.35 million FUA, and no estimate of benefits or cost-effectiveness analysis was made.

Environmental Issues

The report states that the project has no negative environmental impact. As the rehabilitation will make disposal of waste more hygienic, some (unmeasured) positive effects are expected. The wider implications of a better set of health facilities are not addressed, however. These include the attractiveness of urban centers where such facilities are usually located relative to the rural areas, a point that has been made in the ADB's Environmental Paper.

It is unlikely that any one program such as this will have a major impact on population movement but the combined impact of several programs could be significant. It should be part of the ADB's responsibility to look at the overall environmental consequences of its programs in a particular country. Such a strategy would require a separate exercise into which each of the programs such as this one would feed.

3. MALAWI: Study on the Social Aspects of Adjustment

Description of the Project

The project seeks to study the effects on the lower-income groups in Malawi of the macroeconomic adjustment program. No environmental issues are part of its objectives. Although some of its consequences may have indirect effects (for example, through poverty reduction on deforestation), they are not considered relevant to this study. The estimated costs are 860 thousand FUA. The report was submitted in August 1990 and the starting date of the study is fiscal year 1991 (beginning April 1, 1991), with a duration of two years.

Environmental Issues

A study such as this would offer an ideal occasion to integrate the linkages between poverty/income distribution and environmental degradation. One of the hottest debates in the environmental field is the extent to which environmental damage is increasing and sustainable development is being arrested, because of increasing poverty in some countries, where the poor have no option but to degrade their environment. This is disputed (Jagannathan 1989) but the debate remains an important one. The World Bank has been conducting a study of the macroeconomic-environment linkages, and programs such as this one from the ADB would benefit in design from the results of that study.

Conclusions and Recommendations

This paper has examined the issues arising, for the African Development Bank, in the integration of the economic and environmental aspects of sustainable development. The ADB is dealing with these problems on a continent with the gravest environmental crises. Hence the concerns could not be more important. In recognition of this, the ADB has begun to formulate an environmental policy that deals with both project and sectoral policy aspects of its activities. The essential conclusions on the project side are: *(a) there is a need to extend environmental cost and benefit estimation and (b) where this is not possible, there is a need to formalize the use of sustainability criteria to establish guidelines for mitigation action and for resource conservation projects.* However, these are issues that all development banks and bilateral donor agencies are grappling with and the African Development Bank is not alone in facing them. Hence, there may be some sense in a joint effort in addressing many of the issues raised here.

The review of some of the ADB's recent projects reveals that it is taking the environment seriously. However, there is considerable room to extend and integrate the environmental analysis into the economic analysis. The monetary estimation of environmental benefits and costs are confined to a few cases where a dose-response model has been used. These have yielded useful results of benefits in the areas of conservation and should be extended. In addition, there is scope in ADB's project appraisal to apply the other techniques referred to earlier. As mentioned at the beginning of this report, the treatment of positive benefits needs to be strengthened. This will require the use of such techniques.

There is not much to be gained from a retrospective analysis of the projects reviewed here, except in one or two cases where a change in the operation of the project can be made when account is taken of the environmental impacts, or where a compensating project might be justified. On these grounds, the Morocco Dam project and the Tanzanian Road Project could be worth re-investigating. Otherwise, effort needs to be devoted to projects coming up in the near future.

Where mitigation programs are recommended, there is a particular need to look at the wider impacts of the project, so that its indirect consequences can be allowed for. This is particularly the case where land use patterns in a region will change significantly.

On the sectoral/policy lending side, stress is laid on the importance of the links between macroeconomic policy and the environment. Such links are not fully understood, let alone quantified, but some of the research has shown that often it is the underpricing of key commodities that is resulting in their excessive use. This applies to water, and to timber and fuelwood (with low stumpage charges). Such policies result in continuing pressure on certain resources that will remain even if new projects are initiated to increase forest area, or to supply more water for irrigation, and so on. Reducing this pressure, however, runs into several political and social conflicts, created by vested interests. Also, information is needed about the linkages at a quantitative level that is, by and large, missing for most countries. *Thus, it must be a priority to assist countries in the collection of the relevant information in which to base sound policies for sustainable development.*

From the review of programs, it appears that there is a strong need to collect more information on the macroeconomic policy-environment linkages, and to develop a framework for disseminating this to program teams so that they can use it. Again, there is scope for inter-Bank cooperation in this regard.

Bibliography

African Development Bank. 1990a. *Environmental Policy Paper of the ADB Group,* ADB/BD/WP/89/108. Abidjan.

African Development Bank. 1990a. *Environmental Assessment Guidelines for the African Development Bank.* Abidjan: Haskoning Royal Dutch Consulting Engineers.

Bishop, J., A. Markandya, and J. Richardson. 1991. *Macroeconomic Adjustment and the Environment.* London: London Environmental Economics Center and University College.

Boyo, J., K-G. Maler, and L. Unemo. 1990. *Environment and Development*: An Economic Approach. Kluwer Academic Publishers, AH Dordrecht.

Gammage, S. 1990. *Environmental Economics in the Developing World,* Report to U.S. Agency for International Development (U.S.AID). Washington, D.C.

Jagannathan, N.V. 1989. "Poverty, Public Policies and the Environment," World Bank Environment Department Working Paper No. 24. Washington, D.C.

Markandya, A. 1991. *The Economic Appraisal of Projects*: The Environmental Dimension. Washington, D.C.: Inter-American Development Bank.

Markandya, A., and D.W. Pearce. 1991. "Development, Environment and the Social Rate of Discount," *World Bank Research Observer*, Volume 6, No. 2, pp. 137-152.

Markandya, A., and J. Richardson. 1990. "The Debt Crises, Structural Adjustment and the Environment," mimeo. Department of Economics, University College, London.

Panayotou, T. 1990. *The Economics of Environmental Degradation: Problems, Causes and Responses,* Harvard Institute for International Development Discussion Paper No. 355. Cambridge, MA: Harvard University.

Pearce, D.W., E.B. Barbier, and A. Markandya. 1990. *Sustainable Development: Economics and Environment in the Third World.* London: Earthscan Publications Ltd.

Pearce, D.W., and A. Markandya. 1989. *Environmental Benefit Estimation*: Monetary Evaluation. Paris: Organisation for Economic Co-operation and Development.

Repetto, R. 1988. "Economic Policy Reform for Natural Resource Conservation." World Bank Environment Department Working Paper No. 4. Washington, D.C.

Sebastian, I., and A. Alicbusan. 1989. "Sustainable Development Issues in Adjustment Lending Policies," World Bank Environment Department, Policy and Research Divisional Working Paper No. 6. Washington, D.C.

6

The Rural Development and Environmental Protection Project in the Day Forest in Djibouti: A Case Study

Nessim J. Ahmad

The case study covers selected issues in the economic analysis applied in the IFAD appraised Environmental Protection and Rural Development Project in the Day Forest in Djibouti. Using the project as a substrate for discussion, generic opportunities and constraints in the economic valuation and evaluation of environmental changes in marginal areas in developing countries are identified. It is argued that opportunities exist for the routine application in project appraisal of economic valuation methods such as the surrogate market approach, the change in production approach, and the opportunity cost of time approach, while contingent valuation methods (CVM) and the travel cost approach can be considered less suitable. In all cases, judicious use of sensitivity analysis is advocated. In terms of valuation of natural resources on which poor groups depend, it is stressed that the treatment of intra-generational equity is as important as the inter-generational issue.

The case study concludes that the routine application of environmental economics in project appraisal is constrained not so much by methodological gaps, but by difficulties in ensuring that physical estimates of environmental change in "with" and "without" project scenarios are generated in a timely fashion. As such, a case is made for undertaking proactive environmental assessments well in advance of appraisal.

The International Fund for Agricultural Development (IFAD) has a specific mandate to alleviate rural poverty. Its target groups consist of small farmers, landless laborers, artisanal fishermen, nomadic pastoralists, indigenous peoples, and the women who make up these groups. As an outcome of the Fund's efforts to sharpen its focus on the poorest groups, an increasing proportion of IFAD projects are located in marginal, resource-poor environments. In these areas, it is often the case that poverty processes and environmental degradation are closely intertwined. In recognition of this, IFAD projects are increasingly addressing the poverty-environment linkages directly. An example of this trend in IFAD's portfolio is the IFAD-appraised Rural Development and Environmental Protection Project in the Day Forest in Djibouti.

This case study is based on the economic analysis applied in the appraisal of the Day Forest project. The case study does not address the myriad issues associated with the sustainable management of common property and open access resources in dryland areas that are central to the design of the project. Instead, certain valuation aspects of the economic analysis of the project are discussed, with a view to drawing some preliminary conclusions concerning the "economic valuation and evaluation of environmental changes in the context of marginal areas." In line with the objectives of the CIDIE Workshop on Environmental Economics and Natural Resource Management in Developing Countries for which it was prepared, the study focuses specifically on the relevance of environmental valuation techniques for investment decision-making.

The Project

Project Background

The Day Forest is a unique 1,000-hectare remnant of an ancient Juniper forest that once covered the highlands in the Horn of Africa. As such, it constitutes, in a predominantly hyper-arid country, a recognized national patrimony of international biodiversity significance. However, in the absence of timely intervention to introduce more sustainable sylvopastoral resource management practices, the forest is likely to suffer irreversible degeneration. On the basis of trends determined through the analysis of available studies and the interpretation of aerial photograph time-series, the Juniper stand is projected to disappear within ten years. Linked to the disappearance of the forest, rangeland degradation is likely to continue—threatening the livelihood base of pastoralists who subsist in the vicinity of the forest.

In response to a request by the government of Djibouti, the Rural Development and Environmental Protection Project in the Day Forest was identified for possible inclusion in IFAD's portfolio by an IFAD General Identification Mission in March/April 1987 (Report No. 0231-DJ). In April 1988, an IFAD "pre-preparation" mission was fielded to synthesize additional information for project design generated by various pre-investment conservation activities undertaken by the Food and Agriculture Organization of the United Nations (FAO) and United Nations Development Program (UNDP) in the project area. This was followed by a preparation mission fielded by the FAO Investment Centre on behalf of IFAD in November/December 1990 (Report No. 3/91/IF-DJI5). Finally, an IFAD/United Nations Capital Development Fund (UNCDF) mission visited Djibouti in April/May 1991 to appraise the project for possible financing by IFAD.

The objective of the proposed Rural Development and Environmental Protection Project in the Day Forest is to alleviate the poverty of pastoralists in the Day region of Djibouti through the sustainable management of the Day Forest and surrounding sylvopastoral areas on which the pastoralists depend. The project as appraised by IFAD would have a total cost of US$4.37 million over a project life of seven years. The financing plan as originally proposed is as follows: World Food Programme (WFP) would provide a grant of an amount equivalent to US$480,000 (11 percent of total project cost); UNCDF would provide a grant of an amount equivalent to US$1,587,000 (36.3 percent of total project cost); IFAD would provide a highly concessional loan (1 percent interest, ten-year grace period, fifty years repayment) of an amount equivalent to

US$1,388,600 (31.8 percent of total project cost); and the government of Djibouti would contribute an amount equivalent to US$915,100 (20.9 percent of total project cost). The estimated economic internal rate of return at appraisal is 15.23 percent.

Area

The project area, covering an estimated 25,825 hectares, lies to the northwest of the Gulf of Tadjourah and extends northwest from the Day Forest towards Lake Assol. The project area has been defined to include the Day Forest and all other sylvopastoral lands under the direct communal control of the Sekoh Aboussa tribe. In addition, the project area includes an extensive area of untapped potential for grazing, known as the Mak'arrassou, which is under the informal control of the Sekoh Aboussa but which is currently underutilized due to an inadequate distribution of water points. The project boundaries also include certain encampments of the Songo Goda and Bargak Adbara tribes that border the grazing lands of the Sekoh Aboussa.

The project area can be divided into three major geomorphological zones:

- Zone 1. The zone covers an area of about 1,790 hectares. Peaking at an altitude of 1,784 meters, this zone includes the Day Forest.

- Zone 2. A severely desertified zone of about 4,035 hectares covering plateaus and hills on the northwestern fringe of the Day Forest. Altitudes range from 900 to 1,400 meters.

- Zone 3. Covering 20,000 hectares, this zone consists of an extremely rugged topographical unit quite different from the other two zones. Altitude varies between 500 to 1,200 meters.

The climate is tropical semiarid to arid characterized by irregular inter- and intra-annual rainfall, high temperatures, and high potential evapotranspiration. Zone 1, lying within the 300 millimeters isohyet, receives the highest rainfall in the country. Zone 2 lies between the 300 millimeters and 250 millimeters isohyets, while Zone 3 lies between the 250 millimeters and 200 millimeters isohyets. In

Zone 3, 75 percent of rainfall is concentrated in the hot season.

The brown tropical soils and fluvisols found in the area offer some potential for pastoral productivity if properly managed, but are extremely susceptible to erosion in the absence of adequate vegetative cover.

Due to high temperatures, low and uneven rainfall, sparse vegetative cover, and the fissured nature of the bedrock, water is an extremely scarce resource.

Land Use

With certain exceptions, rural land in Djibouti is *de jure* property of the state. This land is *de facto* under the collective control of the tribes and clans who occupy the land. These *de facto* land rights are granted by the traditional authorities and are restricted to usufruct.

Pastoralism is the predominant activity in the project zone. The principal sylvopastoral territory utilized by the Sekoh Aboussa tribe consists of the Day Forest and its fringes, an intermediate zone (Zone 2) and the Mak'arrassou (Zone 3). The Day Forest is under the control of three lineages of the Sekoh Aboussa, while the intermediate zone is divided into several parcels each under the control of one of the five lineages of the Sekoh Aboussa. With the exception of a small portion of the Mak'arrassou under the direct control of one of the Sekoh Aboussa lineages, the Mak'arrassou is an open-access territory shared with other tribes—notably the Songo Goda. However, the Sekoh Aboussa lineages exercise a preeminence over a portion of the open-access Mak'arrassou that is included within the project boundaries and would exercise a right over at least 30 percent of available pasture. This area is shared with those Songo Goda who reside within the project boundaries, as well as with approximately 1,300 Songo Goda based outside the project area.

The territory directly available to the Sekoh Aboussa is not sufficient to support their livestock throughout the year, especially because the current configuration of livestock water points does not allow efficient use of existing resources. Access agreements with other tribes allow the Sekoh Aboussa to transhume to other zones, essentially in the vicinity of

Lake Allol and Lake Assal as well as in Ethiopia. However, transhumance is becoming less frequent as the population shifts towards a sedentarized way of life. As an outcome of this, the Sekoh Aboussa increasingly provide their herds with supplementary feed to cover fodder deficits.

In recognition of the central role that the Day Forest plays in their lives, the three Sekoh Aboussa lineages that control the forest subject its use to strict management. Only dead trees are allowed to be cut. All livestock are excluded during certain periods. In periods when access is allowed, only cattle and some camels are permitted to graze within the forest. Under traditional rules, any animals found in contravention of these principles are slaughtered. In the intermediate zone, where each lineage controls a specific grazing area, all animals are allowed to graze, although cattle are given priority over other animals.

In years of average rainfall, the sylvopastoral management regime is strict, with each lineage exercising full control over its pastoral and sylvopastoral resources. In years of drought, a controlled relaxation of grazing rules is effected to ensure that livestock belonging to the five lineages of the Sekoh Aboussa are safeguarded. Under special circumstances and subject to the explicit consent of the Sekoh Aboussa, other tribes are allowed access to the Sekoh Aboussa pasture lands. At the same time, the dearth of water points within the area controlled by the Sekoh Aboussa renders the tribe dependent on sources of water outside the area of their control.

The pastoral management strategy in dry years consists of forced transhumance outside the project area, supplementation of lactating females and calves, and intensive tree lopping in the forest and its fringes. While the fodder balance is precariously maintained through these coping strategies, a significant pasture resource (in the pastoral facies *Acacia mellifera, Rhigozum somalense, Acacia ehrenbergiana* remains underexploited in the Mak'arrassou due to the lack of water points. The rational exploitation of this resource could provide the Sekoh Aboussa with more than 1,700 metric tons of dry matter units (DM) per year instead of the 388 tons currently provided. An additional

1,906 metric tons of dry matter per year would be available for the livestock of the Songo Goda. In the context of inevitable sedentarization, this resource takes on a critical importance.

Target Group: Income and Economic Activities

The project target group consists of approximately 3,700 seminomadic pastoralists who rank among the most disadvantaged in Djibouti. Per capita income has been estimated to lie in the region of US$160 or 34 percent of gross national product (GNP) per capita (US$475). Ninety-three percent of the target population have a per capita income below US$200, while the remainder fall below US$250.

The population is dependent on several sources of livelihood. A significant source of income is the caravan trade with Ethiopia (40 percent), although the raison d'etre for the trade appears to lie at least partly in the provision of supplementary feed for livestock. Livestock provides a third of revenues, while salaries and pensions contribute less than a quarter. The remainder is made up of remittances from relatives living in Djibouti City.

Income from Livestock

Livestock sales are infrequent and take place primarily to meet contingencies. Because there is currently no livestock market in the vicinity of the Day, the animals are taken to the district capital or as far as Djibouti City, with resultant loss of weight and quality. As a result, prices received are relatively low. Livestock are slaughtered mainly for funerals and religious festivals. Livestock income derives from sales and auto-consumption of milk and meat less supplementary feed used for lactating animals.

Income from Caravans

Caravans provide an important source of income for the population. Involving more than half the families in the zone, these caravans transport salt collected from Lake Assal to Ethiopia and return with cereals and other products. Although significant variations exist between lineages, caravans are mounted an average of seven times a year (the modal average is four caravans a year). It has been estimated that each caravan brings in an imputed net revenue of approximately 30,000 Djibouti francs (DJF) (US$170). However, a proportion of cereals acquired through caravans is used as supplementary feed for the livestock herd.

Income from Salaries and Pensions

In the project zone, forty-three persons have access to employment outside, while twenty heads of household receive pensions. Salaries are in the range of DJF 20,000 (US$113 per head of family) per month, while pensions are roughly half that figure.

Remittances from Outside the Project Area

Remittances from family members working in town or abroad provide an important source of revenue for the population. These can range from DJF15,000 to DJF50,000 per month. Approximately 119 families distributed across most of the encampments have members who work outside the area. In 45 percent of the cases, remittances are sent on a regular basis. Families without access to remittances are assisted collectively.

Description of Project

The rationale for the project lies in the current process of degradation threatening pastoral, forest, and water resources in the project area. In the absence of intervention, and in the context of an inexorable process of sedentarization, the current situation will deteriorate over time, and the natural resources on which the target group depend will no longer provide a means of subsistence.

The linchpin of the sylvopastoralism system practiced by the Sekoh Aboussa is the Day Forest, which is in the process of irreversible degeneration. The multifunctional role of the forest includes its use as a pastoral resource and as a source of fuelwood and minor forest products, its microclimatic functions, and its key role in the region's hydrological balance. The rationale for conserving the Day Forest lies both in its role as a supplier of goods and services to the population who immediately de-

pend on it and as a national heritage and international reserve of biodiversity.

The overall objective of the project is to alleviate the poverty of pastoralists who depend on the Day Forest and surrounding sylvospastoral areas while ensuring that these natural resources are managed in a sustainable way. The project would seek to achieve its objective through a strategy—encompassing economic, environmental, and social elements—that would set in place the conditions for sustainable management of the natural resource base and relieve pressure on the Day Forest and assist its regeneration by:

- Strengthening the capacity of traditional natural resource management institutions

- Enabling a more balanced utilization of overexploited and under-exploited sylvopastoral resources through the strategic siting of livestock water points and through measures to increase the productivity of sylvopastoral resources and the livestock that they can sustain

- Meeting the immediate water-related needs of the population to relieve the burden on women and to foster cooperation between the beneficiaries and the project

- Diversifying the range of income-generating opportunities available to the target group to relieve some of the pressure on the resource base and to increase the viability of rural life

In order to achieve project objectives through the strategy outlined above, the following components were chosen, in consultation with the beneficiaries, for implementation over seven years. The components would be implemented in a phased manner to allow adjustments in response to the findings of a midterm evaluation, the changing needs of beneficiaries, and the evolution of environmental changes.

Sylvopastoral Management Activities

This component includes the progressive introduction of a system of deferred grazing, eventually involving 24,400 hectares; the creation of 750 hectares of permanent pasture; the establishment of 400 hectares of forage plantation; the introduction of improved tree-lopping practices on 200 hectares; and livestock support activities.

Forest Conservation and Regeneration

The project would undertake various actions to support the conservation and regeneration of the Day Forest. The project would promote both artificial and assisted regeneration of *Juniper procera* on various sites in the Day Forest (50 hectares). Windbreaks around the livestock water points would be planted in addition to the planting of 86 hectares of community woodlots.

Water Development Component

The project would provide support to the beneficiaries for the construction of thirty-nine drinking water storage tanks and twenty-five livestock water points. The water points form an integral part of the sylvopastoral management strategy to reduce pressure on the Forest resources.

Soil and Water Conservation

The project would support soil and water conservation (SWC) activities aimed at enhancing the productivity of pasture resources and maintaining the life of water-related infrastructure. SWC measures (stone bunding, water harvesting, terracing, and gully plugging) would be carried out in an area of 900 hectares.

Diversification of Income-generating Activities

The project would support income-generating activities on a pilot basis as a means of diversifying income opportunities. Charcoal production using excess deadwood threatening the forest would be supported, and provisions have been made to promote woodcarving, aviculture, and apiculture.

Project Management Unit and Institutional Support

A Project Management Unit would be created. The project would provide a core of locally and internationally recruited staff, housing, vehicles, training, and monitoring and evaluation (M&E) support. Given the sensitive nature of the project, provisions have been made for a comprehensive M&E system.

Economic Analysis

The economic analysis of the project was projected out over a time horizon of thirty years. Total economic costs and benefits streams are shown in Table 6-1 together with the net benefit stream. For ease of reference, all costs have been aggregated as either investment or recurrent costs. The net present value (NPV) and economic internal rate of return (EIRR) were calculated on the basis of the net benefit stream presented in Table 6-1. The EIRR is estimated at 15.23 percent while the NPV amounts to DJF295,488,200 at a discount rate of 10 percent which reflects the opportunity cost of capital (OCC) in Djibouti.

Quantification and Valuation of Costs

Financial Costs

The financial costs of the project are shown in Table 6-2. The project costs were estimated over the seven years of project life using 1992 (January) as Project Year 1. The exchange rate prevailing at appraisal of DJF177 per US$1 or DJF1 per US$.0056 was applied in the costing.

In conformity with Government of Djibouti practice, the project would benefit from duty-free import of goods and equipment. Only taxes on local salaries and locally purchased goods and services were therefore taken into account in the financial costing. All imported goods were valued at c.i.f. (cost, insurance, and freight)-Djibouti prices obtaining at April 1991 (appraisal), taking into account local transportation costs where relevant.

Because of the relatively open nature of the Djibouti economy and the fact that the DJF is tied to the U.S. dollar, local inflation follows the rate of inflation of Djibouti's principal trading partners, in particular the United States. The local and international inflation rate was estimated at 4.0 percent for the first three years of the project and at 4.5 percent for the last four years. These assumptions were used in estimating price contingencies, with the exception of the salaries of locally and inter-

Table 6-1: Economic Cost and Benefit Streams of Project over Time Horizon of 30 Years

(thousands of Djibouti francs)

Year	1	2	3	4	5	6	7	8	9
Costs									
Investment cost	197,196.00	88,146.00	83,041.00	59,477.00	36,936.00	22,062.00	10,531.00	-	-
Recurrent costs-project	25,164.00	29,240.00	31,520.00	-27,321.00	28,312.00	27,537.00	16,639.00	2,033.00	2,033.00
Total cost	222,360.00	117,386.00	114,561.00	86,798.00	65,248.00	49,599.00	27,170.00	2,033.00	2,033.00
Economic benefits									
Forage production	-42.00	47.00	274.00	539.00	970.00	1,674.00	2,627.00	3,407.00	4,018.00
Price forage	25.00	25.00	25.00	25.00	25.00	25.00	25.00	25.00	25.00
Forage production benefit	-1,050.00	1,175.00	6,850.00	13,475.00	24,250.00	41,850.00	65,675.00	85,175.00	100,450.00
Avoidance of fodder loss	1,227.50	2,455.00	3,682.50	4,910.00	6,137.50	7,365.00	8,592.50	9,820.00	11,047.50
Food production benefit	-	725.00	1,750.00	2,775.00	3,175.00	3,535.00	3,535.00	3,535.00	3,535.00
Charcoal production benefit	7,560.00	14,840.00	14,840.00	7,560.00	7,560.00	7,560.00	7,560.00	7,155.00	7,155.00
Net benefit beebreeding	-	347.00	480.00	1,231.00	1,796.00	2,420.00	2,580.00	2,580.00	2,580.00
Net benefits poultry	-	94.50	154.50	214.50	274.50	334.50	334.50	334.50	334.50
Net benefit woodcraft	320.00	820.00	1,543.00	2,425.00	2,977.00	3,545.00	3,545.00	2,941.00	2,941.00
Total benefit	8,057.50	20,456.50	29,300.00	32,590.50	46,170.00	66,609.50	91,822.00	111,540.50	128,043.00
Total net benefit	-214,302.50	-96,929.50	-85,261.00	-54,207.50	-19,078.00	17,010.50	64,652.00	109,507.50	126,010.00

Table 6-1: Economic Cost and Benefit Streams of Project over Time Horizon of 30 Years
(thousands of Djibouti francs)
Cont'd

Year	10	11	12	13	14-15	16	17-30
Costs							
Investment cost	2,400.00	-	-	2,400.00	-	2,400.00	-
Recurrent costs-project	2,033.00	2,033.00	2,033.00	2,033.00	2,033.00	2,033.00	2,033.00
Total cost	4,433.00	2,033.00	2,033.00	4,433.00	2,033.00	4433.00	2,033.00
Economic benefits							
Forage production	4,381.00	4,680.00	4,849.00	4,851.00	4,851.00	4,851.00	4,851.00
Price forage	25.00	25.00	25.00	25.00	25.00	25.00	25.00
Forage production benefit	109,525.00	117,000.00	121,225.00	121,275.00	121,275.00	121,275.00	121,275.00
Avoidance of fodder loss	12,275.00	12,275.00	12,275.00	12,275.00	12,275.00	12,275.00	12,275.00
Food production benefit	3,535.00	3,535.00	3,535.00	3,535.00	3,535.00	3,535.00	3,535.00
Charcoal production benefit	7,155.00	7,155.00	7,155.00	7,155.00	7,155.00	7,155.00	7,155.00
Net benefit beebreeding	2,580.00	2,580.00	2,580.00	2,580.00	2,580.00	2,580.00	2,580.00
Net benefits poultry	334.50	334.50	334.50	334.50	334.50	334.50	334.50
Net benefit woodcraft	2,941.00	3,291.00	3,291.00	3,291.00	3,291.00	3,291.00	3,291.00
Total benefit	138,345.50	146,170.50	150,395.50	150,445.50	158,445.50	150,445.50	150,445.50
Total net benefit	133,912.50	144,137.50	148,362.50	146,012.50	148,412.50	146,012.50	148,412.50

Table 6-2: Financial Costs by Project Component (thousands of Djibouti francs)

	Sylvo-pastoral management	Soil and water conservation	Hydraul-ic infra-structure	Income diversi-fication	Project manage-ment unit	Total	Physical contingencies		Price contingencies	
							Percent	Amount	Percent	Amount
I. Investment cost										
A. Civil works										
1. Housing	0.0	0.0	0.0	0.0	13,275.0	13,275.0	10.0	1,327.5	2.2	292.0
2. Administrative buildings	0.0	0.0	0.0	0.0	15,930.0	15,930.0	10.0	1,593.0	2.2	350.5
3. Other buildings	0.0	0.0	0.0	5,310.0	24,780.0	30,090.0	10.0	3,009.0	3.0	900.3
Subtotal	0.0	0.0	0.0	5,310.0	53,985.0	59,295.0	10.0	5,929.5	2.6	1,542.8
B. Equipment and vehicles										
1. Agricultural equipment	12,892.0	0.0	0.0	0.0	0.0	12,892.0	0.0	0.0	2.0	257.8
2. Hydraulic equipment	0.0	0.0	34,120.0	0.0	0.0	34,120.0	8.3	2,832.0	2.2	739.0
3. Vehicles	0.0	0.0	14,672.0	0.0	27,781.0	42,453.0	0.0	0.0	7.7	3,270.7
4. Office equipment	0.0	0.0	0.0	0.0	7,844.0	7,844.0	3.8	300.0	2.1	162.9
5. Other equipment	990.0	2,755.5	0.0	4,641.5	0.0	8,387.0	0.6	50.0	3.1	257.7
Subtotal	13,882.0	2,755.5	48,792.0	4,641.5	35,625.0	105,696.0	3.0	3,182.0	4.4	4,685.1
C. Inputs and services										
1. Raw materials and tools	0.0	0.0	43,611.7	0.0	0.0	43,611.7	0.0	0.0	13.6	5,936.3
2. Seeds and plants	28,542.0	0.0	0.0	0.0	0.0	28,842.0	0.0	0.0	16.6	4,775.3
3. Qualified manpower	0.0	0.0	168.0	0.0	0.0	168.0	10.0	16.8	8.1	13.7
4. Food rations	29,152.0	23,540.0	3,000.0	0.0	0.0	55,692.0	0.0	0.0	14.5	8,075.0
5. Compensation indemnity	17,343.1	0.0	0.0	0.0	0.0	17,943.1	0.0	0.0	18.1	3,246.2
Subtotal	75,937.1	23,540.0	45,779.7	0.0	0.0	146,256.8	0.0	16.8	15.1	22,046.5
D. Technical assistance										
1. Technical assistance	21,215.2	0.0	21,215.2	15,580.0	96,000.0	154,010.4	0.0	0.0	7.4	11,457.6
2. Training	0.0	0.0	0.0	0.0	1,416.0	1,416.0	0.0	0.0	2.0	28.3
3. R&D and M&E support	0.0	0.0	0.0	0.0	6,915.0	6,915.0	0.0	0.0	9.1	626.1
Subtotal	21,215.2	0.0	21,215.2	15,580.0	104,331.0	162,341.4	0.0	0.0	7.5	12,112.0
Total investment costs	111,034.3	26,295.5	116,786.9	25,531.5	193,941.0	473,589.3	1.9	9,128.3	8.5	40,389.5
II. Recurrent costs										
A. Civil works maintenance										
1. Buildings	0.0	0.0	0.0	0.0	16,195.5	16,195.5	0.0	0.0	18.1	2,927.9
B. Equipment maintenance										
1. Agricultural equipment	19,020.4	0.0	0.0	0.0	0.0	19,020.4	0.0	0.0	15.8	3,001.7
2. Hydraulic equipment	0.0	0.0	25,117.4	0.0	0.0	25,117.4	0.0	0.0	15.5	3,895.4
3. Vehicles	0.0	0.0	9,933.0	0.0	19,446.7	29,379.7	6.6	1,944.7	13.5	3,961.2
4. Other equipment	0.0	0.0	0.0	0.0	4,200.0	4,200.0	0.0	0.0	15.8	662.8
Subtotal	19,020.4	0.0	35,050.4	0.0	23,646.7	77,717.5	2.5	1,944.7	14.8	11,521.1
C. Personnel salaries and fees	30,826.0	0.0	40,368.0	0.0	41,160.0	112,356.0	0.0	0.0	8.7	9,745.9
D. Other operating costs	0.0	0.0	0.0	1,447.5	13,020.0	14,467.5	9.0	1,302.0	16.6	2,400.7
Total recurrent costs	49,848.4	0.0	75,418.4	1,447.5	94,022.2	220,736.5	1.5	3,246.7	12.0	26,595.6
Total baseline costs	160,882.7	26,295.5	192,205.3	26,979.0	287,963.2	694,325.8	1.8	12,375.0	9.6	66,985.1
Physical contingencies	50.0	0.0	2,848.8	531.0	8,945.2	12,375.0				
Price contingencies	21,193.3	3,287.1	18,578.2	1,869.7	22,056.9	66,985.1	1.0	639.3		
Total project costs	182,126.0	29,582.6	213,632.2	29,379.7	318,965.3	773,685.8	1.7	13,014.3	8.7	66,985.1
Taxes	11,280.1	390.0	16,573.3	0.0	15,855.8	44,099.2	1.4	633.4		
Foreign exchange	118,963.9	29,192.6	133,691.8	25,868.2	206,434.4	514,150.8	1.6	8,198.8		

Values scaled by 1000.0.

nationally recruited staff, to which an indexation of 2.5 percent was applied.

Physical contingencies of 10 percent were applied to buildings, to equipment and inputs, and to operating and maintenance costs for equipment.

The total cost of the project, including physical and price contingencies, was estimated at US$4,365 million or DJF772,072 million. The percentage of costs in foreign exchange is in the order of 66.4 percent. Investment costs of US$2,950 million represent 67.6 percent of total project cost, while recurrent costs of US$1,415 million constitute 32.4 percent of total project cost.

Total project cost is distributed among components as follows: project management unit, 41.3 percent; water development component, 27.6 percent; sylvopastoral management component, 23.4 percent; soil and water conservation component, 3.8 percent; and pilot income-generating activities component, 3.8 percent.

Economic Costs

Economic costs were estimated in constant prices (that is, net of inflation) and were based on financial costs net of taxes and transfers. All quantified economic costs of the project were included in the analysis, regardless of whether they were grant-financed. The valuation of certain economic costs that require further elaboration are discussed below.

Cost of Unskilled Labor. In the financial analysis, the cost of beneficiary labor was taken to be equivalent to the cost of WFP rations provided under the project's food-for-work activities. In the economic analysis, beneficiary labor both under the food-for-work scheme and for other activities was valued on the basis of the local population being willing to provide labor in return for WFP food rations equivalent to DJF400. This can be considered a lower bound estimate of the opportunity cost of their labor, because the experience under pre-investment projects in the area indicates that beneficiaries only engage in food-for-work activities when they perceive the benefits of the work as accruing indirectly or directly to them (for example, soil and water conservation for productivity gain). Thus, it is clear that the

value of the food ration is an underestimate of their opportunity cost of labor. To compensate for this, the economic price of labor was taken to be DJF500 (A conversion factor of 1.25 was applied.)

Cost of Skilled Labor. The scarcity of skilled labor in the Djibouti market implies that its financial price reflects its opportunity cost adequately. Skilled labor was therefore valued at financial prices. However, an exception was made in the case of masons in the project area, whose economic cost was estimated at 50 percent of the financial cost to reflect the fact that this category of labor faces significant underemployment.

Cost of Pasture Resting. The deferred grazing scheme and the forage plantations to be promoted under the project generate an opportunity cost to pastoralists in the form of land taken out of pastoral production in the early years of project life. The project will compensate pastoralists for this loss. While the costs of resting pasture as part of the rotational grazing scheme should be included in the economic analysis, it would constitute double-counting if this value were to be included as a separate cost in addition to the compensation payments already included under the costs ascribed to the sylvopastoral component. Because the costs of compensation reflect the economic loss from pasture resting, no additional economic cost has been included in the cost stream. Compensation in fodder units (FU) per hectare is shown in Table 6-3.

Quantification and Valuation of Economic Benefits

Forage Benefits

As a result of the project's pastoral and sylvospastoral management activities, the project would increase annual forage availability by 113 percent from 4,264 tons in the base year to 9,115 tons at full development. These figures represent "accessible" forage only.

In addition to incremental fodder produced through planting and rangeland management, benefits would accrue in the form of costs of pasture degradation avoided. These benefits would arise from the prevention of the

Table 6-3: Compensation for Pasture Resting

Activity	Year						
	1	2	3	4	5	6	7
Prairie establishment	400	0	0	0	0	0	0
Forage plantation	100	100	50	0	0	0	0
Juniper regeneration	500	500	500	400	300	100	0
Re-afforestation	400	400	300	200	100	0	0

degeneration of Day Forest resources and surrounding pastoral vegetation.

Surrogate Market Technique. Because no market for forage exists, prices prevailing in a surrogate market were used to impute its economic value. Because pastoralists are increasingly relying on supplementary feed to cover fodder deficits, sorghum can be considered a substitute for forage. As such, the price of sorghum feed equivalent can be used as a surrogate for the price of forage.

The price of sorghum feed equivalent was calculated in the following manner: As a first step, the c.i.f. price of sorghum was computed.

- Gulf Port US$96 per ton
- Freight US$100 per ton
- Insurance US$5 per ton
- c.i.f. price US$201 per ton

When local transport costs from Djibouti port to the project area of DJF5,337 per ton are added to the c.i.f. price of sorghum, this results in a price of DJF41 per kilogram. In order to translate this into the price of fodder equivalent, a coefficient of 1.09 was applied, resulting

in a price of DJF37.6 per kilogram. This in turn was converted into dry matter units (DM) using a conversion factor of 2, resulting in a price of DJF18.8 per kilogram of dry matter. Taking the deficit in digestible protein of sorghum (evaluated at 30 percent of the value of its substitute) into account, the price of sorghum equivalent of 1 kilogram of dry matter was estimated to be DJF24.5.

Change in Production Approach. In order to confirm the result provided by the surrogate market technique, another valuation technique, known as the "change in production" approach, was also applied. Under this approach, the valuation of incremental dry matter was based on fodder conversion to milk and meat production. Because of data constraints and to ensure a conservative estimate, the value of hides was excluded and technical production parameters prevailing in the "without project" situation were applied (in other words, projected improvements in the quality and quantity of the herd in the with project situation were not taken into account).

Table 6-4: Livestock Production Parameters

Species	Meat (kilograms)	Milk (liters)
Sheep	4.7	30
Cattle	16.0	400
Goats	6.6	40
Camels	14.0	600
Donkeys	0.0	0

Table 6-5: Sekoh Aboussa Livestock and Feed Requirements

Type	Number	Sorghum feed equivalent	Tropical livestock standard units	Metric tons of dry matter per year
Cattle	1,324	0.73	966.52	2,206.51
Sheep	1,244	0.12	149.28	349.51
Goats	3,331	0.12	399.72	911.75
Camels	472	1.00	472.00	1,076.75
Donkeys	218	0.40	87.20	198.34
Total	6,589		2,074.72	4,734.34

Table 6-6: Evolution of Pastoral Facies without Project

	Year 0		Year 10	
	Area in hectares	Production in tons of dry matter	Area in hectares	Production in tons of dry matter
Jun. procera	820	873	0	0
Acacia etbaica	1,364	812	1,502	894
Aizoon canariense	5,164	2,272	5,846	2,572
Acacia mellifera	6,596	132	6,596	132
A.mell.and others	7,984	120	7,984	120
Rhingo. somalense	2,300	23	2,300	23
A. cherbergiana	1,424	32	142	432
Total	25,642	4,264	25,652	3,733

Table 6-7: Incremental Forage due to Soil and Water Conservation Activities

(thousands of fodder units)

Year	1	2	3	4	5	6	7	8	9	10	11-30
Benefit	0	0	4.5	23.5	51.8	85.1	125.6	146.8	155	160	165.3

Milk and meat production parameters for cattle, camels, goats, and sheep in the project area were derived from available estimates and from the information generated by the project preparation and appraisal missions. The estimated livestock production parameters are shown in Table 6-4.

Data on the size and composition of the herd were collected during pre-investment activities and during preparation and appraisal missions. Herd size and composition for Sekoh Aboussa livestock are shown in Table 6-5.

The value of meat production was calculated by applying the observed price of meat to total meat production of the herd. A more circuitous route was required to derive the total value of milk production. On the basis of an exhaustive household survey carried out at the appraisal stage, the proportion of lactating females was established for each type of livestock. The total number of lactating females of each type of animal was multiplied by the milk production parameter for each respective type of animal. Total milk production was valued at the observed market price of milk of DJF150.

The total value of milk and meat production was estimated to be DJF56,500 million. On the basis of estimated fodder requirements of the herd in kilograms of dry matter (calculated by converting the herd into standard tropical livestock units), the total fodder requirements of the herd were established (see Table 6-5).

The value of a kilogram of dry matter was derived by dividing the value of total meat and milk production by total energy requirements of the herd. This results in an imputed price of DJF12 per kilogram of dry matter. This can be considered a lower bound estimate because the value of hides, the "psychic value" of owning livestock, and other values have not been reflected in the imputed price. In addition, no provision was made for the fact that in the "with project" scenario, the structure and productivity of the herd would improve as a result of the project's livestock support activities.

Valuation of Incremental Production Due to Project. The price of using the surrogate market technique was considered more robust and was applied to incremental forage production in the economic analysis. However, the sensitivity of the EIRR to changes in the value of forage was explored and presented as part of the analysis (please see section on "Uncertainty and Sensitivity Analysis" below).

A basic assumption used in the analysis is that the entire incremental production of forage would be put to productive use. The increase in forage availability due to the project would allow the current rate of increase in Sekoh Aboussa livestock numbers of 3 percent per year to continue, while maintaining a buffer of 30 percent for dry years. Much of the surplus forage available beginning in Project Year 6 would accrue in the Mak'arrassou portion of the project area, where in good years the Sekoh Aboussa allow other tribes to graze under reciprocal arrangements that enable Sekoh Aboussa cattle to graze elsewhere in years when productivity is low in Sekoh Abboussa territory. A certain amount of tolerance for neighboring tribes is also evident in the non-forest grazing areas directly under the control of each of the five Sekoh Aboussa lineages. Accordingly, it was considered reasonable to assume that the forage would be put to productive use.

Benefits in the Form of Forage Loss Avoided

Because the "with and without project" framework forms the basis for the economic analysis, production changes expected to take place in the "without" project scenario should be reflected in the estimation of the net benefits generated by the project. In the "without project" situation, the pastoral resources are expected to degrade over time. In particular, relatively productive species are expected to be replaced by less productive varieties. Notably, the pastoral species of the Day Forest, which represent a pastoral resource of high value if managed properly, are projected to disappear in ten years under the current pastoral management regime. The overall change in the composition and productivity of vegetative cover is given in Table 6-6.

As can be seen from Table 6-6, the reductions in pasture production expressed in metric tons of dry matter per year are quite substantial, representing a decrease of 11.5 percent over ten years. As costs are benefits lost, and benefits are costs avoided, this loss of production was included in the economic analysis as a benefit of the "with project" situation.

Benefits of Soil and Water Conservation

The soil and water conservation activities to be promoted under the project are geared towards increasing forage production and extending the life of livestock water ponds. The soil and water conservation activities will increase rangeland productivity through (a) maintaining soil depth and quality, (b) increasing water retention and soil moisture, and (c) controlling the severe gullying currently taking place.

The incremental forage production in fodder units due to soil and water conservation activities is shown in Table 6-7.

Avoidance of Double Counting. The forage production benefits of soil and water conservation are an integral part of the projected incremental forage production estimates. In order to avoid double counting, these benefits, already subsumed under forage production benefits, were not included as a separate benefit stream in the economic analysis.

The anti-erosion treatment of the 5-hectare catchments of livestock water ponds would reduce siltation by at least 50 percent. This reduction in siltation rates would result in a saving of 100 man-days of maintenance requirements for all livestock water ponds. This benefit was fully reflected in the estimation of annual operating and maintenance costs for the livestock water ponds. It would constitute double-counting if these savings in labor were to be reflected in the economic analysis as a separate benefit.

Downstream Externalities. Soil and water conservation, in addition to increasing on-site productivity, would also generate positive economic externalities through the mitigation of flooding downstream. Floods have occurred with increasing frequency in recent years, causing severe damage to infrastructure and to agriculture. The benefits of mitigating flood damage were not calculated due to the absence of reliable data on downstream farm production and maintenance costs of roads. Data constraints of this nature constitute the norm for project analysis in marginal areas for which secondary sources of data are rarely available.

Benefits of Water Development

The scarcity of drinking water is a severe constraint in the project area and constitutes the main preoccupation of the local population. The drinking water component of the project would provide important social and health benefits that are difficult to value in the absence of epidemiological studies.

Opportunity Cost of Labor Approach. In principle, the economic value of the drinking water benefits could have been imputed using the opportunity cost of time approach. Under this approach, the savings in time resulting from availability of water would have been valued on the basis of the opportunity cost of time. This was not done due to information constraints. Nevertheless, it is clear that a significant amount of time is spent collecting water from distant wells or springs. In the case of many encampments, it was ascertained that women require an entire day to make one round trip to a well. In several cases, women spend up to two days per week on this task. However, for the valuation exercise to have had credibility an in-depth survey of household water collection activities would have been required.

Avoidance of Double-counting. In order to avoid double counting, the benefits of livestock water ponds were not included as a separate benefit stream in the economic analysis. The ponds are an integral part of the rangeland management strategy of reducing pressure on the Day Forest and optimizing the seasonal and spatial distribution of grazing pressure. These benefits are therefore subsumed within the estimates of incremental forage availability resulting from project activities.

Benefits of Wood and Charcoal Production

Direct Market Price Valuation of Wood Production. While the Day Forest does provide a source of wood for certain lineages of the Sekoh Aboussa tribe, there is a need to take a long-term view providing for alternative sources of wood supply. The plantations and forest regeneration activities would result in an annual incremental wood production of 145 cubic meters in Project Year 2, and 350, 555, and 635 cubic meters respectively in the succeeding three years, stabilizing at 707 cubic meters from Project Year 6 onwards. Altogether, wood production would increase by 11,760 cubic meters during project life.

While most of the wood produced would be autoconsumed, the observed market price for wood of DJF5,000 per cubic meter was used for the analysis. The market price of wood reflects primarily the opportunity cost of labor in collecting and transporting wood. While the market price might overestimate the direct user value of wood of encampments close to the forest, it is a reasonable approximation if one considers that for many of the encampments removed from the forest, the availability of fuelwood is an important constraint. This is especially the case for lineages that do not have access rights to the forest. It is primarily in the vicinity of encampments removed from the forest, where fuelwood collection takes place once every two or three days and can occupy an entire day, that the project-supported woodlots would be established. Furthermore, the value of the environmental service functions provided by the trees, which can only be quantified—even in physical terms—with difficulty, is likely to be

Table 6-8: Effect of Time Horizon on EIRR

Time horizon (years)	EIRR (percent)
10	1.84
15	11.05
20	13.82
30	15.24
50	15.57

substantial but is not reflected in the market price.

Other Valuation Approaches. Fuelwood could also have been valued, using the surrogate market technique, by applying the price of kerosene to fuelwood, because kerosene appears to be the closest energy substitute in the project area. However, it was considered that this would overestimate the benefits considerably. Alternatively, the opportunity-cost-of-time approach could have been applied. However, the costs of generating the necessary data were deemed not to justify any incremental accuracy that might have been achieved in the valuation.

Market Price Valuation of Charcoal Production. An important factor contributing to the degradation of the Juniper stand is the presence of the fungus *Armillaria mellea*. The significant amount of deadwood littering the forest contributes to the spread of this parasitical fungus. Total deadwood amounts to 30,000 cubic meters. Of this amount, approximately 5,650 cubic meters would be converted into charcoal. The improved charcoal methods to be extended under the project would allow a net annual gain over wood sales of US$35,000 in Project Years 1, 4, and onwards, with a net gain of US$70,000 in Project Years 2 and 3. These values were based on an estimated charcoal conversion factor of 20 percent and an observed market price for charcoal of DJF200 per kilogram.

Benefits of Income-generating Activities

In order to broaden the income base and provide a more diversified portfolio of income-generating activities for the local population, the project would support a number of pilot income-generating activities. These activities would generate tangible financial and economic benefits. Inputs and products of the artisanal woodcraft, apiculture, and aviculture activities were valued at market prices. Labor costs were valued at the shadow price of unskilled labor. The net benefits of these activities (net of operation costs and labor costs) are shown in Table 6-1.

Other Benefits

In addition to the benefits included in the analysis, the project would generate benefits that are not readily quantifiable in physical, let alone economic, terms. In addition, benefits accruing to future generations have not been taken into account. These benefits can be categorized as user benefits and nonuser benefits.

User Benefits. The Day Forest provides both productive and service functions. While some of its productive functions are reflected in the economic analysis, its service functions are more difficult to identify and to quantify in physical terms and value. In addition, some of the environmental service functions translate into production benefits outside the project boundaries.

Table 6-9: Value of Forage and the EIRR

Valuation method	Price (Djibouti francs)	EIRR (percent)
Surrogate market method	25.0	15.23
Productivity method	12.0	08.77
Average	18.5	12.29

The likely presence of such externalities indicates that the boundaries of analysis for project appraisal should be extended. While there are reasons to believe that the loss of forest cover would upset the hydrological balance in the surrounding areas and reduce groundwater availability downstream, the precise cause-and-effect relationships would be difficult to specify. The prime constraints include the lack of empirical data on the rate of infiltration in the forest area and the difficulty in modelling groundwater recharge in the extremely fissured basaltic substratum characterizing the region. Had it been possible or cost-effective to generate the necessary data in the context of the normal project cycle, it might have been possible to include a proportion of the net value of current production in surrounding areas, which depend on water sources originating in the forest, as a benefit in the form of costs avoided from forest degeneration and the loss of vegetative cover in surrounding rangelands.

Other uses of the forest that were not valued include its role as a recreational resource for residents of Djibouti town as well as international tourists. The travel cost method (TCM) or contingency valuation method (CVM) might have been applied to value these benefits. The TCM approach, entails deriving a demand curve for a resource (generally a recreational resource) using variable travel costs as a surrogate for entrance fees, in order to estimate consumer's surplus.

Certain constraints militate against the application of TCM in this particular situation.

On an operational level, data on visitation rates are extremely patchy, although a limited survey has been carried out by the National Tourism Office. The year-long survey necessary for the proper application of the method was beyond the scope of project preparation activities. On a conceptual level, the approach would have been hampered by the fact that most visitors to the Day Forest begin their journey from Djibouti town. Accordingly, significant variations in travel cost do not occur, and therefore variable entrance costs could not have been simulated meaningfully to derive a demand curve. In the case of international tourists, sophisticated models would be required because of the multipurpose nature of visits to Djibouti.

In principle, the CVM approach could have been used to value the consumers' surplus accruing to recreational users of the forest. Although hampered by several inherent biases, CVM is particularly useful in situations where market data are lacking. However, this approach, like the TCM, is hampered by the surveying constraint and problems in defining the user group. Difficulties in its application for local users would have stemmed from the beneficiaries' lack of integration in markets, which would have hampered the proper functioning of any hypothetical market. Moreover, CVM has not achieved the necessary credibility for application in formal project appraisal.

Nonuser Benefits. Other benefits of protecting the Day Forest are in the form of nonuser benefits or so-called "intrinsic benefits." The existence value or bequest value of the

Table 6-10: Comparison of Dry Matter Productivity in Wet, Normal, and Dry Years

Vegetative cover	Area (hectares)			Productivity Kilograms of dry matter			Total production			Grazing rate (metric tons of dry matter)			Global production (metric tons of dry matter)		
	Wet	Normal	Dry	Wet	Normal	Dry	Wet	Normal	Dry	Wet	Normal	Dry	Wet	Normal	Dry
Jun. procera	820	820	820	2,070	1,775	1,410	1,697.4	1,455.5	1,156.2	0.60	0.60	0.80	1,018.4	873.3	925.0
Term br	na	na	304	na	na	1,100	na	na	334.4	na	na	.80	na	na	267.5
A. et baica	1,364	1,364	1,364	960	850	680	1,309.4	1,159.4	927.5	0.70	0.70	0.90	916.6	811.6	834.8
Alzoon ca	5,164	5,164	5,164	650	550	440	3,356.6	2,849.2	2,272.2	0.80	0.80	0.20	2,685.3	2,272.2	454.4
A. mellifera	6,596	6,596	6,596	460	400	320	3,034.2	2,638.4	2,110.7	0.05	0.05	0.05	151.7	131.9	105.5
A. mel/ others	7,984	7,984	7,984	340	300	240	2,714.6	2,395.2	1,916.2	0.05	0.05	0.05	135.7	119.8	95.8
Rhigo.som	2,300	2,300	2,300	240	200	160	552.0	460.0	368.0	0.50	0.05	0.05	27.6	23.0	18.4
A.Ehren.	1,424	1,424	1,424	520	450	360	740.5	6408	512.6	0.05	0.05	0.05	37.4	32.0	25.6
Total	25,656	25,652	25,956				13,404.6	11,589.5	9,597.8				4,972.4	4,263.8	2,724.1

preparation or during project implemen-
in the sensitivity analysis of this project,
cant of the ERR of changes in variables
as the imputed price of forage, the production of forage over time, the time horizon of

proaches would offer another significant constraint to their application.

Table 6-11: Production Scenarios and the EIRR

Production scenario	EIRR (percent)
Appraisal mission estimate	15.23
30 percent shortfall	12.90
Sigmoid production	15.00
Cyclical drought	14.70

Table 6-12: Without-project Scenario and the EIRR

Without-project scenario	EIRR (percent)
Degradation trend	15.23
Stable production	13.96

forest as a recognized national patrimony is an example of this. There is a also an option value (straddling the distinction between user and nonuser benefits) associated with maintaining the forest as a unique store of biodiversity. The irreversible loss of the forest is a major issue in this regard. However, techniques for the quantification of these relatively intangible values—including CVM—have not reached the stage where they can be considered appropriate the context of formal MFI (multilateral financial institution) project appraisal. The lack of familiarity of decisionmakers with these approaches would offer another significant constraint to their application.

Risk and Uncertainty and Sensitivity Analysis

An obvious means of addressing uncertainty in project appraisal is to invest in more information. However, this is not always possible or cost-effective in the course of the standard project cycle. In cases where uncertainty can be converted into risk, sensitivity analysis can demonstrate the effect of changes in basic assumptions governing the analysis. It can also serve to highlight variables that require closer scrutiny either in the course of further project preparation or during project implementation.

In the sensitivity analysis of this project, the effect on the EIRR of changes in variables such as the imputed price of forage, the production of forage over time, the time horizon of

Table 6-13: Sensitivity of EIRR to Changes in Total Costs and Total Benefits
(percent)

	Changes in total benefits	-10 percent	-20 percent	-50 percent
Changes in total costs	15.23	13.856	12.40	7.43
+10 percent	13.98	12.68	11.31	6.54
+20 percent	12.90	11.66	10.34	5.754
+50 percent	10.34	9.23	8.05	3.87

Table 14. Switching Values
(thousands of Djibouti francs)

Benefit stream	Appraisal present value	Switching present value	Percent change
Forage production	60,783.26	312,375.05	-48.61
Wood production	25,704.47	-269,783.73	-1,149.56
Charcoal production	80,907.38	-214,580.82	-365.22
Avoidance of loss	75,932.39	-219,555.81	-389.15
Apiculture	17,054.27	-278,433.94	-1,732.64
Aviculture	2,396.41	-293,091.80	-12,330.45
Woodcraft	24,008.23	-271,497.98	-1,230.78
Total benefits	833,866.41	538,378.21	-35.44
Total cost	538,378.21	833,866.41	54.88

analysis, and "without project" degradation trends were explored to offer the decisionmaker a better understanding of the economic justification for the project.

Sensitivity of the EIRR to the Time Horizon

Although the time horizon used for the economic analysis of many investment projects is often less than twenty years, in the case of this project it was extended to thirty years to capture some of the longer-term benefits of the project.

It can be seen in Table 6-8 that the choice of time horizon for this project can affect the EIRR for periods below thirty years. When the time horizon is extended beyond thirty years, the change in the EIRR is small. While this reflects the nature of the net benefit stream, it is more directly an outcome of the fact that present values of costs and benefits occurring after thirty years are considerably reduced at any positive discount rate.

It should be noted that extending the boundary of analysis in time reduces the credibility of "with and without" project projections. This must be weighed against the need to reflect benefits or costs accruing in the longer term.

Sensitivity of the EIRR to the Relative Price of Forage

In order to check the sensitivity of the internal rate of return to variations in the imputed price of forage, the EIRR was calculated under different price assumptions. The results of the sensitivity analysis are presented in Table 6-9 below.

It is clear that the EIRR is quite sensitive to the imputed price of forage. However, it should be noted that both the surrogate market technique and the productivity method, as applied in this analysis, underestimate the value of forage. This is because the imputed price only reflects the value of the vegetation as a productive resource and does not capture the environmental service value of the vegetative cover. Thus, a case can be made for choosing the higher rather than the lower estimates for the price of forage.

The case for choosing the higher estimate is further reinforced by the likelihood that the relative price of forage will increase over time. This prediction is based on the plausible assumption that the current dryland degradation trends threatening grazing resources in Djibouti will continue, diminishing opportunities for transhumance outside the project area.

Sensitivity of the EIRR to Changes in Forage Production Assumptions

The sensitivity of the EIRR to changes in assumptions concerning the magnitude and time profile of forage production was explored. The EIRR was calculated using three alternative forage production scenarios. The first scenario entails a 30 percent drop in annual forage production estimates, to simulate below-average rainfall conditions and/or failure to fully adopt the proposed sylvopastoral management activities (see Table 6-10 for forage production in dry, wet, and normal years). The second scenario entails a sigmoid production curve to simulate slow adoption of sylvospastoral management activities, which then accelerates over time before tapering off. The third scenario simulates the occurrence of droughts at five-year intervals. The results of the sensitivity analysis are presented in Table 6-11.

The EIRR is surprisingly robust in the face of plausible changes in the magnitude and time profile of forage production. It is clear, however, that grazing discipline would collapse in the event that severe and persistent drought occurs. Should this happen in the early years of the project, before buffer plantations mature and before the merits of pasture resting, and so forth, are demonstrated, it is likely that the success of the project would be severely jeopardized.

Sensitivity of the EIRR to Changes in Without-Project Assumptions

Forage production in the without-project situation is projected to decline over time. The sensitivity of the EIRR to changes in this assumption is shown in Table 6-12.

Table 6-15: Distribution of Income

Per capita income	Persons	Percent of total
US$200-250	167	7
US$150-200	249	10
US$100-150	1, 235	52
US$100 or less	627	26
Not available	106	5

Sensitivity of EIRR to Changes in Total Costs and Total Benefits Streams

The sensitivity of the EIRR to changes in total costs and total benefits is shown in Table 6-13. The EIRR is quite robust in the face of plausible changes in total benefits and total costs. Drastic increases of total costs or decreases in total benefits do affect the EIRR substantially, with the EIRR being slightly more sensitive to changes in the benefit stream. In the unlikely worst-case scenario with costs increasing by 50 percent and benefits decreasing by 50 percent, the project EIRR would be reduced to 3.87 percent.

Switching Values for Benefit and Cost Variables

The switching value of benefit streams and the total cost stream were calculated using a discount rate of 10 percent. At this discount rate the net present value (NPV) is DJF295,488.2. The results are presented in Table 6-14.

It is clear that forage production benefits constitute the critical benefit stream. Changes in this stream have the greatest impact on the economic viability of the project. At the same time, these benefits would have to fall by 48 percent for the project to be economically unattractive.

Fiscal Impact of Project

Djibouti's external debt outstanding and disbursed (DOD) increased from US$96 million in 1985 to US$163 million at the close of 1989. This rise, amounting to 40 percent of gross domestic product (GDP), is a result of heavy borrowing in the early 1980s to finance public investment projects. The 1991 state budget is an austerity budget, prepared in the context of the Gulf crisis, the closing of the border with Somalia, the collapse in trade with Ethiopia, and the devaluation of the dollar, which—given the fixed parity exchange rate between the Djibouti Franc (DJF) and the U.S. dollar—was fueling inflation. One operational outcome of the austerity plan has been that the government of the Republic of Djibouti is becoming extremely cautious in undertaking new development projects. It is increasingly seeking external grant financing for public investment.

In this context, the fiscal impact of the project takes on special importance. A key element in the project's strategy is the gradual strengthening of beneficiary institutions to allow a gradual devolution of project activities to the beneficiaries themselves, which would serve to reduce the fiscal burden on the government. The recurrent costs after project completion are quite low, amounting to DJF2,033,000 or US$11,485.

However, a characteristic of many environmentally focused projects in marginal areas is that the environmental improvements rarely generate significant cash flows or transfers.

The maintenance of the productivity of a marginal resource base translates—by definition—into marginal economic returns. Even where the economic benefits justify the costs of intervention, these benefits are in the form of gains in subsistence consumption while the costs are in the form of financial flows. Few positive financial cash flows to other sectors of the economy are involved. The imputed economic benefits of environmental improvement do not pay any bills. In this sense, these economic benefits are intangible. Accordingly, the borrowing governments are not in a position to recover costs and might be reluctant to borrow funds for such projects.

Projects that are economically desirable but are not attractive in terms of government cash flow are often grant-financed. In situations where the EIRR is unattractive because environmental benefits have not been valued, projects are also commonly grant-financed. However, in these cases it should be recognized that the presence of grant financing will not alter the EIRR. It will only alter the monetary rate of return to the government.

Income Distribution Effects

As can be seen from Table 6-15, income distribution reflects a modal average in the range of US$100-150. Within the project's overall target group, no explicit measures have been taken to target the poorest of the poor. The nature of this project militates against such an approach; targeting within the context of common property resource management is likely to weaken already fragile traditional management regimes. At the same time, as shown in the table, the entire group falls within the poorest category in the country and therefore meets IFAD's criteria for assistance.

Distribution of Project Benefits

The project's targeted beneficiaries can be divided into four groups. The first group consists of the entirety of the Sekoh Aboussa tribe, who would benefit from all of the project activities. The second group consists of five encampments of the Songo Goda tribe, which border the land controlled by the Sekoh Aboussa and would benefit directly from the construction of water tanks in their encampments

and the construction of livestock ponds in the Mak'arrassou. The third group consists of the population of the Bargak Adbara tribe in the encampment of Menguela, who would benefit from water tanks but whose livestock do not graze in the project area. The fourth group consists of approximately 1,300 additional members of the Songo Goda tribe, who would benefit directly from the creation of livestock water points in the Mak'arrassou. This latter group has access to drinking water from wells recharged from the Day Forest catchment and would not require water storage tanks.

In addition, a large group of nontargeted beneficiaries exist who would benefit from the project through the stabilization of vegetative cover in the project area. This stabilization would reduce soil erosion and environmental damage due to flooding that would otherwise increase over time. It would also maintain and enhance current infiltration rates to ensure availability of groundwater in surrounding areas. The villages of Randa and Bankouele, rangeland in Dorra, and surrounding areas would thus benefit from the stabilization of vegetative cover. A rough estimate of the population that would benefit in this way is on the order of 10,000 persons.

The total of targeted beneficiaries and nontargeted beneficiaries is therefore estimated at approximately 14,000 people. Although irrelevant to IFAD's mandate of rural poverty alleviation, an unknown number of nonrural, nonpoor would also benefit from the conservation of the forest both vicariously and as users.

Income Weighting and the EIRR

Conventional project appraisal as currently practiced does not entail valuing costs and benefits differently according to the income of the individuals affected. However, weighting procedures have been worked out in detail in the cost-benefit analysis literature, involving the use of "income or consumption weights" to reflect the fact that the marginal utility of income (or consumption) is not constant across different income groups. In this way, equity considerations can be reflected in the EIRR, and projects that benefit very low-income groups will appear relatively more attractive.

In projects that are intended to enhance or rehabilitate the environment of the poorest groups, measured benefits valued using an implicit weight of unity can be quite small because environmental enhancement translates into relatively low increases in production. This is especially the case in marginal areas, where the economic value of subsistence production is low. The economic benefits of avoiding environmental degradation are therefore equally low. However, the utility gains accruing to the beneficiary population are quite high. In the absence of income weighting, the EIRR of many environmentally oriented projects in marginal areas is likely to be unattractive and, as a result, such projects may be rejected on allocative efficiency grounds unless significant benefits to other sectors are involved (for example, tourism). Another implication is that, in determining tradeoffs between different groups of users in mutually exclusive uses of the environmental asset, it is the poor that are likely to lose out.

Some Conclusions

The Environmental Protection and Rural Development in the Day Forest Project is an example of a growing number of IFAD interventions that seek to achieve poverty alleviation and environmental objectives in an integrated manner. The case study outlined some of the salient features of the economic analysis of this project. The following are certain generally applicable issues that might warrant attention in the analysis of such projects.

Extending the Boundary of Analysis in Time and Space

The boundaries for project analysis should be extended in time and space to the extent feasible. This would allow externalities to be identified, quantified, and valued during the project cycle. In the context of the Day Forest Project, the time horizon applied in the analysis was thirty years, beyond which "with and without" project projections would have had diminishing credibility. The extension of the geographic boundary of analysis to include off-site effects would have enhanced the economic analysis of the project. However, because these externalities were judged to be positive, their investigation was not considered essential for project design.

Extending the boundaries of analysis requires greater investments in information (see below). This information may not always be directly relevant to the technical design of the project, and the costs of gathering this information must be weighed against the benefits to be derived from it. In the case of the Day Forest Project, information on positive externalities benefiting nontarget groups is not relevant to the project's poverty alleviation objectives but is important for the economic justification of the project. However, it should be noted that in accordance with IFAD's Environmental Principles and Criteria, in cases where negative externalities might be generated, this must always influence project design.

Valuation Methods

Economic valuation methods for environmental changes such as the surrogate market approach, the change in production approach, and the opportunity cost of time approach can be readily applied in project analysis. The extent to which this can be done is subject to the availability of the necessary data, which are often lacking in the context of marginal areas. In many cases, the necessary identification and physical quantification of environmental change can be undertaken in the course of the project cycle. However, specific valuation problems can be encountered when appraising projects that focus on unmarketed environmental goods and services in marginal areas where few markets exist even for surrogate goods.

Valuation approaches such as CVM and TCM require separate information-gathering exercises over an extended period of time and do not lend themselves well to standard project cycle work. Furthermore, the cost of carrying out such exercises may not be justified, given that decisionmakers are not familiar with these techniques and may not accept the results.

While user benefits of environmental goods and services can be valued with varying degrees of ease, nonuser benefits present a challenge. The latter would require the application of CVM and other survey-based methods not thus far applied in IFAD's work.

Fiscal Impact

While it may be true in many cases that "good ecology means good economics," the fiscal impacts of projects that have a strong focus on environmental objectives might be unfavorable. This is especially the case in situations where economic benefits are imputed and no corresponding financial cash flow exists. In marginal areas, these problems are amplified due to the absence of markets and mechanisms for cost recovery. Governments may be reluctant to accept loans for such projects, preferring to seek grant financing.

Equity Concerns

Projects that focus on enhancing the productivity of the natural resources on which subsistence farmers or pastoralists depend may appear unattractive on strict economic criteria. This is especially the case where economic valuation techniques translate environmental changes into changes in productivity. In marginal areas, where the value of production is low, the imputed economic value of environmental changes will be low. Incremental benefits may be relatively small, but utility gains may be high.

One implication of this is that the economic rationale for projects that protect natural resources on which low income groups depend may, in certain cases, rest on nonuser benefits and externalities. It is precisely these benefits, however, that are more difficult to identify, quantify, and value.

Ultimately, decisions to proceed with such projects may rest on non-economic criteria such as intra- and inter-generational equity concerns and other social objectives.

Data Requirements

The economic analysis of projects in marginal areas is hampered by data constraints. When projects are focused on environmental effects, these constraints are amplified because data required to specify environmental cause-and-effect relationships are unlikely to be readily available. In the context of the standard project cycle, many of these data constraints cannot be overcome. Even where environmental change can be predicted, further data constraints face economic valuation techniques such as CVM and TCM, which require additional survey data. The result is that the full range of environmental effects is not identified, physically quantified, and valued during project preparation. At the appraisal stage, there is little time available to capture these effects in the analysis.

The economic analysis of the Day Forest Project benefitted from the fact that extended pre-investment activities were carried out prior to project design, generating a significant amount of relevant data to supplement information acquired during project cycle missions. However, data on which to value nonuser values of the forest, recreational benefits of the forest, and downstream externalities were not generated, because these were not directly relevant to project design. As mentioned earlier, a fundamental problem is that information required to design environmentally sustainable poverty alleviation projects in marginal areas does not always coincide with information required to justify the project on economic grounds.

A case can therefore be made for identifying data needs for economic valuation of environmental changes at the earliest stage of the project cycle. In this regard, the increased use of focused proactive environmental assessments in the preparation of environmental projects in IFAD's work might serve to improve the quality of the economic analysis and, hence, improve decisionmaking. Indeed, IFAD has embarked on a Preliminary Development and Testing Phase of proactive environmental assessments, natural resource management studies, environment-related pre-investment activities, and operational guidelines for sustainable agriculture. Preliminary phase activities, in addition to supporting the design and appraisal of specific IFAD projects, will generate more generally applicable lessons on the most cost-effective means of ensuring that data requirements are identified and met in a timely fashion. These activities will assist IFAD in the challenging task of designing interventions that rehabilitate the natural resource base on which the poor depend, in an economically attractive manner.

Bibliography

Bojo, J., Karl-Göran Mäler, and L. Unema. 1990. *Environment and Development: An Economic Approach*. The Netherlands: Kluwer Academic Publishers.

Dixon, J.A., D.E. James, and P.B. Sherman. 1989. *The Economics of Dryland Management*. London: Earthscan Publications Ltd.

International Fund for Agricultural Development (IFAD). 1989. *Environmental Sustainability and Rural Poverty Alleviation: Operational Issues for IFAD*. (GC 13/L.12). Rome: IFAD, January.

_____. 1990. Report on the IFAD Staff Training Workshop on "The Economic Valuation and Evaluation of Environmental Changes in Marginal Areas." Rome: IFAD.

_____ . 1991. *Progress Report on IFAD's Evolving Approaches to Environmentally Sustainable Rural Alleviation*. (GC14/L.9/Rev. 1). Rome: IFAD, April.

_____. 1991. *Djibouti Rural Development and Environmental Protection in the Day Forest*. Djibouti Appraisal Report. Rome: IFAD, June.

_____ . 1991. *Natural Resource Management for Rural Poverty Alleviation: Preliminary Development Testing Phase of Environmental Assessments, Pre-Investment Activities, Natural Resource Management Studies and Operational Guidelines for Sustainable Agriculture*. (EB 91/44/E.80). Rome: IFAD, December.

7

Incorporating Environmental Costs into Power Development Planning: A Case Study of Sri Lanka

Peter Meier and Mohan Munasinghe

This paper applies economic valuation and multi-attribute decision analysis techniques to the incorporation of environmental considerations into power sector planning, using Sri Lanka as a case study. Unlike most past efforts, the emphasis here is on the long-range planning stage of power system expansion, rather than assessment of project level impacts. Multi-attribute techniques are particularly useful in situations where explicit economic valuation of externalities is subject to great uncertainty or controversy (as in the case of human health effects associated with thermal power generation). The paper illustrates the importance of evaluating the environmental and economic impacts of technology, siting and pollution control options in a systems context, rather than on the basis of stand-alone comparisons, and emphasizes the use of trade-off curves as a tool for assisting decisionmakers.

Background

The environmental impacts of energy development are widely recognized, and they have become an increasingly important topic of public debate in both the developed and the developing countries. In the latter, this debate is part of a broader emerging concern over the relationship between economic policies for sustainable development and environmental costs; and donor agencies and the international financial institutions have become increasingly concerned about implementing new policies that respond more effectively to environmental goals.[1]

The power sector has received particular attention, a consequence of the significant potential impacts associated with the sector. Indeed, historically, many of the most celebrated instances of unanticipated environmental consequences in developing countries have occurred at major power system projects—such as the Akosombo Dam in Ghana and the Aswan Dam in Egypt. Even though it is quite unlikely that one would today encounter unanticipated impacts on the scale encountered at these projects in the past, given the procedures now in place, there is general agreement that the most pressing need is to incorporate environmental concerns into investment planning and decision making rather than simply reacting to environmental problems after they occur.[2]

Exactly how this is to be achieved is still unclear. First, there remains a huge gulf between general discussions of the subject—which typically argue for comprehensive frameworks and the like—and techniques that are operationally practical. This is reflected in the recent experience of the industrialized countries as well. In the United States, despite increasing pressures to do so, many state regulatory commissions have yet to adopt formal procedures for including environmental externalities into their procedures while most of those that have done so have adopted somewhat crude expedients that seem little related to rigorous cost-benefit analysis.

A second feature of the emerging literature on the subject of how to incorporate environmental considerations into energy and power sector planning in developing countries is the perception that somehow the analytical approaches that should be used are "different" than those used in the developed countries, presumably because public sector investment plays a much larger role in many developing countries, and, in the case of electric utilities, because of the substantial differences in the ownership and regulatory frameworks (see, for example, Asian Development Bank [ADB] 1991). That, however, is a matter of the effectiveness of the different policy instruments available, and has nothing to do with the analytical methodology that enables one to quantify the linkages between the configuration of the power system, economic costs, and environmental quality.[3] Whether, for example, investments are made by state-owned electric utilities (as in developing countries) or by privately owned utilities under regulatory supervision (as in the United States) does not alter the linkage, say, between a requirement for flue gas

The writers acknowledge the contributions to this study made by a team of Sri Lankan consultants: Professor K. K. Y. W. Perera (Leader), H. S. Subasinghe, K. D. Arudpragasam, Sunith Fernando, Shavi Fernando, J. Kotalawala, P. Illangovan, L.R. Sally, and T. Siyambalapitiya.

---

[1] For a good general discussion of the major issues, see International Atomic Energy Agency (IAEA) 1991. Also see World Bank 1989; or Giampaoli 1988.

[2] For example, a U.S. Agency for International Development (AID) report (Oct. 1988) concludes "In the near term, this calls for devising a strategy that encourages developing countries to assess the costs and benefits of environmental protection—as well as those of competing alternativesat the investment planning stage of energy sector development rather than after project investment decisions have been made."

[3] For example, the ADB report argues (p. 4) that ".. by contrast, a relatively stronger role is played by public investment in developing countries and this is a major factor determining the choice of approach. In fact, in the absence of efficient markets and effective enforcement mechanisms for government regulation and revenue measures, investment decision-making may well be the most effective policy instrument developing country governments have to influence the nature

desulfurization systems and ambient air quality; it makes different only how a policy that would require such systems might be implemented.

In fact, the literature is quite limited, a reflection of the very few attempts that have been made to formalize the process into operational models. The recent review of models and the literature by Markandya (1990), despite its stated focus on power systems planning, found that most of the emphasis to date has been on modifying much broader energy systems models to deal with environmental constraints or objectives. For example, the MARKAL, an energy system optimization model developed a decade ago under the auspices of the International Energy Agency (IEA), has been modified to deal with CO_2 emissions, and is being used in a number of developed countries to study technological options for greenhouse gas emissions control. The only model that can be regarded as a power systems model for which any attempt has been made to incorporate environmental considerations, and which has been used extensively in developing countries, is the Wein Automated System Planning (WASP) model for which a so-called IMPACTS module was developed a few years ago by Argonne National Laboratory.[4] However, this module calculates only the quantity of pollutants emitted (or "residuals"), together with cost estimates for any pollution control devices: it does not deal with impacts per se.

Given this methodological vacuum, it is hardly surprising that most of the attention to date has been given to improving environmental assessment procedures at the project level. Thus the World Bank, for example, now has extensive new procedures in place to ensure inclusion of environmental concerns in the project cycle. Nevertheless, even if done well, there are inherent limitations to the degree to which

an environmental assessment (EA) and a benefit or cost analysis at the project level can address many of the most important environmental issues. The project-level EA deals well with local, site specific questions, and the options for project level mitigation (such as resettlement questions at dams, loss of wildlife habitat, local socioeconomic impacts associated with construction). However, the project-level EA deals less effectively with regional (for example, downstream water quality impacts), national (for example, acid rain) and global scale (for example, greenhouse gas) issues. These can really be addressed only at a much broader scale than that of the single project—namely at the scale of the system plan. At this level of the planning process, the fundamental question is not whether the impact of any single project is environmentally acceptable, but what are the relative environmental costs and benefits of alternative power sector development strategies.

Indeed, there are widespread perceptions that project-level EAs are nothing more than ex post justifications of decisions already made.[5] In Sri Lanka, the first full-scale EA for a power project was prepared for the proposed Trincomalee coal fired power plant (Black and Veatch International [BVI] 1988) and many of the public comments reflected just this perception:

> ...it is therefore evident that the entire feasibility study process, terminating with the EIA [environmental impact assessment], has followed a policy known as "decide-announce-defend"....The EIS [environmental impact statement] is an ex post facto document seeking to environmentally justify a project which was formulated without any environmental considerations whatsoever.... [t]his EIA is a

---

and location of economic activity and consequent environmental impacts."

[4] However, Markandya notes that "... in practice, this model has not proved easy to apply, or particularly useful. None of the World Bank staff involved in the power sector used it" (Markandya 1990: p.20). A new version of the IMPACTS module that is part of the broader energy planning package called ENPEP (for ENergy and Power Evaluation Package) has since become available, and is equipped with a modern user interface that makes it much easier to use than previous versions.

[5] For a broad review of the environmental assessment procedures in Asia see, for example, A. L. Brown, R. A. Hindmarsh, and G.T. Macdonald 1991. Reporting on a workshop on EIA, the authors noted "... a perceived futility of some environmental assessments in terms of their ability to modify the project. ...[M]ost construction projects starts before the EIA work begins. [T]he EIA work should begin at the planning stage of the project."

post planning exercise, whereas it ought to have been an ongoing exercise from the inception of the project.

Although it is perhaps easy to dismiss such comments as mere rhetoric, in fact we know of no EIS prepared for a power project that has ever concluded that the project should not go forward. It is probably fair to assert that the twenty years of experience with EISs has shown that while they have succeeded in forcing project developers to become more sensitive to environmental issues, and in ensuring that mitigation options are fully integrated into the project design, they have proven to be inadequate as a tool for ensuring that environmental considerations are incorporated into the planning decision process itself.[6]

In response to these issues, the Environmental Policy and Research Division of the World Bank initiated a case study of the power sector of Sri Lanka, one of a series of research efforts that seek to explore alternative approaches to quantifying and valuing environmental impacts in different sectors. The express objective of this effort is to develop methodologies that can be implemented in practical ways, and whose potential impact on decision rules is clearly demonstrable. This paper summarizes some of the key findings of the case study: the reader is referred to the detailed report for a more complete presentation of methodological issues and research findings (Meier and Munasinghe 1992).

Traditional Power System Planning

In the past, the principal planning objective for the development of the power sector has been to deliver the anticipated need for electrical energy at "least cost." Indeed, largely at the insistence of the World Bank and other international financial institutions, developing countries have had to demonstrate that

facilities proposed for financing are in the "least cost" plan. In practice this has meant the application of sophisticated capacity expansion optimization models— such as the WASP model that is very widely used in developing countries—whose objective function is the minimization of the present value of system expansion costs over some planning horizon and for some given level of system reliability.

Yet, in the complex regulatory environment of the industrialized countries, few utilities use the results of mathematical optimization models to develop their capacity expansion plans. The most common approach is to develop a small number of discrete options, with revenue requirements and environmental impacts derived in some detail as part of the necessary regulatory submissions. Moreover, "least cost" planning in countries such as the United States has come to encompass a much broader perspective than the traditional stress on minimizing the costs of supply expansion for some exogenously specified level of demand, since the demand itself is subject to modification by so-called demand side management approaches.[7] Indeed, as noted earlier, over the past few years a number of U.S. state regulatory commissions have expanded the operational definition of "least cost" planning even further by introducing specific techniques for including the costs of environmental externalities.

The problems of an excessive reliance on supply-side optimization models as a basis for planning in the developing countries has become broadly recognized of late, not least within the World Bank itself (see, for example, Crousillat 1989). Perhaps the most important objection to the use of the traditional models such as WASP is the difficulty with which they deal with the huge uncertainties currently faced by the sector, ranging from uncertainties in the prices of imported fuels to the impacts of

---

[6] That the EIS is an inefficient vehicle for evaluating anything more than the very local site-specific impacts is well illustrated by the American experience: because there was little if any public and environmental input to fundamental questions on the generation mix, EISs prepared for proposed nuclear plants proved to be the only focus for such input, resulting in long delays as fundamental questions on the generation mix, on the role of energy conservation, and on nuclear safety were endlessly re-examined.

[7] In its modern usage in the United States, least-cost planning has been defined a process that "... explicitly includes conservation and load management programs as capacity and energy resources; it considers environmental and social factors as well as direct economic costs; it involves public participation; and it carefully analyzes the uncertainties and risks posed by different resource portfolios and by external factors" (C. Goldman et al. 1989). The Electric Power Research Institute (EPRI) prefers the use of the term "integrated resource planning" to capture the idea of a balanced consideration of demand and supply side options.

construction cost overruns and droughts. In other words, the so-called "least cost" plan may in fact be optimal only for the particular set of external circumstances assumed, and may deviate from optimality for most other combinations of external factors.

In the traditional approach to power sector planning, environmental considerations have generally been deferred to at least the siting stage of the process. In other words, decisions about the generation mix, and the basic technology choices, have been made entirely on the grounds of direct costs, in the case of hydro projects, however, easily quantified mitigation and opportunity costs—such as the cost of re-settlement, or the opportunity costs of foregone production from inundated land—are now routinely incorporated into economic analysis.

Attempts at quantifying environmental factors at the siting stage—efforts that are quite common in the United States and growing in developing countries—have tended to be based on some very ambiguous ranking and weighing schemes, with an ubiquitous reliance on "judgment and experience of siting experts." It is quite unclear whether such approaches have in fact improved the quality of siting decisions.

Quantification at this level of analysis has generally meant the application of mathematical models of the fate of pollutants in the environment—such as atmospheric dispersion models for air pollutants, and thermal plume models for predicting ambient temperature increases from cooling water discharges. The thrust of such modelling studies is to demonstrate compliance with ambient standards: if these are not met, mitigation options are explored to bring the facility into compliance. An analysis of actual impacts—say in the case of air quality an estimation of the health risks associated with pollution exposure—is rarely part of such assessments.

In general, not much detail is presented on the impacts at alternative sites, whatever may be the regulatory requirement that alternatives to the proposed action need to be examined. More often than not, in an EIS of several hundred pages, there is but a section of a few pages of discussion about alternative sites, most of which is in the nature of undocumented (and almost always unquantified) assertion.

Planning Process in Sri Lanka

This general characterization of the planning process described above applies almost perfectly to Sri Lanka. The annual planning cycle begins with load forecasts, which are used in turn by the Generation Planning Branch as a basis for their Generation Plan, for which the WASP-III model is currently used. Hydro scheduling is done with the SYSIM model, which was developed as part of the Electricity Masterplan sponsored by the German assistance agency GTZ. (For a description of this model, see Nanthakumar 1990.)

Both the Masterplan system expansion studies and the present CEB (Ceylon Electricity Board) Generation plan have in the past restricted their consideration of environmental issues to a few calculations of residuals: yet the usefulness of such calculations and their graphical portrayals could be improved and may have very little to do with the actual environmental impacts that might be expected. For example, in Figure 7-1, the simple horizontal "stacking" of SO_2, NOx, and ash emissions provides a visual implication that tons of these very distinct pollutants could be arithmetically added together to yield some form of aggregate impact.

The approach followed in the early 1980s with respect to the coal plants followed very much the traditional pattern: environmental issues were really only addressed in any detail, as part of the project-level EA, once the basic siting decision—for a coal-burning baseload station at Trincomalee—had already been made. The subsequent decision to examine a site on the South Coast, followed by another political decision to drop further consideration of that site—illustrates the largely ad hoc nature of how environmental considerations were being addressed. More recently, the Kukule hydroelectric project has come to the forefront of public debate and controversy; again the danger is of public perception increasing that the feasibility study that is currently underway will inevitably lead to the plant's construction.

The need for a more systematic and early approach to analyzing the environmental aspects of power system alternatives in Sri Lanka is quite clear. The ad hoc procedures of the past, in which major projects are examined one

Figure 7-1: Master Plan Portrayal of Emissions

Masterplan for the Electricity Supply of Sri Lanka - Clients: GTZ & CEB - Consulting Engineers: Lahmeyer   SEXSI LISTI

EXPECTED EMISSION FROM THERMAL PLANTS

SCENARIO: SCBAR029

Emission from thermal plants   (kton)

Year	SO2	NOx	Ash
1991	3	5	0
1992	3	5	0
1993	5	9	0
1994	8	12	0
1995	11	17	0
1996	15	24	0
1997	19	29	0
1998	19	23	14
1999	19	18	26
2000	24	26	26
2001	29	33	27
2002	30	28	41
2003	37	39	41
2004	37	33	55
2005	45	45	55
2006	45	38	69
2007	48	36	82
2008	57	50	82
2009	55	36	107
2010	64	49	109
Total	573	555	734

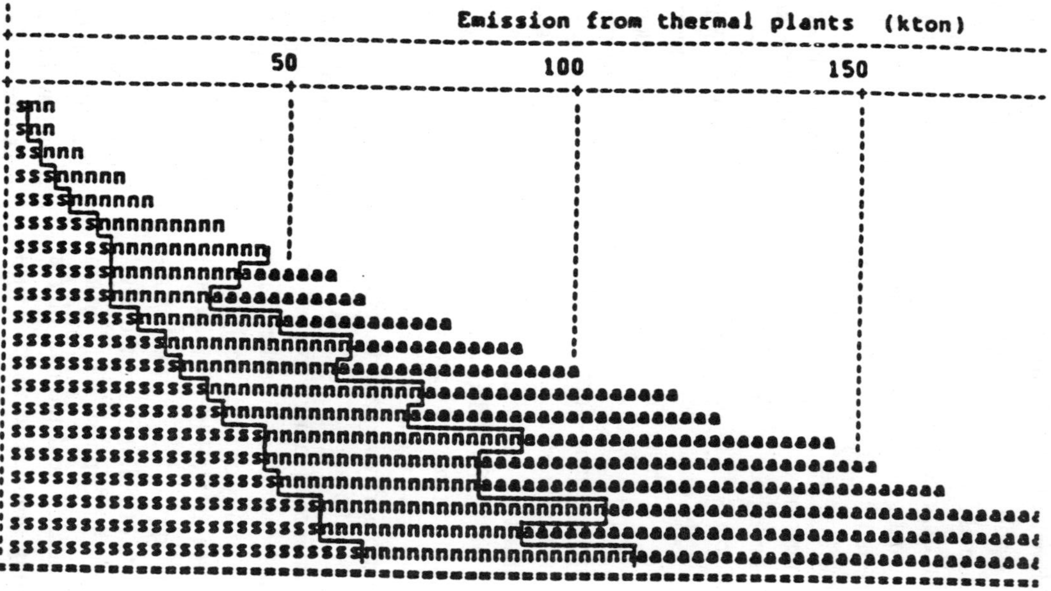

Type of emission

s   Type of emission   SO2
n   Type of emission   NOx
a   Type of emission   Ash

at a time, and rejected one at a time, will create substantial problems in the future unless a more proactive approach is taken.

Environmental Issues of Power Sector Development in Sri Lanka

Because hydroelectricity dominates the present power system, it is logical that the principal environmental issue that the power sector has had to deal with in the past has been that of resettlement. In recent years, the few thermal plants in the system (the diesels at Sapugaskanda, and the combustion turbines and steam plant at Kelanitissa) have been only sporadically operated, and neither facility is seen to have major environmental problems. (However, during times of drought [as most recently in April 1992], these thermal units may run twenty-four hours a day, with the remaining limited hydro resources used for peaking purposes.)

The Samanalawewa hydroelectric project, currently in the final stages of construction, illustrates well the kind of environmental issues associated with hydro development in Sri Lanka. An earlier Overseas Development Administration (ODA) (1990) evaluation of the Victoria project highlighted a number of social and environmental issues, and several ODA missions were undertaken during construction of the Samanalawewa project to ensure implementation of mitigation measures. The issues addressed in their 1990 report were as follows:

Construction phase issues

- Water table drawdown during power tunnel construction.

- Removal of biomass from the area to become inundated.

- Need to ensure adequate irrigation water supply immediately downstream of the reservoir for a 2,000-acre rice paddy irrigation scheme (and the possible need for compensatory water supply).

- Resettlement issues: (a) need to extend attention from families with property to landless laborers, tenants, and traders whose customers move from the area; (b) need to establish more formal counseling service arrangements.

- Archeology: a preliminary assessment discovered some unique iron smelting sites dating to the sixth to ninth centuries AD; ODA recommended a complete excavation of the site prior to inundation.

Long-term issue

Need for an environmental management plan (for both upstream and downstream areas).

As the system gradually shifts towards a greater role for thermal plants, the major issues will also shift towards those associated with such plants. Clearly, the issues related to thermal plants are of a quite different nature from those at hydro plants, and how to compare the two types of quite different impacts—primarily air and thermal discharge issues at thermal plants, against land use issues at hydro plants—is one of the main themes of this case study.

The comments received in response to the Trincomalee EIS is a good indicator of what these new concerns are likely to be. As required by regulations, the document was circulated for public comment, and on Figure 7-2 we illustrate the results of an analysis of the 154 comments received. That air quality would be the major concern at a coal-fired plant is to be expected: perhaps less expected is that the second most frequent concern was over the process by which a coal-fired power plant had been selected for this particular site. As noted earlier, widespread dissatisfaction was expressed by nongovernmental organizations (NGOs) and others over the way in which decisions had been reached.

Land Use and Resettlement

Sri Lanka is one of the more densely populated countries of the world, and land availability to support a growing population is an important issue. In general, hydro sites are in the wet zone areas where there is little available land nearby for resettled inhabitants to be re-located; and such land as is available at greater distances (mainly in the newly irrigated dry zone areas of the Mahaweli schemes) is often seen by potential evacuees as undesirable because of questions concerning the availability of adequate water supply.

Figure 7-2: Public Comments to the Trincomalee EIS

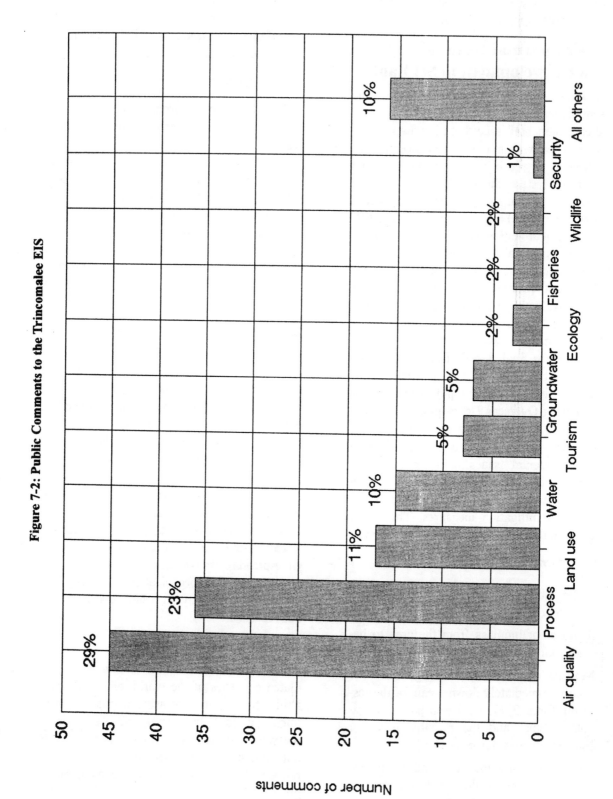

On the basis of the recent experience at Samanalawewa, where some new ideas have been tried by the CEB, the resettlement issues at most of the remaining major hydro sites appear to be tractable. At Samanalawewa itself, as of fall 1992, the families from the power station site have already been moved and resettled in a tea estate, and some 365 families remain to be resettled. Of these, 68 have agreed to move to the Mahaweli area, 80 are still negotiating, and 120 have agreed to find on their own land for resettlement in return for an additional cash payment. This has the merit of giving evacuees the opportunity to resettle in areas of their choice, and reducing the pressure on government organizations to meet the demands of evacuees.

The one major hydro project where substantial resettlement issues are likely to occur in the future is at Kukule. Although there are a number of variants of this project currently under study, the GTZ Masterplan variant of the Kukule Ganga Hydropower Project, which at 2,080 hectares has the largest reservoir size of any of the remaining hydro projects, estimates that some 9,100 persons would need to be evacuated. This represents four times the number of potential evacuees as at Samanalawewa, and will therefore require very careful management.[8]

On the other hand, it should be noted that this Kukule project variant will also provide substantial irrigation benefits, calling for some 68,000 hectares to be irrigated in the southeastern dry zone, of which some 95 percent would be new land. The net increase in agricultural production would substantially offset the production losses in the area affected by reservoir inundation, and would provide substantial employment in an area of high youth unemployment.

A comprehensive feasibility study of the Kukule project is currently underway. In the Progress Report of January 6, 1992, preliminary analysis suggests that the most attractive option may be a run-of-river project, that involves the resettlement of only some 27 families.

Deforestation

The progressive loss of Sri Lanka's natural forest over the past fifty years is well documented, and represents one of the country's most important environmental concerns. Power sector projects will likely be scrutinized very carefully for their potential impact on what natural forest areas remain, even if it is true that the power sector per se has been a relatively minor contributor to the loss of forest lands. The main causes of deforestation in the past have been planned agricultural development and settlement schemes, chena cultivation, encroachment by unplanned settlement and cropping, illicit logging, and uncontrolled fuelwood and timber extraction.

Air Quality

Relatively little is known about ambient air quality in Sri Lanka, except perhaps on a very general level: in most parts of the country the air quality is fairly good, a reflection of the limited extent of industrialization (except in Colombo) and the natural ventilation provided by strong monsoonal wind regimes. In Colombo, however, the sharp increase in automobile and bus traffic over the past decade has led to strong indications of increasing deterioration of urban air quality. Between 1970 and 1990 the number of vehicles registered annually in Colombo has increased fourteen-fold. It is estimated that vehicles produced 98 percent of carbon monoxide emission, 79 percent of NOx, and 46 percent of SO_2. With 60 percent of the country's vehicles registered in the Colombo area, and with about 60 percent of the total industry, the outlook for air quality in Colombo, while still nowhere close to the levels experienced in other Southeast Asian cities, is still poor in the absence of appropriate actions.

The first major effort to monitor air quality began in 1989 when the National Building Research Organization (NBRO) initiated a three-year program for monitoring air quality in Colombo; in a first phase, a citywide survey of

---

[8] Again, however, it is useful to make a comparison to the scale of projects elsewhere where the resettlement impacts have become matters of major national (and international) debate. The two Narmada projects in India (Sardar Sarovar and Narmada Sagar), for example, would require resettlement of 170,000 people, but provide over 2 million hectares of irrigated land (see, for example, Dixon, Talbot, and Le Moigne 1989).

dustfall and sulfation rates is being conducted, with detailed measurements of SO_2, particulates, and NOx to follow in phase two for those areas with unsatisfactory air quality. This program is viewed as a necessary first step not just to develop a data base for Colombo, but also to assist in the formulation of national air quality standards, and to establish a permanent monitoring capability.

Based upon what we do know about patterns of energy utilization, certain inferences can be drawn. It is fairly certain that at present the power sector contributes only marginally to air pollution in Sri Lanka. The existing thermal plants in and around Colombo presently need not be run at all during a normal hydro year. Once the anticipated coal burning power plants are added to the system beginning in the late 1990s, however, this is expected to change significantly; from essentially zero in 1991, the power sector is expected to contribute 80 percent of SO_2 and 70 percent of NOx emissions by 2010. Clearly the potential for significant degradation of air quality is the major environmental concern associated with coal-burning power plants, and the options to minimize such air pollution impacts—whether by technology choices (say by application of some of the newer clean coal technologies such as fluidized bed combustion [FBC]), by impact mitigation options (say by the use of flue gas desulfurization system [FGD]), or by locational choices—is one of the main themes of this paper.

Another major uncertainty is the air quality impact of the use of traditional fuels, particularly in the congested lower-income areas of Colombo where fuelwood and agricultural wastes are still widely used as a cooking fuel. The release of carcinogens may be a particularly important concern.

Acid Rain

Acid rain is likely to become an increasingly important environmental issue in the Asia-Pacific region given the fact that the energy plans in many countries, in India and China in particular, call for rapid development of fossil energy systems. Acid rain is largely a long-range phenomenon, and it is fairly obvious that the extent to which acid rain is or will be experienced in Sri Lanka is as much a function of

emission trends of acid rain precursors (SO_2 and NOx) in India as in Sri Lanka itself. As suggested by the predominant wind directions in South Asia, the most significant source of acid rain precursors to Sri Lanka would be coal-burning power plants on the East Coast of India.

In light of these observations, it is clear that the debate over the potential acid rain consequences of the Trincomalee coal-fired plant, as evidenced by the discussion in and comments to the EIS, was not very well founded. What is most relevant is the matter not of SO_2 emissions in North America (which was used by the consultant as the yardstick of comparison), but of emissions in India.

It is probably true that from a local acid-rain perspective, the best location for a large coal-burning power plant would be the south-/southeast coast, since the plumes from this location would be overland for a much lesser distance than at either the Colombo or Trincomalee areas. However, different intensities of the two monsoons that would transport the plumes (about 12 kilometers per hour during the northeast monsoon, and 19 kilometers per hour in the southwest) make even such simple comparisons quite uncertain.

Global Warming

Global warming (and transnational acid rain) are conceptually different from local environmental impacts, since in the former case the impacts will occur predominantly in other countries. If the main economic objective is to maximize welfare in Sri Lanka, decision makers in Sri Lanka would be unwilling (quite justifiedly) to incur additional costs (for example, to reduce CO_2 emissions) if the benefits of such actions accrue mainly to other nations. The assumption here is that Sri Lanka will be reimbursed by the international community for the incremental costs of global warming mitigation efforts, or that the Government would have signed an international agreement committing itself to undertake certain CO_2 emission reduction measures. In either event, power sector planners would need to consider the impact of alternative expansion strategies on greenhouse gas emissions.

Carbon emissions in Sri Lanka, both in absolute terms and in per capita terms, are extremely low, a reflection of the dominance of hydro in the electric sector, and of low energy intensity of the industrial sector. Beyond the year 2010, however, CO_2 emissions will rise very sharply as the electric sector generation mix moves toward fossil fuel. This has important consequences for the negotiating posture of Sri Lanka in the event that a consensus emerges for tradable CO_2 emission rights; it will be in the interests of small developing countries whose present electric systems are hydro dominated to argue that the initial allocation of emission rights be based on population, or income, rather than on present fossil fuel consumption.

Indeed, Sri Lanka may be an example of a country that may be as much affected by the global measures to reduce CO_2 emissions, as by the physical impacts of any global warming that may in fact occur. Some of the recent studies of measures that might be necessary to stabilize CO_2 emissions have staggering implications for developed and developing countries alike. At the June 1991 meeting of the Energy Modelling Forum, whose focus was the energy sector impacts of greenhouse gas emission control strategies, a number of models suggested that the level of carbon taxes necessary to stabilize emissions (typically defined as 1990 emission levels by 2005) should begin now at over $100 per ton of carbon, rising, in some cases, to as much as $550 per ton by 2005.

Such tax levels are perhaps not very likely to materialize. Yet much more modest rates of carbon tax, even if imposed only in the industrialized countries, will have substantial implications for relative fuel prices, and the ratio of coal to oil prices in particular has relevance for fossil fuel importing countries such as Sri Lanka.

On the other hand, the impacts of global warming that might be experienced by Sri Lanka are also quite speculative. Some researchers expect an intensification of the monsoon in tropical latitudes, which may increase soil erosion and adversely affect stability in the hill country watersheds where deforestation rates already represent a threat to the sedimentation rates experienced by hydro and irrigation reservoirs. Unlike many other countries in Southeast Asia, the tectonic conditions are relatively stable, with little significant seismic activity of the type that has produced significant surface depressions of coastal areas in the Philippines. Nor are the major cities presently threatened by major subsidence problems caused by excessive exploitation of groundwater.[9] Nevertheless, extensive areas of the coast, especially in the south and southwest, are already threatened by coastal erosion (that can, at least in part, be attributed to large-scale mining of coral reefs), and there are extensive areas of highly populated coastal areas that would be severely affected by sea level rises of one to three meters. In the north, one of the immediate consequences of sea level rise is likely to be contamination of the limestone aquifers that are important sources of groundwater for that area.

Whatever may be the resolution of these uncertainties, it seems clear that power sector planners, at the very least, will need to be much more aware of this debate than in the past, and should be cognizant of the implications of alternative expansion strategies on CO_2 emissions, especially in relation to any future global agreements on emissions and their financial and technical ramifications. We therefore include CO_2 emissions as one of the environmental factors to be considered in this study.

Biodiversity

Because Sri Lanka is a small island, which has been isolated for relatively long periods, it is the home to a large number of endemic (unique) species. Among Asian countries, Sri Lanka has the highest levels of biological diversity. Indeed, the U.S. National Science Foundation's Committee on Research Priorities in Tropical Biology identifies Sri Lanka as demanding special attention. Biological diversity is under threat in Sri Lanka primarily from the progressive reduction in its natural forests and

---

[9] The classic example is Shanghai, which subsided some 2.5 meters between 1920 and 1965. An artificial recharge program was, however, successful in arresting further subsidence. Parts of Bangkok are now subsiding several centimeters per year, and many other coastal cities in Southeast Asia face potentially serious subsidence problems.

other ecosystems and the selective exploitation of species (particularly for timber).

The main biodiversity issue for the power sector is the degree to which hydro projects and transmission line corridors affect forest lands of high biological diversity, and to which thermal generation projects on the coast affect the high diversity coastal systems (particularly coral reefs and seagrass beds).

It is not merely the loss of acreage that is of potential concern. Since most ecosystems require minimum contiguous areas for stable existence, fragmentation of habitats will be of significance for long-term survival. Many of the high biodiversity wet zone forests are already highly fragmented—for example in the Matara district, the 160 square kilometers of remaining wet zone forest is fragmented into 30 patches, the largest of which is no more than 1,000 hectares.

Detailed site specific studies need to be conducted at the project level EIS stage to examine whether or not a proposed project will in fact affect an endemic species. At the planning stage, however, information at this level of detail is not likely to be available. The best that can reasonably be done, therefore, is to develop a quantitative index that predicts the probability that a particular project, or combination of projects in a sectoral development plan, will have an effect on endemic species or destroy habitats of high biodiversity.

Coastal Zone

As the generation mix shifts from one that is predominantly hydro, to one in which large baseload fossil-fueled plants play an increasing role, it is inevitable that sites will need to be found on the coast to accommodate such thermal plants. Since imported coal is the most likely fuel for those plants, the implication is that any inland location would incur substantial additional transportation cost penalties.

The economic importance of preventing environmental degradation in the coastal zone is well established (Energy and Science Authority 1991). Foreign tourism, an important source of foreign exchange, is largely focused on its sandy beaches and coastal estuaries and lagoons, with over 80 percent of hotel rooms located on the coast. Also, the marine fishery industry provides employment to some 100,000 persons, and is the largest source of animal protein for the island. The main concern related to the power sector is the discharge of heated effluents into shallow waters that contain valuable ecosystems.

The range of impacts will depend on the existence of a thermocline and the depth of the well-mixed layer. Two surveys by the Norwegian oceanographic survey vessel *Nansen* give a broad idea of the temperature structure of shelf in Sri Lanka. The thermocline lies at depths of 50 meters, differing slightly on the west coast with season, and showing greater variation on the east coast. The well-mixed layer extends down to about 50 meters. Approaching the shore, therefore, coastal waters will be well mixed.

In Trincomalee Harbor, where depths well in excess of 50 meters exist within the harbor area, an effluent led into the surface water will not reach the bottom, and major communities will remain unaffected. However, in shallower coastal waters, because the well-mixed layer reaches the bottom, impacts of the thermal effluent are likely to be quite drastic.[10]

Outline of the Proposed Methodology

Based on the experience with the Sri Lanka case study, one can outline the following seven-step approach to incorporating environmental issues into the planning stage of power systems development in developing countries: the key steps are depicted on Figure 7-3.

Step 1. Selection of Attributes

Perhaps the most important criterion in deciding which environmental issues to address is to be clear about the scale of analysis that is required at the system planning level. Many impacts that are purely local in nature can safely be deferred to the project-level EIS stage without running any significant risk that these would ultimately stand in the way of

---

[10] At the Turkey Point plant in the state of Florida (United States), where water temperatures are comparable to those in Sri Lanka, thermal discharges went directly into Biscayne Bay, which has a depth of about 1 meter and is semi-enclosed. Thermal effluent killed or damaged 118 hectares of benthic organisms in the first two years of operation.

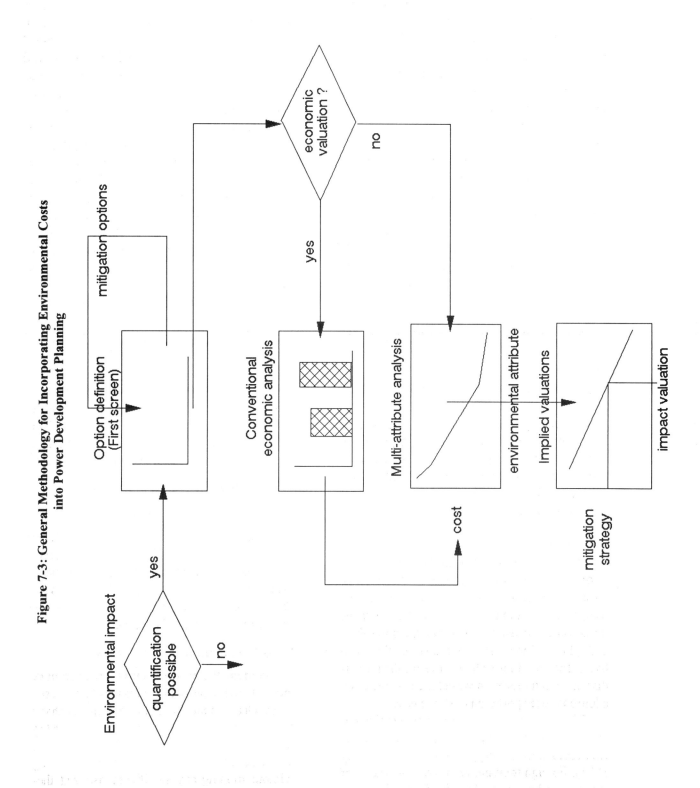

Figure 7-3: General Methodology for Incorporating Environmental Costs into Power Development Planning

implementing a strategy identified at the planning stage. Thus, in the case of Trincomalee, while it may well be true that a number of very vocal interest groups raised objections based on very narrow issues (whale watching, oyster beds), the issue that in fact prevailed was the view held by the broader environmental community that discharge of effluents into shallow waters constituted a broad risk to aquatic ecosystems. The trade-off to be examined in system planning studies, therefore, concerns the cost of various cooling system options to limit thermal discharges, not the presence or absence of specific species at specific locations. The latter is, however, the proper concern of the project-level EIS.

Judgments must still be made; and there may be some impacts that at some projects may turn out to be purely local, but at others prove to be of national significance. Resettlement at hydro plants is a good example: at some projects, the resettlement impacts may be quite small, and would neither strain the ability of local authorities to manage, nor be likely to become a political issue at a national scale. But at other sites, the scale of resettlement needs may be such that indeed it may require the attention of national decision makers. Certainly if the high dam variant of the Kukule project is built, the need to resettle some 9,100 people defines an issue of national importance; on the other hand, the run-of-river variant would displace only 135 people in 27 families.

Many applications of multi-attribute methods suffer from the same malady that afflict environmental impact statements: in their desire to be comprehensive, they become tedious recitations of all possible impacts, with not much

thought given to what is really important.[11] For example, in the scoring system used in testimony in a Vermont (United States) proceeding (which attempted to deal with the question of the relative environmental impacts of hydro imports from Canada, demand-side management measures, and decentralized renewables), 36 different attributes were used (Mintzer et al. 1990). These included separate attributes for each of the following material uses: steel, concrete, aluminum, silicon, glass, plastics, and non-ferrous metals.[12] Exactly what environmental concerns the consumption of these materials implies that is not already reflected by other attributes is unclear.

A proliferation of attributes tends to make weighing more difficult (and may introduce a bias simply because one is reluctant to weight any particular attribute as near zero). Moreover, trade-offs become difficult to understand and display to decision makers in comprehensible form if there are too many of them. The guiding principle ought to be that one starts from what are the most important impact issues (greenhouse gas emissions, health effects of fossil fuel pollution, the risk of groundwater contamination, the risk posed to aquatic ecosystems from thermal plumes, and so on), and then select one attribute for each of these concerns.[13]

One of the issues at this stage is how to draw the boundaries of analysis. In this case study we have bounded the problem in such a way that we have examined only that set of environmental issues that are likely to be of direct importance to national decision makers. Thus we have not included the environmental impacts associated with the extraction of

[11] This was a major problem in the United States in the early years of the Environmental Protection Agency (EPA). In 1977, in response to EISs of increasingly encyclopedic proportions, President Carter directed the Council on Environmental Quality, the entity established a monitor EPA, to issue new regulations "... designed to make the EIS more useful to decision makers and the public and to reduce paperwork and the accumulation of extraneous background data in order to emphasize the need to focus on real environmental issues and alternatives" (Executive Order, May 24, 1977). This led to the development of the so-called scoping process as a means to direct effort to real problems.

[12] This study also proposed an interesting approach to the determination of weights, based on the reversibility of the impact as the most important factor: high level radioactive waste from a nuclear power plant would be assigned a high weight because it remains radioactive for thousands of years while thermal pollution of a river during low flow periods would be assigned a low weight. What is critical to validity, however, is whether or not the weights actually reflect the trade-offs that decision makers would be prepared to make in practice.

[13] All these points have long been established in the decision sciences literature, and were validated in a large number of applications in the 1970s to power plant siting, particularly by Keeney and his colleagues (see, for example, Keeney and Raiffa [1976], and Keeney and Nair [1977]). The 1981 EPRI report by Woodward-Clyde (Keeney et al. 1981) is one illustration of a well-founded application of decision theory to utility resource planning (a coal/nuclear choice).

imported coal (that would arise in Australia or South Africa), except in the sensitivity analysis to coal prices: if in fact Australian policy makers do decide to include the cost of environmental externalities associated with extraction (say by imposition of rigid land reclamation requirements on the coal mining companies), then that would simply be reflected in a higher coal price to Sri Lanka.

On the other hand, we have included the question of greenhouse gas emissions; this is because Sri Lanka decision makers will need to deal with the issue as part of the international discussions that are now underway, and any international agreements that are reached will surely have repercussions in Sri Lanka itself.

Finally, attributes (and criteria) should be conceptually distinct, that is, preference independent. Decision analysis differentiates between statistical independence and preferential independence; the former refers to the correlation structure of the alternatives, the latter to structure of the user's preferences—a distinction that might be characterized as "facts" versus "values." Additive value functions—such as those used in weighing and summation methods—assume certain type of value independence, but statistical independence is irrelevant to the validity of the additive form.

Step 2. Physical Quantification

To some extent, of course, the physical quantification is not unrelated to the selection of attributes: clearly there is not much point in selecting criteria that cannot be quantified. That of course does not imply that only quantifiable criteria are relevant or important: it means only that such unquantifiable criteria need to be considered through some other means.

As an example, the health impacts associated with exposure to very high voltage transmission lines may be viewed as significant. There is presently no basis for quantifying that health effect. Therefore, the way to include an assessment of the issue is to define a technology scenario that eliminates the need for EHV transmission (for example, by moving the baseload coal plants from the remote areas in the south and Trincomalee to the major load center in Colombo), and then asking whether one is

willing to incur the incremental health costs of this option (associated with exposure to fossil plant air pollutants) in order to avoid the health impacts of EHV transmission.

The measure used for quantification is especially important. For example, the attribute "solid waste disposal" expressed as tons of waste generated, is often encountered. Yet, precisely why the quantity of solid waste is relevant is unclear, except that it is easy to estimate. Since a large part of the land required may be for solid waste disposal, there may in any event be double counting if there is also a criterion for "land use" (expressed in acres). Moreover, in fact the relevant environmental risk associated with ash and scrubber sludge disposal is the risk of toxic leachates contaminating nearby aquifers, which has very little relationship to the quantity of waste produced, but rather to characteristics such as soil permeability, depth to the groundwater table, and rainfall.

Step 3. Preliminary Screening/Option Definition

A great deal of care must be taken in any preliminary screening exercise. Some exclusionary screens can be applied with great confidence: no facilities in designated wildlife sanctuaries, no nuclear plants in areas of known geological faults, and so on. However, many other screens routinely applied by engineers in a siting study involve judgments that may reflect only some personal viewpoint (even if supported by personal experience)—such as a presumption that a coal-based plant must be "near" its coal receiving port. What does this really mean? Obviously there are costs associated with intermediate truck or conveyer belt transport, but these have to be put in the context of other costs associated with particular sites.

Indeed, one of the most important considerations at this stage is to properly define the universe of alternatives to be studied. A priori judgments that certain technology and mitigation options need not be considered further are particularly to be avoided. This is again clearly indicated by the history of the Trincomalee site selection process. In the early stages, the advantages of the deepwater harbor were deemed so compelling that south coast sites were not further considered. Then, at the subsequent prefeasibility stage, the only technology options considered for Trincomalee Bay were conventional, once-through cooled plants with discharge into the shallow waters of the bay. Once the environmental community came to the conclusion that the resulting thermal impacts were unacceptable, attention then reverted back to the south coast. Yet it is entirely unclear that the additional costs of an alternative cooling system at Trincomalee, which would mitigate the impacts of the thermal effluents, are greater than the additional costs of coal transportation at a south coast site.

In the particular case of Sri Lanka, security considerations, and a temporary reduction in the rate-of-demand growth, made it relatively easy to suspend discussion of first the coal plant at Trincomalee, and then of its replacement at Mawella. Nevertheless, as a matter of methodological procedure, the important point is that all reasonable technological configurations should be considered for all reasonable sites at the stage of the initial analysis of environmental trade-offs.

Step 4. Economic Valuation

Clearly the most difficult valuation issue concerns the value of human life, and the economic cost of illness. Indeed, one of the major findings of a recent comprehensive literature review is that a substantial fraction of the environmental damages associated with particulate, SO_2, and NOx emissions is related to health impacts and visibility impairment (Pace University Center for Environmental Legal Studies 1990). American valuations of these impacts indeed suggest damages that are higher than the costs of pollution control now imposed by American standards. Whether that is true for developing countries is an interesting and important question, and indicates the need for some country-specific contingent valuation studies to establish the willingness to pay to avoid illness.

In general, we are of the view that where valuations involve a high degree of uncertainty,

one is better off not to attempt them, and simply use the physical impact quantification in a subsequent multi-attribute analysis of trade-off curves. In this study, therefore, we have avoided use of dose-response functions in the multi-attribute analysis, but instead used the population exposure to specific pollutants as the proxy for health damages. In any event, since the main purpose here is to provide a basis for comparison of practical options, rather than to establish some absolute measure of impact, the population exposure measure still provides a great deal of relevant information.

Step 5. Multi-attribute Analysis

Multi-attribute decision analysis has been developed expressly for situations where decisions must be made upon more than one objective that cannot be reduced to a single dimension. Its central focus is the quantification, display, and resolution of trade-offs that must be made when objectives conflict. In the case of application to the power sector, there may well be strategies that have beneficial impacts on environmental and on economic objectives—most energy efficiency investments that are economically justifiable also bring about a reduction in emissions and hence improve environmental quality as well as economic efficiency. In most other cases, however, there are economic penalties associated with investments designed to reduce emissions or improve environmental quality. It could be argued that if economic valuation of the environmental costs and benefits were in fact possible, these might well outweigh the short run- costs. However, from a practical standpoint, expressed in terms likely to be understood by laymen decision makers, the trade-off is indeed one of short-run economic costs (or the present value of readily quantifiable costs) against longer-term benefits to environmental quality.

Multi-attribute decision analysis, even if not formally described as such, has been used for some time for power plant siting and transmission corridor routing,[14] including in Sri Lanka itself. More recently, attempts have been made to use such techniques for broader

[14] It is hard to evaluate whether cases in which formal models were used for siting decisions were any better than in cases in which they were not. It is certainly true that the most celebrated siting controversies in the United States, from the Storm King Mountain pumped storage project to the Shoreham and Seabrook nuclear plants, would not have been resolved sooner, or at less cost to the economy, had formal siting models been applied. But these siting decisions were in

studies of energy-environmental interactions (for example, ADB 1991). Finally, the technique has come into increasing use by state regulatory commissions in the United States in an attempt to develop practical approaches to considering environmental objectives in the power sector.

Step 6. Implicit Valuation

Implicit valuations can be most useful to guide resource allocation decisions. For example, we estimated the valuation of a human life implied by a hypothetical decision to install an FGD system at Trincomalee. The particular value of $1.5 million is important not as an estimate of human life per se, but what it implies about health expenditures of the Government as a whole. Clearly it makes no sense to spend $1.5 million to avoid one death at a coal-fired power plant by installation of an FGD system, if the expenditure of $100,000 on improved medical diagnostic equipment at a hospital might avoid 10 deaths. Implied valuations can also be derived from the trade-off curves themselves.

Step 7. Decision Rule

There are a number of reasons to avoid the use of formal decision rules at this stage of environmental debate in Sri Lanka. For example, we might have ranked the policy options studied using a weighing summation rule to derive an overall merit score for each strategy. However, that would inevitably force attention on whether or not our weights were correct, or whether we had elicited weights from the appropriate group of decision makers. Moreover, a number of methodological problems arise in the application of procedures to elicit valid weights, which can be described as still being subjects of research.

We believe that for those countries where the process of setting clear environmental priorities are still at a very early stage, the first step is to first try to focus on the nature of the trade-offs themselves, and to attempt to identify policy options that are robust with respect to the many uncertainties that arise, and that may be completely independent of what economic values are attributed to environmental externalities, or what relative weights are placed on particular impacts. Of course it is unlikely that options can be found that are completely—in other words, that they are best across all criteria. Nevertheless, as demonstrated in our case study, certain policy and technology options —such as demand side management measures and certain clean coal technologies—do appear to be desirable from both environmental and economic perspectives over a wide range of conditions.

Finally, it is almost certainly true that whatever the shortcomings of the sort of analysis conducted in this study, and whatever the level of uncertainty that is associated with both physical quantification and economic valuation of environmental externalities, existing practices are so flawed that the application of almost any rigorous analytical approach represents a significant step forward.

Evaluating Options

The key step in the multi-attribute analysis is the identification of the best set of candidate options, from the large number of candidate plans, that merit close study for implementation.

A first criterion is that of dominance. Let the set of such plans be denoted P_1, P_2, and so forth. Suppose for the sake of clarity that there are only two attributes: cost, and an environmental attribute reflecting the population exposure to SO_2. Figure 7-4 depicts the solution space for this problem, in which we plot the values of the two attributes for each plan.

The plan P_1 is said to strictly dominate plan P_2 if P_1 is better than (or equal to)—that is, dominates—P_2 in terms of every attribute. Thus, as illustrated on Figure 7-4, P_1 is better than P_2 in both cost and SO_2 exposure. P_1 strictly dominates all of the plans beyond the boundary AP_1B. By repeating such comparisons for all pairs of plans, and discarding all dominated plans, the remaining plans constitute

---

fact made in the 1960s, and the use of formal siting models was significantly improved in the 1970s as a direct consequence of the problems encountered at these (and other) plants. The most important lesson from the application of formal siting models in the United States is the need for public participation in the decision process: it was very quickly realized that as decision models forced explicit quantification of values and preferences, this could no longer be done by the self-appointed "siting experts" of the utilities and their consultants.

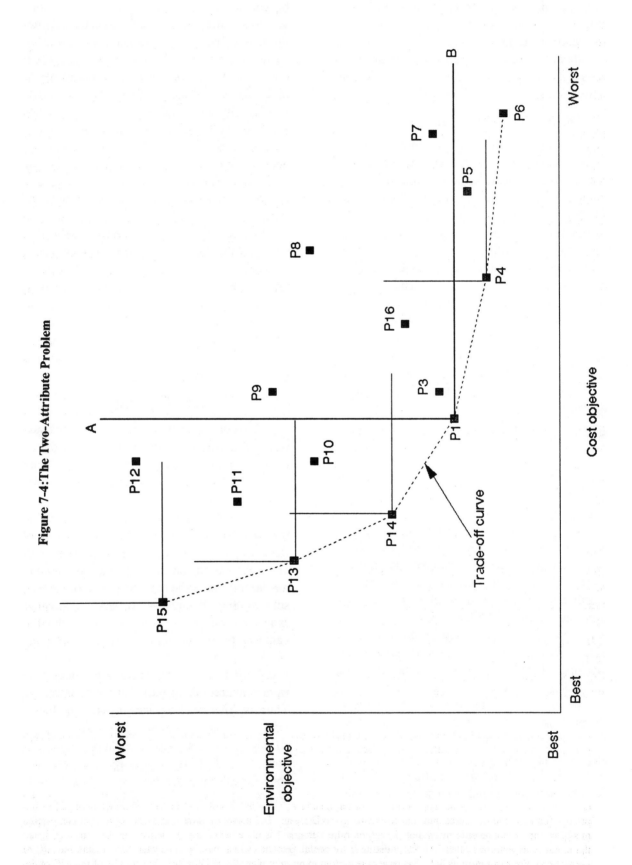

Figure 7-4:The Two-Attribute Problem

the set of the so-called non-inferior solutions —in our case the set of plans $\{P_6, P_4, P_1, P_{14}, P_{13}, P_{15}\}$. These points, in turn, define the trade-off curve, as indicated on Figure 7-4.

This procedure will in general provide a means for reducing a very large number of possible plans to some smaller number of plans—a "short list" or "candidate list" that is to be presented to decision makers. In the example shown, using the concept of strict dominance, plan P_3 would not appear on the resulting short list. Yet one might argue that while P_3 is somewhat worse in both attributes than P_1, it is not significantly worse (as opposed to, say, P_{16} and P_8, which are significantly worse in both attributes). In particular, because of uncertainties associated with the calculations, one may be reluctant to discard a plan that is not significantly worse than another from a final short list.

This idea is captured by the concept of significant dominance (as defined by Crousillat and Merrill 1992). P_1 is said to significantly dominate P_2 if $a_i(P_1) + m_i < a_i(P_2)$ for at least one i, and if $a_i(P_1) - e_i < a_i(P_2)$ for all i, where m and e are significance parameters or tolerances. m_i is the smallest difference in values for attribute a_i such that one plan is considered to be much worse than the other, and e_i is the largest difference between values such that one plan is considered equivalent to another.

These concepts are illustrated on Figure 7-5. P_1 significantly dominates all of the plans in the shaded region. Note that P_2, which is not strictly dominated by P_1, is significantly dominated. That is, significant dominance also rejects solutions where the improvement in one attribute (in this case in the environmental objective) is bought at great cost in the other (in this case in cost). In other words, from the environmental perspective, for a plan to be

significantly better than P_1, it must have a value less than $P_1 - e_i$.

The knee set is the set of plans that are not significantly dominated. In the example of Figure 7-5, redrawn on Figure 7-6, the knee set is $\{P_1, P_4, P_9\}$. Note that this set differs from the non-inferior set, defined by the trade-off curve, which is the set $\{P_2, P_1, P_5\}$. From the practical standpoint of decision making, the knee set is clearly the more useful, since the non-inferior set also includes solutions where slight improvements in one objective are bought only at great cost in the other—such as P_5 and P_2. Another way of expressing this is that the knee set consists of that set of plans for which decision makers representing different objectives are most likely to agree upon: in the above example, both P_5 and P_2 are unlikely candidates for agreement, even though both lie on the trade-off curve.

The knee set will be a function both of the values of the significance parameters used, and the shape of the trade-off curve. In the situation of Figure 7-6, the knee set is relatively compact, because the trade-off curve exhibits a sharp rate of change of curvature at P_1. However, in the situation shown on Figure 7-7, there are no sharp changes in curvature of the trade-off curve: here the knee set is the same as the non-inferior set.

A third criterion for identifying desirable plans is the set of options that lies in the third quadrant with respect to the base case (see Figure 7-8). Plans that lie in this quadrant are better than the base-case in both criteria; consequently no trade-off is involved because both interests (in our case both cost and environmental objective) are served by adopting them.

Plans that lie in quadrant I are inferior in both cost and environment, and both objectives are served by avoiding plans in this quadrant.[15]

---

[15] Presently the CEB uses the following measure to evaluate alternative generation options: the net present value of total system costs (capital and operating costs of new facilities plus operating costs of existing facilities) over the next 15 years is divided by the present value of generation requirements over the same period less the present value of generation from existing hydro. This measure is a good approximation for the average incremental cost (AIC) of generation (since in the average hydro year, the current energy demand is almost exactly met by the existing hydro plants). However, for our study this is not the appropriate criterion, insofar as some of the policy measures examined here reflect improved demand-side measures and improvements in T&D losses. Therefore, in order to provide for a valid comparison of supply- and demand-side measures, the appropriate numeraire is incremental energy demand at the consumer level; the result is an estimate of the AIC of meeting incremental demand (which will be somewhat higher than the AIC of generation). For example, for the CEB base case system expansion plan, the ENVIROPLAN estimate of the AIC of demand is 5.81 U.S. cents per kilowatt-hour, while the AIC of generation is 5.65 U.S. cents per kilowatt-hour. The latter

Figure 7-5: Significant Dominance

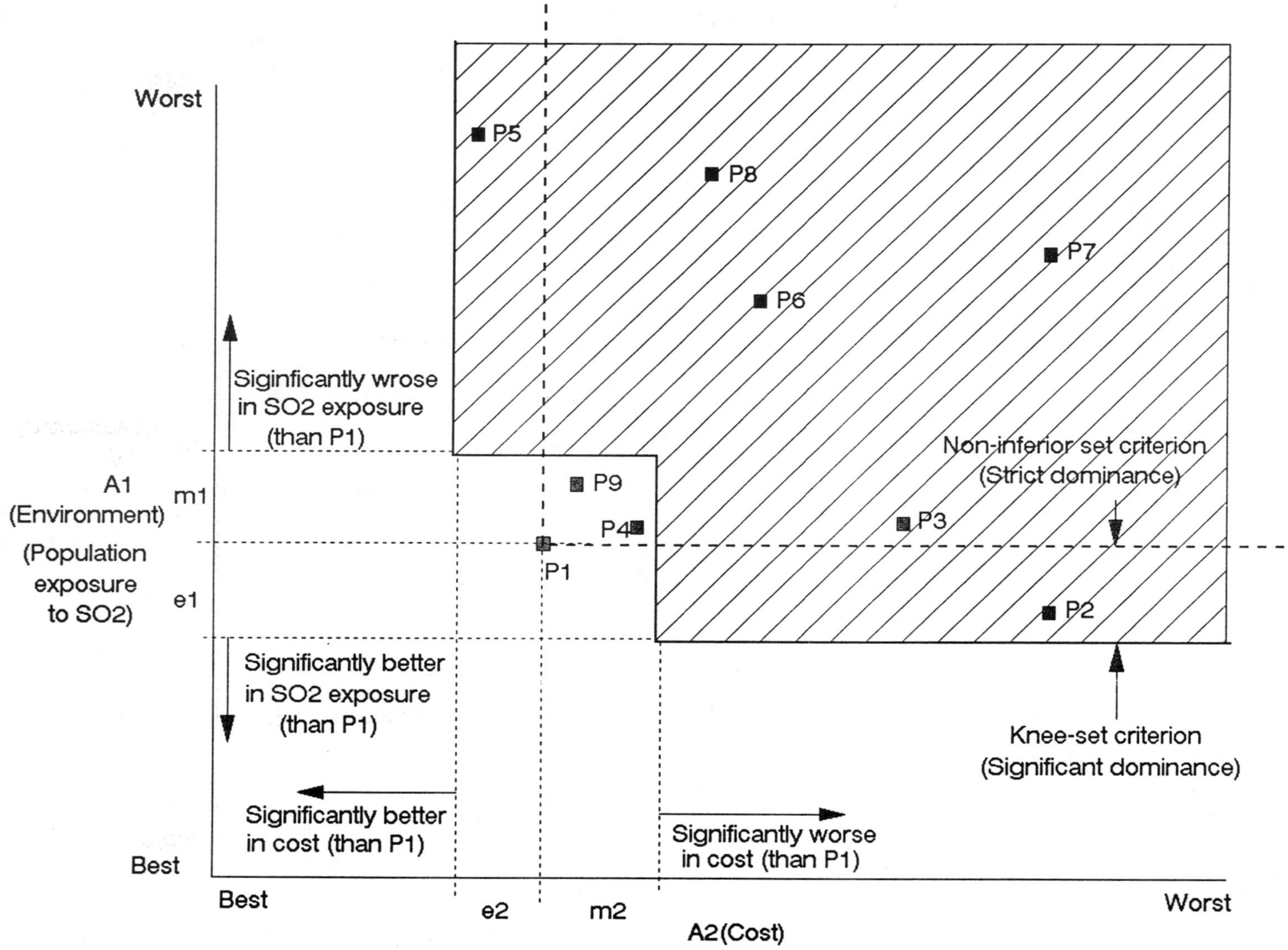

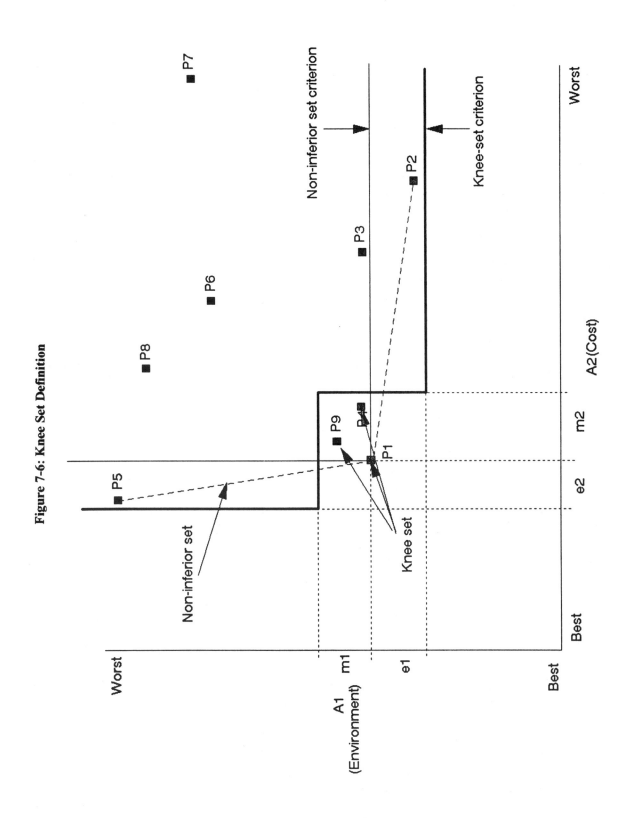

Figure 7-6: Knee Set Definition

Figure 7-7: Knee Set Equivalent to the Non-inferior (Trade-off Curve) Set

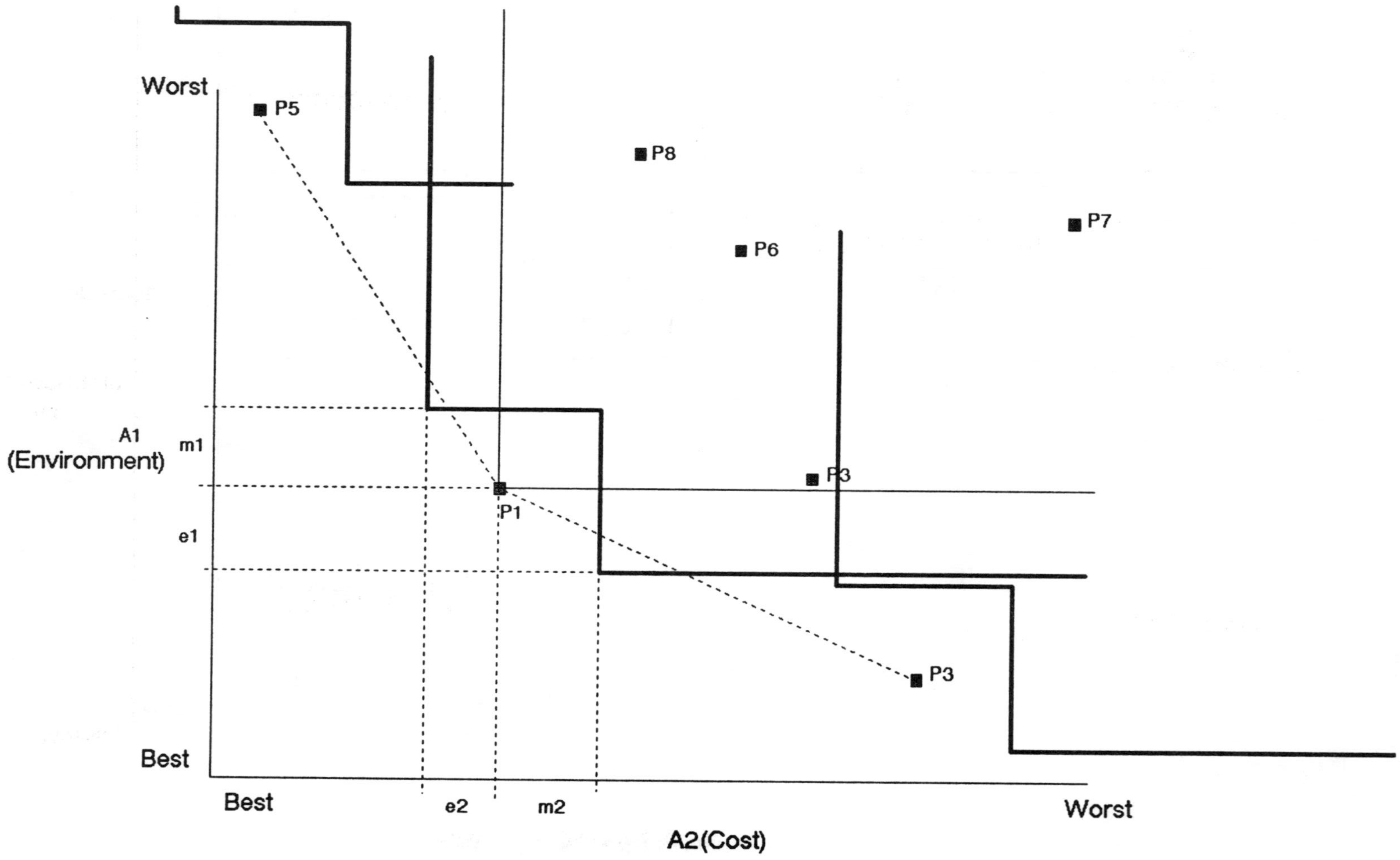

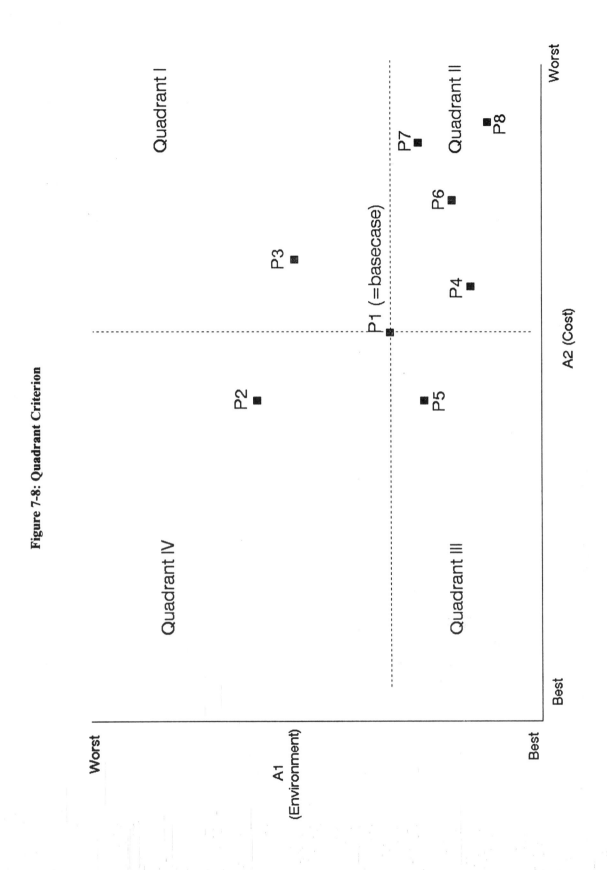

Figure 7-8: Quadrant Criterion

It is in quadrants II and IV where trade-offs must be made—where an improvement in one objective necessarily implies worsening in the other.

Extension to Multiple Dimensions

All of the mathematical definitions of knee sets and non-inferior sets continue to be valid when there are more than two dimensions. In this case, one should properly refer to the trade-off surface, say $S = S(C, A_1, A_2, ... A_n)$, which is an n-dimensional non-inferior hypersurface, where C is the cost attribute, and A_i (i=1,..n) are n environmental attributes.

A rigorous definition of the trade-off between any two of these attributes would require that the values of all of the others are held constant. In practice that is rarely possible—for example, finding a series of plans that all had the same water impact, but varied only in cost and air quality impact would be hard to find. What can be done is to simply plot the values of two attributes (for example, C versus A_1), and to assume that the variations in the other attributes may be ignored. In other words, in the three-dimensional case, the third dimension is in effect projected onto the two-dimensional plane of the two attributes being displayed, ignoring variations in the third dimension.[16]

It might be noted, however, that while looking at attributes only two at a time provides great insight, it may not in fact reveal all of the members of the non-inferior set. This is discussed in some detail in the main report (Meier and Munasinghe 1992).

Assumptions for the Case Study

Although cast as a research study, we nevertheless deemed it to be important that the results were properly aligned to the work of the CEB. Thus, for example, rather than derive our own demand forecasts, we elected to use official forecasts of the CEB, which include a set of low, base case, and high forecasts of the type that we needed to examine the robustness of our findings to alternative load growth assumptions.

The System Load Curve

An analysis of the impact of demand side management and nondispatchable technologies requires much more detailed assumptions about the nature of the load curve than what is provided by the simple aggregate characterization as the system load factor (SLF). We, therefore, used a linearized, trapezoidal representation of the annual load duration curve of the form shown on Figure 7-9. This curve was then manipulated algebraically to depict the impact of measures such as reductions in transmission and distribution (T&D) loss rates,[17] demand-side management measures, or, as depicted on Figure 7-9, wind energy—which, as a nondispatchable technology, is modelled as negative demand. Because early field tests of wind energy availability on the south coast show little impact on the peak, the principal impact is on intermediate demand, as indicated.

Fuel Prices

The question of fuel price projections are obviously of critical importance, because they are a critical factor in determining the generation mix. But it is not just the absolute level of prices that matters. For Sri Lanka, a critical variable is the ratio of coal to heavy fueloil price, because that ratio will determine the balance of diesel and coal plants in the generation mix, in turn of central importance to the environmental impacts that follow. Again, as a base case we use the September 1991 projections of the CEB. These in turn are based on the December 1990 projections of the World Bank.

Historically, the ratio of fueloil to coal price has shown great fluctuations, ranging

---

is very close the CEB's estimate of 5.61 U.S. cents per kilowatt-hour.

[16] In the literature, there are a number of examples of such trade-off curves dealing with economic-environmental trade-offs in the power sector. The first example that we encountered is Ferrell (1978), who examined the trade-off between cost and SO_2 emissions. Other examples include Meier and Ruff (1979), and Amagai and Leung (1991), who looked at CO_2 emissions trade-offs.

[17] It is important to recognize that T&D losses are proportional to the square of the load. This means that if T&D losses are specified in the conventional way as some percentage of total energy generated, this value cannot simply be applied across the entire load duration curve in a uniform manner. In other words, if annual energy losses are reduced, say, from 13 to 12 percent, the benefit to the peak load will be much greater than this average value, and the benefit to the off-peak period will be smaller.

Figure 7-9:Impact of Wind Energy on the Load Duration Curve

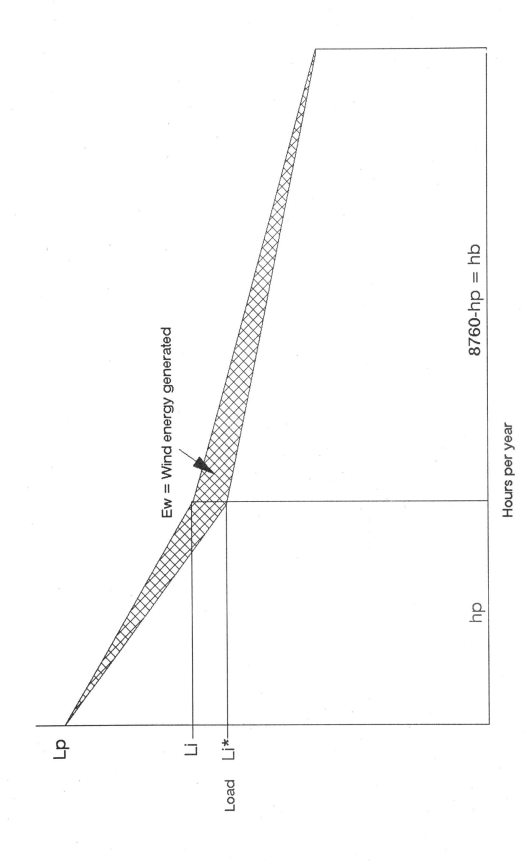

from 3 in late 1984, to less than 1 in early 1986 and late 1987: indeed, this was a time when many dual-fueled plants, which had been converted from oil to coal in the late 1970s, switched to residual oil.

From an environmental policy viewpoint, the relationship between fuel price and sulfur content is of particular interest. The relationship between low sulfur (0.5 percent sulfur by weight) and high sulfur (3.5 percent) fueloil traded on the Singapore spot market is fairly constant: in the three-year period 1989-1991, the average premium for the low sulfur fueloil was about 27 percent, equal to about $4 per barrel.

On Figure 7-10 we graph the low sulfur fueloil price as a function of the high sulfur fueloil price. There are two periods, one in spring of 1990, the second in October and November 1990, when the price of low sulfur fueloil is unusually high, and falls outside the general trendline; these deviations are seen to be of short duration and can be ignored for long-term projection purposes.

The relationship between price and sulfur content of internationally traded coal is less clear. A regression analysis of recent prices of coals traded in the Pacific rim market[18] produced the following relationship:[19]

$$P = -0.342 + 0.003686\ H\quad 2.577\ \text{sulfur percent} - 0.744\ \text{ash percent};$$

$$R2 = .558\quad (0.0013)\ (9.41)(0.451)$$

where H is the heat value in British thermal units (Btu) per pound and P is in dollars per ton. The figures in parentheses indicate the standard errors. The heat value and ash terms have the expected sign, but the sulfur content term has an unexpected sign (one would expect the relationship to show that lower sulfur contents have higher price, as with ash). The range of variation in sulfur content is too small for a statistically significant relationship to be established.

A reasonable conclusion would be that in the export markets in the Indian Ocean/Pacific rim area, sulfur content is not as important a consideration as it is in Europe or in the Eastern part of the U.S.; both 0.6 percent or 1 percent sulfur coals would be regarded as "low" sulfur, that would not generally require FGD systems. High sulfur coal (3 percent and above), for which a substantial discount would be expected, is simply not available as an export fuel in this market.

Hydro Assumptions

As a result of a close re-examination of the historical hydrological records, the assumptions for hydro energy availability have been revised downwards by the CEB. The result is that in the 1991 Generation planning study, total hydro energy of existing plants has been reduced from 4,070 gigawatt-hours to 3,869 gigawatt-hours, with corresponding reductions in projected energy from new projects as well.

The changes in hydro assumptions, and the differences in the relative fuel prices between residual oil (the fuel used in diesels) and coal, have a dramatic impact on the optimal generation mix as determined by the WASP model—as indicated on Figure 7-11. This shows capacity additions built in the periods through 2000 and 2005. As one might expect, given lower hydro energy, fewer hydro plants are built in the 1991 study. But the most dramatic difference is the mix of diesels and coal plants; in the 1991 study, by 2005 some 900 megawatts of coal fired plants would be needed, as opposed to only 300 megawatts in the 1990 study. The differences in the environmental impacts that follow from these two very different generation mixes are obvious.

The Analytical Model

Although a review of the literature reveals a great many different approaches to the problem of identifying the non-inferior set, three methods account for the bulk of practical

---

[18] We excluded, for example, internationally traded coals from the east coast of the U.S. and Poland, since these would be unlikely sources for Sri Lanka.

[19] Time and resource constraints did not permit a comprehensive analysis of likely coal costs, c.i.f. Sri Lanka, as a function of all of the parameters of importance. In addition to sulfur, ash, and heat contents, other significant characteristics include moisture content, volatile matter contents, Hardgrove grindability Index, and assessments of corrosion, fouling, and slagging potential, among others. These were all considered in the Black and Veath International (BVI) Trincomalee Fuel Supply and Transportation Study (March 1985), although no statistical analysis was presented.

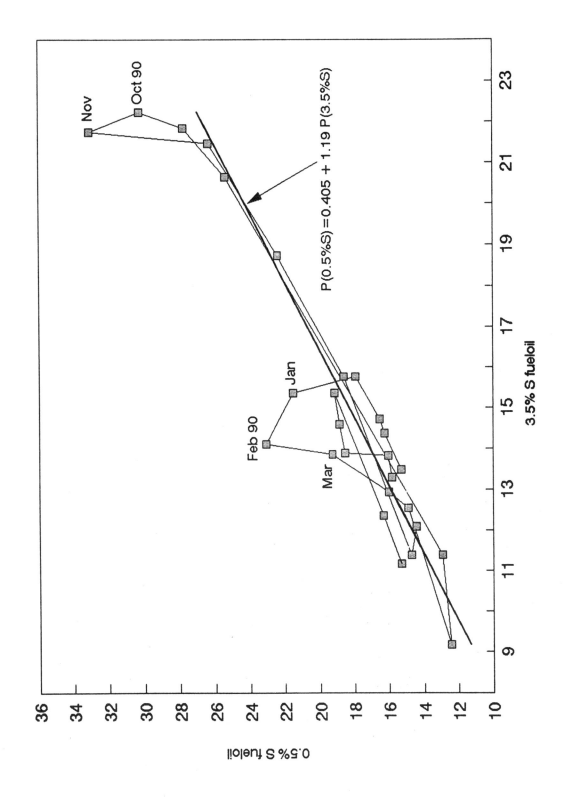

Figure 7-10: Relationship between Low and High-Sulfur Fuel Oil

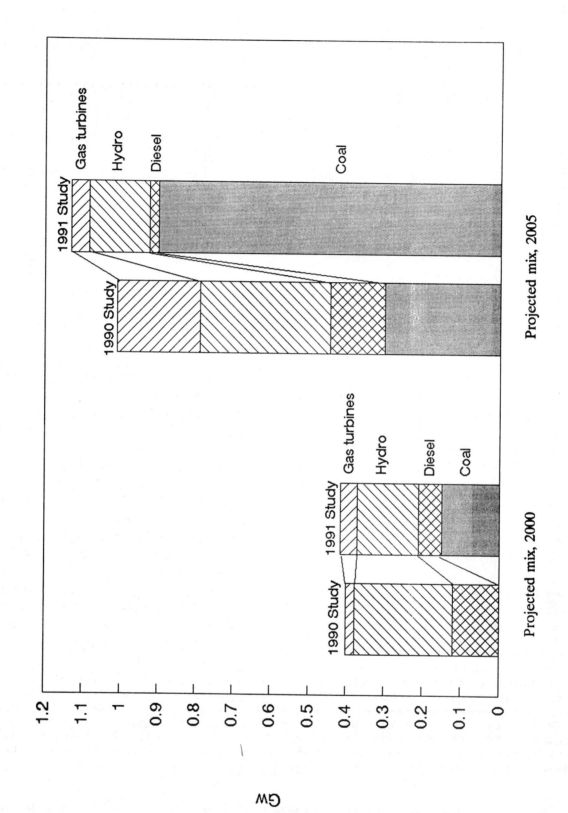

Figure 7-11: Generation Mix Additions in the 1990 and 1991 Studies

applications. The first two, the so-called constraint method, and the weighing method, are derived from the theory and practice of multi-objective mathematical programming; the third is simply to generate the solution space of discretely defined plan alternatives in a simulation model, and determine the trade-off curve and knee set by inspection.

Even though a number of existing optimization models appear suited to either the constraint or the weighing method, we rejected the mathematical programming approaches in favor of direct simulation.[20] The most important reason is that we are interested in not just the non-inferior set, but also those solutions that are near this curve, and in particular the plans in the knee sets. Solutions that are close to the optimum are not normally generated by the commonly available LP software packages. Of course, all of the algorithms will pass through near-optimal solutions as they make their way through the solution space, but to examine them individually is not generally possible.

The direct simulation model has a number of advantages for practical policy making that offset the problem of not being sure that all of the points in the non-inferior set have in fact been looked at. Besides the ability to identify knee sets, one may also be interested in identifying very poor programs and policy packages, namely those that never occur in any of the knee sets. The main requirement, therefore, is for a model that can examine very quickly perhaps several hundred different expansion plan variants, given the very large number of combinations of different site locations, pollution

abatement options, and technology variations: the use of a complex engineering model such as WASP or EGEAS (for Electric Generation Analysis System) is simply unsuited for the sort of sensitivity analysis required here.

In any event, a second problem with the existing models such as WASP concerns their scope: while they provide great detail on the supply side, they have very limited capability of examining demand side issues beyond simply using alternative exogenously specified load forecasts. IAEA, which supports the WASP model, does provide a demand side model for use with WASP called MAED: but this model is not currently installed in Sri Lanka. Moreover, even if it were available, the MAED-WASP combination is still very cumbersome, and ill suited to the requirements of our case study.

Several other existing models were reviewed as possible candidates for our case study, including GEMIS/TEMIS, developed in Germany;[21] ENPEP/IMPACTS, developed at Argonne National Laboratory;[22] EGEAS/COMPASS, developed by EPRI;[23] and LEAP, developed for the Beijer Institute of Sweden.[24]

All of these models contain some parts of what we needed: reviews of these models are provided in the annex to chapter 10 of the main report. None contained all of the necessary features. Most importantly, none had the direct capability of multi-attribute analysis integrated into a credible characterization of the electric sector, and suitable for extensive sensitivity analysis. And because all involved the use of compiled program environments (PASCAL, FORTRAN, C, and so on),

[20] One LP model in particular that has multi-objective capability is MARKAL. Developed as a mainframe model fifteen years ago for the International Energy Agency (IEA) to examine long-term energy R&D strategies, it has recently been moved to a microcomputer environment and has seen new use in the United States to examine the implications of CO_2 emissions reduction strategies. The model has also been used in some developing countries, notably Indonesia. Whatever the merits of the new user-interface, we viewed this model as being simply too unwieldy for application to our study.

[21] GEMIS: for Gesamt-Emissions-Modell Integrierter Systems; see OKO Institute (1989). An English version of the model, known as TEMIS (for Total Emission Model for Integrated Systems) was developed in 1990 with support from the U.S. Department of Energy. The model provides a total fuel cycle analysis of residuals—in which residuals are calculated in a consistent way from the point of fuel extraction to the point of use.

[22] See Buehring et al. (1991). The WASP model is widely used in developing countries for capacity expansion optimization—indeed it has been used for this purpose by the generation planning branch of Sri Lanka's CEB for some years. Argonne National Laboratory has developed a microcomputer version of WASP that has been integrated into a broader energy planning packaged called ENPEP (for ENergy and Power Evaluation Package). This includes a module called IMPACTS, which provides the capability for calculating pollution residuals and pollution control costs.

[23] For a brief description see, for example, Stone & Webster Management Consultants, Inc. (1989). For a more detailed description, see EGEAS Capabilities Manual, April 1989, also available from Stone and Webster.

[24] See Raskin (1985).

Figure 7-12: Major Features of ENVIROPLAN Computer Model

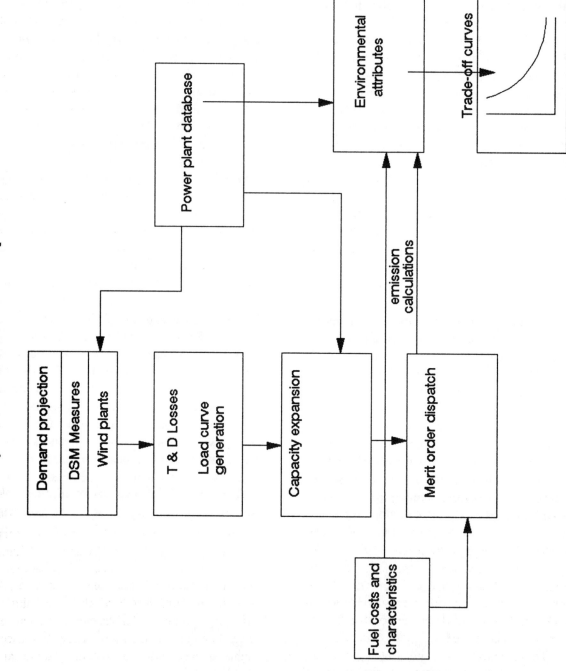

modification would have involved considerable programming effort that was beyond the resources of our study.

In the end, we decided to use ENVIROPLAN, a LOTUS 1-2-3 model expressly designed to analyze the environmental impacts of the power sector in a multi-attribute analysis.[25] With the entire set of calculations in a single spreadsheet, including the generation and display of trade-off curves and knee sets, sensitivity analyses that permit the examination of wide ranges of assumptions and policy and program alternatives are relatively easy to conduct. And as a spreadsheet, modifications and enhancements could be easily added as the study progressed.

The main features of ENVIROPLAN model itself are indicated on Figure 7-12. The process starts with the demand projection, which is aligned to the CEB forecasts as described in the previous section, and also as noted above, adjusted to reflect the impact of demand-side management (DSM), wind energy, T&D losses, and so forth.

Generation capacity expansion is based on the anticipated peak load plus some reserve margin. ENVIROPLAN has several available generation expansion algorithms: the one used in the Sri Lanka case study is based on a heuristic, such that the model builds plants in the same sequence as WASP, but adjusts the timing in such a way as to maintain an exogenously specified planning reserve margin. This is a much less sophisticated approach than the probabilistic dynamic programming of WASP that provides an optimization subject to loss of load probabilities (LOLP); however, experience indicates that this provides a reasonable approximation if the changes to the load curve are small. Thus, as we perturb the original load curve, say to provide for energy conservation, ENVIROPLAN will defer the construction sequence in light of the lower peak demands.

These concepts are illustrated on Figure 7-13. The "target margin" is the smoothed (5-period) reserve margin as yielded by the WASP solution. The "minimum planning

reserve margin (PRM)" is what is used as the expansion criterion by the "adjusted " algorithm: the next plant is added if the reserve margin would otherwise drop below this minimum level.

However, the actual expansion path is iteratively adjusted in such a way as also to meet a maximum unserved energy requirement, taken here as 1 percent of total annual energy. That is, if after merit order dispatch, the unserved energy exceeds this minimum in any year, the target margin is increased incrementally for that year, and the expansion calculations are repeated.

ENVIROPLAN makes merit order dispatch calculations for each of the three hydro conditions used by the CEB for WASP simulations, and the "average" dispatch, which is used to calculate fuel consumption and pollutant emissions from thermal plants, is then the weighted sum of the three individual dispatch conditions. This will provide a much better alignment of ENVIROPLAN to WASP than the much simpler procedure of dispatching into "average" hydro conditions.

The merit order itself is calculated in the usual way by incremental marginal cost. ENVIROPLAN may yield a marginally lower estimate of fuel consumption for thermal plants because fuel consumption is calculated at the full load heat rate; we do not distinguish between heat rate at minimum load and the incremental heat rate as does WASP.

Technology and Policy Scenarios

Six major policy scenarios were examined. Each scenario is translated into a set of specific technological assumptions necessary to quantify the impact of these policies in practice, as shown on Table 7-1. It should be noted that the specific measures examined are purely illustrative; for example, the replacement of incandescent lighting by high efficiency fluorescent lights is only one of a potentially quite large number of DSM measures that might be examined. The same observation applies to the wind power example as well, since

---

[25] ENVIROPLAN uses version 2.4 of LOTUS 1-2-3. In contrast to version 2.2, spreadsheets of essentially unlimited size can be handled, because cell pointers are stored in expanded memory rather than in conventional memory. In version 2.2, the size of spreadsheets was limited by the 640 kilobytes of conventional memory; in version 2.4, the size is limited only by the amount of expanded memory available. ENVIROPLAN runs comfortably on 386 machines with 1 megabyte of conventional and 3 megabytes of expanded memory.

Figure 7-13: Reserve Margin Definitions

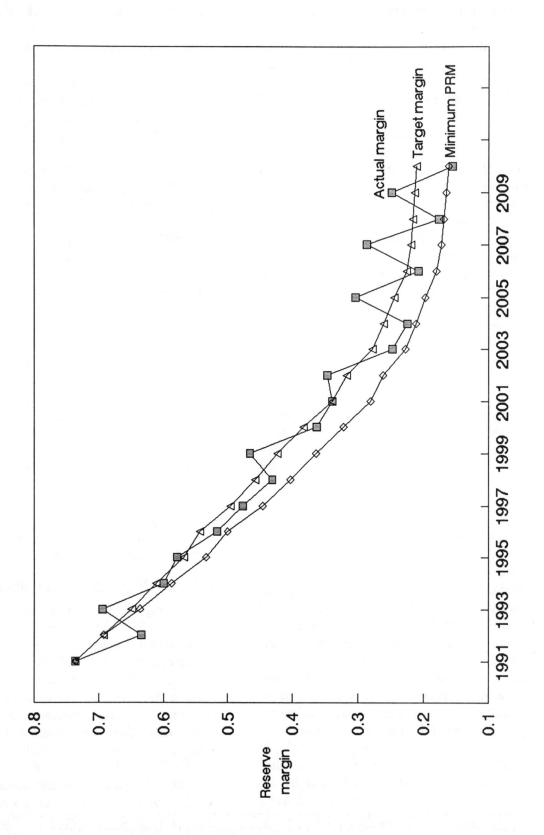

photovoltaics and direct solar might be also examined as renewable energy technologies. As a research study, the intent here is primarily to demonstrate how the methodology can treat different types of technologies and policies, rather than reach definitive conclusions. Finally it should be noted that although we examine these policies individually, they are by no means mutually exclusive: a discussion of strategies that combine some of these options together is presented later.

Power System Efficiency

One of the most important ways of reducing the environmental impacts of power sector development is to ensure that the technical efficiency of the system is at its economically efficient value. For example, a T&D system that has only 2 percent losses might certainly be technically feasible, but would entail the use of technology (such as superconducting transmission) that is prohibitively expensive. On the other hand, loss rates of 20 percent and more, commonplace in some developing countries, are clearly also economically inefficient, and investments to reduce losses by rehabilitation of the T&D system are frequently justifiable on economic grounds alone. But if technical losses are reduced, then to produce the same level of benefits to consumers, less fossil fuel will be required to produce these same benefits, and pollution emissions will decrease (per unit of benefit to society).[26]

However, whether or not efficiency improvements do, in fact, lead to environmental benefits is illustrated in Figure 7-14. Consider a coal burning power plant at X, which selects a fuel with a sulfur content that is such that it exactly meets the ambient standard; for example, in order to meet the maximum 24-hour standard, coal with a sulfur content no higher than 0.8 percent might be used; the emission level is at A, the corresponding cost at K.

Efficiency improvements have the general effect of shifting the non-inferior curve toward the origin—all other things equal, higher efficiency means some combination of lower costs and lower emissions. Suppose, for example, that the heat rate of the plant is improved; the non-inferior curve shifts from FF to GG. All other things equal, less fuel is required per kilowatt-hour produced, so fuel consumption, and SO_2 emissions, decrease; and the net cost to the utility goes down (fuel costs less the amortized costs of the investment that produced the heat rate improvement). But now the utility has an incentive to move to Y: by buying cheaper fuel, with higher sulfur contents, further savings can be achieved without violating the standard—with the result that there is no environmental benefit, but only lower costs. From the environmental perspective, the desired response would be to W: implying that the savings from better heat rates be applied to the purchase of still lower sulfur coal, say 0.7 sulfur by weight.

In Sri Lanka, where there is no large inventory of old, inefficient thermal plants (as exists, say in India), the most important system efficiency issue is T&D losses. Substantial progress in loss reduction has already been achieved, but the question might be posed whether the present 12 percent loss reduction target of the CEB ought to be further reduced, and what environmental benefits might result.

Demand-side Management

A systematic assessment of demand-side management (DSM) options has yet to be conducted in Sri Lanka: indeed, comprehensive DSM assessments have been conducted for only a very few developing countries to date.[27] Nevertheless, there are indications that there

---

[26] It should be noted that this reasoning applies only to the reduction of technical losses: The environmental consequences of reduction of nontechnical losses through improvement of collection procedures, elimination of pilferage, and so forth, will depend upon assumptions made about the resulting financial impact on the utility, and on the price elasticity of demand of those consumers who would now pay the going tariff. If, for example, improved revenue collection eliminates the need for a tariff increase in order to meet given balance sheet ratios, then overall consumption would tend to increase (given normal price elastic behavior). On the other hand, with the same assumptions about price elastic behavior, consumers who were forced to pay for previously pilfered consumption would presumably reduce their consumption. On balance, one suspects that these effects offset each other, with the result that it is primarily the reduction of technical, rather than nontechnical losses, that has a direct environmental benefit.

[27] Such assessments have recently been conducted for India (as part of a recent World Bank/U.S.AID power sector review) and Costa Rica (see U.S.AID 1991).

Table 7-1: Policy Options

Policy emphasis	Illustrative measure
System efficiency	T&D loss reduction
Demand-side management	Fluorescent lighting
Renewable energy technology	Wind power
Pollution control policy	FGD systems
Clean coal technology	Pressurized fluidized bed combustion (PFBC)
Fuel switching	Low-sulfur coal imports Low-sulfur fueloil imports

exist some significant opportunities for the introduction of energy efficient end-use technologies in Sri Lanka. Both the World Bank power system efficiency study of Sri Lanka (see UNDP/World Bank 1983) and the GTZ Masterplan made some preliminary estimates of the potential for load management and energy conservation by the systematic replacement of incandescent lights by fluorescent lights. This measure is, therefore, used in this study as the illustrative example; the analytical framework is capable of analyzing other potential DSM measures in a similar way.

Renewable Energy Technology

Although there are a number of renewable energy technologies that may be considered for Sri Lanka, the technology with the largest potential impact on the operations of the CEB is wind energy. Utility-scale solar thermal plants appear to have little potential, while the use of photovoltaics probably has greatest potential in remote rural areas that do not have grid access. The extent to which it might actually be possible to displace one or more coal fired units with wind plants in Sri Lanka, and at what cost, is of obvious environmental interest.

Wind energy activities in Sri Lanka were started on a very modest scale as far back as 1978. Early activities were focused on the development of small wind pumps mainly for application in the agricultural sector for small-scale irrigation during the dry season. At least one small-scale workshop is now engaged in the commercial-scale production of these machines.

After a preliminary assessment of Sri Lanka's wind resources, using past meteorological data, the southern coastal region was identified as a potential region for harnessing wind energy for large-scale applications such as electricity generation. On the basis of that study, a more detailed study of wind energy resources in the southern region was initiated in early 1988, funded by the government of the Netherlands. The first interim report of this study will be available shortly.

Based on the analysis completed so far, the southern coastal belt, extending from Hambantota towards Palatupana on the southeast, has been identified as the region that offers highest potential for wind power generation. Specific electrical outputs of about 800 to 900 kilowatt-

Figure 7-14: The Impact of Efficiency Improvements

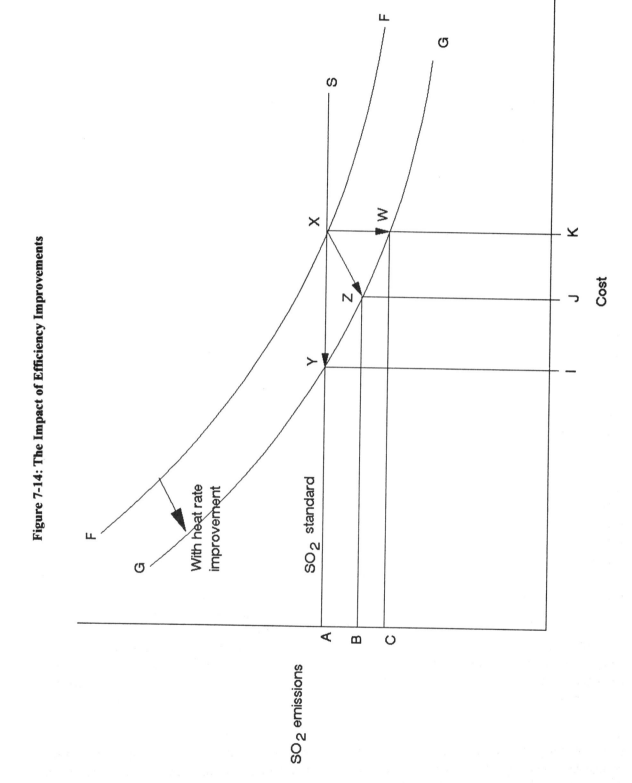

hours per square meter and plant factors of about 20 percent have been estimated for this region. The wind power potential within the five-kilometer wide stretch of coastal land between Hambantota and Palatupana has been estimated as 200 megawatts. The estimate is based on a power density of 8 megawatts per square kilometer and a 50 percent land utilization factor after excluding forest cover, agricultural land, homesteads, and the Bundala Bird Sanctuary.[28] Specifically, our scenario for wind energy development assumes a first 5-megawatt demonstration plant, followed by three 50-megawatt facilities built over a subsequent six-year period.

Clean Coal Technology

The shortcomings of conventional approaches to deal with the air pollution impacts of coal plants have long been recognized: rather than fix individual emission problems separately— SO_2 control by FGD systems, NOx control by burner modifications—a much better approach is to use fundamentally different combustion technologies. Over the past decade a substantial research effort has therefore been mounted into so-called clean coal technologies, including such technologies as atmospheric and pressurized fluidized bed combustion (AFBC, PFBC) and integrated gasification combined cycle (IGCC). A number of these are at or very close to commercial availability at the utility scale in the industrialized countries, and have lately been proposed for application in developing countries as well. In India, for example, IGCC is viewed as an attractive way of dealing with very high ash coals, and in Pakistan, fluidized bed combustion is under consideration as a way of dealing with the high sulfur contents of the Lakhra coals.

In this study we hypothesize the general commercial availability of PFBC technology by the end of the 1990s, in combination with the use of a combined cycle.[29] Even though oil-

fired combined cycle plants, as examined in the CEB's 1991 generation planning study, have been found to be uneconomic, this is largely a consequence of high oil costs. But if coal can be used to drive a combined cycle plant, the inherently higher efficiency of such units is a major advantage where coal must be imported, and where freight costs may account for a third of the delivered price.

For the purpose of examining the environmental impacts of this technology, we assume the use of 150 megawatts of PFBC units for the Trincomalee coal plant. The assumption here is that Trincomalee would be built after Mawella. With the earliest start-up data for Trincomalee estimated presently at 2002, and a six-year lead time, this would imply a technology commitment by 1996. That appears to be a reasonable assumption given the state of large scale demonstration projects in the industrialized countries. It would probably be unreasonable for Mawella, which may be needed as soon as 1998, implying a technology commitment by 1993. But certainly by 1996, the technology can reasonably be projected as commercially available.

Pollution Control

Fuel gas desulfurization (FGD) is taken as the representative pollution control measure. This technology is being widely advocated for SO_2 control in developing countries despite high capital costs (that may increase by 15 percent to 20 percent) and difficult operation and maintenance problems (such as sludge disposal).

Fuel Switching

A variety of fuel switching options are examined, including (a) 1 percent sulfur coal at coal burning plants, 2.5 percent residual oil for diesels (the base case); (b) 1 percent imported residual oil used at diesel plants; 1 percent sulfur coal at coal burning plants (identified in the

---

[28] The western part of this area has long ago been declared a bird sanctuary that is considered the habitat for numerous species of migratory birds. Although the danger of wind turbines for bird life has not been proved conclusively, it seems safer to exclude this region for the moment from wind energy development plans.

[29] There are four utility-scale demonstration plants presently at or very close to commercial operation: a 200-megawatt unit at Tidd, Ohio; the 330-megawatt Philip Sporn plant in West Virginia; a 200-megawatt plant at Escovar, Spain, which will burn black Lignite that has 6.8 percent sulfur, 20 percent moisture, and 36 percent ash; and a 135-megawatt plant in Stockholm, which is configured not as a combined cycle but to also produce 225 megawatts (thermal) of steam for district heating.

trade-off curves as "low S resid"); and (c) 0.7 percent sulfur coal at coal burning plants ("low S coal").

One might note the distinction between fuel switching (as defined above) and environmental dispatch. In the case of Sri Lanka the conventional and environmental dispatch merit orders are not likely to be significantly different; both call for hydro to be dispatched first, followed by the coal plants, as they become available, then diesels, and finally the combustion turbines. Wind energy would also be used whenever available under both criteria. The relatively remote location of the coal plants would place these plants high on the merit order even under the criterion of minimizing impacts (rather than emissions). However, in other countries there may well be significant differences in economic and environmental dispatch rules.

Results

We have attempted to keep the number of attributes small, in the interests of being able to focus on what are important environmental impacts from the national viewpoint, and that properly need to be included at the strategic planning stage. Purely site-specific impacts (such as visual intrusion of structures, or temporary changes to groundwater tables during tunnel construction), amenable to mitigation at the project stage, and in any event better addressed by established EIS procedures, have been purposely excluded. Table 7-2 summarizes the attributes used in the case study.

Demand-side Management

Some preliminary runs indicated that when policies were examined one at a time, DSM occurred in every non-inferior and knee set, and lay in the third quadrant in every case. That this should be so is hardly surprising, because, in general, improving the efficiency of end-use generally (but not always) results in across-the-board reductions in emissions.

Indeed, it is conceivable that because DSM has the effect of making it possible to defer capacity additions, it is a hydro capacity addition that may get deferred; and that in turn fossil plants may be run in those years at a level higher than if the hydro plant had been built earlier—with the result that emissions in these years are higher than they would have been if the hydro plant had been built earlier. In the case of Sri Lanka, for example, if DSM permits, say, the Broadlands hydro plant to be delayed for several years, then emissions from Sapugaskanda and Kelanitissa may be higher in those years. However, DSM also has the effect of reducing energy demand, which tends to offset this effect.

Figure 7-15 illustrates the impact of DSM on SO_2 emissions. In the early years until 2000, the reduction in SO_2 emissions is substantial. However, beyond 2001, because Broadlands and Ging Ganga are deferred, emissions are indeed higher (as the existing thermal plants operate more hours per year). In fact, over the entire planning horizon, the net present value of SO_2 emissions is 2.5 percent lower for DSM (but 6 percent lower for NOx, and 4.4 percent lower for CO_2 emissions). These, to be sure, are modest reductions, a consequence of the fact that fluorescent lighting, while having a big impact on the evening peak demand, has a relatively small impact in terms of energy. Other DSM measures may well have higher energy impacts (and hence result in larger reductions in emissions).

Given the conclusion that, in light of its economic and environmental advantages, DSM ought to be part of all policy packages for the development of the power sector,[30] we therefore redefined the base case as including DSM: that is, as we examined combinations of programs and policies, DSM was always a component of the combined strategy. For example, what is identified on Figure 7-16 as "no coal" not only replaces coal plants by a mix of diesels and hydro, it also includes DSM. The CEB base case is identified as "no DSM."

Greenhouse Gas Emissions

The relationship between global CO_2 concentrations and the actual physical impacts that may follow, such as sea level rise or changes in

---

[30] Just such a recommendation was adopted by the report of the Official Committee to study Sri Lanka's power needs, appointed by the Cabinet Subcommittee on Foreign Investments in April 1992. Recommendation (3) urges a number of DSM measures for immediate- (including high-efficiency lighting) and medium-term implementation.

Table 7-2: Summary of Environmental Attributes

Attribute	Units	Impact
Emissions of carbon dioxide	[1,000 tons]	global warming
Population exposure to air pollutants	person-microgram per square meter per year	human health impacts
Biodiversity index	[ ]	diminution of biodiversity; impact on habitat of endemic species
Surface temperature> 1°C	[hectare]	ecosystem impacts from thermal plumes
Employment		discounted incremental employment
Emissions of acid rain precursors	[1,000 tons per year]	potential for acid rain damages

monsoonal rainfall patterns, are still poorly understood, and in any event are very unlikely to be captured by simple linear correlations. However, since Sri Lanka's contribution to worldwide emissions will remain extremely small, the assumption of linearity is not unreasonable. In any event, since the focus of current international efforts is primarily on reductions in CO_2, in the first instance Sri Lanka decision makers will still require information on emissions (especially in light of the possibilities of CO_2 taxes or tradable emission rights that have been advocated by some).

On Figure 7-16 we show the trade-off curve for CO_2 emissions against average incremental cost (AIC). As one might expect, the trade-off curve includes the acceleration and addition of hydro plants (Upper Kotmale and Uma Oya), and the elimination of coal from the expansion plan (in which a combination of hydro and diesels replace Mawella and Trincomalee). The other options in quadrant III include the Kukule run-of-river project, and PFBC.

If the knee set is defined on the basis of symmetrical and equal tolerances of plus or minus 5 percent, then it contains the options on the non-inferior set plus Kukule run-of-river. Here is an example of where there is no pronounced knee-set, typical of situations where the non-inferior curve shows no marked change in gradient.

If the reduction in other environmental impacts is valued at zero, then a comparison of plans in quadrant IV—where improvements in the environmental objective imply a worsening of the cost objective—indicate that although wind energy has an implied cost of $60 per ton of CO_2 emissions avoided, the no coal option has an implied cost of $44 per ton, and the construction of the Upper Kotmale hydro project by 2001 only $6 per ton.

Air Quality and Health Impacts

Prior efforts to quantify air quality impacts associated with different thermal generation technologies and with different sites in Sri Lanka have been very crude. "Air quality" was one of the attributes used in the Black and Veatch thermal generation options study: alternative sites were assigned an air quality score in the weighing summation method that was used to select sites for different generating stations.

The most serious problem with such expert judgment scales is not that expert judgment may be incorrect, but that the relationship between the score and possible mitigation actions is not demonstrable. In other words, there is no way of subsequently performing a sensitivity analysis that might explore the use of alternative fuels, alternative pollution control strategies, or alternative technologies.

In our study we made a much more precise calculation, by estimating the actual population exposure, namely

$$X = \Sigma \; C_j \, P_j$$

where   X is the cumulative population exposure to the incremental ambient concentration attributable to the power plant.

P_j is the population in the j-th grid square.[31]

C_j is the incremental average annual concentration in the j-th square, attributable to the emissions from the source in question.

The C_j is estimated by application of the standard Gaussian plume model

$$C_j = \frac{Q}{\pi u \sigma_y \sigma_z} \; \exp \left(-\frac{y^2}{2\sigma_y^2} - \frac{H^2}{2\sigma_z^2} \right)$$

where   u is the mean wind speed (in meters per second).

Q is the source term (in grams per second).

H is the stack height (in meters).

It is important to state the implied assumptions involved in the definition of such an attribute as a measure of health damage. First is the assumption that the dose-response function is linear through the origin: neither thresholds nor non-linearities are assumed; this is equivalent to saying that one individual experiencing a dose of two units has the same impact as two individuals experiencing a dose of one unit each. In fact, it is reasonably well established that acute episodes of high pollutant concentration, even of short duration, are much more damaging, particularly to the aged already suffering from respiratory ailments, than chronic exposure to lower levels. Nevertheless, whatever the limitations of the simple linear model implied, the main issue is whether the procedure as a whole provides a more objective way of comparing the potential air quality impacts of alternative sites, technologies, and pollution mitigation strategies than the purely subjective assessments of "air quality impact" of the type usually made in siting studies.

This model is no substitute for detailed air quality simulations that might be conducted at the EIS stage to demonstrate compliance with specific regulatory requirements. But for application to system planning and site selection studies we believe the model to be a material improvement over the sort of purely subjective "expert judgment" scale commonly encountered.[32]

The health impacts trade-off curve is illustrated on Figure 7-17. The non-inferior curve is defined by the low-sulfur fuel options, PFBC, and, again, an increased use of hydro.

There are two particularly instructive findings here. First is that the no coal option, and the replacement of Mawella by diesels, worsens the health impacts unless accompanied by the use of low-sulfur fuels. This is simply a consequence of the likely locations of the diesels that would replace the coal plants: located in or close to urban areas, and therefore in much greater proximity to population, the associated health impact will be larger than that of coal plants located far from the population centers.

The second relates to the effectiveness of FGD, which is neither in the non-inferior set,

---

[31] Populations were estimated for each 500x500 meter grid square using census data and land use maps. Unfortunately, detailed land use maps were not available for the Trincomalee area, and therefore the population data was estimated on the basis of very crude approximations that have limited reliability.

[32] A further problem concerns the extent to which the presence of a major power plant itself acts as a growth pole, and attracts additional population. For major cities this is not likely to be an issue, and it can safely be ignored for Colombo. For both the Trincomalee and south coast sites, however, it is conceivable that population may grow faster than would otherwise be the case in the absence of any major power plant. In light of the difficulty associated with making local area population projections, fine tuning the population estimates would be a somewhat specious exercise, and the population estimate for each area was therefore simply taken as constant.

208

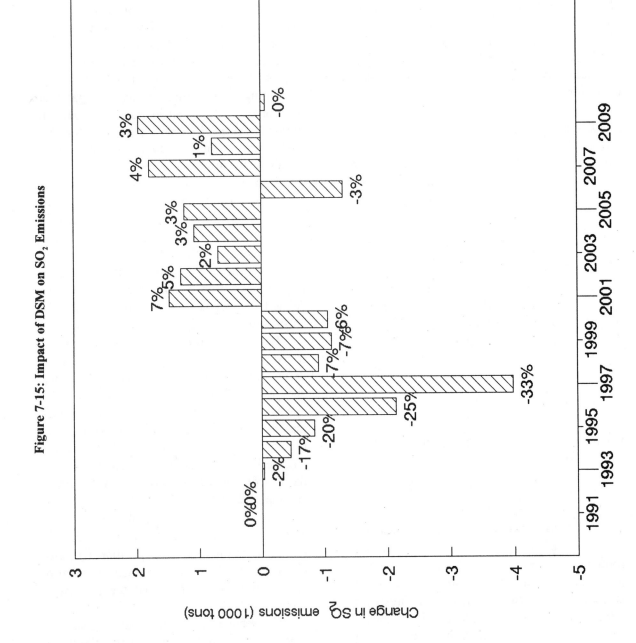

Figure 7-15: Impact of DSM on SO₂ Emissions

Figure 7-16: Greenhouse Gas Emissions

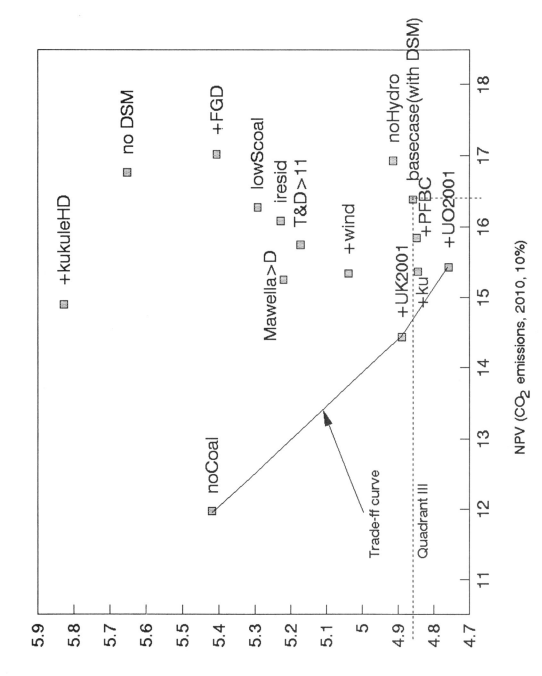

nor in the knee set. On the other hand, PFBC is in the knee set (and also lies in quadrant III). When one also takes into account the CO_2 emissions trade-off curve, for which FGD is in quadrant I (that is, worse than the base case in both cost and CO_2 emissions), the superiority of PFBC (and possibly other of the newer clean-coal technologies not examined here) becomes evident.

Indeed, a comparison of the health impact and SO_2 reduction trade-off curves is useful: if one looks only at emissions, it comes as little surprise that FGD does now lie on the trade-off curve (Figure 7-18). However, the low-sulfur fuel option is not significantly dominated, and is included in the knee set. The point here is that strategies that may appear effective from the standpoint of reducing emissions may or may not be effective to reduce impacts in a cost-effective way.

These results are a function of the assumption made for the sulfur content of domestically produced residual oil, whose specification for sulfur is no more than 3.5 percent by weight. Because the refinery at Sapugaskanda has been running low sulfur crudes over the last few years, actual sulfur contents are considerably lower than this: in this case study we have assumed 2.5 percent. Unfortunately, no reliable data are available on the sulfur content of the residual oil actually produced at Sapugaskanda. This is an area where better data needs to be developed before definitive conclusions are derived.[33]

Employment

Employment creation is an important objective of national policy, and in Sri Lanka there has occurred frequent discussion of the need for employment creation in the south, where youth unemployment rates are especially high. It should be noted at the outset that what is captured in this attribute is the separate and purely political objective of employment creation, which is to be distinguished from strictly economic benefits that would captured by the use of shadow wage rates appropriate to reflect high unemployment in the construction cost estimates.

The employment creation attribute used in this study is based on the estimates of local construction and operating phase employment impacts developed as part of the GTZ Masterplan. The total man-year construction phase impact is spread uniformly over the construction period; all employment data are then discounted to calculate the following index:

$$E = \sum_t \frac{\sum_k (O_{tk} + C_{tk})}{(1+r)^t}$$

where O_{tk} is the number of operational staff required in year t at the k-th facility.

            C_{tk} is the number of persons employed during the construction phase at the k-th facility in year t.

            r is the discount rate.

It is implicitly assumed that the nominal value of each person employed is the same across time periods (before discounting). This corresponds to the democratic political objective of the attribute—as noted above, wage rate differences among employees is captured in the economic attribute by appropriate wage rate computations. Finally, the bulk of the additional jobs created are for semiskilled workers and new jobs for unemployed. According to the analysis conducted by the GTZ Masterplan, total employment at existing hydro plants in 1988 was 988 individuals. The largest single categories were 260 security guards, 121 unskilled laborers, 101 semiskilled laborers, 80 switchboard operators, and 93 other casual and unskilled jobs; these five categories comprise 66 percent of the total.

As one might expect, the non-inferior curve for employment (Figure 7-19) is defined by the large hydro projects that require a relatively large local construction workforce. Note that since employment generation is a benefit from the national perspective, the non-inferior curve curves to the right, rather than to the left as in the previously presented cases of costs. (Whether this is also true from the local perspective is a matter for the project-level

---

[33] Another issue is the degree to which there is an adequate supply of high-sulfur oil available from the Sapugaskanda refinery: at the moment this is in excess, but towards the late 1990s it is expected that domestic demands will utilize all residual production. Consequently, heavy fueloil would need to be imported for those options that require extensive use of diesels.

Figure 7-17: Health Impact Trade-off Curve

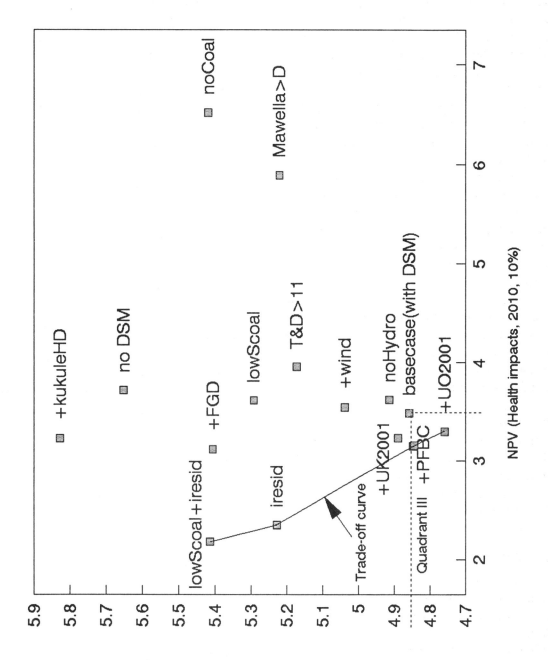

environmental assessment. Large construction projects in relatively remote sites may strain the ability of local communities to handle the influx of temporary workers.)

We have assumed no incremental employment effect for DSM; however, it might be noted that a number of studies in the industrialized countries indicate that the number of new jobs created by energy efficiency projects is greater than the number generated by an equivalent supply-side project.[34]

Biodiversity

Given that at the planning level detailed site-specific information at potential power plant sites is unlikely to be available, the only quantification that appears possible is to derive a probabilistic index that gives the decision-maker information about the likelihood that the detailed EIS will reveal the presence of an endemic species;[35] significantly affect ecosystems of high biological diversity; or affect a habitat already in a marginal condition. It should be noted that endemicity and biodiversity are not necessarily correlated: an endemic species may be encountered in an area of low biodiversity, and areas of high biodiversity may contain no endemic species. It is certainly true, however, that extinction of an endemic species would very likely constitute a "show-stopper" at the project stage; and it is also true that at least as far as Sri Lanka is concerned, its endemic species are most likely to be encountered in areas of high biodiversity.

Such an index will have several constituent elements. First is the nature of the impacted ecosystem itself. On Table 7-3 are ranked the main ecosystem types encountered in Sri Lanka, and assigned to them a value, w_j, that captures the relative biodiversity value of different habitats.

The second element concerns the relative valuation, because the value of the area lost is a function of the proportion of the habitat that is lost. For example, the loss of the last hectare

of an ecosystem would be unacceptable, and hence assigned an infinite value (even if the habitat involved were of low biodiversity, such as a sand dune), whereas the loss of one hectare if 1,000 hectares remain would be much less.

Such an approach to valuation of biodiversity is subject to several caveats. First, as noted, ecosystems may require some minimum area for long-term survival, which implies that the value function would need to tend to infinity as it approaches that minimum value.

Second, and perhaps more importantly, the argument is sometimes made that the value to be ascribed to the loss of habitat associated with some regulatory or governmental decision depends upon whether what remains is secure. For example, the cost of the loss of 1 hectare of a habitat if 1,000 hectares remain might be valued as negligible, if that remaining habitat is protected from encroachment. On the other hand, if the remaining 1,000 hectares are vulnerable to encroachment, then the loss of that 1 hectare under consideration might be assigned a much higher value. Although not often put explicitly in these terms, this line of reasoning has in effect been much used by environmentalists to oppose power facilities. For example, the reasoning goes, because coastal wetlands are ecologically valuable, power plants should be sited elsewhere. Yet, a much greater threat to coastal wetlands is posed by uncontrolled real estate development, but since this is harder to control, attention is focused on power plants that make much better targets for attack.

Such reasoning is not logical, because there is a confusion between costs and benefits. On the cost side, it really does not matter whether the loss is attributable to a power plant, or to agricultural development, or even to illicit felling: the loss is the same in both cases. On the other hand, the benefits to society of these two activities may be quite different. Yet it is only land use planning at the local and regional level that can address the costs and

---

[34] See, for example, the study by the Council on Economic Priorities, Jobs and Energy (1979). This study, which examined energy options for Long Island, concluded that a conservation strategy generated more than twice the regional employment than what would be required by an equivalent supply-side strategy; the national employment effect was estimated at 1.5 times higher for the conservation strategy. As in Sri Lanka, Long Island has no heavy electrical equipment manufacturing industry, so the bulk of the equipment associated with supply-side generation projects need to be imported (in the case of Long Island, from other areas of the United States).

[35] A species is said to be endemic to Sri Lanka if it occurs nowhere else in the world.

Figure 7-18: Trade-off Curve for SO₂ Emissions

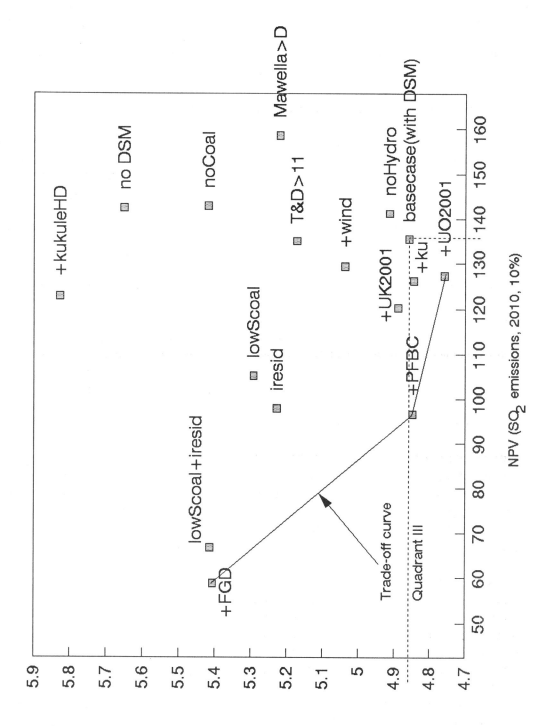

Figure 7-19: Non-inferior Curve for Employment Impacts

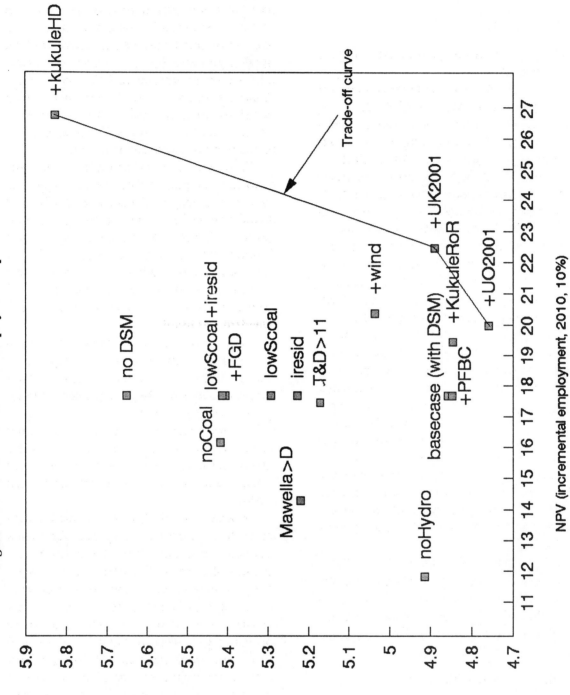

benefits of alternative uses in a systematic way.

Thus, the biodiversity index associated with site i, B_i, is therefore simply defined as

$$B_i = \sum_i A_{ji} W_j$$

where A_{ji} is the hectare of ecosystem of type j at site i.

   w_j is relative biodiversity value of type j (as defined in Table 7-3).

As it turns out, it appears that the biodiversity index is strongly correlated with reservoir size, as indicated on Figure 7-20. This is simply a consequence of the fact that all of the larger projects inundate relatively large amounts of natural forest of high biodiversity value: this would not necessarily be the case elsewhere. However, when one excludes the five very large projects with reservoir sizes in excess of 15 square-kilometers, the correlation is quite poor, reflecting the diversity of ecosystem types encountered at the smaller projects.

The biodiversity impact trade-off analysis is depicted on Figure 7-21. The non-inferior curve obviously has as one of its endpoints a "no hydro" option (in which Broadlands, Ging Ganga, and Uma Oya are all forced out of the base case): the assumption here is that all of the thermal projects that would replace the hydro plants would be at sites of poor biodiversity value close to load centers. Certainly the high dam variant of Kukule implies a potential loss to biodiversity value (B=530) that is eight times that of the majority of the policy options (B=50 to 70).

Although the wind plants would require a rather large land area, the vegetation of the area on the south coast has rather low biodiversity value, and therefore the overall increase in biodiversity impact of this option is judged small.

Aquatic Ecosystem Impacts

The valuation and quantification of potential environmental damages from thermal discharges is extremely difficult. The most important problem stems from the fact that extrapolations from one aquatic ecosystem to another is very complex. Thus, for example, even if reliable studies were available concerning, say, the impact of thermal discharges on coral reefs in Australia, or on the Red Sea, it is unclear what applicability they would have on the unique conditions of Sri Lanka. Certain general principles are easy to state; for example, water temperatures off the coast of Sri Lanka are already fairly close to known lethal threshold temperatures for corals. But predicting the impact of a 1, 0.1, or 0.001 degree temperature rise is essentially impossible.

The current set of standards are of little guidance: the present requirement is only that no discharge may be of greater temperature, at the discharge point, than 45C; the design temperature of the once-through cooling system discharges for Trincomalee was set by BVI as 37C, which is well below the standard—a fact that is repeatedly mentioned by the EIS.[36] However, it is unclear upon what basis the 45C standard was based.

The general effects of thermal discharges into coastal waters are well recognized. Discharges into the well-mixed surface layer would usually have the general tendency to repel fish. On the other hand, if the discharge is below the thermocline, thermal discharges would have a generally beneficial effect, as the up-welling effect caused by plume buoyancy brings nutrients into the layers nearer the surface.

However, attaching specific numerical estimates to the values of this general function is essentially impossible. One is simply not able to make statements of the type that a 1C average surface temperature increase over an area of x square-kilometers would cause fish-catches to decline by y percent. What can be done as a generic calculation that can be used to compare different sites is to begin with a definition of what is considered to constitute an acceptable environmental risk; for example, say a temperature increase of no more than 1C at the surface. One then calculates the surface area over which this criterion is exceeded as a function of the cooling system design proposed.

---

[36] For example, "... it should be noted that the design conditions for thermal discharge were based upon the standard set by CEA that stated maximum discharge temperature was limited to 45C. As a mitigation measure the power plant is designed for a maximum discharge temperature of 35C (with 37C as a worst case situation), which allows for a significant safety margin" (Trincomalee EIS, Volume I, p. 8-51).

Table 7-3: Relative Biodiversity Value of Main Ecosystem Types in Sri Lanka

Rank	Ecosystem	Weight (W_j)
1	Lowland wet evergreen forest	0.98
2	Lowland moist evergreen forest	0.98
3	Lower montane forest	0.90
4	Upper montane forest	0.90
5	Riverine forest	0.75
6	Dry mixed evergreen forest	0.5
7	Villus	0.4
8	Mangroves	0.4
9	Thorn forest	0.3
10	Grasslands	0.3
11	Rubber lands	0.2
12	Home gardens	0.2
13	Salt marshes	0.1
14	Sand dunes	0.1
15	Coconut	0.01
16	Forest plantations	0.01
17	Tea plantations	0.001
18	Rice paddies	0.001

Source: This scale was developed by Professor K. D. Arudpragasam, Professor of Zoology at the University of Colombo and former Chairman of the Central Environment Authority.

There are a number of cooling system options that might be considered as alternatives to once-through cooling with discharge directly into shallow bay waters, including long outfalls (with or without diffuser systems), cooling ponds, and mechanical or natural draft cooling towers. Although the alternatives to the base case configuration all reduce the thermal impacts and involve higher costs, however, some of them also introduce new environmental impacts—such as salt drift and visual intrusion (in the case of natural draft towers). While a detailed engineering study of these alternatives is beyond the scope of this case study, in our view the potentially most suitable alternative is some kind of long outfall with diffuser system, perhaps involving a different site to that

recommended by BVI, but with discharge to the much deeper waters of Koddiyar Bay.

That such long ocean diffuser system outfalls are technically feasible is illustrated by a number of power plants in the United States. For example, at the San Onofre power plant in California,[37] the intake is about 1 kilometer offshore, while the diffuser discharge section on the outfall starts about 2 kilometers offshore and extends for about another kilometer.

To be sure, such a system involves additional costs. However, the alternative of moving the coal plant to the south coast also involves very severe fuel cost penalties. We estimate the present value of the incremental fuel-costs for 900 megawatts over a 30-year lifetime of the plant at US$142 million,[38]

[37] Whatever may have been the licensing difficulties at this nuclear power plant, the cooling system design was never an important issue.

[38] The annual cost differential calculates as follows: 900 [megawatts] x 0.6 x 8760 [hours per year] x 1000 [kilowatts per megawatt] x 2500 [kilocalories per kilowatt-hour] x 1.20 [dollars per million kilocalories fuel penalty] = $13 million per year. The fuel cost differential is taken from the 1991 CEB Generation planning report (p.45); Mawella fuel costs

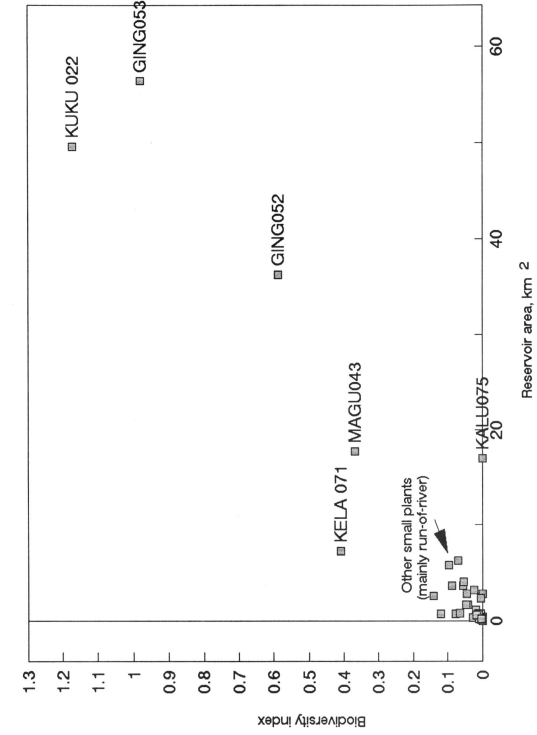

Figure 7-20: Biodiversity Index Correlated with Reservoir Area

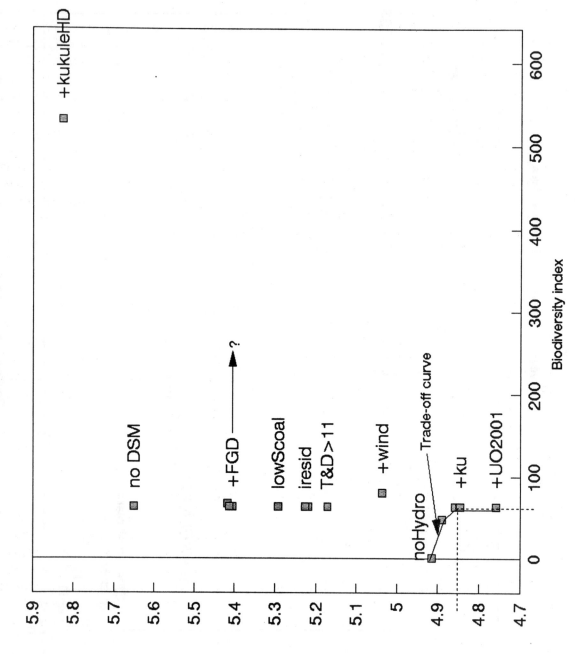

Figure 7-21: Trade-off Curve for Biodiversity Index

whereas the incremental costs of a diffuser system are likely to be in the range of $25-50 million.

On Table 7-4, we compare the differential site costs, as indicated in the Trincomalee EIS. The item for "circulating water" includes a capitalization of the operating cost differential associated with different pumping heads at the different sites. The total cost of site 3A-2 is seen to be only marginally higher than that of the BVI recommended site 2A-2. As already noted in a previous chapter, BVI's incorporation of "environmental factors" into the site ranking process seems somewhat unreliable: it is certainly true that no thermal modelling results are presented for site 3A-2. Because this site is nearer to the deeper waters of Koddiyar Bay, and because aquatic ecosystem effects are demonstrably the most important environmental impact to be considered, we consider this site to be potentially attractive.

With thermal plume modelling studies in hand for both these sites and for a variety of cooling system configurations, and for comparable representative locations on the south coast, Table 7-4 could be expanded on the cost side, and a trade-off curve constructed. For the moment, we have only one point on this curve: from the modeling studies for once-through cooling at site 2A (see Figure 7-22), the area of the thermal plume with a 1C rise above ambient, located in well-mixed shallow waters, is 160 hectares (for the full 900-megawatt development at the site).

Candidate List and Policy Implications

Although the discussion here has thus far been focused on the two-dimensional trade-off curves, examination of the two-dimensional plots alone is insufficient to establish the complete trade-off surface, as noted previously. Only the application of the set definition rules in the n-dimensional attribute space provides a rigorous definition. On Table 7-5 we summarize the set of plans and policies that emerge by application of each criterion. A discussion of the policy implications follows.

Demand-side Management

The first conclusion, already noted, is the attractiveness of demand-side management (DSM) from both the economic and environmental standpoints. Our representative DSM measure, fluorescent lighting, enters the short list of attractive policies for all attributes examined; and we therefore redefined the base case to include DSM. A detailed study of a broader set of potential DSM opportunities in Sri Lanka ought to be given high priority.

Because the peak use of lighting occurs in the early evening hours at the time of the daily system peak, it has an unusually large impact on the system peak, and hence an unusually large impact on capacity requirements. Other DSM measures would be expected to have a considerably smaller impact on capacity requirements, but may on the other hand also save larger amounts of energy. Indeed, our representative wind energy scenario, which foresees 155 megawatts of wind capacity on the south coast by 2001, will provide significantly more energy than fluorescent lighting may save; however, as noted previously, wind plants will not reduce the peak capacity requirement. This also underscores the need to examine alternative options in a systems context, for comparisons of technologies in isolation of their systemic context simply cannot capture such interactions.

Tall Stacks

Tall stacks are expressly excluded as means of assuring compliance with ambient air quality standards in the United States. This was a rational modification of policy, since tall stacks were used mainly at large mine mouth power plants in the central United States; the prevailing weather patterns with westerly winds for most of the year meant that long-range transport aggravated air quality problems in the northeastern United States and Canada.

The view that since tall stacks are inappropriate for the United States and Europe, they should also be disallowed in developing countries as a compliance device is quite widely held. While we certainly are not advocating tall stacks as a compliance mechanism, it

---

are estimated at 755 cents per million kilocalories, Trincomalee at 635 cents per million kilocalories.

Table 7-4: DIfferential Site Costs

	1	2A-2	3A-2	4
Transmission	5,790	2,670	70	0
Coal handling	0	3,270	1,630	3,840
Circulating water	41,830	0	10,440	14,390
Site clearing	16,380	9,940	0	23,190
Foundations	0	0	0	0
Ash disposal	6,010	8,170	11,950	0
Transportation	3,120	0	0	3,460
Total	73,100	24,050	24,090	89,680

would seem that the option ought not to be dismissed without a careful case-by-case examination for tropical islands, given the very high costs of alternative means of SO_2 reduction. For example, at the Mawella location, the distribution of prevailing winds is strongly bimodal, corresponding to the southwest and northeast monsoons. Long range transport in this case disperses pollutants entirely over the ocean during the northwest monsoon, and after a short overland distance during the southeast monsoon. Consequently, if, in fact, short-range air quality standards might be violated in the vicinity of Mawella, tall stacks would be a perfectly rational solution since any long-range deposition (that typically occur over distances between 200 and 800 kilometers) would occur almost entirely over the Bay of Bengal or the South Indian Ocean.

Health-based Standards

Whatever may be the difficulties of explicit valuation of environmental externalities, the effort ought still to be made provided one is mindful of the assumptions and limitations. While the argument that in the absence of damage valuation studies one ought simply to be conservative has a certain political appeal, adopting the environmental and ambient standards of the industrialized countries may imply a serious misallocation of resources.

Suppose for the moment that the standard for the United States is properly defined at (or near) A, based on the American damage curve Z—as illustrated on Figure 7-23. Assume further that the cost function for pollution abatement, say X, is the same in both the United States and Sri Lanka—a reasonable assumption for FGD systems equipment, for example. But suppose the damage curve in Sri Lanka is W, which implies an optimum at D, not A. Since a large part of the total environmental damage relates to the costs of health care and societal valuations of morbidity and mortality, there seems little question that this damage function does indeed lie below that incurred the United States. It follows that use of the American standard implies an over-investment in pollution control by the amount Q.

Perhaps the most important point is that even if it is true that environmental standards are not strictly optimal in economic terms, at least in the industrialized countries there are institutional mechanisms that ensure extensive and informed public discussions of proposed regulations; the U.S. Environmental Protection Agency, for example, is required to conduct a detailed economic impact analysis of proposed emission standards on the affected industries. Such a debate is still almost entirely absent in most developing countries, and the resource allocation decisions implied by the adoption of standards, or "environmental guidelines,"

Table 7-5: Candidates for Plans and Policies

Quadrant test[1]	Non-inferior set	Knee set
{DSM}[2]	{DSM}[2]	{DSM}[2]
	{no coal}	{no coal}
{PFBC}	{PFBC}	{PFBC}
{Uma Oya}	{Uma Oya}	{Uma Oya}
	{imported resid}	{imported resid}
	{low S coal+ imported resid}	{low S coal+ imported resid}
	{FGD}	{FGD}
	{Upper Kotmale}	{Upper Kotmale}
{kukule RoR}		
		{Mawella>D}
		{T&D losses>11 percent}
	{no hydro}	
	{kukule HD}	

1. This is the multidimensional equivalent of the two-dimensional "Quadrant III" criterion: these are plans that are better than the base case in at least one attribute, and no worse in any others.

2. DSM is included in the base case, as discussed in the preceding text.

222

Figure 7-22: Estimated Thermal Plumes at Site 2A

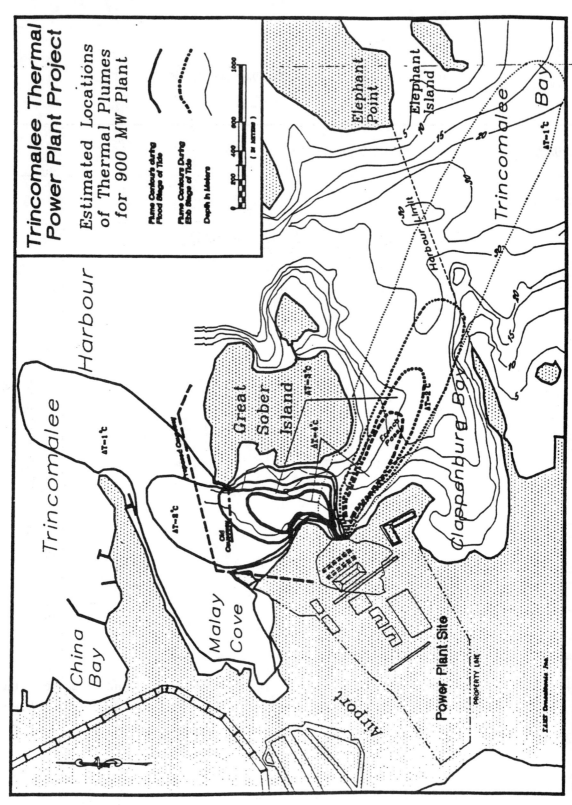

Source: BVI EIS, Figure 8.6-4.

**Figure 7-23: Comparison of Damage Functions and Environmental Standards
Sri Lanka and the United States**

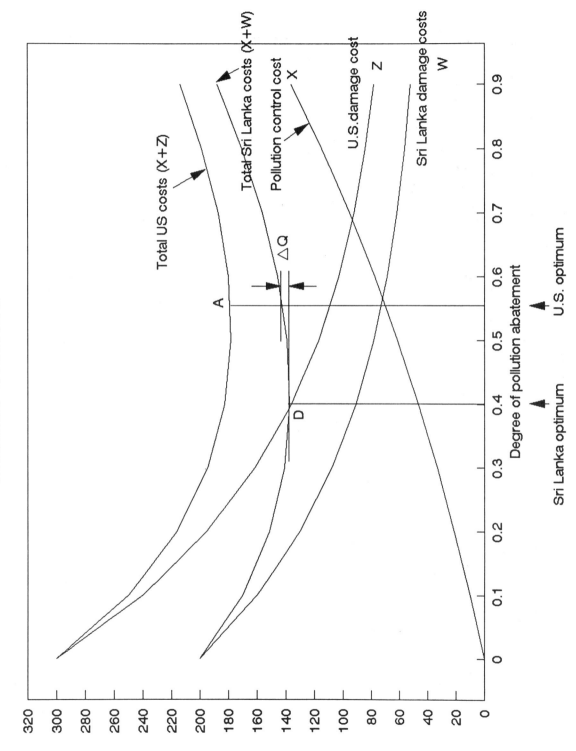

ought almost certainly not be made by well-meaning functionaries at the international financial institutions responding to pressures from American environmental groups.

The argument that health-based standards should be absolute—meaning that the value of a human being is the same wherever he or she may be—may have ethical merit, but its selective and isolated application to power sector projects is irrational. Why should the Sri Lanka government be forced to accept an implied valuation of $1,500,000 per human life necessary to justify an FGD system, when expenditures on road safety, anti-smoking, and basic health care imply human life valuations one if not two orders of magnitude less. Expressed differently, if the Sri Lanka government can justify increased expenditures on human health care, these resources should be applied where they have maximum benefit. The reality in most developing countries is that there are many more pressing public health problems than respiratory diseases induced by incremental ambient concentrations of sulfates and fine particulates caused by power plants.

FGD Systems

Our results show that if one wishes to spend resources on SO_2 emission reductions, the importation of low-sulfur fueloil for use at diesel plants costs less than one third per ton of SO_2 removed than by FGD systems. And when population-weighted health impacts are considered, the value of FGD systems in the relatively remote locations being considered for coal plants is even less, compared to fueloil sulfur removal at diesel plants located close to populated areas.

Coal Projects

It seems fairly clear that from a cost standpoint, Trincomalee is a superior site for coal plant development to any south coast location: Mawella has specific costs about 20 percent greater than Trincomalee. This conclusion remains unchanged when the cost of environmental damages is taken into account: there is no reason to assume that the environmental damages of a plant on the south coast are any smaller than those of a plant in the Trincomalee Bay area that has been properly designed to

mitigate undesirable impacts of thermal effluents.

The present assumption is that Mawella would be developed before Trincomalee. The only justification for developing a higher-cost site before a lower-cost site would be security considerations that might preclude Trincomalee from earlier development. However, the results of this study suggest that if security reasons do in fact prevent Trincomalee development before 2003 (that is, before a construction start in 1997), then it is not clear that one would still want to develop Mawella. The critical assumption here is the location and sulfur content of the fuel of the diesels that would be required to eliminate coal at Mawella.

More importantly, our analysis of the aquatic ecosystem impacts of a coal plant on Trincomalee Bay show that if the reason for denying a permit is the potential environmental risk to the aquatic resources of the Bay, there are more cost-effective ways of dealing with that risk than to build the plant at Mawella. In particular, the study indicates that the additional costs of $8 per ton of coal incurred at Mawella (because of the lack of a deepwater harbor that can accommodate vessels of the size possible at Trincomalee) are larger than the incremental costs of a long outfall that would discharge heated effluents at greater depth out in the Bay, rather than close to shore as envisaged by the present design. We have not conducted a detailed feasibility study of such an option, but the evidence is sufficiently strong to warrant closer examination.

CEB Planning Procedures

At present, the CEB does not include the costs of resettlement or the opportunity costs of lost production at hydro plants in its generation planning studies. For some major hydro projects, this is a significant issue, increasing capital investment by as much as 10 percent (although at many others, such as at Broadlands, there are no resettlement costs). While one can reasonably be against the inclusion of opportunity costs in investment decisions, resettlement costs represent an unambiguous incremental cash outlay during the construction phase, and need to be included. In any event, since the costs of NOx control are added to the capital costs of diesel plants, exclusion of direct mitigation costs for hydro plants is illogical.

The ability of the WASP-III model to deal with the generation planning options in Sri Lanka is subject to some serious question. Not only are the shortcomings of the model with respect to hydro treatment fairly well recognized, but this study has raised a number of issues concerning the robustness of the so-called "optimal" solutions. At the very least, the WASP runs should be verified by runs of a detailed production simulation model.

The set of options that are currently examined in the generation planning studies needs to be expanded. This case study suggests that the following options merit serious consideration: (a) replacing Mawella with diesels (leaving Trincomalee to be the first coal plant to be built, perhaps as a PFBC); (b) replacing the high dam variant of the Kukule project (as in the 1990 and 1991 studies) by the run-of-river variant.

T&D Loss Reduction

The most important result of our analysis with respect to T&D loss reduction is its relationship to the implementation of DSM measures. Whether or not DSM is implemented, a four-year delay in reaching the 12 percent target (that is, from 1998 to 2002) increases both costs and emissions—as illustrated on Figure 7-24 for the cost-CO_2 emission trade-off.

However, when one examines the possibility of reducing T&D losses to 11 rather than 12 percent then whether or not DSM is also implemented makes a significant difference. In both cases, CO_2 (and indeed other) emissions will decrease further. However, in the absence of DSM, the further reduction also reduces costs, whereas if DSM is also implemented, the cost increases.

This result is not unexpected: since the particular DSM measure considered in this analysis—fluorescent lighting—has a sharp impact on the peak demand, and since reduction of T&D losses brings a disproportionate benefit to the peak period (because losses vary with the square of the load), the two measures interact through their respective impacts on the load duration curve.

Although we do not claim to have made any detailed engineering study of these issues—and our cost estimates of bringing losses down to 11 percent are subject to considerable uncertainty—nevertheless the conclusion is an important one because it illustrates once again the need for evaluating options in a systems context.

PFBC

Pressurized fluidized bed combustion using the combined cycle appears to be an extremely attractive technology for Sri Lanka. Even if the installed cost per kilowatt is comparable to that of a pulverized coal plant with an FGD system, its suitability to be employed in a combined cycle means that the incremental costs (compared with a coal plant without FGD) are largely offset by coal savings that follow from improved heat rates.

In any event, since PFBC also results in substantial NOx reductions, and because of heat rate savings lower CO_2 emissions per net kilowatt-hour from an overall environmental viewpoint PFBC-CC is much more attractive than merely fitting an FGD system to a PC plant (which, all other things equal, increases CO_2 emissions per net kilowatt-hour).

The main question concerns the commercial availability. However, the prospects for the general commercial availability of 75 to 200 megawatt units by the end of the decade seems reasonably assured.

Towards a Robust Energy-environmental Development Strategy

The results of this preliminary investigation need to be confirmed by more detailed prefeasibility studies that are beyond the scope of this report. Nevertheless, there are a number of conclusions that may be drawn at this point:

1. The fluorescent lighting program to reduce the evening peak load appears to be both economically and environmentally attractive. However, a more systematic examination of other DSM options appears to be justified.[39] Moreover, we have not addressed here the implementation issues of a fluorescent lighting replacement program.

Table 7-24: Impact of T&D Alternative Loss Reduction Targets

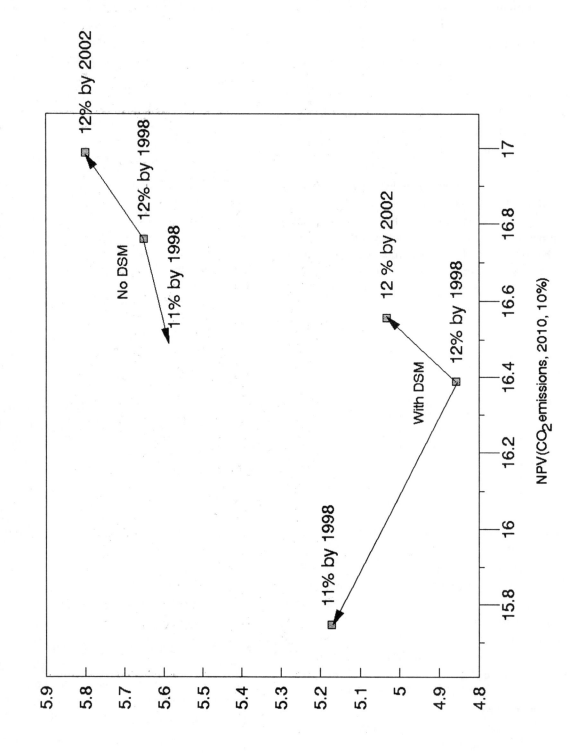

2. Examination should be made of the possibilities of reducing T&D losses to an 11 percent rather than to the 12 percent target presently envisaged by the CEB. As noted previously, however, the economics of such a step is likely to be strongly dependent on any concurrent implementation of DSM measures.

3. An initial pre-feasibility study of PFBC should be conducted. Preliminary discussions might be held with ASEA-Brown Boveri, the manufacturer of all of the important utility scale PFBC projects to date, on issues such as commercial availability, suitability to imported Australian coals, local availability and cost of sorbents, likely cost, and performance.

4. Examination should be made of the possibilities of replacing the Mawella coal units by diesels. Either conventional coal (or PFBC) might then follow in 2001 at Trincomalee. In any event, unless environmental studies are begun very soon for a Mawella site, a south coast coal plant cannot be realized by the late 1990s (as required by the 1991 CEB generation plan).

5. Finally, it seems clear that the most urgent priority for environmental study is in the area of thermal plume modelling. The sort of detailed analysis provided in the BVI EIS for Trincomalee, for once-through cooling at the Clappenburg Bay-French Pass site (SITE 2A) needs to be extended, at a minimum, to SITE 3A on Koddiyar Bay, and to one or two representative sites on the south coast. The modelling should be done not just for once-through cooling, but for a range of options to include ocean outfalls, with and without diffuser systems, and for cooling towers. Cost estimates for the various options should also be developed. Only with this information in hand can the trade-offs across the various siting options be realistically assessed.

Bibliography

Amagai, H., and P. Leung. 1991. "The Trade-off Between Economic and Environmental Objectives in Japan's Power Sector," *The Energy Journal*, 13:3, p.95.

Asian Development Bank. 1990. *Economic Policies for Sustainable Development*. Manila.

_____. May 1991. *Environmental Considerations in Energy Planning*. Manila.

Black and Veatch International (BVI). March 1985. Trincomalee Fuel Supply and Transportation Study. Report to the Ceylon Electricity Board, Colombo, Sri Lanka.

_____. March 1988. *Social and Environmental Assessment, Trincomalee Thermal Power Project*.

Brown, A.L., R.A. Hindmarsh, and G.T. Macdonald. 1991. "Environmental Assessment Procedures and Issues in the Pacific Basin and the Southeast Asia Region," *Environmental Impact Assessment Review*, 11, pp. 143-156.

Buehring, W., et al. 1991. *ENPEP: An Integrated Approach for Modelling National Energy Systems*. Argonne, Illinois: Argonne National Laboratory, Environmental Assessment and Information Sciences Division.

Council on Economic Priorities, Jobs and Energy. 1979. *The Employment and Economic Impacts of Nuclear Power, Conservation and Other Energy Options*. New York.

Crousillat, E. 1989. *Incorporating Risk and Uncertainty in Power System Planning*. Energy Series Paper #17. Washington, D.C.: Industry and Energy Department, World Bank.

Crousillat, E., and H. Merrill. 1992. *The Trade-off/Risk Method: A Strategic Approach to Power Planning*. Washington, D.C.: Industry and Energy Department, World Bank.

Dixon, J., L. Talbot, and G. Le Moigne. 1989. *Dams and the Environment: Considerations in World Bank Projects*. Technical Paper #10. Washington, D.C.: World Bank.

Ferrell, G.C. April 1978. *Coal, Economics and the Environment: Tradeoffs in the Coal-Electric Cycle*. International Institute for Applied Systems Analysis (IIASA) Report PP-78-2. Vienna: IIASA.

---

[39] A good model for what seems indicated for Sri Lanka was recently completed in India, where a comprehensive evaluation of DSM options was undertaken as part of the World Bank-U.S.AID Power Sector Review. The options examined included a diversity of measures from the rehabilitation of agricultural pumpsets to high-efficiency industrial motors. Clearly the efficacy of different measures will vary considerably from country to country, depending on the devices used in agricultural and industrial sectors. See Office of Energy, U.S.AID 1991, for details of the India analysis.

Giampaoli, D. 1988. *Policies and Strategies of the Inter-American Development Bank for the Energy Sector and the Environment.* Washington, D.C.: Inter-American Development Bank.

Goldman, C., et al. 1989. *Least Cost Planning in the Utility Sector: Progress and Challenges.* Report LBL 27310. Berkeley, California: Lawrence Berkeley Laboratory.

Hobbs, B. August 1979. *Analytical Multi-objective Decision Methods for Power Plant Siting.* NUREG/CR-168. Washington, D.C.: U.S. Nuclear Regulatory Commission.

International Atomic Energy Agency (IAEA). 1991. *Senior Expert Symposium on Electricity and the Environment: Key Issues Papers.* Vienna: IAEA.

Keeney, R.L., and K. Nair. 1977. "Nuclear Siting Using Decision Analysis," *Energy Policy,* 5(3): 223-231.

Keeney, R.L., and H. Raiffa. 1976. *Decisions with Multiple Objectives: Preferences and Value Trade-offs.* New York: Wiley and Sons.

Markandya, A. 1990. "Environmental Costs and Power Systems Planning," *Utilities Policy,* 1, pp. 13-22.

Meier, P., and L. Ruff. 1979. *The Spatial Dimension of Regulatory Cost Assessment.* Washington, D.C.: National Commission on Air Quality.

Meier, P., and M. Munasinghe. 1992. *Incorporating Environmental Concerns into Power Sector Decision-making: A Case Study of Sri Lanka.* Washington, D.C.: World Bank.

Mintzer, I., et al. July 1990. *Environmental Externality Data for Energy Technologies.* College Park, Maryland: Center for Global Change, University of Maryland.

Munasinghe, M. 1990. "Energy-Environmental Issues and Policy Options for Developing Countries," *Proceedings, International Conference on Energy and Environment,* Bellagio, Italy. Delhi, India: Tata Energy Research Institute.

Nanthakumar, J. 1990. "Generation Expansion Planning in a Hydro Dominated System," paper presented at the Fourth RCA Workshop on Energy, Electricity and Nuclear Power Planning. Daejon, Korea.

Natural Resources, Energy & Science Authority of Sri Lanka. 1991. *Natural Resources of Sri Lanka.*

OKO Institute. 1989. "Umweltanayse von Energie Systemen: Gesamt-Emissions-Modell Integrierter Systems (GEMIS)," Darmstadt, Germany: Ministry for Economy and Technology of Hessen.

Overseas Development Administration (ODA). February 1990. *Social and Environmental Issues at the Samanalawewa Hydro Electric Project.* London: ODA.

Pace University Center for Environmental Legal Studies. 1990. *Environmental Costs of Electricity Report.* New York: Oceana Publications.

Raskin, P. 1985. "LEAP, A Microcomputer System for Energy Planning," in *Microcomputer Applications for Energy Planning in Developing Countries.* New York: United Nations.

Stone & Webster Management Consultants, Inc. 1989. *Least Cost Planning Using EGEAS/COMPASS/STAFF.* Boston, Massachusetts. EGEAS Capabilities Manual, April 1989, also available from Stone and Webster.

UNDP/World Bank Energy Sector Management Program. July 1983. *Sri Lanka Power System Loss Reduction Study.* Report 007/83. Washington, D.C.: World Bank.

U.S.AID. October 1988. *Energy and Environment: An Appraisal of Energy Assistance Strategies for Minimizing Environmental Impacts in Developing Countries.* Washington, D.C.: Office of Energy, United States Agency for International Development.

_____. February 1991. *Costa Rica: Power Sector Efficiency Assessment.* Washington, D.C.: Office of Energy, United States Agency for International Development.

_____. June 1991. *India Power Sector Review: Demand Forecasting and Investment Planning.* Washington, D.C.: Office of Energy, United States Agency for International Development.

Woodward-Clyde Consultants, Inc. 1991. *Decision Framework for Technology Choice: A Case Study of One Utility's Coal-Nuclear Choice,* Electric Power Research Institute (EPRI) Report EA 2153. Palo Alto, CA: EPRI.

World Bank. 1989. *Environment and Development: Implementing the World Bank's New Policies,* Development Committee Paper #17. Washington, D.C.

8

National Economic Cost of Soil Erosion in Zimbabwe

David Norse and Reshma Saigal

Loss in productivity due to soil erosion has an impact at all levels of society. The central focus of the paper is to provide a systematic method for assessing the economic cost of land degradation, and particularly soil erosion. It describes a methodology developed in the mid-1980s to assess the national economic cost of soil erosion in Zimbabwe. Such cost, it was estimated, could exceed 16 percent of Zimbabwe's agricultural GDP, equivalent to 3 percent of the country's total GDP. These estimates were based on the highly significant relationship between soil loss and losses of nitrogen, phosphorous and organic carbon.

The paper recognizes that the Zimbabwe case study suffers from some limitations. They include whether national economic costs can be reflected by the equivalent cost of nutrient replacement because local fertilizer prices are only indicative of the actual cost. In addition, the link between the loss of plant nutrients and loss of production is not established. A more complete analysis of the economic cost of soil erosion would need to consider the levels of loss under different soil conditions, rain regimes and crops grown, as well as natural regeneration of the soil. The paper goes on to describe a later study that attempts to fill these gaps from an analysis of soil nutrient depletion in 38 sub-Saharan African countries for 1983 and 2000. While the results of the two studies were broadly similar, many difficulties remain in establishing a quantifiable relationship between soil productivity and erosion.

Loss in productivity due to erosion has an impact at all levels of society. At the farm level, declining crop yields lead to falling profits as a result of lower output. Farmers may thus be forced to make changes in the mix of crops and the level of input use and in extreme cases even withdraw land from cultivation leading to marginalization and increasing migration to urban areas. Off-site consequences place more pressure on the local environment in terms of sedimentation and silt that can clog up irrigation channels and lower the water storage capacity of dams, thus increasing expenditure to governments for infrastructure and conservation measures.

The central focus of this paper will be to provide a systematic method of identifying and ensuring the economic cost of land degradation and more specifically that of soil erosion. It describes a methodology developed in the mid-1980s to assess the national economic cost of soil erosion in Zimbabwe.

The Food and Agriculture Organization (FAO) has been involved since the early seventies with the issues of assessment and monitoring of the problem of land degradation (Sanders 1991). According to recent estimates by FAO, global loss of productive cropland due to soil erosion and degradation is estimated to be nearly seven million hectares annually (FAO 1991).

The principal objective of the Zimbabwe case study undertaken in 1986 for FAO's Soil Conservation Programme was to collect, collate, classify and analyze data available in order to quantify the impact of erosion. The underlying policy rationale of the study was to bring home to decisionmakers the real but "hidden" cost of not investing in soil conservation, which it was estimated could exceed 16 percent of agricultural gross domestic product (GDP) and 3 percent of total GDP.

The research was carried out by Michael Stocking[1] in collaboration with the Institute of Agricultural Engineering, Ministry of Agriculture, Zimbabwe. It was based on data gathered during the late 1950s and early 1960s in the course of a series of experiments on soil loss, runoff, and nutrient losses conducted at the Henderson Research Station in the then Southern Rhodesia. The analysis showed highly significant relationships between soil loss and nitrogen, phosphorus, and organic carbon losses from the experimental plots. These findings were then extrapolated to quantify the national cost of the erosion-induced nutrient loss (Stocking 1986).

This paper reviews the approach and findings of the study, broadly following the CIDIE prescribed format. It is divided into four parts: the first discusses the global and the conceptual context and sets out the basic problem; the second summarizes the methodology used; the third describes the physical and country context and highlights the main findings of the study; and the final part assesses both the limitations and the relevance of the methodology, suggesting a number of refinements.

Impact of Soil Erosion on Productivity

Much of the discussion on the land degradation issue centers around the causes and forms of degradation, the extent and rate of damage resulting therefrom, and the impact of such damage on land productivity. There is, however, only limited quantitative information available on rates of erosion in different soils and ecosystems, and much of it is largely anecdotal. The reason is mainly the complexity of the underlying relationships. Current literature, while replete with broad estimates, does not present a systematic conceptual framework for a coherent analysis of the various elements involved in the physical and ecological processes underlying land degradation.

The relationship between land degradation and production is difficult to quantify, because data are lacking on the link between erosion, plant production, and economic returns. To estimate the economic significance of soil erosion, it would be necessary to develop a model of the physical dimensions of erosion, link these to changes in crop production and farming systems, and, finally, value these changes.

To date such research on the impact of erosion on crop yield has been largely confined to the United States, Canada, and Australia,

---

[1] Dr. Michael Stocking, School of Development Studies, University of East Anglia, U.K.

where it tends to focus on field plot trials and artificial de-surfacing to simulate the removal of successive layers of topsoil.

Soil erosion is a major form of environmental degradation in the developing world, especially the tropics (due to intense rainfall, and high temperature, for example). The build-up of population pressure and the direct dependence on natural resources for livelihood further accentuates the natural process of erosion (through deforestation, overgrazing, and so forth).

For developing countries there is a virtual absence of tropical experimental data relating soil erosion to yield losses. Another problem is the disparity of extrapolating from the U.S. temperate experimental data or empirical models derived therefrom. Notwithstanding these limitations, a study conducted by W. Magrath and P. Arens (1989) in Java established the total on-site and off-site costs of declining soil productivity at US$340 million to US$406 million or 0.5 percent of total GDP. More recently, for Zimbabwe's neighbor, Malawi, on-site losses from soil erosion have been estimated to be in the range of 0.5 to 3.1 percent of GDP (Bishop 1990).

Table 8-1 provides an overview of global soil degradation and excessive soil loss. Of the 4,700 million hectares of agricultural land, some 900 million (17 percent) are moderately and 300 million (6 percent) are strongly degraded (Oldeman, Hakkeling, and Sombroek 1990). The major man-made causes are deforestation (120 million hectares between 1973 and 1988), followed by mismanagement of arable land and overgrazing. The most frequent type of degradation is water erosion, followed by wind erosion.

Erosion lowers soil productivity through a variety of mechanisms, notably the loss of soil moisture-holding capacity, restriction of rooting depth, and loss of soil nutrients and organic matter. Erosion selectively removes the finer and more fertile particles in a soil, thereby reducing soil fertility. Eroded soil particles contain up to twelve times the concentration of nutrients as the original soil. Erosion also affects soils physically in the form of crusting, compaction and increased strength with "deleterious" consequences on plant growth.

There is little agreement, however, on exactly how productivity is related to erosion, or on the quantitative impact of erosion on yields. In part, this arises from the difficulty of defining fertility as well as the difficulty of conducting controlled experiments to identify and measure erosion-related yield changes. In this respect the most substantial tropical yield data is from Nigeria (Lal 1989) where, experiments on Alfisols showed that mechanical removal of the top 10 centimeters of the soil resulted in yield declines of 73 percent for maize.

Much of the research on assessment of land degradation concentrates on the physical aspects, such as rates of soil loss through wind and water erosion. Hence, the 1986 Zimbabwe study represents a significant attempt in a developing country to focus on the issue of nutrient depletion from of soil erosion.

The approach adopted by Stocking is however not the only one available. At the conceptual level four possible techniques can be identified.

The Productivity Approach considers the cost of production foregone due to erosion-induced productivity decline, summed for the whole country. If national estimates of soil erosion costs are to be meaningful, however, several qualifications need to be made. What is production in the eroded case measured against? Is it the farm management situation prevailing at the time without declining yields (that is, static rather than falling production)? Or should the benchmark be an improved management system that may include several non-conservation benefits (such as fuelwood and crop residues)? The latter would be appropriate for a conservation project but not for assessing national costs of soil erosion.

The Land Value Approach has erosion-induced losses thereby reducing its value capitalized into the price of agricultural land. This approach, however, may be more applicable in a developed country context in which rural real estate markets are well established.

The Defensive/Preventive Expenditures technique considers the cost of avoiding erosion on a national scale by estimating how much it would cost to modify or eliminate the problem.

Table 8-1: Soil Degradation by Type and Cause
(classified as moderately to excessively affected)

	Water	Wind erosion	Chemical	Physical	Total
Regions	*(in millions of hectares)*				
Africa	170	98	36	17	321
Asia	315	90	41	6	452
South America	77	16	44	1	138
North and Central America	90	37	7	5	139
Europe	93	39	18	8	158
Australasia	3	-	1	2	6
Total	748	280	147	39	1,214
Major causes	*(in percent)*				
Deforestation	43	8	26	2	384
Overgrazing	29	60	6	16	398
Mismanagement of arable land	24	16	58	80	339
Other	4	16	12	2	93
Total	100	100	100	100	1,214

Source: Adapted from ISRIC/UNEP (Oldeman, Hakkeling, and Sombreok 1990).

Replacement Cost is the approach adopted for the Zimbabwe study. This estimates the cost of replacing the degraded "productive asset," considering it as an indicator of the damage incurred by degradation.

Methodology of the Study

The primary objective of the research was to quantify the impact of erosion by measuring the nutrients lost in the eroded sediments and the cost of replacing them. The underlying policy rationale of the study was to bring home to decisionmakers the real but hidden cost of not investing in soil conservation.

The methodology had three main components:

- Compilation and refining of the empirical data collected from experimental plots
- Analysis of data to determine the quantitative relationships between soil loss and losses of nitrogen, phosphorus and organic carbon
- Extrapolation of the findings to the dominant farming systems of Zimbabwe, quantifying soil loss at the national level of three major nutrients and computing the equivalent cost of fertilizers needed to replace the lost nutrients

Data Base

An intensive erosion research program in Zimbabwe was instituted during the period of the Federation of Rhodesia and Nyasaland between the years 1953 and 1964. The data base is drawn from this source and covers 400 plot years of experiments conducted at the Henderson Research Station.

This study represents a notable attempt at classifying, documenting, and analyzing the full record of soil loss and run off, storm by storm and annually, for the many treatments and for the four soil types used in the experiments conducted by Stocking during 1970-76. A new model of soil loss estimation, SLEMSA (a modification of the Universal Soil Loss Equation) was constructed for the specific field conditions of Zimbabwe.

The raw data consisted of sludge measurements taken from the collecting tanks on the erosion plots. This gave records of nutrient concentration in percent for nitrogen (N) and organic carbon, and parts per million for phosphorous (P). These three nutrients represented the major quantitative impact of erosion on soil chemistry. Further details of the methodology together with data summaries are available in the FAO report of the study (Stocking 1986).

Analysis of Quantitative Relationships between Erosion and Nutrient Loss

Through correlation and regression analysis of the refined annualized data, predictions were made as to losses of nutrients under given levels of erosion.

The agricultural land resource was grouped into two main categories—commercial lands (41.4 percent) and communal lands 41.6 percent). Each of these categories was further sub-divided into grazing lands and arable lands.

The extrapolation exercise consisted of the following main steps:

- Categorizing of land area into broad farming groups and systems by degrees of erosion hazard

- Estimating the rate of erosion on each system

- Applying regression equations to obtain the loss of nutrients corresponding to the estimated rates of erosion

- Summing up of each farming group to obtain the total loss of nutrients from Zimbabwe

- Calculating the cost of these nutrients as calculated from current fertilizer prices

The above sequence for calculating total cost to Zimbabwe of the nutrients removed by erosion is diagrammatically shown in Figure 8-1.

Main Findings of the Study

The main findings of the study could be summarized as follows:

1. Statistically significant relationships were established between soil loss and the losses of nitrogen, phosphorus, and organic carbon from experimental plots. Statistically valid rates of nutrient loss for different levels of erosion were calculated.

2. Variations in mean annual losses of soil, nitrogen, organic carbon, and phosphorus were dependent on soil type, crop, and year. The two most important variables in explaining this effect were the rainfall pattern and the crop type.

3. The erosion process is considerably selective in removing nutrients from the soil. The ratios were highest in areas where run-off was highest, an important finding in evaluating physical conservation measures that are designed to detain soil but allow run-off. Extrapolating the experimental plot findings to the four main farming systems of Zimbabwe, these variations in erosion rates were found:

- *Commercial grazing lands* with low densities of livestock and relatively complete vegetation cover had a low rate of erosion.

- *Commercial arable lands* demonstrated similar moderate rates of erosion. This can be attributed to the maintenance of physical conservation measures in nearly all cases (such as contour bunds, terraces, and waterways).

- *Communal arable lands*, though adopting similar physical conservation measures,

234

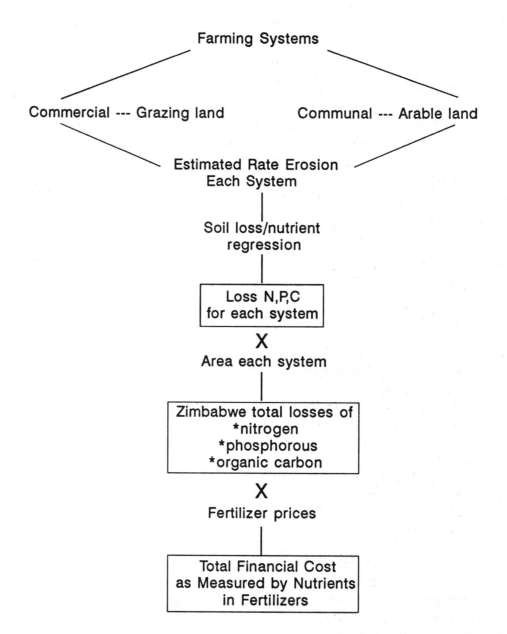

Figure 8-1: Flow Diagram Illustrating the Calculation of the Financial Cost of Erosion

Table 8-2: Losses of Nutrients and Organic Carbon from Zimbabwe's Soils
(thousands of tons)

Farm system	Nitrogen	Organic carbons	Phosphorous
Commercial grazing	57	454	5
Commercial arable	19	148	2
Communal arable	134	1,324	20
Communal grazing	1,425	13,679	209
Total losses	81,635	15,605	236

had considerably higher rates of erosion compared to commercial areas. This was largely due to their poor state of maintenance, open access to grazing, and inadequate vegetation cover.

• *Communal grazing lands* were the most eroded of all. Livestock numbers exceeded the carrying capacity of the land. This combined with a succession of droughts denuded the vegetation cover.

On average, 1.6 million tons of nitrogen, 15.6 million tons of organic matter, and 0.24 million tons of phosphorus are lost annually by erosion (Table 8-2 provides details). The arable lands alone lose 0.15, 1.5, and 0.02 million tons respectively. These nitrogen and phosphorus losses from arable land were about three times the level of total fertilizer application in Zimbabwe in the 1984—85 season, and they do not include losses of nutrients dissolved in runoff water.

To monetize the physical losses of nitrogen and phosphorus, the equivalent cost of fertilizers containing these nutrients was calculated. For the total nutrient losses from the four farming groups, the financial cost based on mineral fertilizer replacement was US$1.5 billion per year (at 1985 market fertilizer prices and rates of exchange). For the arable lands alone, where there is the greatest investment in terms of food production and fertilizers, the financial cost amounted to US$150 million.

On a per hectare per year basis, the financial cost of erosion was found to vary from US$20 to $50 on arable lands, and US$10 to $80 on grazing lands, according to the level of erosion.

If these estimates are correct, they represent a substantial percentage of the financial return per hectare of arable land in Zimbabwe. This can be illustrated by hybrid maize, which is grown in the relatively better managed commercial lands. The 1984 estimates of variable costs and returns on one hectare of maize production (Windmill Pvt. Ltd. 1984) are illustrated in Table 8-3.

Thus, a US$50 per hectare additional cost of replacing nutrient loss would represent between 13 percent to 60 percent of the gross returns per hectare of arable land under maize production. Although these estimates must be considered provisional for reasons considered below, they imply a massive hidden cost on the

Table 8-3: Annual Yield and Return of Hybrid Maize

		Land Type	
	Low yield	Average yield	High yield
Yield (kilogram per hectare)	4,000	6,000	8,000
Income (at 180 Z$ per ton)	720	1,080	1,440
Variable costs (Z$ per hectare)	588	700	812
Gross margin (Z$ per hectare)	132	380	628
or (US$ per hectare)	82.5	237.5	392.5

economy of Zimbabwe and an undermining of its resource base for the future.

Physical and Country Context Results

Only part of the physical processes by which soil erosion affects soil productivity can be captured by the empirical data. The impacts can occur on and off site, and they can be manifested in the use of the soil, and in changes in soil characteristics.

The impact on the *use of soil* may, for example, be a combination of (a) crusted and compacted soils that are too hard to be plowed using animals, resulting in delayed planting and lower yields, excess runoff, and associated moisture deficiency; (b) forced changes in land use and farming systems occasioned by lower levels of productivity; and (c) off-site damage such as siltation and sedimentation of drainage channels and reservoirs, and inundation of fertile top soils.

The impact on *soil characteristics* and productive potential commonly takes the form of (a) nutrients consistently lost in the eroded sediments in proportional amounts greater than

in the original soil, a hypothesis confirmed by the findings (as to enrichment ratios) of the Zimbabwe study; (b) acidification, which in turn causes aluminum toxicity in soils; (c) decreased water availability due to loss of water-holding capacity, reduced soil depth, and other factors; and (d) loss of the soil's structural stability through increased bulk density or loss in organic matter.

These changes in soil characteristic have significant implications for crop yields, and the costs of sustaining present yields as more and more fertilizers are required to make up for the eroded nutrients. However, research efforts so far have not been successful in quantifying fully these diverse but interrelated impacts.

Because the basic data consists of nutrient and carbon losses from Zimbabwe soils and measurements are limited to assessing the erosion effects on nutrient availability, the study's cost estimates are incomplete.

Limitations of the Study

Stocking's study undoubtedly represents an important step in quantification of soil erosion impact. The analysis, however, is partial in nature and based on a number of assumptions and generalizations which need refinement.

It is questionable whether financial costs can be quantified sufficiently accurately by the equivalent cost of nutrient replacement. Inorganic fertilizers supply nutrients in a different chemical form, and eroded soil undergoes physical and chemical changes that make the soil less efficient in supplying nutrients to plants. Fertilizer prices, therefore, can only be indicative of the actual cost.

Another limitation of the study is that it does not establish a link between the loss of nutrients and the loss of production, thus, making it difficult to assess the profitability of their replacement. In fact, the fertilizer cost may not be a good estimate of the economic costs of on-site soil loss. The true measure of is the loss of productivity. One would need to take into account organic matter losses, downstream or off-site damages (sedimentation, for instance) in addition to the on-site productivity losses to obtain a total estimate of the costs of soil erosion. Furthermore, damage from naturally occurring erosion is likely to be much greater than that produced in artificial experiments, mainly because natural erosion tends to remove preferentially the most productive constituents of the soil.

Stocking's analysis also does not take account of the social cost of worsening food security and replacement of food losses incurred by erosion with food imports and aid. Such an approach could internalize in part the intergenerational externality incurred by erosion, since it is future generations who would be burdened with debt repayment for food imports.

The data base appears to be biased towards the better protected soils, and consists mainly of low values of soil and nutrient loss. Stocking moreover seems to down-play the significance of variations in nutrient losses for different crops, in different years and between soils, despite extensive evidence of such variations. Lal (1989) and other researchers, for instance, have emphasized differences between soil types. The only exception in the study is the conclusion that "the higher rates of erosion on the nutrient-poor granite sands yield rather lower nutrient concentrations."

If data were available to assess erosion impact on crop-yields, the Stocking study could have been extended to incorporate cost-benefit analysis. The economic costs of nutrient loss could be expressed in terms of potential loss of production. This could then be compared with the costs of soil conservation or other remedial actions. Such an approach is particularly relevant in assessing the economic justification of environmental protection projects.

Soil erosion on arable lands is a function of several variables, such as rainfall, management and conservation practices, and land use systems. Other factors that should be distinguished from erosion include climate variability, salinity, and structural collapse, for example. Erosion rates alone may also be poor indicators of productivity loss, particularly net national losses. Erosion rates may hide the fact that soil is redistributed within a catchment and is not necessarily lost to agriculture. For some soils, even improved management techniques may restore their productivity (generally soils that have a concentrated distribution of nutrients in the topsoil or shallow rooting depths).

A more complete analysis of soil erosion impact would therefore need to consider the natural replenishment of the organic nutrient content of the soil through manure, deposition, and sedimentation, as well as differentiate losses under different rainfall regimes and crops. A number of such possible refinements are considered below.

The Winand Staring Centre Study

A later study supported by FAO (Stoorvogel and Smoling 1990) and undertaken by the Winand Staring Centre of the Netherlands developed a methodology that attempts to accomplish some of these aspects. It assesses the state of agricultural soil nutrient depletion in 38 sub-Saharan African countries for 1983 and the year 2000. The analysis measures the net removal of the macronutrients nitrogen, phosphorous and potassium from the rootable soil layer using production figures for 1983 and projected production figures for 2000 provided by FAO by crop and country. These figures were disaggregated into six land/water classes with different rainfall and soil moisture regimes: low, uncertain, and good rainfall

238

Table 8-4: Annual Nutrient Losses from Arable Land

| | Stocking Study | Winand Staring Study | | |
	Erosion loss	Adjusted for output factors[1]		Overall country balance
N (thousands of tons)	(–)153.0	(–)99.5	(–)66.2	(–)127.5
P 2, 5 (thousands of tons)	(–)22.0	(–)37.2	(–)32.4	(–)19.4
Area (millions of hectares)	3.0	-	-	4.1
Estimated financial cost (Z$ millions)[2]	240.0	263.2	204.4	
(US$ millions)	150.0	164.5	131.9	127.8

1. Adjusted for compensatory nutrient accruals due to manure, deposition, nitrogen fixation, and sedimentation, but not for mineral fertilizer application.

2. Prices as per Stocking study of Z$888 per ton for elemental nitrogen and Z$4,700 per ton for elemental phosphorous in 1985. (One US$ = Z$1.6.)

areas (rainfed agriculture); problem areas; and naturally flooded and irrigated areas. Data from 1983 and projections for 2000 were used to estimate fertilizer use by country and by crop.

The factors determining the nutrient flow into and out of the soil were defined and quantified for each land/water class taking into account variables such as rainfall, soil fertility, cropping pattern, farm management level, fertilizer and manure application, crop residue management and rate of erosion. These were incorporated into a land use systems model. It was assumed that each land use system was homogeneous and thus became the unit for the calculation of the nutrient balance. The nutrient balance of each land use system was assumed to be governed by five input and five output factors.

The input factors were mineral fertilizers, manure, nutrient deposition by dust and rain, nitrogen fixation, and sedimentation. The output factors were harvested product, crop residues, leaching, gaseous losses, and erosion.

The results of this study demonstrated that nutrient depletion is already severe in sub-Saharan Africa, and is projected to get worse.

Using this more elaborate methodology, the arable land (4.11 million hectares) nutrient balance loss for nitrogen and phosphorus for Zimbabwe for 1983 were estimated to be 127.5 thousand tons and 19 thousand tons respectively.

In contrast, the Stocking study placed the average annual loss of nitrogen at 153 thousand tons and that of phosphorus at 22 thousand tons, since it did not take into account the output factors which offset the losses of nutrients (Table 8-4).

The Stocking study apparently may have overestimated the costs of soil erosion by almost 20 percent due to the neglect of natural nutrient inputs. Although the figures in both studies are remarkably similar, the Staring Centre study incorporates a number of useful methodological refinements that provide an improved basis for assessing nutrient losses. The Stocking study, however, provides more reliable estimates of soil erosion losses per se. Both approaches, however, only consider the cost of nutrient losses.

Secondary and Off-site Costs

As pointed out in the previous section, there are a number of other costs to be brought into the calculation. Some examples are soil crusting and compaction, soil acidification, declining response to mineral fertilizer inputs; reduction of soil water availability (and consequently increased yield variability); greater competition from aggressive weeds; changes in land use and farming systems; and off-site damages.

These additional costs cannot be determined at the national level with any precision because situations and responses are very heterogeneous. Nonetheless, they could be very significant. Soil crusting and compaction, for example, could delay land preparation and planting, resulting in crop yield losses of 10 to 20 percent. If this problem was prevalent on just a fifth of the arable land area, the cost would be of the order of Z$30 to $60 million.

Similarly, off-site damage resulting in the siltation of irrigation channels and reservoirs, such that their effective working life is reduced by 25 percent, could involve multimillion dollar costs.

Empirical Corroboration of Production Trends

Nutrient depletion caused by soil erosion no doubt has an adverse impact on levels of production and productivity. However, this adverse impact can be offset by countervailing factors, such as introduction of improved technical packages and support services, agricultural intensification, or simply by favorable weather conditions. Consequently it may be difficult to corroborate the expected loss in production due to soil erosion with the aid of actual empirical data on levels of production. In the case of Zimbabwe this can be seen in the context of communal areas, which according to the Stocking study were affected quite severely by soil nutrient losses. (The predicted rate of erosion in the case of communal arable lands was estimated at approximately 50 tons per

hectare per hectare compared to 15 tons per hectare for commercial arable lands.)

Many difficulties thus remain in indicating a clear-cut relationship between soil productivity and erosion. Experiments in this area are site-specific. General trends in yield loss are difficult to evaluate because experiments rarely specify initial yield, stage of erosion, and detailed soil type, especially at the national level. In both developed and developing countries there are severe limits to the availability of reliable data on the rate at which soil erosion takes place on different soils, the impact of this erosion on crops, farmer responses, and nonfarm factors that determine the social losses caused by erosion.

In conclusion, it is becoming increasingly apparent that the costs of soil erosion in the case of Zimbabwe could be well in excess of 16 percent of agricultural GDP and 3 percent of total GDP since these are costs of nutrient loss from arable land alone. It is critically important, therefore, to proceed with the refinement of the methodologies for cost/benefit analysis and particularly for soil productivity and yield loss relationships. FAO is, consequently, expanding its activities in this area.

Bibliography

Bishop, Joshua. 1990. "The cost of soil erosion in Malawi," draft report for the World Bank Malawi Country Operations Division. Washington, D.C.: World Bank. November.

Food and Agricultural Organization of the United Nations (FAO)/Netherlands Conference on Agriculture and the Environment. 1991. Background document No. 2. April 15-19.

Lal, Rattan. 1989. "Effects of Soil Erosion on Crop Productivity" in *CRC Critical Reviews in Plant Sciences*, 5:4, pp. 303-367.

Magrath, William, and Peter Arens. 1989. "The Cost of Soil Erosion on Java: A Natural Resource Accounting Approach." World Bank Environment Department Working Paper No. 18. Washington, D.C.: World Bank. August.

Oldeman, L.R., R.T.A. Hakkeling, and W.G. Sombroek. 1990. World map of the status of human-induced soil degradation: maps and explanatory note. In cooperation with

International Soil Reference and Information Center, Wageningen, United Nations Environment Programme, Nairobi, Winand Staring Center, Food and Agriculture Organization of the United Nations, International Institute for Aerospace Survey and Earth Sciences.

Sanders, D.W. 1991. "International activities in assessing and monitoring soil degradation," paper presented at the International Workshop on Assessment and Monitoring of Soil Quality. Emmaus, Pennsylvania: Rodale Research Center. July.

Stocking, Michael. 1986. *The Cost of Soil Erosion in Zimbabwe in Terms of the Loss of Three Major Nutrients*. Rome: Soil Resources, Management and Conservation Service, Food and Agricultural Organization [of the United Nations] (FAO).

Stoorvogel, J.J., and Ema Smaling. 1990. *Assessment of Soil Nutrient Depletion in Sub-Saharan Africa 1983-2000*. Winand Staring Centre for Integrated Land, Soil and Water Research, Wageningen/FAO Rome.

Windmill Pvt. Ltd. 1984. *1984 Zimbabwe Profit Planner*. Harare, Zimbabwe.

9

Environmental Management:
An Economic Proposal for Uruguay

Roberto Alfredo Recalde

This paper provides an economic analysis of the main national environmental problems of Uruguay and proposes a set of specific economic measures to deal with those problems. The paper (1) shows that the administration of most environmental resources of the country have been in the hands of the state and followed a command-and control approach; (2) discusses an economic strategy to environmental management and proposes its use as a complement to the existing methods; (3) reviews the main environmental problems of the country, as identified in the National Environmental Study; (4) assesses the importance of these environmental problems and identifies their causes through economic analysis; (5) proposes a number of economic-based mechanisms of environmental management for incorporation in the overall economic policy of the country; and (6) formulates, through an application of those mechanisms, packages of specific economic measures to deal with those activities which create the most pressing national level environmental problems (e.g., erosion caused by intensive agricultural production; industrial emissions; water resource management; erratic natural ecosystems management; commercial exploitation of public goods; human occupation of coastal areas; weak management of scenic and cultural urban resources; and uncontrolled disposal of urban garbage).

This document provides an economic analysis of the main problems Uruguay has with the management of its natural and environmental resources, and a proposal of concrete economic measures for incorporation into the country's economic policy or environmental action plan. (It does not involve specific investment projects or legislative, institutional, and educational measures, which have been dealt with separately by the National Environmental Plan (NEP).

As in most other Latin American countries, Uruguay's management of natural goods[1] is basically in the hands of the government, which essentially follows a "command and control" approach, as it is called in the literature. This approach, also referred to as the "regulatory" or "normative" approach, seeks to regulate the behavior of individuals and institutions utilizing the country's resources. It does so by laws, norms, and rules (that set maximum levels of pollutant emissions, prohibit or restrict use of resources, adopt urban and ecological zoning, and so forth), then enforces them.

Other government responsibilities include (a) implementing environmental education and public awareness programs; (b) allotting permits or licenses for the exploitation or enjoyment of environmental resources (such as fishing, consumption of irrigation water, and hunting); (c) directly providing certain services that involve natural goods (such as potable water and sewage, maintenance of protected areas, collection and treatment of waste, and programs of technology development and technical assistance on environmental matters); and (d) executing projects or works for the maintenance and rehabilitation of natural goods.

The experience of other developing countries, and economic analysis, indicate that the regulatory approach has severe limitations when applied in isolation from other measures. First, laws, regulations, and bans, are openly

ignored (even by governmental organizations) or cleverly evaded. Second, government usually lacks funds to adequately to monitor compliance with the law, maintain and improve the resources involved, develop suitable technologies, and conduct public awareness campaigns, for instance. Third, the technical standards, quotas, and bans are economically inefficient since they usually bring about underutilization and deficient allocation of resources (that is, the conservation of resources is achieved at the expense of unnecessary loss of production or well-being). Fourth, the existence of quotas and bans, and the concession (generally gratis) of licenses, create situations conducive to favoritism or bribery. Finally, adoption and enforcement of technical norms demand expensive information and expertise on ecological, technological, and sanitary matters that the government does not have.

Although the regulatory approach is valid and valuable in the formulation of environmental objectives and goals, it provides only partially for the instruments needed for their implementation. To overcome this limitation, various countries—especially the industrialized ones—have begun to adopt economic instruments for the management of environmental resources. These instruments have shown themselves to be particularly useful for (a) assessing the importance and priority of environmental problems on the basis of an economic calculation of their impact; (b) allocating environmental resources more efficiently and ensuring their sustainable use; (c) providing a system of economic incentives that makes private individuals and institutions cooperate with the administration and conservation of those resources; and (d) generating the financial resources for meeting the costs of operation and investment demanded by the management of natural goods.

This paper was prepared under the auspices of the Department of Regional Development and Environment, of the Organization of American States (OAS), as part of the project "National Environmental Study," under an agreement with the Inter-American Development Bank and the Government of Uruguay. The author's views do not necessarily represent those of the OAS.

[1] In this document, "natural goods" and "environmental resources" refer to natural resources, ecosystems, natural systems, biological resources, and other products of nature that meet the definition of an economic good: they are scarce

In Uruguay, the application of economic instruments for the management of natural resources and ecosystems is practically nonexistent. As a general rule, economic considerations are not incorporated into the formulation of environmental policy nor are environmental factors considered in the formulation of economic policy, suggesting that the country could benefit significantly by adopting an economic approach that complements the existing regulatory one. A proposal to achieve that purpose is set forth below.

Objectives of the Proposal

Based upon the above discussion, the proposed economic measures should contribute toward three objectives:

First is the incorporation of economic criteria into the formulation of laws and environmental policies, as well as environmental considerations in the formulation of the country's economic policy. The proposed approach provides an initial step in that direction by putting forward specific measures to be incorporated into economic and environmental policies.

Second, environmental regulations and policies must be formulated and applied on the basis of *feasibility* (not just *desirability* as has been the case until now). The mere enactment of environmental laws and the creation of a specialized agency are not sufficient for implementing environmental goals. Economic criteria and instruments are necessary for formulating realistic laws and regulations, making their application feasible, and complementing other instruments (such as institutional reform, and education and public awareness programs). The proposal pursues that objective through (a) the introduction of explicit mechanisms for financing costs of maintenance, replacement, and administration of environmental resources; and (b) the incorporation of the private sector (through economic incentives) in the conservation and administration of those resources.

Lastly, objectives of economic growth and conservation of environmental resources should be reconciled through the productive and sustainable utilization of those resources. It is

assumed, in this regard, that the government wishes to achieve its objectives of environmental management without sacrificing those of economic growth and equitable distribution. To this end, the suggested approach includes measures for an appropriate valuation of the country's natural resources and ecosystems, and an efficient allocation of those resources (that is, based on their real value or cost to society as a whole).

Problems Identified

The problems of greatest economic interest are those of loss of the quantity, quality, or productivity of environmental resources. Quantity or quality losses are economic when the production or consumption activities that generate them bring about a present welfare gain that is lower than the loss of future well-being from reducing the country's base of productive resources. The losses of productivity are also relevant from a conservationist standpoint: their recuperation permits not only increasing economic production but also diminishing the pressure on fragile resources (that is, lower inputs of them are required to obtain the same level of production).

Water and Land Management

The environmental problems identified as part of the National Environmental Plan are primarily related to water and land: loss of soil through erosion, deterioration of water quality through contamination, and loss of water productivity through deficient allocation.

Soil Erosion

Serious soil erosion is taking place in farming areas, especially on the country's richest lands—the zone of influence of the city of Montevideo. The problem causes an annual gross loss of 31 tons of soil per hectare, which compares unfavorably with the 12-ton per hectare of the United States; the irreversible (or net) loss amounts to 24 tons per hectare, which is equivalent to a total for the country of 14 million tons per year. Its greatest impact has been (a) a significant loss of land productivity, which in some areas has led to the impoverishment and migration of the rural population; and

(or will be in the future) and have alternative uses.

(b) a high degree of silting (estimated at 11 million tons per year), which chokes rivers, irrigation canals, and reservoirs, thus raising the costs of water treatment, maintenance of waterways, and hydroelectric generation. The resultant silting has in the past led to the embankment and loss of the port of Paysandu on the Uruguay River.

Water Pollution

The country's water pollution has increased slowly but continuously and is reaching dangerous levels in certain places. Surface streams are receiving increasing runoffs of sewage, solid household wastes, and industrial effluents in urban areas, and residues of agricultural and livestock production (fertilizers, pesticides, and biological wastes) in rural areas.

Often, the very slowness of the polluting process masks its insidious nature. Thus the gradual contamination of the Montevideo bay (through the activity of the port and its related industries) led to the practically irreversible loss of what used to be the city's most highly prized beaches, residential area, and landscape. Consideration of the devaluation suffered by the properties and land around the bay gives only an inkling of the huge economic loss involved.

Meanwhile, the list of problems is mounting:

- Multiple and critical deterioration of the Santa Lucia basin, which stores and supplies potable water for 60 percent of the country's population

- Serious pollution of the watercourses of the city of Montevideo, including the coastal waters (with the dumping of sewage) and the Pantanoso, Miguelete, and Carrasco arroyos (with household and industrial effluents and solid wastes)

- Grave eutrophication of the Paso Severino reservoir and the Laguna del Sauce, potable water supplies of Montevideo and Punta del Este

- Serious deterioration of the sub-basins dedicated to rice production and intensive cultivations on the banks of the Uruguay River, polluted with pesticides, fertilizers, and biological wastes

- Significant loss of fish, in volume and number of species, in the Rio Negro, for reasons still not understood (the projected expansion of the thermoelectric plant of Candiota, Brazil, may aggravate not only the pollution of this river but also that of the Laguna Merin)

- Urban and industrial pollution of watercourses in certain coastal areas of the Atlantic seaboard resulting from heavy population and tourism pressures, with significant problems in Maldonado and Punta del Este

Inadequate Allotment of Water Resources

Although no adequate figures are available on the productivity of the water resource in its manifold applications, indications are that its use is seriously inefficient; that is, its productivity and quality (and, consequently, its contribution to the growth of production and quality of life) are probably far below that obtainable if allocations were based on economic criteria. In view of the multiple uses of this resource (consumption, hydroelectric generation, irrigation, waste and sediment disposal, fishing, and navigation, for example), some of which are complementary or competitive, achieving its efficient allocation would require (a) careful programming based on use priorities, capitalizing on what is complementary and minimizing conflicts, and (b) a pricing system that reflects the true cost of the resource in each alternative application.

In Uruguay, none of these conditions are met. The use of the resource is determined much more by historical circumstances in the localization of population and production rather than appropriate programming. In addition, the price of the resource varies arbitrarily among alternative uses and, in general, does not even cover its most direct costs. This situation can lead only to waste of a resource that is growing scarcer and more important.

The economic losses through improper use of water have not been calculated but may well turn out to be the largest of those presented here.

Management of Other Sources

Many of the country's other resources are subject to problems of loss, deterioration, or inefficient utilization. Among the outstanding ones are:

- Deterioration of urban ecosystems, especially that of Montevideo, because of the disorderly and unhealthy disposal of solid wastes (household, medical, and industrial), especially by scavengers, and emission of atmospheric pollutants (industrial and automotive).

- Deterioration or loss of coastal resources, especially scenic, through haphazard, spontaneous, and speculative recreational and tourism development in large sections of the coast, and by the disposal of non-degradable (recreational and naval) wastes on beaches and in seas.

- Generalized loss of habitat by native animal species; this fact in combination with hunting, has led to the loss of important species (particularly, the large carnivores, the peccary, and the swamp deer).

- Deterioration or loss of natural ecosystems as a result of conflicts of use with farming. Particularly grave is the gradual loss of wetlands of high productivity and biodiversity in the Laguna Merín basin as a result of (a) the draining of those lands for rice cultivation and cattle raising, and (b) the interference of pesticides and fertilizers in the trophic chains of the ecosystem.

- Deficient use or abuse of various public natural resources as a result of inadequate monitoring and consequent law evasions. Major examples are commercial exploitation of native species, building on beaches of facilities with high touristic or recreational value; stumping of native woodlands, especially for firewood; and, in general, commercial use of urban lands, parks, beaches, or government-owned and public-access property.

Analysis of Causes

Analysis of these problems suggests a variety of explanations (ethical, cultural, technological, institutional, administrative) and, consequently, a diversity of solutions. There is, however, a common, continuing basic cause for most of the problems described. That is that the management of natural goods has been left in the hands of a government that lacks both (a) the funds, technology, and institutional apparatus necessary to properly manage those goods; and (b) the economic motivation for ensuring the profitable exploitation of those goods and counteracting the vested interests of the groups that exploit or pollute them. The principal problems created by this type of management are set forth below.

Free Use of Natural Goods

A major problem resulting from government administration of a large number of natural goods is that of free exploitation or enjoyment. Private access to such goods is initially gratis; this situation gradually leads to overexploitation of the good and, consequently, to its undue loss or deterioration. Then, when this latter problem becomes critical or irreversible, such access is banned or restricted with quotas. In economic terms, the government assigns the good a zero price initially and, subsequently, an unlimited price, thereby abstaining from applying the economically relevant price (that is, the opportunity cost of the good).

Free use is the most frequent practice in Uruguay, which is as often the case when access is unrestricted as when banned by law. And so, the watercourses and other public places are used freely for dumping sewage and a large variety of solid wastes, effluents, and sediments; such resources as surface water, native species, river fish, and beach sand are exploited as though they were gratis. Individual decisions as to activities that remove or degrade resources of the rest of the community (extraction of ground water, application of pesticides, cultivation of highly erosive crops, etc.) are taken as though such losses cost nothing at all. Free access to public goods is general; when a price is charged, it reflects transportation and processing costs, and not the value of the good in itself.

Free government provision of natural goods seems to stem from tradition or unwritten law and manifests itself in many forms. Neither the tax nor the custom system, for instance, is designed on the basis of a valuation of natural goods. Consequently, there are no taxes or duties aimed at correcting problems of loss of natural resources or of environmental deterioration. Furthermore, licenses or permits for exploiting environmental resources are issued for practically no charge. When it is necessary to ration them, the allotment is made not by pricing but according to non-economic criteria. Finally, as noted before, the users of public natural goods are not charged anything for service received nor are fined for polluting.

The zero price provides the worst possible economic incentive. It leads to inefficient and inequitable utilization of the resource. It is inefficient because its value of use (that is, its productivity or consumption value) is much less than the cost of replacing or rehabilitating the good, or the value it would have in alternative uses. The resulting overexploitation (that is, non-sustainable exploitation) also leads to the undue loss or deterioration of the base of the country's resources. It is inequitable because it benefits only those utilizing the good and harms the rest of society, which suffers the consequences of environmental decay and loss of national wealth.

The situation with free natural goods contrasts markedly with that of those which are duly valued, as is the case with forest resources and certain native species that are privately owned and commercially exploited. For them there is no indication of loss of the base of resources but rather an expansion thereof. The industrial consumption of firewood, for example, has increased 4.5 times over the last 10 years, but has been accompanied by an even greater increase in production. This is in sharp contrast with the experience of other countries where the forests and firewood, which are state property and available gratis, are continuously being lost).

The contrasts noted above permit correction of two frequent misconceptions. One is that the excessive exploitation of natural resources and systems is the inevitable consequence of the development process. The Uruguayan situation suggests that such excess exploitation results from a deficient economic valuation of natural goods rather than from a development-conservation conflict. The

overexploitation of resources resulting from their free use contributes neither to the conservation of natural goods, nor to the country's economic growth. The economic loss (in resources and quality of life) that results from allocating scarce resources to inferior uses cannot but diminish the country's present and future development.

Another misconception is that given that natural goods belong to the community, they cannot but be turned over to it. The effect of free use, however, is exactly the opposite: while the benefits accrue to a few (the users), the community as a whole loses in resources and well-being.

Assignment of Use Rights

For a number of public resources (natural or otherwise), especially those subject to commercial exchange (such as irrigation water, mineral resources, fish, certain native fauna, and routes for urban public transportation), the government controls their use by granting use rights, such as licenses, permits, or quotas.

By contrast, when the end sought is limitation of the amount exploited and when control is effective, an unofficial market in licenses quickly appears. Although the original price charged by the government for the licenses is zero (except in the case of mineral resources) their market price is usually very high; for instance, even though taxi and public bus fares in Montevideo are carefully controlled, and even though the possession of licenses for operating those vehicles is unstable, their market price is around US$35,000 for taxis and US$54,000 to US$72,000 for buses. (The total cost of existing licenses in the city is approximately US$90 million for taxis and US$100 million for buses).

Given that this appreciation is a good measure of the economic value of the resource (that is, of the present value of its rent), the mechanism of license assignments is economically equivalent to an arbitrary transfer of the property of the resource to a privileged private group. Paradoxically, the government thus turns over the income obtained from the resource but retains the burden (costs) of maintaining it.

A major problem, therefore, of licensing public goods for use in Uruguay is the improper transfer to private groups of the income obtained from those goods. Any change in that mechanism, as far as public natural goods are concerned, should, in consequence, ensure that a greater share of that income is captured by the government and dedicated to the maintenance and renovation of those assets. The new mechanism could be similar to that being applied to mineral resources.

Price Distortion

Innumerable experiences of many countries (developed and developing) show that some of the problems in the exploitation of natural goods are caused by government-imposed economic incentives or disincentives created for purposes unrelated to that exploitation. For instance, the policy of high customs duties and prices for imported fuel oil appears to have had a dramatic impact on consumption and production of firewood in the country, and could have been responsible for the rapid development of forestry now underway.

In Uruguay, the major problem that leads to distortions is the disassociation of economic from environmental policy. This creates a wide opening for serious, unexpected environmental problems. Recent economic studies show, for instance, that the government's pricing policy has been responsible for most of the nation's soil erosion, because it favored growing crops (such as fruits and vegetables) that bring about the greatest erosion. The historical low-price policy for fertilizers and pesticides may have worsened this problem.

A special problem worthy of further economic study is the loss of wetlands caused by the expansion of rice cultivation areas in the department of Rocha. It appears that this expansion has no legitimate economic basis and has been prompted by the high profitability of the crop stemming from two undue incentives: (a) the low implicit cost of water, the principal input in the activity, and (b) the low existing tax rate on cultivated lands, which is not based on the actual use of those lands but on their (low) potential productivity for cattle-raising.

Budgetary Constraint

The drafting of proposed laws, policies, and environmental actions in Uruguay suffers from the same problem in other sectors—and in most other developing countries—failure to take proper account of the drastic limitation that governmental revenue imposes on the fulfillment of the objectives and recommendations put forward. Each proposal is prepared as though the government were going to allocate all the necessary funding. This approach leads to other significant problems:

- The objectives and recommendations (presented in laws, policies, and studies of specialists) turn out to be more a listing of all desirable means for solving each problem than of what would be feasible to implement with limited resources.

- Those objectives and recommendations are prepared without identifying the sources of funds or the mechanisms for generating them.

- The failures of the government to implement the recommendations of experts are normally viewed as negligence on the part of the authorities or disregard for environmental issues, rather than the result of specific economic constraints, which could well be the basic cause.

- The shortage of funds to finance all recommendations forces the government to select only some of them for implementation; most policies, laws or studies, however, provide no priorities or criteria for their selection, which makes the whole planning process ineffectual.

Avoidance of such problems calls for a systematic and explicit incorporation of budgetary constraints in the formulation of proposals. Emphasis should be placed on the definition of feasible objectives, the establishment of priorities for recommendations, and the identification of financing mechanisms. The present proposal seeks to contribute to that end.

Proposed Economic Measures

Based on the foregoing analysis, a number of economic measures suggest themselves for possible adoption in Uruguay. These measures imply considerable modification of existing economic policies and may, for that reason, not be feasible in the short term. They are designed, however, not for immediate implementation, but rather for pinpointing technically appropriate instruments that may lead to permanent solutions. Some of the measures can be put to immediate use: others, in contrast, can be used only as technical options that may facilitate the discussion of alternative solutions.

The country has two valuable opportunities for simultaneously increasing economic growth and conserving its natural resources and ecosystems: eliminating (a) unproductive uses of natural goods resulting from a false valuation of them, and (b) uses that are much more detrimental to society than they are beneficial to user groups. The following measures seek to take advantage of those opportunities.

Mechanisms for General Application

Proposed here are six economic management mechanisms that may be employed singly or in various combinations. The next section describes specific measures for carrying out these mechanisms.

Valuation and Sale of Resources

The valuation of each resource should be based upon its estimated opportunity cost, and users charged accordingly. The opportunity cost is a technical concept that appropriately adds all costs involved in the provision of the resource (such as maintenance and replacement, loss of welfare occasioned by its use by the rest of society, and productivity in alternative uses.

Forcing users to pay the opportunity cost of the good seeks to prevent them from giving it a use value below that of its replacement cost or its value in alternative uses. This approach avoids the overexploitation of the good (that is, its exploitation above sustainability levels). Given also that the natural good is available to any user who agrees to pay its opportunity cost, payment of the opportunity cost avoids underutilization (resulting from banning or excessive curtailment measures that cause unwarranted loss of production).

In view of the fact that, in general, no appropriate markets exist for the purchase or sale of natural goods, their "sale" could be made by the government through such mechanisms as fees, taxes, fines, and customs duties, or through competitive bidding for use rights. Any of these mechanisms can be used as an economic incentive for the user to dispose of or transfer the good on the basis of its opportunity cost.

The possibility of selling natural goods through taxes or fees is easier to conceptualize when the good is a productive resource (such as timber or minerals) than when it is an intangible good. Nevertheless, the sale of the resource for its opportunity cost is just as necessary. Consequently, a tax on industrial emission of toxic pollutants is best viewed as the price the government charges for the dissipation service lent by the resource "atmosphere."

This tax achieves the desired effects of (a) discouraging pollution by making the industrial firm—and, indirectly the consumers of its product—pay for the pollution; (b) encouraging the industrial firm to invest on its own (that is, without direct pressure from the government) in pollutant-treatment plants or production processes that reduce emissions; (c) encouraging industrial plants to locate in other areas of lower pollution density (where the tax will be lower or nil); and (d) generating funds necessary for financing the programs for pollutant research, monitoring, and control.

In the application of the proposed incentives (such as fees, duties, and taxes), certain principles should be followed: (a) The cost of the natural good should be paid by its users (that is, by whoever exploits or pollutes it); and as in the previous example, the tax should be paid by the polluting industry itself, reducing the burden of pollution on the neighbors of the plant. In selected cases, however (especially when the polluters are low-income groups), a contrary criterion may be advisable (that is, to pay those groups for abstention from polluting). (b) The incentive should also be specifically applied to the polluting or exploiting activity. For example, to discourage the use of pesticides, a tax on their sale is better than one on farm products that require pesticide-intensive cultivation). (c) It is preferable to immediately apply a tentative (and, insofar as possible, conservative) quantification of the opportunity cost than to wait indefinitely for a technically solid evaluation of that concept. In most cases one can simply set a tentative price for the natural good, then adjust it subsequently on the basis of market reactions to it.

Self-financing

For each environmental good, funds generated by the "sale" of the good (by taxes or user charges, for instance) should be wholly allocated to the agency responsible for its management. In addition, they should be allocated exclusively to the administration of the good, that is, to defraying the costs of its maintenance, replacement, monitoring, and oversight. In this way, the cross-subsidies that usually result from the combination of budgets for different activities of the same agency are avoided. Finally, self-financing of investment and operation costs should be made an explicit goal of management, insofar as possible.

Probably the strongest criticism to be levied against self-financing mechanisms is that the charges for natural goods increase the cost of living and therefore lead to lesser social welfare. It should be clarified, however, that the higher cost and reduced welfare are only apparent. If management programs are financed by the government instead of by users of natural goods, their cost would in any case be paid by society through other means (inflation, higher indebtedness, taxes, or loss of other services). Furthermore, the sale of natural goods leads to a net gain in production and welfare for society as a whole (although it may occasion losses for some users of goods); this gain, if properly handled, could be used to diminish or eliminate the welfare loss of users, especially when they are low-income groups. Some of the measures proposed below pursue the latter objective.

Management by Interested Parties

The management of natural goods should be decentralized and transferred insofar as possible from the central government to groups directly interested in the good: direct beneficiaries, nongovernmental organizations,

or local authorities (when the good directly concerns them). Priority will be given to direct beneficiaries whenever it is possible to organize them in a suitable association. The formation of such associations should be subsidized.

The experience of many societies shows that the behavior of a group of beneficiaries is quite different from their behavior as individuals. Individually, beneficiaries generally exploit the good to their individual satisfaction without taking due account the impact that its loss or deterioration has on the rest of society. Collectively, on the contrary, the group seeks to defend the general interest through careful management of the good, and to distribute equitably its usufruct as well as the burden of its administration. This mechanism is not always feasible (depending, as it does, on the nature of the good), however, and the simple grouping of beneficiaries does not guarantee its success. The form taken by the association and its by-laws are determinants of its success. In Montevideo, for example, associations providing urban public transportation (those exploiting the resource "urban transportation routes") have functioned much better as corporations than as cooperatives (a basic difference between their by-laws is that, in the former, each bus is owned by one or a few members while, in the latter, the entire fleet is the joint property of all members).

The government has various advantages in delegating the management of the good to its beneficiaries: (a) the association is an appropriate vehicle for making direct beneficiaries pay for management costs; (b) the cost of subsidizing the formation of the association and monitoring its operation is usually much lower than if the state conducted the operation; (c) the beneficiaries have the economic incentive to conserve the good and are consequently much more zealous in carrying out that task; and (d) the associates have a powerful informal knowledge about who uses or abuses the good, which allows them to take corrective measures more effectively than the government can.

Tradeable Rights

For the reasons set forth in the previous section on causes, it is proposed that the allotment of licenses or permits for the exploitation of goods be conducted by public bidding, that those licenses may be traded between private parties, and that their market price be used explicitly as the criterion for decisionmaking regarding the management of the good. The scope of concessions granted through the licenses will depend upon the nature of the good. The government should be able to increase or reduce the number of licenses outstanding (through their sale or repurchase at market prices) in accordance with its environmental policy.

Licenses already issued will remain in force, at least for a reasonable period in order to avoid private capital losses (for license holders). In the future, however, any capital gain accruing from appreciation of these licenses will be appropriately taxed.

The number of licenses issued and the income obtained from their sale will be instruments for environmental management. Their number will be determined on the basis of an estimate of critical volumes of exploitation. Thus, for fishing, the critical volume will be that which assures sustainable levels of production; for the discharge of industrial wastes in watercourses, it will be that which fully utilizes the watercourse's capacity for sound waste dissolution. Income derived from license sales should finance such management costs as estimating critical volumes and monitoring the amount and quality of exploited resources.

Temporary Incentives

In order to modify civic conduct on a basis of noneconomic factors (moral, cultural, educational, and so forth), the government is already taking a series of important measures aimed particularly at environmental education and public awareness. Those measures should be complemented with temporary economic incentives geared for reinforcing them.

Most of these incentives will be aimed at engaging people in new environment-friendly activities (for example, the subsidy suggested for establishing associations of beneficiaries). In general, these incentives should be temporary; they should be removed as soon as individuals learn whether the subsidized activity is worthy. Consequently, it is important that the subsidy be adopted along with the schedule for its removal, in order to avoid the perpetuation of favoritism. The removal will be made even if it is accompanied by abandonment of the subsidized activity, since this merely implies that the new activity is not worthwhile.

Other such incentives (especially fines) are particularly useful for dealing with marginal segments of the population who do not respond readily to awareness campaigns or moral persuasion and whose bad example discourages the rest of the population.

Taxes on Land Appreciation

The service provided by certain public goods (for example, urban parks and beaches) is hard to valuate or "sell" to its beneficiaries. Investment in improvement of these services nevertheless translates into ostensible appreciation in the value of the properties bordering on the resource, these values being reasonably easy to estimate through econometric techniques. In some cases, the appreciation stems from the elimination or improvement of sources of noise, objectionable odors, or pollution (such as airports, swamp water, or industrial plants).

In all these cases, at least part of the financing of improvements should come from taxes based on the enhanced value (caused by those improvements) of the adjoining properties. The advantage of this type of financing is that payment is made by the direct beneficiaries of the improvements and is not a net burden for them since it is deducted from actually accrued benefits.

Specific Measures

Presented below are the packages of economic measures that it would be advisable to adopt in order to solve each of the main environmental problems discussed previously. At this stage, however, they are only illustrative of how to apply the six economic instruments discussed above to specific problems rather than being definitive proposals. The latter would be elaborated in consultation with the specialists and institutions involved and after verification of the feasibility of applying each instrument to each situation.

Erosion and Silting

The existing system of taxes on farmlands, which is based on their potential productivity, will be complemented by a mechanism of taxation or surcharges based on land use. This mechanism will tax crops and agricultural practices that cause either higher erosion (for example, fruit and vegetable cultivation); loss of ecosystems (for example, rice cultivation); or negative effects on other properties (for example, eucalyptus cultivation). For technical reasons, the tax will be based only on the losses occasioned outside the farm being taxed. For example, it will involve the costs of erosion and silting outside the farm (such as dredging of ports and reservoirs, and water treatment for eutrophication), but not the loss of soil productivity within that farm.

Temporary incentives will be introduced, such as free technical assistance and concessionary credits, for stimulating investment by farmers in soil conservation works and technologies. To guarantee their adoption, the activities promoted with technical assistance must be earmarked as much for soil conservation as for significant production increase. Loan payments could be tied to actual production increases.

All subsidies—direct or implicit—related to fertilizers and pesticides will be withdrawn. Additionally, consideration will be given to a selective adoption of taxes on the use of pesticides and fertilizers based on an estimate of their social impacts on human health, water treatment costs, and so forth.

The taxes proposed on land use and on pesticides and fertilizers shall finance the costs of temporary subsidies and research on the impact of erosion and silting.

Industrial Wastes and Emissions

A tax will be levied on industrial dumping of effluents and solid wastes into watercourses and emissions into the atmosphere. Based on the amount of contaminants discharged, its level will depend initially upon the existing density of contamination of the resource (air or water) at the plant's location. Subsequently, it will be periodically adjusted on the basis of the results obtained and until the overall pollution of the dissipating resource (water or air) attains a pre-established basic standard of maximum density. Obviously, the higher the concentration of industrial plants and the lower the dissolving and dissipating capacity of the resource, the higher the tax.

When the existing overall density is much higher than the basic standard, a temporary schedule of short-term standards will be established accordingly. The affected industries will be consulted (through their associations, insofar as possible) on the design of temporary standards in order to identify technological trade-offs and lower cost alternatives for achieving equivalent goals. When the existing density is below the basic standard, the tax could be zero; in this case, however, it will be necessary to define and disseminate, as far in advance as possible, the critical emission levels beyond which tax levels will become positive.

Alternatively, in line with the arguments put forward above, tradeable pollution permits will be issued which may be freely bought and sold. The total amount of pollution authorized through the permits (for each major category of pollutants) will have to be consistent with the predetermined standard (temporary or basic). Under this arrangement, the market determines the price of the right to pollute (with the tax, that value must be established a priori); the management of pollution levels will be based on that price.

Initially, basic pollution standards will be higher than those of industrialized countries. Since either the amount of taxation required to reach those standards or the market price of tradeable permits provides a suitable measure of the economic cost of attaining them, it is suggested that definitive standards be established only after that cost is known. This procedure may require a change in existing legislation on toxic pollution.

Water Pricing

A national system of water charges will be established for selling water (or its services) at the opportunity cost it has in different applications. The price of this resource must, therefore, adequately reflect its scarcity and incorporate all relevant costs, such as those of maintaining its quality or increasing the local or national supply. The design of local rate schedules (of residential and industrial consumption in urban centers, and of irrigation in certain rural areas, for instance) can remain in the hands of the local water agency. But the overall "wholesale" price for each major application must be established at the national level on the basis of demand, supply, and aggregate water balances. The central purpose of sound water pricing is the reallocation of water at both national and local levels, through cost-based charges, that transfer it from lesser uses (which is presently the case as the cost to consumers is low or zero) to more productive uses (which is the case when water is rationed among users). Local charges must include, in addition to the basic price, the costs of operating, maintaining, and expanding the installed equipment and plants.

When a system of quotas is in place, as is the case with irrigation for rice production, those quotas will be sold by competitive bidding. The price obtained (which is an appropriate indicator of water productivity in that use) will be the yardstick for determining whether water for that activity should be reduced or increased.

In supplying urban potable water, the structure of consumption that results from the present system of consumption-based charges will be continuously monitored. The system provides sufficient incentives (discouraging excessive or wasteful consumption) but may require periodic adjustments based on actual consumption patterns. The monitoring of the physical quality of water must be accompanied by the monitoring of economic indicators (such as quantity and prices of bottled water consumed, and percentage of households with water treatment equipment) in order to facilitate the programming of water-treatment investments.

Management of Natural Ecosystems

In correcting market price distortions that affect the use of natural goods, priority will be given (that is, immediate application) to removing distortions that lead to the destruction of natural ecosystems. Consequently, to prevent further losses of wetlands in the department of Rocha, measures must be immediately taken in that region for adjusting irrigation water charges and land use taxes.

Given that lands with natural ecosystems are generally privately owned and that preserving those ecosystems is of greater benefit to society than to the individual owner (especially when alternative uses are more profitable to the owner), incentives for such use will be provided. Therefore, the tax on rice cultivation proposed will be complemented with tax credits (or with zero tax) for wetlands use. The rice tax/wetland credit gap can be self-financing and broadened until the current process of wetlands loss is reverted. One important advantage of this mechanism is that the mere announcement of a debate on its legislation will already have the desired effect: the owners of wetlands will tend to hold on to them in expectation of the outcome. This would not happen, for example, with the announcement of a possible land expropriation or a rice cultivation ban, since owners would rush to drain the wetlands in order to avoid such expropriation or ban.

Simultaneously with measures for water charges and tax credits, a program of gradual government purchase of areas to be protected will be launched. Given that protection of natural ecosystems is of global (worldwide) interest, the funding for these purchase should be obtained as much as possible from interested outside sources (for example, with debt-for nature mechanisms).

With establishment of the system of protected areas proposed by the National Environmental Plan, differential (foreign/national) fees will be charged for access to eco-touristic areas. Initially, the schedule of fees will be based on the cost of operating those areas and subsequently (if justified by the demand) on the carrying capacity of each (that is, on the maximum volume of visitors its fragile nature will allow).

Commercial Use of Public Resources

In selling public resources, the government will favor a mechanism of tradeable licenses. This mechanism will be applied mainly to public natural resources (that is, owned or administered by the government) which are already being commercially exploited, such as beach and river sand, fishing resources, certain species of native fauna, and navigable waters. (Forest resources—such as firewood, timber, and seedlings—are excluded because of being privately owned.) The mechanism could be based on the one already being applied to mineral resources. In all cases, the government will seek to control the total amount of the resource exploited through the number of permits issued and the amount permitted each license. When there is a licensing system in place (as in the case of fishing), the expiration time of outstanding licenses will be shortened and a tax levied on their appreciated value.

An alternative mechanism could be to establish a system of taxes or fees for resource use. When feasible, however, the system of license is to be preferred because of the advantages mentioned before: the government does not have to calculate the price of the resource (the market does that); the administration of the resource is more easily decentralized; and it is easier for the government to impose a high license price than a high tax.

The advice of license holders will be sought, so that they may contribute to assuring the sustainable use of the resource and the checking of infractions by members and non-members. However, license holders should play no part in determining the number of licenses to be issued since they will seek to limit that number in order to increase the profits from their activity (as is apparently the case in Montevideo with holders of licenses for taxis and commercial fishing).

For public non-natural resources (especially urban transportation routes) similar sale mechanisms may be employed (that is, tradeable licenses, fees, or taxes), using part of the income obtained for eliminating or mitigating the environmental problems stemming from the involved activity. In the case of buses and taxis, for instance, the sale of licenses (whose current market value is, as was seen, approximately US$190 million) could be employed in part to finance the costs of reducing smoke and toxic emissions from their vehicle fleets.

Haphazard Occupation of Coastal Areas

The zoning of coastal areas proposed by the National Environmental Plan will be complemented by a system of taxation on the use of coastal lands and of sale of use rights. Taxes will apply to existing land uses (for example, the subdivision and sale of fragile and scenic lands) in conflict with zoning regulations. Sale of use rights will seek to increase the value of the scenic resource and the cost of its alteration, and to finance works for its improvement. These rights will refer to certain uses of private property (for example, construction of a commercial building) which (a) are restricted (but not prohibited) by zoning; or (b) capitalize on nearby scenic or touristic resources (or on projects for improving them); or (c) modify their value. The price of those rights will be based on zoning criteria and on the impact on the scenic resource concerned.

The depreciation of properties stemming from zoning restrictions and land use taxes will be monitored. The tax level can be adjusted to ensure that such depreciation acts as a fine or deterrent on speculative practices in fragile or scenic areas but not as a cause of big capital losses (since many owners have paid property taxes over many years). Consequently, it will also be advisable, in selected cases, to grant tax breaks for land depreciation.

A long-term program will be implemented for the gradual buying up of coastal lands involving a public interest. This program will take advantage of the depreciation of properties mentioned above.

Associations of the beneficiaries of tourism activities (businesses, hotels, tourism, agencies, and so forth) or of scenic/recreational resources (landowners of properties adjoining beaches, parks, and scenic spots) will be promoted as much as possible in order that they will cooperate with local institutions in the administration of these resources.

Urban Scenic and Cultural Resources

In view of the fact that over 80 percent of the population of Uruguay lives in urban centers, the conservation and development of these resources must be given corresponding priority.

Mechanisms similar to those proposed for coastal scenic resources, including the sale of use rights (based on existing zoning) and subsidies for the formation of beneficiary associations, will be applied to these resources. Some use rights may be traded between private parties (for example, the right to erect buildings of more than a certain height could be sold to the owner of an adjoining property who wishes to preserve a given view). It should be pointed out that the sale of urban use rights satisfies a demand on the part of owners of real property willing to reconcile their own interests between one another and the municipal administration. Properly handled, this mechanism could serve to orient the physical and aesthetic development of the city and generate funds for advancing the municipality's scenic/cultural projects.

Municipal taxes could be applied on the valuation of properties adjacent to scenic/recreational resources in order to finance investment projects (such as improvement of urban beaches and parks, and elimination of sources of noise, objectionable odors, and toxic emissions) that benefit the owners of those properties. Associations of beneficiaries who would cooperate in the administration of these resources could be formed.

In order to finance the maintenance and renovation of privately owned cultural resources that benefit society as a whole (for example, antique residences of historical value), direct subsidies will be granted to the owners (such as technical assistance, subsidized loans, tax breaks, and even financial contributions). The administration of community cultural and scenic resources (for example, the Old City of Montevideo) will be subsidized, as will the formation or consolidation of associations of interested parties, with technical and financial assistance. It should be noted that while subsidies (especially financial) for the formation of associations of beneficiaries will be temporary, those for associations interested in community heritage could be permanent.

Garbage Disposal

A selective and differential rate system for garbage collection and treatment, will be introduced to cover the total cost of the service. The system will be experimental and its adoption graduated. When the collection of fees is not feasible (either in certain cities or certain low-income sections of a given city), a zero-base system could be adopted. Under this system, the price of the service will be zero for those

users who follow certain procedures for garbage disposal and sorting; those who do not will be charged the cost of the service. When the collection of fees is feasible, a system of zero-average subsidy (that is, a system of high charges in high-income sections and low or zero charges in low-income ones, equalling, on average, the cost of the service) is proposed. Even in this case, the use of zero-base (instead of zero) charges in low-income sections is suggested.

Different methods of providing garbage collection services will be tried in different cities or in different collection zones within each major city. This experience will be used to extend the adoption of the most successful methods to other urban zones or centers.

A gradual privatization of the service will be sought, if the above experience proves its convenience. Insofar as possible, more than one private company will be kept in operation in the largest cities, with limited-term contracts and assignment by zones, in order to maintain a certain degree of competition.

The income of scavengers will be increased by assigning them certain remunerated tasks of collection, which may both complement their main activity of sorting and put a stop to their disorderly disposal of wastes all over the city. Such methods will be tried out first in selected zones of Montevideo and used also as a means for incorporating the scavengers into private collection companies. To this end, the formation of informal associations of scavengers will be encouraged.

Systems of deposit/refund will be adopted for non-biodegradable goods (tires, containers, certain plastics, batteries, etc.). Under this system, consumers of these goods will pay a high deposit, which will be refunded only after the used good is returned to certain collection centers. No receipt stubs will be used, in order that any person, including the scavenger, will be able to make the return. The amount of deposit will, at a minimum, cover the cost of collecting the discarded good in accessible public places.

Bibliography

Anderson, Dennis. 1990. *An Economic Perspective on Management in the Public Sector.* Paris: Organisation for Economic Co-operation and Development (OECD).

Asian Development Bank (ADB). 1990. *Economic Policies for Sustainable Development.* Manila: ADB.

Lutz, Ernst, and Michael Young. 1990. *Agricultural Policies in Industrial Countries and their Environmental Impacts: Applicability to and Comparisons with Developing Nations.* Washington, D.C: World Bank.

McGaughey, Stephen. 1988. *The Role of Multilateral Agencies in Promoting Sustainable Development.* Washington, D.C.: Inter-American Development Bank.

Munasinghe, Mohan. 1990. "Managing Water Resources to Avoid Environmental Degradation: Policy Analysis and Application." Washington, D.C: World Bank.

Munasinghe, Mohan, and Ernst Lutz. 1991. "Environmental-Economic Evaluation of Projects and Policies for Sustainable Development." Washington, D.C: World Bank.

Myers, Norman. 1990. "The Environmental Basis of Environmental Development." Washington, D.C.: World Bank.

Organization of American States (OAS). 1984. *Integrated Regional Planning: Guidelines and Case Studies from OAS Experience.* Washington, D.C.: General Secretariat, OAS.

_____. 1990. *Environmental Accounting: An Application to Environmental Soil Loss.* Washington, D.C.: General Secretariat, OAS.

_____. 1991. *Managing the Region's Natural Resources: A Development Challenge for the 1990's.* (mimeographed). Washington, D.C.: General Secretariat, OAS.

_____. 1992. *Uruguay—National Environmental Plan.* Washington, D.C.: General Secretariat, OAS. (in print).

Organisation for Economic Co-operation and Development (OECD). 1991. "Environmental Management in Developing Countries—A Conference Summary." Paris: Environmental Management Programme, OECD.

Panayotou, Theodore. 1990. "The Use of Fiscal Incentives." Paris: OECD.

Pearce, David, and Anil Markandya. 1989. "Marginal Opportunity Cost as a Planning Concept in Natural Resource Management." Washington, D.C.: World Bank.

Pearce, David. 1990. "Recent Thinking in OECD Countries." Paris: Organisation for Economic Co-operation and Development (OECD).

Repetto, Robert. 1988. "Economic Policy Reform for Natural Resource Conservation." Washington, D.C.: World Bank.

_____. "Economic Incentives for Sustainable Production." Washington, D.C.: World Bank.

Rodgers, Kirk. 1990. "Strengthening Government Capacity for Environmental Management in Latin America." Washington, D.C.: General Secretariat, OAS.

United Nations Environment Programme (UNEP). 1990. "Action Plan for the Environment in Latin America and the Caribbean." Regional Office for Latin America and the Caribbean, UNEP.

Warford, Jeremy. 1989. "Environmental Management and Economic Policy in Developing Countries." Washington, D.C.: World Bank.

10

Integrated Environmental and
Economic Accounting: A Case Study for Mexico

Jan van Tongeren, Stefan Schweinfest, Ernst Lutz,
Maria Gomez Luna, and Francisco Guillen Martin

This paper presents the results of a case study carried out in 1990 and 1991 jointly by UNSO, the World Bank, and the National Institute of Statistics, Geography, and Informatics (INEGI) in Mexico, with the objective of integrating and linking environmental and economic information and to explore whether environmentally-adjusted national product aggregates for Mexico can be derived. This work was carried out within the overall analytical framework developed in UNSO's Draft Handbook on Environmental Accounting.

GDP for 1985 was 47,391 million pesos. Depreciation of produced capital was 5,331 million pesos. Therefore, NDP is 42,060 million pesos. Two Environmentally-Adjusted net Domestic Products (EDPs) are calculated. EDP1 is derived by deducting from NDP the environmental uses related to depletion, deforestation, and land use; it is estimated to be 39,662, i.e. about 94 percent of the traditional NDP. EDP2 is obtained by further deducting the cost of degradation, and is estimated to be 36,448 million pesos, i.e. about 87 percent of NDP. In reviewing the results of this pilot study, one needs to keep their tentative nature in mind. The main emphasis in the first stage of developing the SCEEM was on identifying the relationship between different economic aggregates and environmentally-adjusted aggregates. There was less emphasis on the quantitative accuracy of the environmental adjustments.

This paper reports the conclusions of a case study carried out in 1990-91 jointly by the United Nations Statistical Office (UNSO), the World Bank, and the Mexican "Instituto Nacional de Estadistica, Geografia e Informatica" (INEGI), with partial funding from the United Nations Development Programme (UNDP), to compile, on an experimental basis, environmentally adjusted economic aggregates for Mexico.[1] The aggregates were to be developed within an analytical framework of environmental accounts linked to the national accounts of Mexico, and based on concepts elaborated in the UNSO's Draft Handbook on Environmental Accounting (United Nations 1990). Given that environmental and economic information has traditionally been collected by different agencies, a special effort was made to establish contacts between INEGI, the Urban and Environment Ministry (SEDUE), and other relevant agencies with data and expertise in these areas.

This paper covers the following topics. First, information is given on the orientation and organizational context of the work on environmental accounting in Mexico. Next, the paper describes the environmental concerns, distinguishing between three concerns—oil extraction, deforestation and land use, and degradation concerns. It summarizes for each of the concerns (a) the data sources of physical environmental indicators that are compiled in order to measure the impact of the concerns (and the adjustments that are made to these data in order to use them for integrated economic-environmental analysis), and (b) the principles of valuation applied in order to arrive at monetary valuation of the environmental impacts. Lastly, this report describes and analyzes the effects of incorporating data into an accounting

framework for joint economic-environmental analysis, called *Sistema de Cuentas Economicas y Ecologicas de Mexico* (SCEEM): It starts with a presentation of the traditional Mexican national accounts framework for economic analysis, called the *Sistema de Cuentas Nacionales de Mexico* (SCNM), and extends SCNM to SCEEM, successively integrating into the analysis the resource balances in physical terms that reflect oil extraction, deforestation and land use, and degradation concerns, and applying the valuations developed to arrive at a SCEEM macroanalysis in monetary terms that permits a comparison of SCNM and SCEEM aggregates. The macroaggregates in monetary terms are broken down by economic activities, which permits comparative evaluation of environmental impacts and use of natural resources by different economic activities in Mexico.

The analytical data presented in the tables throughout the paper refer to 1985. In that year, a detailed input-output table for Mexico was compiled, facilitating the adaptation of SCNM to the integrated economic and environmental analysis of SCEEM.

General Orientation of the Pilot Project

There has been much discussion in Mexico about environmental concerns, and a variety of studies have been carried out to quantify the impacts on production and the quality of life.[2] Public opinion and politicians in Mexico are aware that many of the environmental concerns are linked to economic activities and that environmental impacts can be mitigated through a combination of incentives and regulations affecting economic activities. In order to assess

The authors are grateful to Sweder van Wijnbergen and Mohan Munasinghe for supporting this work, and to Dale Jorgensen and Michael Ward for valuable comments. Also, the authors would like to thank Hector de Alzua Romo, Jaime Rodriguez Carranza, Joel Villegas Tovar, J. Dulce Ma. Martinez Moreno, Fernando Perez Conde, Gerardo Calderon Fierros, Alma Morales Lozado, Hilda Martinez Diego, and Silvia Jaime Leija from INEGI for valuable assistance. Finally, the authors would like to thank the World Bank's Research Committee and UNDP's Mexico Program for providing funding for the study.

[1] The annexes to the case study present a detailed account of data sources and valuation methods and include the quantitative results of the project in considerable detail. Since the annexes are voluminous, they are not included as a part of this book.

[2] For example, the recent report "Mexico in Transition: Towards a New Rate for the Public Sector" (World Bank Report No. 8770-ME, May 22, 1991) discusses environmental policy issues in considerable details.

the economic ramifications of environmental interventions, there is a need to link economic analysis with analysis of environmental impacts. Such linkage makes it possible to determine in which economic activities environmental regulations would be most effective from an environmental point of view and at the same time be optimal from an economic point of view. The development of such a linkage between economic and environmental accounting was an important objective of this pilot study.

One of the difficulties encountered in developing a joint economic-environmental analysis was the separation between different disciplines which deal with economic analysis and with analysis of environmental impacts. In mexico, as in may other countries, the different orientations of economic and environmental analysis not only are reflected in different disciplines and experts supporting those disciplines, but also are represented by different institutions. In preparing government policies in fields related to the present study, the two disciplines are mainly represented by INEGI, which has developed macro economic accounts that are used by the government in economic policy making, and SEDUE, which is the focal point in the government for environmental policy making. The first step in implementing the project in Mexico was to establish the necessary contacts between experts in economic accounting in INEGI and resource accounting in SEDUE and other Mexican institutions dealing with natural resources.

An accounting framework was developed that could be used as the quantitative instrument through which environmental data analyzed by SEDUE and other Mexican institutions , and macroeconomic data elaborated by INEGI, could be linked. The joint economic-environmental accounting framework SCEEM is based on the *System of Economic Environmental Accounts* (SEEA).[3] SEEA was adapted to the Mexican circumstances and requirements, such that economic accounts included in SCNM and compiled by INEGI, and resource balances known by experts from

SEDUE and other Mexican institutions working in the area of natural resources, were separately identified. This facilitated discussion and further reconciliation of common concepts, valuations, and so forth, and also made it possible to confront available economic and environmental data sets, which were used in the past for separate analyses, and use them in a joint analysis to bring out the interactions between economic activities and environmental effects. Furthermore, within the resource balances of SCEEM, a distinction was made between different resource balances representing different environmental concerns, so that the quantitative interactions between economic activities and each of those environmental concerns could be separately assessed.

In line with the orientation of SEEA, SCEEM was compiled in an integrated manner, with much emphasis on identifying, quantifying, and establishing the relation between the environmental effects on different macroeconomic aggregates and less emphasis on quantitative accuracy of the environmental adjustments. The reason for this emphasis is our belief that first the orientation of the integrated environmental-economic analysis should be established, thus, integrating expertise, concepts, and data, and only at a later stage when there is common understanding of concepts and format of such integrated analysis, data improvements can be attempted, which would not only lead to improved accuracy of isolated data, but would also lead to improvements in the integrated analysis.

For instance, after completion of the environmental project in Mexico, detailed studies may be carried out with regard to soil erosion caused by agricultural production or with regard to air and water pollution caused by economic activities in the Federal District of Mexico. In such studies, economic and environmental data would have to be compiled in the same classification detail and on the basis of compilation methods that are compatible in terms of valuation, estimation procedures, and so on.

---

[3] SEEA is the accounting framework that is included in the Draft Handbook on Environmental Accounting that is being developed by a consultant to the United Nations Statistical Office. In the remaining text, reference will be made either to SEEA or the Handbook.

Improvement of data for integrated environmental and economic analysis should not be the only objective of future activities in environmental accounting, though. There should be also much emphasis on further developing the rudimentary analyses of environmental impacts on growth and performance, which are presented later in the paper. Only through such improvements of the analytical tools would the improved data have an impact on policy making through the replacement of traditional economic analyses by integrated analyses that are based on environmentally adjusted aggregates.

Environmental Concerns Addressed and Measured

The environmental concerns examined as part of the project activities deal with quantitative and qualitative effects on natural resources. They are grouped together in the present report in three main groups: oil extraction concerns, deforestation and land use concern, and degradation concern. The first two groups are also called the depletion and land use concerns.

The oil depletion concern is dealing with the quantitative exhaustion of a natural resource that is an important source of revenues for the Mexican economy. It is reflected in oil extraction and findings of new oil reserves. The traditional economic aggregates do not take into account any allowance for depletion, which constitutes a loss of future revenues; in other words, the oil resources are considered as free goods in traditional economic analysis. The oil depletion aspect is analyzed here separately from environmental impacts, that is, the air and water pollution caused by oil extraction and the subsequent oil refining activities; these environmental impacts, which affect the quality of natural resources (air, water), are dealt with under the degradation concern described below.

The deforestation and land use concerns deal with two aspects of deforestation. These include the loss of timber as a result of commercial and noncommercial logging at a speed beyond the capacity of nature to replace it through natural growth, and the transfer of unexploited forest areas to uses in economic activities, either in the form of agricultural land, land used for holding cattle, or land transferred

for the purpose of urbanization. The transfer of land also affects the practice of cultivation, which is sometimes carried out by burning forests for temporary cultivation and abandoning the land after a few harvests. Both the logging of timber and the transfer of forest areas to economic uses generally involve not only the exhaustion of depletable resources—timber and forest land—but also the destruction of these natural resources as ecosystems. While the latter loss of the forest as an ecosystem is an environmentally critical concern, it is not dealt with under the deforestation and land use concern as defined here, which solely deals with the quantitative reduction of two natural resources, that is timber and forest land.

The degradation concerns do not deal with the quantitative exhaustion of natural resources, but rather with the qualitative degradation of the ecosystem. They include in the present study the contamination of air and water through the generation and deposit of residuals, and also the environmental impact of leaving garbage and solid wastes behind as a result of production, including domestic production activities of households. Also covered under the degradation concerns are land erosion and ground water loss.

In further analysis of the impacts of the three types of environmental concerns, it has been assumed that the quantitative depletion and land use concerns of oil extraction, deforestation, and land use presented above have an immediate impact on the productive and income-generating capacity of the Mexican economy. The depletion of oil and the loss of trees immediately affects the future income-generating capacity of the oil extraction and logging activities. Also, land transferred from the environment to economic activities in agriculture, livestock holding, and for purposes of urbanization will have an immediate (in this case positive) impact on the income-generating capacity of economic activities. The qualitative degradation concerns, on the other hand, have almost immediate effects on the welfare of the population and long-run effects on the productive and income-generating capacity. The effects are on the quality of life through effects of air, water, and solid waste pollution on health, through the effects of land erosion on the quality of recreational areas, and through ground water loss which immediately affects households in their consumptive activities. Ultimately, the degradation concerns will have an impact on production, either through health effects of workers in the production processes or through secondary effects on growth of products in agriculture, fishing, and forestry which, in turn, affects the generation of net product in these economic activities. These secondary effects on production are, however, more difficult to identify and analyze because many effects—and not only environmental ones—may operate together, and time lags of the effects on production may be very considerable.

The distinction between immediate effects on production and the long-run effects on production through primary effects on well-being, does not entirely coincide with the distinction between the two groups of concerns. Oil depletion may also have long-run effects through the air and water pollution caused by oil extraction activities. Deforestation may have severe long-run effects: the loss of ecosystems may affect productivity, particularly in agriculture, and through health effects on the productivity of workers in other industries, and in general it may have a deteriorating effect on the quality of life. On the other hand, some of the degradation effects such as land erosion and ground water loss may have immediate effects on productivity, particularly in agriculture.

Data Sources

The compilation of additional data on physical indicators with regard to balances of natural assets was accompanied by an extension of the present SCNM to include asset balances of produced assets as well. The information used to extend the SCNM in this manner took as a point of departure the SCNM data regarding gross capital formation. Additional information was obtained from the Economic Census 1986, supplemented by data from the Census of Commerce and Services 1980, and the Survey of Capital Formation in the Enterprise Sector, both carried out in 1980 by the Banco de Mexico.

A variety of data sources were used for compiling physical indicators that reflect the three types of environmental concerns mentioned above. They are summarized below and described in detail in the annexes to the case study.[4]

Information on proven reserves of oil was obtained from published information by the publicly controlled Mexican Petroleum Company PEMEX. Annual extraction data were also obtained from this source. New discoveries are not published but obtained as a residual from the published data on oil deposits and oil extraction.

Information on the (opening and closing) stock of forest resources was obtained from the National Forest Inventory, a report prepared by the Secretaria de Agricultura y Recursos Hidraulicos. The report included information on land surface covered by forests expressed in hectares and also data on the volume of trees in cubic meters. There was no detailed information on the type of trees. The same Secretaria de Agricultura and Recursos Hidraulicos also compiled a Regional Inventory of the Use of Land, which provided information on land use in general and not only for forest areas. Information on changes in the use of land was obtained on the basis of assumptions that were based on studies about the relation between increases in the use of land and the corresponding growth of agricultural production, growth of production in cattle farming, and growth of urban centers. As a result of these assumptions, decreases in the forest area over time could be calculated.

Data regarding the degradation concerns were compiled with regard to land erosion, air and water pollution, ground water use, and the generation of solid wastes.

Land erosion was estimated on the basis of the General Ecology Report elaborated by the Comision Nacional de Ecologia. The report identifies areas with very severe, severe and moderate land erosion and presents an average erosion per hectare (27.54 tons per hectare) at the national level. The information on erosion per hectare was applied to the areas used for agriculture, cattle farming, and forestry and thus national totals in tons were derived and

---

[4]   See footnote 1.

allocated to the three economic activities mentioned. Reconditioning of soil, resulting in the elimination of some of the soil erosion, was deducted from soil erosion in agriculture.

The main source of information on air pollution were 1989 reports resulting from a long-term program carried out by the Federal District of Mexico, called the "Programa Integral Contra la Contaminacion Atmosferica." Based on the results of this project, contamination coefficients could be calculated for five types of contaminants—sulfur dioxide, nitrogen oxide, hydrocarbons, carbon monoxide, and full suspended particles. The contamination coefficients related the emission of these substances to the number of motor vehicles, the output of the oil refining industry, the output of electricity plants, and the output of other manufacturing industries. The coefficients were used to calculate national totals for each of the contaminants, based on the total number of vehicles in Mexico and the output of a variety of industries causing air pollution.

The extent of water pollution was measured in terms of biochemical demand of oxygen (DBO). This is an effective measure because additional oxygen is needed in order to break down excess of organic substances found in the water. The sources of information were private studies. Contamination coefficients expressed in DBOs were estimated for a variety of industrial sectors and also per capita to cover water pollution by households. Application of the coefficients to output in each industry and total population provided national totals on DBOs.

Information on ground water resources was obtained from a variety of reports, but the main one was the General Ecology Report prepared by the Comision Nacional de Ecologia. The use of ground water was estimated on the basis of water used per capita and water used per unit of industrial production in a number of industries including agriculture, cattle farming, and electricity production. The reduction in the ground water resources would be the difference between this use and what is annually replenished through precipitation.

The generation of solid wastes was only calculated for the household sector; industrial wastes were not covered. The main source of information was the General Ecology Report prepared by the Comision Nacional de Ecologia, which provided information on the daily average generation of solid wastes at the national level (.693 kilogram) and at the Federal District level (.987 kilogram). The report distinguishes between different solid residues, which are grouped together in the preparation of data between biodegradable and nonbiodegradable. This information was used together with population data to arrive at a national level of solid waste generation by households.

Valuation

As will be shown below environmental accounts in physical terms can give indications of the direction in which environmental costs and capital would affect the traditional economic aggregates. However, for an integrated analysis, it is essential that environmental variables be expressed in the same monetary units as the economic variables.

Two types of criteria are used in valuing the natural assets and changes therein. The first type calculates the value of stocks of assets as the sum of discounted values of future income streams; the value of changes in the stock of natural assets is based on the changes in future income streams as a consequence of additions to the reserves of natural assets, or depletions. The second type of valuation, which is only used for valuing quality changes in the natural assets, is based on the cost of avoiding such changes. These general criteria translate into more specific methods for each of the natural resources and environmental concerns covered in SCEEM.

For exploitation of oil and timber reserves, two alternative valuation methods are used. the first one is the net rent method as developed in projects carried out by the World Resources Institute projects (Repetto 1989), and the second one is the method developed by El Serafy (1989), which is based on the calculation of a depletion allowance. The net rent method calculates the value of natural resources in the ground as the difference between the market value of lumber and oil and the cost it takes (including a normal profit) to extract this resource for commercial exploitation. The net rent value is calculated separately for opening and closing stocks as well as for changes in those stocks as a result of depletions and additions.

The method developed by El Serafy values the natural resource as a function of the sum of the discounted values of future income streams that are generated by it. It assumes that a part of operating surplus of mining and forestry would have to be reserved for re-investment (depletion allowance) in order to assure that the sum of the discounted income streams (covering net operating surplus and compensation of employees) over the limited life of the natural resources would be equal to the sum of discounted income streams over an infinite period obtained if net product were reduced by the depletion allowance and the depletion allowance were re-invested. The amount of the depletion allowance per unit of production is obtained as a result of these assumptions. The values based on the net rent and El Serafy methods have their own economic meaning and are, therefore, used in combination in the integrated analysis of this paper.

The value of land is generally based on the sum of the discounted value o f future income streams in the different economic activities in which land is used. It is calculated separately for forest land, land used in agriculture, land used for holding of livestock, and land used for urban needs. In each type of economic activity, the value per hectare of land is based on the sum of the discounted values of net value added per year per hectare of land. In the case of forest land, the value of the land is based on net value added in forestry. Only forest land as an environmental asset has been given an economic value; other land not used for economic purposes other than forest land has not been valued. Revaluation of land within the same activity between the beginning and end of the period is not taken into account, only changes in the value of land when transferred from one activity to another.

All types of degradation have been valued on the basis of avoidance cost per unit of contaminant or other unit of degradation. In the case of land erosion, this cost was valued as the cost of fertilizer to maintain the productivity of the land as it was before erosion took place. For ground water loss, the cost was assumed to be equal to what it would cost to re-inject water into underground water reservoirs. The cost of water and air pollution was estimated on the basis of the cost it would take to reduce such pollution to acceptable levels.

Accounting for Environmental Impacts on Economic Activities

In order for the integrated environmental and economic analysis to have maximum effect, the existing analysis taken as a point of departure should be the one that is frequently used as a basis for government policy decisions and that furthermore includes a maximum number of variables in which environmental impacts could be incorporated. The analysis that best fits these conditions in the Mexican case is input-output analysis that is based in Mexico on the highly developed data base of SCNM. It is convenient to take SCNM as point of departure when developing SCEEM, as the SCNM data base and its analytical features are easily understood by both users and producers of such statistics in Mexico, where in the past extensive use has been made of input-output data and analyses for policy purposes. By structuring SCEEM in a manner similar to SCNM, both producers and users of SCNM can easily compare the data base of SCNM with the expanded data set of SCEEM and can thus appreciate how aggregates of SCNM change when redefined in SCEEM. Also, for analytical users it would be easy to see how the SCEEM analysis would differ from the analysis that is traditionally carried out in the context of SCNM.

The present section starts with a macroanalysis of the economic and environmental data, followed by a similar analysis in which separate economic activities are identified.

Macroanalysis

Features of "Sistema de Cuentas Nacionales de Mexico" (SCNM)

Behind the present national accounts of Mexico, that is, SCNM, is a very simple analytical model, which serves a variety of analyses. The simple model includes a supply and use identity and production functions. With help of Table 10-1, some basic features of

Table 10-1: Mexico Input/Output Scheme (SCNM)
(billions of Mexican pesos)

| | Economic activities | | | |
	Production	Rest of world	Final consumption	Produced capital
Economic supply Total	P 75,706,918	M 4,897,328		
Economic uses Total	Ci 28,315,216	Ex 7,305,293	C 34,948,897	I 10,034,840
Gross product	Y 47,391,702			

Table 10-2: Enlarged Input/Output Scheme with Produced Asset Balances
(billions of Mexican pesos)

| | Economic activities | | | |
	Production	Rest of world	Final Consumption	Produced Capital
Opening assets produced assets				Ko. p. ec 111,162,310
Economic supply Total	P 75,706,918	M 4,897,328		
Economic uses Total	Ci 28,315,216	Ex 7,305,293	C 34,948,897	I 10,034,840
Depreciation	Depr. 5,331,186			–Depr. (5,331,186)
Net product	Yn 42,060,516			In 4,703,654
Revaluation produced assets				Rev. p. ec
Closing assets produced assets				K1. p. ec 115,865,965

SCNM can be described.

The supply and use identity can be written as

$$P + M = Ci + C + I + Ex \quad (i)$$

in which P is production,

> M is imports,
> Ci is intermediate consumption,
> C is final consumption,
> I is gross capital formation (or investment), and
> Ex is exports.

A second identity defines gross product or value added (Y) as the difference between production and intermediate consumption:

$$Y = P - Ci \quad (ii)$$

When substituting this income definition into the first identity, a third identity is derived, which links gross product and expenditures:

$$Y = C + I + (Ex - M) \quad (iii)$$

The supply and use identity (i) is represented in Table 10-1 as the identity between the totals of the second and third row, that is,

$$75,707(P) + 4,897(M) = 28,315(Ci) + 34,949(C) + 10,035(I) + 7,305(Ex).^5$$

The product identity (ii) is shown in the first column as the difference between total economic supply or output (P) minus total economic uses or intermediate consumption (Ci); that is, gross product (Y) is

$$47,392(Y) = 75,706(P) - 28,315(Ci).$$

The product-expenditure identity (iii) is not immediately obvious from the presentation of the table; it is reflected in the identity between Y on the one hand and the sum of C, I, and (Ex-M) on the other, that is,

$$47,391(Y) = 34,949(C) + 10,035(I) + [7,305(Ex) - 4,897(M)].$$

The first step in deriving SCEEM, in which asset balances of environmental assets

or natural resources play an important role, is to expand SCNM with the corresponding asset balances of produced assets, which are not regularly compiled in Mexico, but which form an integral part of the system of national accounts. This expansion of SCNM, which is represented in Table 10-2, changes the input-output (i/o) scheme from one that can only be used for static analysis of the input-output type to a dynamic input-output model in which capital output ratios can be identified and used in analysis of growth. The extended scheme of Table 10-2 includes three additional elements as compared to the scheme of Table 10-1, that is: $K0_{(p.ec)}$ is opening stock of produced assets; $K1_{(p.ec)}$ is closing stock of produced assets; and Depr is depreciation.

The three elements are used to define the additional asset balance identity, which explains the relation between the opening and closing stocks of produced assets —$(K1_{(p.ec)}$ and $K0_{(p.ec)})$— on the basis of changes in produced capital. Further changes are reflected in (net) product and (net) capital formation. Both were defined gross in Table 10-1 and are replaced by net versions after deduction of depreciation in Table 10-2.

The asset balance presented in the last column of the table has the following format:

$$K1_{p.ec} = K0_{p.ec} + (I - Depr) + Rev_{p.ec}$$

One element, $Rev_{p.ec}$ (standing for revaluation of produced economic assets), is added for the purpose of completeness. In Table 10-2 no value has been entered for this element, however, as revaluation of produced assets is not taken into account in the additional data that were compiled. The asset balance in monetary units as presented in Table 10-2 therefore takes the following quantitative format:

$$115,866(K1_{p.ec}) = 111,162(K0_{p.ec}) + [10,035(I) - 5,331(Depr)]$$

Because one of the elements that explains the change in the value of produced assets is depreciation, incorporation of depreciation is an essential element of changing the static i/o model of SCNM to a dynamic one. The

---

5   For ease of presentation, the last three digits of the figures presented in the tables are omitted in the text.

incorporation of asset balances into the expanded version of SCNM is therefore accompanied by a corresponding change from using gross product (Y) in Table 10-1 to net product (Yn) in Table 10-2—and gross capital formation (I) to net (In)—and this changes the national accounts identity presented above as follows):

$$Yn = C + In + (Ex - M)$$

in which Yn and In are net product and capital formation concepts from which depreciation has been deducted.

Conceptual Framework of "Sistema de Cuentas Ecologicas e Economicas de Mexico" (SCEEM)

SCEEM takes SCNM as the point of departure in its design, while introducing a number of modifications. It includes a wider asset boundary, covering not only produced assets, but also nonproduced natural or environmental assets. Thus, SCEEM includes imputations for additional expenditure items that are related to depletion and degradation of nonproduced assets. Furthermore, taking into account the imputed items, SCEEM incorporates modified concepts of net product or value added, which are derived by deducting not only the traditional cost items, but also imputed items that correspond to environmental cost of depletion and degradation. Finally, SCEEM changes the concept of capital formation as used in the traditional analysis of SCNM and introduces a new concept of capital accumulation, which takes into account not only changes in produced assets as a result of production and depreciation of such assets, but also changes in the stock of nonproduced assets resulting from new finds of nonproduced assets and deteriorations of nonproduced assets as a consequence of economic activities.

The modified features of SCEEM can be easily appreciated from the presentation of Table 10-3. They can be compared with the features of the traditional SCNM, which are identified by the shaded areas in the table.

SCEEM in Table 10-3 includes to additional columns for the incorporation of asset balances of nonproduced assets alongside those of the produced assets that were included in SCNM. The first additional column refers to nonproduced assets that are directly "used" in economic activities together with produced assets; both groups are labeled economic assets. The second additional column refers to assets that are only "affected" by economic activities—so-called environmental assets. Economic assets are used as production factors in the generation of output, and production analysis requires that full balances including stocks of economic assets are available. Environmental assets are not considered as production factors in this sense; their contribution to the generation of output is not fully understood or perceived in existing analysis and this is generally reflected in the nonavailability of information on asset balances, including data on stocks of those assets.

In the case of Mexico, oil reserves and land used in agriculture, livestock management, and urbanization are treated as nonproduced economic assets, while water (including ground water), air, soil (lost through erosion), and also all forests are dealt with as environmental assets. Forests are included as environmental assets because it was not possible to distinguish in the data between virgin forests and forests that are used for commercial logging and that should have been treated as an economic asset in the same manner as oil. Both ground water and soil are treated as nonproduced environmental assets either because their contribution as a production factor to the generation of output is not sufficiently clear (ground water) or because no asset balances could be obtained from available data (soil).

Corresponding to the incorporation of a wider asset boundary in SCEEM, additional costs are incorporated that reflect the use or deterioration of nonproduced assets as a result of economic activities. In Table 10-3, two types of imputed costs are represented. The first type (Ci_{depl}) are imputed costs related to depletion and losses reflecting deterioration of land that is transferred from the environment to economic activities, and the second type of imputed cost (Ci_{degr}) covers the deterioration of the environmental assets as a consequence of economic activities. For purposes of this pilot study, the cost of depletion includes the cost of depleting

Table 10-3: System of Economic Accounts of Mexico (*Sistema de Cuentas de Mexico (SCEEM)*): Basic Structure

	Economic activities					Environment
				Economic assets		Nonproduced environmental assets
	Production	Rest of world	Final Consumption	Produced assets	Nonproduced assets	
Opening assets				Ko.p.ec	Ko.np.ec	Ko.np.env
Economic supply	P	M				
Economic uses	Ci	Ex	C	I		
Depreciation	Depr			Depr		
Net domestic Product (NDP)	Yn			In		
Environment uses:					I.np.ec	−I.np.env
Depletion and land use concerns	Ci.depl				−Dpl.np.ec	−Dpl.np.env
Environmentally adjusted net product	Ynl			IAn.ec1		−IAn.1env
Degradation concerns	Ci.degr					−Degr.np,env
Environmentally adjusted net product	Yn2			IAn.2ec (=IAn.1ec)		−IAn.2env
Revaluation				Rev.p.ec	Rev.np.ec	Rev.np.env
Closing assets				K1.p.ec	K1.np.ec	K1.np.env

oil, timber, and ground water reserves. The imputed cost of land use refers to the trees—representing the ecosystem—that are lost as a consequence of transfer of forest land to agricultural land, land used for holding of cattle, and land used for the purposes of urbanization. The imputed cost referred to as cost of degradation includes the cost of air and water pollution, the cost associated with solid waste materials, and also the cost of land erosion and ground water loss.

Following the introduction of imputed cost items in SCEEM, two modified net product concepts are introduced, called environmentally adjusted net domestic product 1 and 2 (EDP1 and EDP2). EDP1—or what is represented in the table as Yn1—is derived by deducting from net domestic product (NDP) in SCNM the environmental uses related to depletion and land use, that is

$$Yn1 = Yn - Ci_{depl}$$

and EDP2—or Yn2—is obtained by further deducting the cost of degradation, that is,

$$Yn2 = Yn - (Ci_{depl} + Ci_{degr})$$

There are two reasons why a distinction is made between EDP1 and EDP2. The first is that the valuation of depletion cost and the cost of land use as summarized above is directly linked to the market value of the assets that are depleted or transferred to economic use. On the other hand, imputations for the cost of degradation are much less close to market valuations and therefore much more controversial elements in the analysis. A related reason is that the cost of depletion and land use taken into account in the calculation of EDP1 relates to the use of economic assets, whereas in the derivation of the EDP2 not only the cost of depletion of nonproduced economic assets is taken into account, but also the cost of affecting nonproduced environmental assets such as air, water (including ground water loss), and soil (soil erosion).

Another feature of SCEEM that is different from SCNM is the introduction of two new concepts of net capital accumulation. One such concept refers to net accumulation of economic

assets (IAn_{ec}) and the other to net accumulation of environmental assets (IAn_{env}).

Net accumulation of economic assets is defined as the change in the productive capacity, that is, capital used in production, including not only produced assets, but also nonproduced economic assets. Net accumulation of environmental assets is the net change in the quantity and quality of environmental assets as a result of economic activities.

The enlarged concept of net accumulation of economic assets includes net capital formation and two additional elements related to nonproduced economic assets, including an element representing "investments" in nonproduced assets, that result from the transfer of environmental assets to economic activities ($I_{np.ec}$), and another element representing the depletion of nonproduced economic assets ($Depl_{np.ec}$). In the case of Mexico, the "investment" element includes the transfer of land and mineral reserves to use in economic activities, while the depletion element refers to the depletion of oil. Depletion of timber and ground water is not included in net accumulation of economic assets, as timber and ground water are not treated as economic assets but rather as environmental assets. Also excluded from net accumulation of economic assets is revaluation of produced assets ($Rev_{p.ec}$), nonproduced economic assets ($Rev_{np.ec}$), and nonproduced environmental assets ($Rev_{np.env}$).

The table distinguishes between net accumulation of economic and environmental assets related to Yn1 and Yn2, which are defined as follows:

$$IAn_{1ec} = IAn_{1ec} = In + (I_{np.ec} - Depl_{np.ec})$$
$$IAn_{1env} = -(Inp.env + Depl_{np.ec})$$
$$IAn_{2env} = -(Inp.env + Depl_{np.ec} + Degr_{np.ec})$$

When approaching Yn1 and Yn2 from the expenditure side, while using the above definitions of IAn_{ec} and IAn_{env}, the following identities hold:

$$Yn1 = C + (IAn_{1ec} - IAn_{1env}) + (Ex-M)$$
$$Yn2 = C + (IAn_{2ec} - IAn_{2env}) + (Ex-M)$$

Both identities show clearly the change in the traditional national accounts identity, after incorporation of environmental assets. Net accumulation of economic assets (IAn_{ec}) is only partly reflected in Yn. An important component of net accumulation of economic assets is directly based on the transfer of environmental assets to economic activities; and this is reflected in a negative entry for IAn_{env}.

SCEEM Applied to Environmental Concerns

The conceptual scheme explained above is applied below to the three environmental concerns separately.

1. *Oil Extraction*. The incorporation of the oil extraction concern in Table 10-4 is very simple. It includes only two elements of environmental uses, that is, oil depletion and new finds of oil, both of which are expressed in physical terms. Oil depletion (1,265 million barrels) is shown as an extra environmental cost ($C_{i.depl}$) and a reduction in the value of nonproduced economic assets ($Depl_{np.ec}$). New finds of oil (415 million barrels) is presented as an addition to nonproduced economic assets ($I_{np.ec}$) and as a reduction in the quantity of environmental assets ($-I_{np.env}$).

As a result of the incorporation of these two elements, there are changes in EDP1 as compared to NDP, and in net accumulation of economic assets as compared to net capital formation of SCNM in Tables 10-1 and 10-2. Even though the environmental uses are in physical terms, it is easy to see the direction in which these macroaggregates would change. EDP1 (Yn1) would decrease with the amount of oil extracted ($C_{i.depl}$) and net accumulation would change as a result of the difference between what is extracted ($Depl_{np.ec}$) and the new finds of oil reserves ($I_{np.ec}$). The difference between the decrease of Yn1 and net accumulation of economic assets would be the decrease in nonproduced environmental assets (oil reserves) that are transferred from the environment to economic uses ($-I_{np.env}$). The asset balances of oil are presented in the column for nonproduced economic assets, which shows the following quantitative

relation between closing and opening assets of oil in terms of million of barrels:

$$K1_{np.ec} = K0_{np.ec} - (Depl_{np.ec} - I_{np.ec})$$
$$70,900 = 71,750 - (1,265 - 415)$$

2. *Deforestation and Land Use*. The concern of deforestation and land use is represented in Table 10-5. It includes three separate elements of environmental uses—the logging of trees as part of the forestry activity (7,626 thousand cubic meters); the transfer of forest land to economic activities in agriculture, livestock holding, and urbanization (277,589 hectares), and finally the losses in terms of trees resulting from the transfer of land from the environment to economic uses (35,474 thousand cubic meters).

The cost of logging of trees is presented as intermediate cost of production ($C_{i.depl}$) and as forests are treated as environmental assets, a counterpart reduction in nonproduced environmental capital ($Depl_{np.env}$). The transfer of forest land to economic uses is reflected in an increase in nonproduced economic capital ($I_{np.ec}$) and a decrease in nonproduced environmental capital ($-I_{np.env}$). The transfer losses resulting from this transfer of land are shown as intermediate cost of the activity (an example for such an activity might be the construction industry, which is responsible for the output called "improvements to land"), which carries out the preparation of land for economic use ($C_{i.depl}$), and a reduction in environmental capital ($-Depl_{np.env}$).

EDP1 (Y_{nl}) is reduced as a result of logging costs and losses of trees due to the transfer of land to economic uses. Net accumulation of economic assets (IAn_{lec}) as compared to net capital formation, though, is increased with the amount of forest land transferred to economic uses. The difference between the reduction in Y_{nl} and the change in net accumulation of economic assets as compared with net capital formation, is entirely reflected in losses of environmental capital as presented in the column of the environment ($-IAn_{lenv}$).

The asset balances that are affected by the deforestation and land use concerns are those for land in economic uses, which are presented in the column for nonproduced economic assets; forest land, which is included in the

Table 10.4: Enlarged Input/Output Scheme with Asset Balances (billions of Mexican pesos) and Adjustments for Net Changes in Oil Reserves (physical units)

	Economic activities			Economic assets		Environment	Physical unit of measurement
	Production	*Rest of world*	*Final consumption*	*Produced assets*	*Nonproduced economic assets*	*Nonproduced environmental assets*	
Opening assets							
Produced asset							
Oil				Ko.p.ec 111,162,310	Ko.np.ec 71,750	Ko.np.env	millions of barrels
Economic supply							
Total	P 75,706,918	M 4,897,328					
Economic uses							
Total	Ci 28,315,216	Ex 7,305,293	C 34,948,897	I 10,034,840			
Depreciation	Depr 5,331,186			-Depr (5,331,186)			
Environmental uses:							
Oil extraction concerns							
Oil depletion	Ci.depl 1,265				-Depl.np.ec (1,265)		millions of barrels
New finds of oil					I.np.ec 415	-I.np.env (415)	millions of barrels
Net product: EDP1	Yn1			, IAn1.ec		IAn1.env	
Closing assets							
Produced assets				K1.p.ec 115,865,965	K1.np.ec 70,900	K1.np.env	
Oil							millions of barrels

Table 10-5: Enlarged Input/Output Scheme with Asset Balances (billions of Mexican pesos) and Adjustments for Changes in Land Use and Deforestation (physical units)

	Economic activities			Economic Assets		Environment	
	Production	Rest of world	Final consumption	Produced assets	Nonproduced economic assets	Nonproduced environmental assets	Physical unit of measurement
Opening assets							
Produced asset							
Timber				Ko.p.ec 111,162,310		Ko.np.env 3,125,268	thousand cubic meters
Land					Ko.np.ec 139,741,568	56,078,532	hectares
Economic supply total	P 75,706,918	M 4,897,328					
Economic uses total	Ci 28,315,216	Ex 7,305,293	C 34,948,897	I 10,034,840			
Depreciation	Depr 5,331,186			-Depr (5,331,186)			
Environmental uses:							
Deforestation concerns	Ci.depl					-Depl.np.env (7,626)	thousand cubic meters
Logging	7,626						
Forest land transfer to economic uses					I.np.ec 277,589	-I.np.env (277,589)	hectares
Transfer losses	35,474					-Depl.np.env (35,474)	thousand cubic meters
Net product: EDP1	Yn1			IAn1.ec		-IAn1.env	
Closing assets							
Produced assets							
Timber				K1.p.ec 115,865,965		Ko.np.env 3,082,168	thousand cubic meters
Land					K1.np.ec 140,019,157	55,800,943	hectares

column for environmental assets; and timber, which is also presented in this column. The three asset balances in quantitative form are as follows:

$$K1_{np.ec} = K0_{np.ec} + I_{np.ec}$$
140,019,157= 139,741,568 + 277,589
land used for economic purposes (hectares)

$$K1_{np.env} = K0_{np.env} - I_{np.env}$$
55,800,943 = 56,078,532 - 277,589
forest land (hectares)

$$K1_{np.env} = K0_{np.env} - Depl_{np.env}$$
3,082,168 = 3,125,268 - (7,626 + 55,474)
trees lost (thousand cubic meters)

3. *Degradation*. Table 10-6 incorporates the effects of degradation. These include soil erosion in terms of tons of soil lost, solid waste materials resulting from household activities—also in tons—ground water used in terms of thousand cubic meters, water pollution in terms of the bio-chemical demand for oxygen (DBO) used by nature to destroy the foreign substances in the water, and finally air pollution in terms of tons of various chemicals that are emitted by industrial production processes. The cost of degradation is presented as environmental cost of production (Ci_{degr}), with counterpart entries in the column for the environment, representing the deterioration of environmental capital ($-Degr_{np.ec}$).

The effect of including these environmental uses is to lower EDP2 (Yn2) in comparison with NDP (Yn) included in the traditional SCNM. There is no effect on net accumulation, as all degradation effects are recorded as affecting nonproduced environmental capital. The difference between the negative effect on Yn2 and no effect on net accumulation of economic assets as compared to net capital formation is entirely reflected in the degradation effects reducing the quality of environmental capital ($-Degr_{np.env}$) presented in the column of the environment.

Comparison between SCNM and SCEEM Aggregates and Analyses, in Monetary Terms

In order to overcome some of the limitations of the above analysis in physical terms, a parallel analysis in monetary terms is presented below. The monetary analysis is presented in two tables. Table 10-7 includes the monetary valuation of the depletion and land use concerns, including oil extraction, deforestation, and land use concerns. The table arrives at a concept of EDP1 (Yn1) as defined earlier in Table 10-3. Table 10-8 presents a similar analysis in monetary terms for the degradation effects that are added in this table to the monetary valuation of the depletion effects. After incorporation of both effects into the latter table, the concept of EDP2 (Yn2) is obtained.

1. *EDP1*. Table 10-7 reflects in monetary terms the same environmental effects as presented in Tables 10-4 and 10-5. By applying valuations to the elements of the depletion concerns related to oil, deforestation, and land use presented in those tables in physical terms, estimates are obtained for EDP1 and also for net accumulation of economic assets (IAn_{1ec}) and environmental assets ($-IAn_{1env}$). The net product and corresponding expenditure items are presented on the line for EDP1. Because different values have been used for opening and closing stocks and flow items, revaluation elements ($Rev_{np.ec}$ and $Rev_{np.env}$) have been incorporated additionally in the table.

2. The national accounts identity without environmental adjustments, which was in Table 10-2, formulated as

$$Yn = C + In + (Ex - M) \text{ or,}$$

in quantitative terms:
42,060,516 = 34,948,897 + 4,703,654 + (7,305,293 - 4,897,328)

changes in Table 10-7 to:
$$Yn1 = C + (IAn_{1ec} - IAn_{1env}) + (Ex-M) \text{ or,}$$

39,662,772 = 34,948,897 + (24,245,455 - 21,939,545) + (7,305,293 - 4,897,328)

Table 10-6: Enlarged Input/Output Scheme with Asset Balances (billions of Mexican pesos) and Adjustments for Degradation of Air, Water, and Land (physical units)

	Economic activities			Economic assets		Environment	Physical unit of measurement
	Production	Rest of world	Final consumption	Produced assets	Nonproduced economic assets	Nonproduced environmental assets	
Opening assets							
Produced asset				Ko.p.ec 111,162,310			
Land					Ko.np.ec	Ko.np.env	
Water							
Air							
Economic supply							
Total	P 75,706,918	M 4,897,328					
Economic uses							
Total	Ci 28,315,216	Ex 7,305,293	C 34,948,897	I 10,034,840			
Depreciation	Depr 5,331,186			-Depr (5,331,186)			
Environmental uses:							
Degradation concerns							
Land	Ci.depl					-Degr.np.env	
Soil erosion	420,992,059					-420,992,059	tons
Solid wastes	18,228,157					-18,228,157	tons
Water							thousand cubic meters
Ground water use	2,456					-2,456	
Water pollution	2,359,275					-2,359,275	tons DBO
Air							
Sulfur dioxide	6,646,070					-6,646,070	tons
Nitrogen oxides	1,804,408					-1,804,408	tons
Hydrocarbons	2,383,030					-2,383,030	tons
Carbon monoxide	17,967,872					-17,967,872	tons
Suspended particles	477,529					-477,529	tons
Net Product: EDP2	Yn2			IAn2.ec (=IAn1.ec)		-IAn1.env	
Closing assets							
Produced assets				K1.p.ec 115,865,965	K1.np.ec	Ko.np.env	
Land							
Water							
Air							

The elements in the above expression that have changed are net product and net accumulation. All other elements are unaffected.

The table includes revaluations for oil, timber, and land. The revaluations for oil and timber are residuals obtained as the difference between the value of closing minus opening stocks and the net changes due to new finds and depletions, which are all valued separately. The revaluation of oil and timber therefore includes two elements: the first one refers to the change in the value of resources remaining between the opening and closing balance sheets, and the second reflects the revaluation of the extracted oil or timber between the opening balance sheet and the moment of extraction.

The revaluation for land used in economic activities is negative. The reason is that land is transferred at its value as forest land, which is derived as the sum of discounted revenues accruing if all timber would be harvested for purposes of lumbering; this value was estimated to be 38.15 million pesos per hectare. Once incorporated into the column for nonproduced economic assets at this value, the land is then revalued to the value per hectare of its use in economic activities. In most instances this value was much lower than the value per hectare of forest land (agriculture: 2.64 million pesos per hectare; livestock holding: 1.99 million pesos per hectare); forest land that was changed to waste land after use in shifting agricultural cultivation was assumed to have no value after this use. In the case of urbanized land, the value was higher, that is, 75.50 million pesos per hectare. As a result of these generally lower land values in economic uses, the revaluation element (-18,290) is negative in Table 10-7.

The valuation used for oil and timber in Table 10-7 is the net rent value, that is, the market value minus cost including a normal profit. An alternative value proposed by El Serafy (1989) suggests that both oil and timber be valued as the sum of discounted values of depletion allowances that would be needed to secure a continuous income stream (after deduction of the depletion allowance) even after the natural resource has been depleted. Both for oil and timber the depletion allowance is much lower than the net rent. For oil the net rent is 1,162 Mexican pesos per barrel and the depletion allowance is only 160 Mexican pesos per barrel; for timber the net rent is 21.527 Mexican pesos per cubic meter, while the depletion allowance is only 1.46 pesos per cubic meter. If these much lower valuations would be applied to the extraction of oil and timber, the cost of depletion would be much lower and thus EDP1 would be higher. The quantitative result of these alternative valuations as presented in Table 10-7a, supplement, shows that EDP1 would increase from 39,662,772 to 41,795,147, and the element of revaluation due to extraction would be correspondingly decreased with the same amount from 84,820,456 to 82,688,08[6]

2. EDP2. Table 10-8 presents the same degradation elements as were included in Table 10-6 in physical terms. All counterparts of the degradation cost presented as CIdegr in the column for production are included in the column for the environment. None of the degradation therefore affects net accumulation of economic assets: the only effects are on net accumulation of environmental assets (IAn2env).

The revised national accounts identity is presented in the row of net product, that is,

$$Yn2 = C + (IAn2_{ec} - IAn2_{env}) + (Ex-M)$$

or, in quantitative terms:

---

[6] The large differences between the two valuations are due to the long period in which oil and timber would be available. Several questions may be asked with regard to the alternative valuation. Would it indeed be feasible to find in a country like Mexico an alternative investment potential that would be able to absorb the depletion allowances of oil and timber production. If that were the case, why would oil and timber not be exploited more rapidly? However, if resources were exploited more rapidly, prices of the products (oil and timber) may drop as a result of increased supply, and alternative investment possibilities may be reduced, which would result in lower interest rates. This would mean, that in the long run, the net rent method and the El serafy method may result in similar valuations.

Table 10-7: Enlarged Input/Output Scheme with Asset Balances and Adjustments for Oil Depletion, Land Use, and Deforestation (billions of Mexican pesos)

	Economic activities			Economic assets		Environment
	Production	Rest of world	Final consumption	Produced assets	Nonproduced economic assets	Nonproduced environmental assets
Opening assets				Ko.p.ec	Ko.np.ec	Ko.np.env
Produced asset				111,162,310		
Timber						46,988,404
Oil					66,584,000	
Land					339,259,491	1,483,758,406
Economic supply	P	M				
Total	75,706,918	4,897,328				
Economic uses	Ci	Ex	C	I		
Total	28,315,216	7,305,293	34,948,897	10,034,840		
Depreciation	Depr 5,331,186			−Depr (5,331,186)		
Environmental uses:						
Oil extraction concerns	Ci.depl				−Depl.np.ec	
Oil depletion	1,469,930				−1,469,930	
New finds of oil					I.np.ec 482,320	−I.np.env −482,230
Deforestation concerns						
Logging	164,165					−Depl.np.env −164,165
Forest land Transferred to economic uses					I.np.ec 20,529,501	−I.np.env −20,529,501
Transfer losses	763,649					−Depl.np.env −763,649
Net product: EDP1	Yn1 39,662,772	Ex − M 2,407,965	C 34,948,897	IAn2.ec: 24,245,455		−IAn1.env −21,939,545
Revaluation				Rev.p.ec	Rev.np.ec	Rev.np.env.
Produced assets						
Timber						32,368,256
Oil					52,452,200	
Land					−18,290,522	
Closing assets				K1.p.ec	K1.np.ec	Ko.p.ec
Produced assets				115,865,965		
Timber						78,428,847
Oil					118,048,500	
Land					341,498,470	1,463,228,905

**Table 10-7a: Supplement EDP
and Asset Balances Alternatively
Valued on the Basis of Net Rent
and a Depletion Allowance
(billions of Mexican pesos)**

Openings stock	
Timber	46,988,404
Oil	66,584,000
Oil	
New finds of oil	482,230
Depletion	
Valued on basis of:	
Net rent	(1,469,930)
Depletion allowance	(202,400)
Timber, net reduction	
Valued on basis of:	
Net rent	(927,814)
Depletion allowance	(62,969)
Adjustment to EDP1	2,132,375
EDP1	39,662,772
EDP1.ADJ.	41,795,147
Revaluation, based on	
depletion allowance	82,688,082
Net rent	84,840,456
Adjustment to revaluation	(2,132,375)
Closing stocks	
Timber	78,428,847
Oil	118,048,500

36,448,314 = 34,890,558 + (24,245,455 - 25,095,664) + (7,305,293 - 4,897,328)

which is different in a number of respects from the traditional identity in SCNM defined in Table 10-2 as

$$Yn = C + In + (Ex - M) \text{ or,}$$

in quantitative terms:
42,060,516 = 34,948,897 + 4,703,654 + (7,305,293 - 4,897,328)

Net capital accumulation of economic assets minus that of environmental assets is negative as compared to a positive value for capital formation in economic accounting, and this results in a much lower value for Yn2 as compared to Yn. It should furthermore be noted that in the derivation of Yn2, an additional deduction has been made for environmental services produced by the government in the form of sanitation services. They are treated as intermediate consumption of (domestic) household production activities. Because these expenditures (58,339) are dealt with as final expenditures in SCNM, this treatment lowers final consumption (C) from 34,948,897 (in Table 10-2) to 34,890,558 and correspondingly reduces Yn2 further as compared with its value in previous tables.

The incorporation of values for output of environmental protection services into the table permits comparison with the corresponding degradation effects. From the macro presentation in Table 10-8 it can be observed that the total value of environmental protection services (151,194= 92,855+58,339) is only 5 percent of the total value of environmental degradation cost (3,156,119). It is questionable, however, how to interpret these figures, as it is not certain whether the degradation effects measured are gross, that is, before the protection services were carried out, or are net values after incorporation of the effects of these services. Given the manner in which the degradation effects are estimated, it is likely that at least some of the effects measured are gross effects and

Table 10-8: Enlarged Input/Output Scheme with Asset Balances including Adjustments for Degradation and Environmental Protection Expenditures (billions of Mexican pesos)

	Economic activities					Environment
				Economic assets		
	Production	Rest of world	Final consump-tion	Produced capital	Nonproduced economic assets	Nonproduced environmental assets
Opening assets				Ko.np.ec	Ko.np.ec	Ko.np.env
Produced assets				111,162,310		46,988,404
Timber						
Oil					66,584,00	
Land					339,259,491	1,483,758,406
Water						
Air						
Economic supply	P	M				
Total	75,706,918	4,897,328				
Economic uses	Ci	Ex	C	I	I	I
Total	28,315,216	7,305,293	34,948,897	10,034,840		
of which: Environmental Protection services	P.envp			P.envp		
Industry	92,855			291,385		
Households	58,339					
Depreciation	Depr			-Depr		
	5,331,186			-5,331,186		
Environmental uses	Ci.depl				I.np.ec	-Depl.np.env.
Oil extraction, deforestation, and land use concerns					-Depl.np.ec	
(total)	2,397,744				19,541,801	-21,939,545
Degradation concerns	Ci.degr.					-Degr.np.env.
Land						
Soil erosion	448,880					-448,880
Solid wastes	197,269					-197,269
Water						
Ground water use	191,568					-191,568
Water pollution	662,456					-662,456
Air						
Sulfur dioxide	234,792					-234,792
Nitrogen oxides	137,442					-137,442
Hydrocarbons	127,409					-127,409
Carbon monoxide	1,072,826					-1,072,826
Suspended particles	83,427					-83,477
Subtotal degradation	3,156,119					-3,156,119
Net product: EDP 2	Yn2	Ex - M	C	IAn.ec2 (=IAn.ec1)		-IAn.env2
	36,448,314	2,407,965	34,890,556		24,245,455	-25,095,664
Degradation				Rev.p.ec	Rev.np.ec	Rev.np.env
Produced assets						
Timber						32,388,256
Oil					52,452,200	
Land					-18,290,522	
Closing assets				K1.p.ec	K1.p.ec	K1.p.ec
Produced assets				115,865,965		
Timber						78,428,847
Oil					118,048,500	
Land					341,498,470	
Water						1,463,228,905
Air						

that therefore there is some double counting, because the cost of environmental protection services and the degradation they try to eliminate are deducted at the same time to arrive at EDP2.

3. *Comparative Analysis of EDP1 and EDP2.* The analysis presented above is summarized in Table 10-9. The table shows in dramatic form how changes in net product from NDP to EDP1 and EDP2 would have consequences for analysis. The table shows that final consumption is 83 percent of NDP and net capital formation is 11 percent. When changing to EDP1, final consumption increases to 88 percent of EDP1 and net capital accumulation is less than 6 percent. It is true that net accumulation of economic assets would be nearly 12 percent of EDP1, but the effect of this increase is eliminated because a large part of the net accumulation in economic assets is directly taken from the environment (the environmental capital is reduced by 6 percent of EDP1). When extending the analysis to EDP2, final consumption is further increased to nearly 96 percent and net capital accumulation becomes a negative -2 percent, which is the net result of an increase in net accumulation of economic assets to nearly 13 percent of EDP2 and a decrease of environmental capital which amounts to -15 percent of EDP2.

Analysis by Economic Activities

Comparison of SCNM and SCEEM Aggregates by Economic Activities

The analysis above of environmental impacts on economic aggregates has been carried out in macro format, showing how main aggregates of net product are affected by the incorporation of depletion and degradation effects; how net capital formation changes into a concept of net accumulation that refers to all economic assets, produced as well as nonproduced; and finally how final consumption and net product are affected by a different treatment of environmental expenditures that are included in final consumption of SCNM. While such macroanalysis is useful, it does not provide the information that would be needed

for operational government policies. Therefore, the analysis has been extended below to identify the depletion and degradation effects by economic activities and determine the sectors that are using the economic assets in their production processes. The sectoral analysis focuses, among others, on three elements: value added, balances of economic assets including produced as well as nonproduced assets, and also the environmental protection expenses made by different sectors. The quantitative results of this study are reflected in Tables 10-10 and 10-11.

Value added. Table 10-10 presents a breakdown of the production data by economic activities, including not only the traditional output and intermediate consumption components, but also the values of depletion, degradation, and land use effects. Environmental protection expenditures are also identified in the table for each industry and (domestic) household production activities, and presented as "of which" items that are reflected in the output and intermediate consumption figures of each industry. The net product concepts—NDP, EDP1, and EDP2—have been identified in each of the three sections of the table: NDP is calculated first, followed by EDP1 after incorporation of the depletion and land use effects, and then EDP2 is calculated after incorporation of the degradation effects. The environmental uses presented are the same as in Tables 10-7 and 10-8; the totals for the national economy between Table 10-10 and those two tables coincide.

An additional economic activity, called household production activities, is introduced in Table 10-10 in order to allocate the environmental impacts of household consumption. This column also includes the environmental expenses made by households. The environmental protection expenses made by government on behalf of households, which are treated in SCNM as final consumption and thus added to NDP, are deducted in the table for the calculation of EDP2 in the same manner as this was done in Table 10-8.

The oil concern presented in the table only covers oil depletion that is recorded as environmental cost of the oil industry. New finds of oil are not dealt with in this part of the table,

Table 10-9: Comparative Analysis of Expenditure Distribution of NDP, EDP1, and EDP2

	NDP	*Percent of NDP*	*EDP1*	*Percent of EDP1*	*EDP2*	*Percent of EDP2*
Net product/expenditure	42,060,516		39,662,772		36,448,314	
Final consumption	34,948,897	83.09	34,948,897	88.12	34,890,558	95.73
Capital accumulation, net	4,703,654	11.18	2,305,910	5.81	−850,209	−2.33
Economic assets	4,703,654	11.18	4,703,654	11.86	4,703,654	12.90
Environmental assets			−2,397,744	−6.05	−5,553,863	−15.24
Exports−imports	2,407,965	5.73	2,407,965	6.07	2,407,965	6.61

because they are treated as net accumulation of economic assets with a counterpart negative entry for net accumulation of environmental assets. The oil industry includes only extraction and not refining.

The deforestation concern includes two elements: logging and transfer losses due to the transfer of environmental land to economic uses. The depletion cost of logging is allocated to the forestry industry. Reforestation is assumed to be the result of forestry activities and therefore deducted from trees lost through logging of timber in forestry. The transfer losses are allocated to agriculture and animal farming and breeding, insofar as they concern the losses due to transfer of environmental land to these economic activities. Losses allocated to agriculture also include losses due to forest fires and losses of trees due to the conversion of forest land into waste land; allocation of these losses to agriculture is based on the assumption that these losses are caused, for example, by shifting cultivation. Transfer losses due to the transfer of land for urbanization purposes is allocated to the construction industry, because this industry includes all the cost related to construction for purposes of urbanization.

Soil erosion is only identified for agriculture, animal farming and breeding, and forestry. Ground water use is only measured for agriculture, animal farming and breeding, manufacturing, other services, government services, and household production (that, consumption) activities.

Air and water pollution are mainly allocated to the oil industry, manufacturing, electricity production, transport, other services, and household production activities. Solid wastes are assumed to be only generated by households in their capacity as consumers. Therefore all environmental impacts of solid wastes have been allocated to the column for household production activities.

Capital Stock and Capital Accumulation. The balances of economic assets by economic activities are presented in Table 10-11. The rows of the table include, for each sector, asset balances for produced assets and relevant nonproduced assets. The table distinguishes between fixed assets and stocks. For the fixed assets, the asset balances include as columns the opening and closing stocks, gross fixed capital formation, consumption of fixed capital and net accumulation of economic, nonproduced fixed assets. The closing balance of fixed assets is equal to the opening balance plus gross fixed capital formation, minus consumption of fixed capital plus net accumulation of nonproduced economic assets. For stocks, the asset balances also include the opening and closing stocks as well as separate columns for changes in stocks of produced assets and nonproduced assets. In this section of the table, closing stocks are equal to opening stocks plus changes in stocks of produced and nonproduced assets.

The table refers exclusively to economic assets that are used in production and thus contribute directly to the generation of output and value added. The nonproduced economic assets included in the fixed asset section of the table refer only to land used for agriculture, animal farming and breeding, and urbanization. The nonproduced economic assets included in the

Table 10-10: Breakdown of Production Data by Economic Activity (billions of Mexican pesos)

	Agriculture	Animal farming and breeding	Forestry	Fishing, hunting, etc.	Oil	Other mining	Manufac-turing
Economic supply Total	3,241,866	2,285,331	283,943	249,551	1,901,465	900,951	25,874,013
Economic uses Total	619,948	1,003,947	35,676	94,512	229,920	354,982	14,805,379
of which: Environ-mental protection services Industry Households			767		12,555	4,155	5,162
Depreciation	261,074	171,435	22,805	20,097	200,091	138,686	2,285,025
NDP (Yn)	2,360,844	1,109,949	225,462	134,942	1,471,454	407,283	8,783,609
Environmental uses:							
Oil concerns Oil depletion New finds of oil					1,469,930		
Deforestation concerns Woods Forest land transfer to economic use Transfer losses	137,687	517,983	164,165				
EDP1 (Yn1)	2,223,157	591,966	61,297	134,942	1,524	407,283	8,783,609,
Degradation							
Land Soil erosion Solid wastes	107,709	250,701	90,470				
Water Ground water use Water pollution	86,582	830					14,173 424,849
Air Sulfur dioxide Nitrogen oxides Hydrocarbons Carbon monoxide Suspended particles					6,709 3,164 21,795 40,384 2,592		12,275 11,629 11,299 4,992 9,464
EDP2 (Yn2)	2,028,866	340,435	-29,173	134,942	-73,120	407,283	8,294,927

Table 10-10: Breakdown of Production Data by Economic Activity (billions of Mexican pesos) (continued)

	Electric, gas, water	Construc- tion	Trade, hotels & restaurant	Transport, storage & communica- tion	Other services (excluding govern- ment)	Government services	Household production activities	Total production activities
Economic supply								P
Total	900,798	4,897,862	16,014,145	4,596,322	12,637,004	2,016,522	0	75,799,773
Economic uses								Ci
Total	451,937	2,827,735	2,707,691	1,431,195	3,180,714	664,435		28,408,071
of which: Environ- mental protection services	68,747				1,469			92,855
Industry								
Households							58,339	58,339
Depreciation	119,029	351,550	231,712	761,207	764,701	3,774		5,331,186
NDP (Yn)	329,832	1,718,577	13,074,742	2,403,920	8,691,589	1,348,313		42,060,516
Environmental uses:								Ci depl.
Oil concerns								
Oil depletion								1,469,930
New finds of oil								
Deforestation concerns								
Woods								164,165
Forest land transfer to economic use		53,602				54,377		763,649
Transfer losses								
EDP1 (Yn1)	329,832	1,664,975	13,074,742	2,403,920	8,691,589	1,293,936	0	39,662,772
Degradation								Ci. degr
Land								
Soil erosion								448,880
Solid wastes							197,269	197,269
Water								
Ground water use	1,204				280	21,453	67,046	191,568
Water pollution							237,607	662,456
Air								
Sulfur dioxide	197,697			13,602	3,887		623	234,792
Nitrogen oxides	48,394			56,901	1,515		15,839	137,442
Hydrocarbons	580			54,726	32		38,976	127,409
Carbon monoxide	3,212			613,876	139		410,223	1,072,826
Suspended particles	59,537			5,918	2,153		3,813	83,477
EDP2 (Yn2)	19,208	1,664,975	13,074,742	1,658,898	8,683,582	1,272,483	-1,029,735	36,448,314

Table 10-11: Balance Sheets for Produced and Nonproduced Economic Assets, Classified by Economic Activity (millions of Mexican pesos)

Concept	Opening balance fixed assets	Net capital accumulation (including revaluation)		
		Produced assets		Nonproduced assets
		Gross fixed capital formation	Consumption of fixed capital	
Total				
Produced assets	103,156,227	9,048,296	5,331,186	
Nonproduced assets	339,259,491			2,238,979
Agriculture				
Produced assets	5,559,424	398,062	261,074	
Nonproduced assets: land use	91,575,665			95,790
Animal farming and breeding				
Produced assets	3,797,518	280,611	171,435	
Nonproduced assets: land use	207,572,243			434,336
Forestry: Produced assets	485,614	34,771	228,805	
Fishing: Produced assets	427,951	30,642	20,097	
Extraction of crude oil & gas				
Produced assets:	5,235,811	167,754	200,091	
Nonproduced assets: oil				
New findings: oil				
Depletion: oil				
Revaluation of reserves				
Subtotal				
Minings (excluding oil)				
Produced assets	1,388,660	962,285	138,686	
Subtotal other industries:				
produced assets	86,261,250	8,040,171	4,516,998	
Manufacturing	21,863,054	2,202,818	2,280,025	
Construction	3,172,062	570,380	351,550	
Electric, gas, and water	7,321,540	1,184,763	119,029	
Trade, restaurant & hotels	12,680,012	1,184,119	237,712	
Communication and transportation	21,974,698	1,609,092	761,207	
Services	19,249,884	1,288,998	764,701	
Public administration and defense			3,774	
Nonproduced assets: land use	40,111,582			1,708,853

Table 10-11: Balance Sheets for Produced and Nonproduced Economic Assets, Classified by Economic Activity (millions of Mexican pesos) (continued)

Concept	Closing balance fixed assets	Opening balance stocks	Changes in stocks		Closing balance stocks
			Produced assets	Nonproduced economic assets	
Total					
Produced assets	106,873,338	8,006,083	986,544		8,992,627
Nonproduced assets	341,498,470	66,584,000		51,464,500	118,048,500
Agriculture					
Produced assets	5,696,412	61,472	-16,448		45,024
Nonproduced assets: land use	91,671,455				
Animal farming and breeding					
Produced assets	3,909,994	155,676	80,981		236,657
Nonproduced assets: land use	208,006,579				
Forestry: Produced assets	497,580	796	8,821		9,617
Fishing: Produced assets	434,496	38,926	7,774		46,700
Extraction of crude oil & gas					
Produced assets:	5,203,474	246,185	26,583		272,768
Nonproduced assets: oil					
New findings: oil				482,230	
Depletion: oil				-1,469,930	
Revaluation of reserves				52,452,200	
Subtotal		66,584,000		51,464,500	118,048,500
Minings (excluding oil)					
Produced assets	1,346,259	125,276	6,125		131,401
Subtotal other industries:					
produced assets	*89,784,423	7,377,752	872,708		8,250,460
Manufacturing	21,780,847	4,755,565	398,318		5,153,882
Construction	3,390,892	313,403	25,037		338,440
Electric, gas, and water	8,387,274	64,573	4,266		68,839
Trade, restaurant & hotels	13,632,419	1,949,790	386,695		2,336,485
Communication and transportation	22,822,583	98,164	19,468		117,632
Services	19,774,181	196,258	38,923		235,181
Public administration and defense					
Nonproduced assets: land use	41,820,436				

* The closing balance of fixed assets incorporates a deduction for consumption of fixed assets for government assets, even though no stocks of assets are measured for the government sector.

stock section of the table cover only oil reserves. Other nonproduced assets, such as standing timber, forest land and also air and water are not included in the table because these are treated as nonproduced environmental assets.

Nonproduced assets specified by industry are land used in agriculture and animal farming, and oil reserves depleted by the oil industry. Land used for purposes of urbanization is allocated to a group of industries together that include all except agriculture and animal farming, forestry, and oil and other mining.

The balances of produced assets by economic activities were especially compiled for the purposes of the present analysis in order to be able to determine the total stock of produced as well as nonproduced assets used in production. Opening and closing balances of produced fixed assets and stocks are obtained for all sectors, except for the government sector (public administration and defense).

Two revaluation elements are incorporated implicitly. The first one refers to revaluation of land when it is transferred from the environment (forest land) to economic sues. Contrary to what was done in Table 10-7, where land transferred was valued as forest land, land transferred to economic uses is valued in Table 10-11 at its value in economic uses (in agriculture, livestock holding, and urbanization). Therefore, any change in its value from forest land to land used for economic purposes is not explicitly presented in the table but included with net accumulation of nonproduced economic assets. The other revaluation element concerning oil is explicitly included in the stock section of the table as changes in stocks of nonproduced assets.

Comparative Analysis of Performance and Growth in SCNM and SCEEM

The information on value added and capital balances by activities can be used to assess each sector's performance and growth potential, using alternatively estimates that are linked to NDP, EDP1, and EDP2. This done in Tables 10-12 and 10-13 below. Table 10-12 has three sections: one presenting alternative distribution of NDP, EDP1 and EDP2 by economic activities; a second section comparing

the distribution of capital when using NDP or EDP1; and a third section comparing capital output ratios between the three types of concepts. Table 10-13 compares the environmental protection expenses made by each sector with the corresponding values of degradation effects.

The first section of Table 10-12 shows that there is a considerable change in the distribution of value added when environmental uses are incorporated. The sectoral contributions negatively affected are those of animal farming, forestry, and oil: The contribution of animal farming drops from 2.64 percent for NDP to 1.49 percent for EDP and to .93 percent for EDP2; the contribution of forestry drops from .54 percent through .15 percent to a contribution of -.08 percent; the oil sector's contribution drops from 3.50 percent through 0.00 percent to a -.20 percent. There are three sectors' contributions that increase or remain the same in the case of EDP1 and decrease again when degradation effects are taken into account for EDP2: The first sector is agriculture, whose contribution remains the same between NDP and EDP1 (that is, 5.61 percent) and decreases in the case of EDP2 to 5.57 percent; the contribution of electricity,gas, and water increases from .78 percent to .83 percent in the case of EDP1 and decreases to only .05 percent when also degradation effects are taken into account for EDP2; transport, storage, and communication is the other sector whose contribution increases from 5.72 percent to 6.06 percent for EDP1 and then decreases to 4.55 percent in the case of EDP2. On the other hand, the manufacturing contribution increases from 20.88 percent of NDP to 22.15 percent of EDP1 and 22.76 percent of EDP2, and the same applies to construction (4.09 percent of NDP, 4.20 percent of EDP1, 4.57 percent of EDP2), and there are minor increases for services, which are generally less depleting or degrading.

The second section of the table shows the changes in the distribution of capital between sectors, first including only produced assets (CAP), which is compatible with the concept of NDP, and then including produced as well as nonproduced economic assets (CAP1), which is compatible with the concept of EDP1. CAP

Table 10-12: Net Product Generated and Economic Assets Used in Economic Activities:
Comparative Analysis between NDP, EDP1, and EDP2 (billions of Mexican pesos)

	Agriculture	Animal farming, and breeding	Forestry	Fishing, hunting, etc.	Oil	Other mining	Manufac-turing	Electric, gas, water
Net product								
NDP	2,360,844	1,109,949	225,462	134,942	1,471,454	407,283	8,783,609	329,832
Percent distribution	5.61	2.64	0.54	0.32	3.50	0.97	20.88	0.78
EDP1	2,223,157	591,966	61,297	134,942	1,524	407,283	8,783,609	329,832
Percent distribution	5.61	1.49	0.15	0.34	0.00	1.03	22.15	0.83
EDP2	2,028,866	340,435	-29,173	134,942	-73,120	407,283	8,294,927	19,208
Percent distribution	5.57	0.93	-0.08	0.37	-0.20	1.12	22.76	0.05
Economic assets used								
CAP	5,681,165	4,048,273	496,803	476,037	5,479,119	1,495,798	26,776,674	7,921,114
Percent distribution	5.00	3.57	0.44	0.42	4.83	1.32	23.59	6.98
CAP 1	97,304,725	211,837,664	496,803	476,037	97,795,369	1,495,798		
Percent distribution	23.77	51.74	0.12	0.12	23.89	0.37		
Output/Capital Ratios (percent)								
NDP/CAP	41.56	27.42	45.38	28.35	26.86	27.23	32.80	4.16
EDP1/CAP1	2.28	0.28	12.35	28.35	0.00	27.23		

**Table 10-12: Net Product Generated and Economic Assets Used in Economic Activities:
Comparative Analysis between NDP, EDP1, and EDP2 (billions of Mexican pesos)
(continued)**

	Construc-tion	Trade, hotels & restaurant	Transport, storage & communica-tion	Other services (excluding government)	Government services	Subtotal other industries	Household production activities	Total production activities
Net product								
NDP	1,718,577	13,074,742	2,403,920	8,691,589	1,348,313	36,350,582		42,060,516
Percent distribution	4.09	31.09	5.72	20.66	3.21	86.42		100.00
EDP1	1,664,975	13,074,742	2,403,920	8,691,589	1,293,936	36,242,603		39,662,772
Percent distribution	4.20	32.96	6.06	21.91	3.26	91.38		100.00
EDP2	1,664,975	13,074,742	1,658,898	8,683,582	1,272,483	34,668,815	-1,029,735	36,448,314
Percent distribution	4.57	35.87	4.55	23.82	3.49	95.12		100.00
Economic assets used								
CAP	3,607,399	15,299,353	22,506,538	19,727,752	Non-available	95,838,829	Non-applicable	113,516,025
Percent distribution	3.18	13.48	19.83	17.38		84.43		100.00
CAP 1						136,804,839		409,406,417
Percent distribution						33.42		100.00
Output/Capital Ratios (percent)								
NDP/CAP	47.64	85.46	10.68	44.06		37.93		37.05
EDP1/CAP1						26.49		9.69

Table 10-13: Intersectoral Comparison between the Imputed Cost of Environmental Degradation and Environmental Protection Expenditures (billions of Mexican pesos)

	Agriculture	*Animal Farming and Breeding*	*Forestry*	*Fishing, hunting, etc.*	*Oil*	*Other mining*	*Manufac-turing*	*Electric, gas, water*
Environmental Degradation	194,291	251,531	90,470		74,644		488,681	310,624
Environmental Protection Expenditures								
Current			767		12,555	4,155	5,162	68,747
Capital			3,128		6,472	7,320	4	319,522
Total			3,895		19,027	11,475	5,166	388,269
Environmental protection expenditures								
As percentage of environ-mental degradation			4.31		25.49	Very High	1.06	125.00

Table 10-13: Intersectoral Comparison between the Imputed Cost of Environmental Degradation and Environmental Protection Expenditures (billions of Mexican pesos) (continued)

	Construc-tion	Trade, hotels & restaurant	Transport, storage & communica-tion	Other services (excluding government	Government services	Subtotal other industries	Household production activities	Total production activities
Environmental Degradation			745,022	8,007	21,453	1,573,787	971,396	3,156,119
Environmental Protection Expenditures								
Current				1,469		75,378	58,339	151,194
Capital				654		320,180	245,670	582,770
Total				2,123		395,558	304,009	733,964
Environmental protection expenditures As percentage of environ-mental degradation				26.52	Not Applicable	25.13	31.30	23.26

and CAP1 refer to average stock of capital between opening and closing stock, including changes in the closing stock due to revaluation. Only a CAP1 concept compatible with EDP1 is used, because there is no change in the stock of economic assets between EDP1 and EDP2. The changes in the capital distribution are particularly dramatic for agriculture, whose capital contribution increases from 5.00 percent to 23.77 percent; animal farming, where the increase is from 3.57 percent to 51.74 percent, and oil where it changes from 4.83 percent to 23.89 percent. The increase is matched by a dramatic decrease in the capital contribution of other industries, which drops from 84.43 percent to 33.42 percent in spite of the land used for urbanization, which is included in this category.

The considerable changes in the value added contributions to net product and capital participations of each sector between NDP, EDP1, and EDP2, result in equally drastic changes in the third section of the table, which examines the output/capital ratios, that are an indication of productivity in each sector. For agriculture (41.56 percent to 2.28 percent), animal farming (27.42 percent to .28 percent), forestry (45.38 percent to 12.34 percent) and oil (26.86 percent to 0.00 percent), there are considerable reductions, and for other industries there are minor reductions (37.93 percent to 26.49 percent). For the economy as a whole, this results in a reduction of the output/capital ratio from 37.05 percent to 9.69 percent.

When comparing in Table 10-13 the current and capital expenses by each industry on environmental protection services with the imputed value of degradation effects, there are also large differences. The average value of environmental protection expenses as a percentage of the total value of degradation effects for the economy as a whole is 23.26 percent. The percentage for individual industries is very high—that is, more than 100 percent—for other mining and for electricity, gas, and water. It is very low—that is, less than 5 percent—for agriculture, animal farming and breeding, forestry, manufacturing and transport, storage, and communication. Average percentages are found for oil, other services, and household consumption.

Limitations of the Study and Follow-up

In reviewing the results of this pilot study, one needs to keep their tentative nature in mind. First, a number of environmental and resource concerns were not covered (for example, biodiversity, ecosystem services, fisheries, marine environment, historical monuments). Second, the work represents only an initial pilot effort. The main emphasis in the first stage of developing the SCEEM was on identifying the relationship between different economic aggregates and environmentally adjusted aggregates. There was less emphasis on the quantitative accuracy of the environmental adjustments. Follow-up studies, to be undertaken by INEGI and others, are intended to improve the accuracy of data or estimates in selected areas, and also to provide analyses for other years, so that the effects of environmental adjustments on growth can be determined.

Bibliography

Ahmad, Y.J., S. El Serafy, and E. Lutz, eds. 1989. *Environmental Accounting for Sustainable Development.* Washington, D.C.: World Bank.

Bartelmus, P. C. Stahmer, and J. van Tongeren. 1991. *Selected Issues in Integrated Environmental-Economic Accounting.* International Association for Research in Income and Wealth, Special Conference on Environment Accounting, Baden (Austria) May.

Lutz, E., and M. Munasinghe. 1991. "Accounting for the Environment." in *Finance and Development,* Vol. 28, No.1, March, pp. 19-21.

Repetto, R. and others. 1989. *Wasting Assets: Natural Resources in the National Income Accounts.* Washington, D.C.: World Resources Institute.

United Nations. 1990. Revised system of national accounts, preliminary draft chapters (provisional).

United Nations. 1990. Prelimianry draft of "Part I: General Concepts," in *SNA Handbook on Integrated Environmental and Economic Accounting.* New York.

World Bank. 1991. "Mexico in Transition: Towards a New Role for the Public Sector," Report No. 8770-ME, May 22. Washington, D.C.

11

Issues and Options in Implementing the Montreal Protocol in Developing Countries

Mohan Munasinghe and Kenneth King

The global benefits of protecting the stratospheric ozone layer far outweigh the costs of doing so. A more efficient approach than merely meeting the fixed schedules of the Montreal Protocol would be to encourage an even faster phaseout of ozone depleting substances. A more equitable approach than merely reimbursing the low abatement cost countries (generally the developing countries) would be to share the global net benefits of ozone layer protection. Both objectives can be met if the global community provided financial incentives for early phaseout in the form of transfers that exceed incremental costs.

The paper discusses the special factors that affect the incremental costs and their relationship to national policies and strategies.

The depletion of the stratospheric ozone layer that protects the biosphere from harmful solar radiation has become a matter of increasing concern worldwide. Almost all of the past chlorofluorocarbon (CFC) accumulation, which is the primary cause of the ozone layer depletion, has been the result of economic activity in the industrialized world. Meanwhile, it is the inhabitants of higher latitude regions where the ozone layer appears to be thinnest that are more vulnerable. There is also an unknown but potentially serious global effect due to the generalized impact of increased ultraviolet rays on plant and animal life.

It is not surprising, therefore, that the initial recognition of the problem and impetus for action to limit the emission of ozone depleting substances (ODS) has arisen in the developed world. At the same time, the developing countries share the deep worldwide concerns about environmental degradation, and some are already taking steps to protect the ozone layer. However, they also face other urgent issues like poverty, hunger and disease, as well as rapid population growth and high expectations. The paucity of resources available to developing countries constrains their ability to undertake costly measures to protect the global commons. In brief, the crucial dilemma for them is to find ways to reconcile development goals and the elimination of poverty—which will require increased use of environmental resources—with responsible stewardship of the environment, and doing so without overburdening already weak economies.

Balancing Growth and Environmental Needs

The recent report of the Bruntland Commission (WCED 1987), which has been widely circulated and accepted, has presented arguments around the theme of sustainable development, which consists of the interaction of two components: needs, especially those of the poor segments of the world's population and limitations, which are imposed by the ability of the environment to meet those needs. The development of the presently industrialized countries took place in a setting which emphasized needs and de-emphasized limitations. The development of these societies have effectively exhausted a disproportionately large share of global resource—broadly defined to include both the resources that are consumed in productive activity (such as oil, gas and minerals), as well as environmental assets that absorb the waste products of economic activity and those that provide irreplaceable life support functions (such as the ozone layer). Clearly, any reasonable growth scenario for developing nations that followed the same material-intensive path as that of the industrialized world would result in unacceptably high levels of future ODS accumulation as well as more general depletion of natural resources.

A division of responsibility in this global effort emerges from the above arguments. The unbalanced use of common resources in the past should be one important basis on which the developed and developing countries work together to share and preserve what remains. The developed countries can afford to substitute environmental protection for further growth of material output. On the other hand, the developing countries can be expected to participate in the global effort only to the extent that this participation is fully consistent with and complementary to their immediate economic and social development objectives. Since most developing countries can hardly afford to finance even their present industrial development, to address global environmental concerns they will need financial (and technical) assistance on concessionary terms, that is in addition to existing conventional aid.

The Montreal Protocol

The international community, reacting through the United Nations, has recognized the danger presented by ozone destruction and decided to limit the damage and the risk by stopping the emissions of ODS (CFCs, halons, and substances having similar effects). This resolve took the form of the Montreal Protocol, signed in September 1987. The Protocol establishes schedules for gradual reductions in the consumption of ODS based on use within each participating country during 1986. The Protocol also places restrictions on trade in ODS with nonparties to the Protocol.

The Parties to the Protocol recognized the special situation of developing countries and undertook to facilitate their access to environmentally safe alternative substances and technology and to assist them in making expeditious use of such alternatives. The Parties also undertook to facilitate bilateral or multilateral subsidies to developing countries for that purpose. They recognized, in essence, that the reluctance of developing countries to ratify the Protocol was due to lack of financial resources necessary to meet the obligations without impairing their development efforts. Consequently, a special Multilateral Fund was set up to provide concessional finance and outright grants additional to those available from existing aid programs.

The Fund is jointly administered by the World Bank, the United Nations Development Programme, and the United Nations Environment Programme, with the World Bank handling the project financing arrangements. Grant financing is to be made available to eligible countries (that is, developing countries who are Parties to the Protocol and who consume less than 0.3 kilogram of ODS per person annually for eligible expenditures (the incremental costs of various phase-out projects). The expenditures that are reimbursable are listed in the London Agreements of June 1990. These include such items as incremental costs of production (for example, to reconfigure a plant to produce substitutes), equipment manufacture (for example, to retool refrigerator manufacturing to use alternatives to ODS), recycling, technical assistance, and training.

The phase-out in each country takes place in a policy context comprising overall economic policy, industrial strategy, and specific measures adopted to comply with the Protocol's provision for a National Ozone Policy (NOP). As financing from the Multilateral Fund is, in a sense, compensation by the developed countries for developing country action toward mitigating a global problem, it is not conditioned upon any policy reform or change in industrial strategy. Signatory countries are required, however, to produce a national implementation plan for their phase-out activities. It must show that the projects proposed for financing will meet the obligations under the Protocol and do so at least cost. Specific institutional steps and

regulations or other instruments of NOP will also be needed.

There are three broad requirements one might reasonably expect that both the Fund and National Ozone Policy to meet and which are discussed in this paper. They are: *Economic efficiency* (Can the goals be met in a cheaper way?), *Equity* (Who bears the burden of adjustment and will they be compensated fairly?), and *Effectiveness* (Will the specific mechanisms proposed be effective in achieving the goals?).

These broad requirements generally are in conflict. This is also the case in implementing the Protocol.

Issues in the Implementation of the Multilateral Fund

At the outset, it is interesting to consider how the efficiency of the Protocol as it now stands compares with alternative approaches. First, as shown in Figure 11-1, if we assume that global benefits (B) of ODS reduction exceed the costs (C) of implementation, then the Protocol-bounded path yields significant net benefits over the unbounded base case. Since the Protocol specifies a minimum compliance scenario, the basic objective for LDCs is to identify the path, such as D, which will satisfy the Protocol requirements at minimum incremental cost to the country.

Suppose the global net benefit of ODS reduction is $NB = B - C$. If the objective of the world community is to maximize NB, and if the benefits of a unit ODS reduction greatly exceed the costs (at least, for initial decreases), then the optimal path may be E which lies inside D. In fact, depending on how high incremental benefits are relative to costs, there will be a family of curves (such as E and F) all of which favor faster ODS phase-out than the Protocol. This still leaves us with the difficult practical problem of valuing the economic benefits of ODS use reduction.

Finally, if (as is very likely) administrative, institutional, human resource, and other problems place implementation constraints on the rate of ODS phase-out in developing countries, then curve G may be the appropriate limiting scenario. In this case, the valuation of benefits is not required in practice.

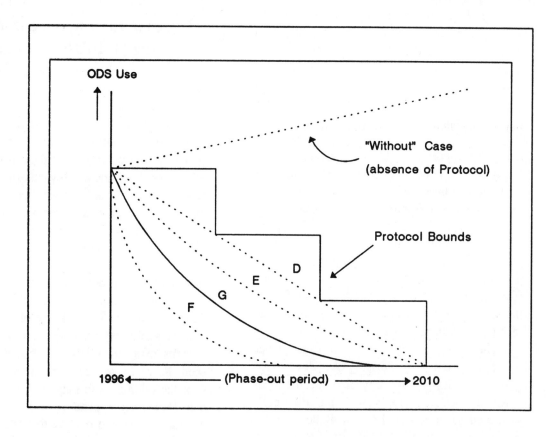

Figure 11-1: Benefits and Costs of ODS Phase-Out

Two issues arise from the foregoing discussion. The first concerns the extent to which incentives should be provided for countries to do better than the Protocol, perhaps to the limit of their implementation capability. The second concerns the exploitation, through market mechanisms and economic incentives, of the significant gains in speeding up ODS reduction in certain countries relative to others.

First, let us consider the issue of incentives for accelerated phaseout. In Figure 11-2, IC_D is the curve of incremental costs for phasing out ODS in a typical developing country, and IC_I is the corresponding curve in a relatively higher cost industrialized country. *IB* is the overall benefit to the global community, and this is assumed to greatly exceed incremental costs.

MN represents the typical compensation received by the developing country for eliminating one unit of ODS. The net global benefit of this activity (that is, global benefit minus the cost of providing compensation) is *NS*. This large surplus accrues to the global community generally; only a small fraction represents benefits for the host nation. Since *IB* is unknown (but large), suppose we use *MR* (that is, *KL*) as a proxy for benefits based on the known, *avoided* incremental cost in the industrialized country. Even with this conservative assumption, there is still a net global benefit *NR* associated with the ODS eliminating activity in the developing country.

The conclusion from the foregoing is that, if indeed incremental costs such as *MN* are small compared to net potential benefits, then the compensation provided to the developing country is the minimal amount. Therefore, some part of the significant net global benefit or surplus (for example, *NS*, or more conservatively *NR*) could be used as an *added* incentive to accelerate ODS phaseout.

Factors Affecting Incremental Costs

A number of general factors will affect the incremental costs of the transition, apart from those applying to individual ODS. These are the role of market forces, the timing of intervention in developing countries, expenditure on informational and administrative matters, and the overall strategy adopted.

Market Forces

The significant reductions in CFC use to date have been market driven in most countries. In some cases the use of ODS alternatives has actually been cost-effective and operating costs have been reduced (for example,, in replacing CFCs in aerosols). Export and local markets have been protected where industries have stopped ODS use before being required to do so by bans. Where satisfactory alternative technology exists, consumer preferences have been satisfied by non-ODS devices and preferences.

External markets also exert a powerful influence over the user sectors. For example, Brazil exports compressors to the United States and elsewhere, and Tunisia expects to export more than half of its refrigerator production to Europe. The ODS ban and new standards in these large markets which are Protocol signatory countries, will by itself force compliance in the exporting countries. Exports of foam products and aerosols will be similarly affected. Imports of ODS and equipment will bear the international price of these substitutes.

In other cases, where the objectives of the Protocol cannot be met by the free market, policy instruments that use market mechanisms are important because they can ensure that adjustment takes place in a cost-effective manner.

Timing

The developing countries have been given a ten-year grace period under the Montreal Protocol. That is, while developed countries are assigned a 1986 baseline consumption (from which the percentage reductions are computed) developing countries can continue expanding consumption until 1996 after which the reductions take effect. There is some evidence that this has introduced a note of complacency in developing countries who do not feel the urgency underlying the Protocol, and also led to certain other concerns discussed below.

The first concern is that because developing countries will be using a 1996 baseline for ODS use, the potential exists for unintentional or deliberate misforecasting of the 1996 ODS consumption level. The second concern is that the Protocol, by not providing incentives for

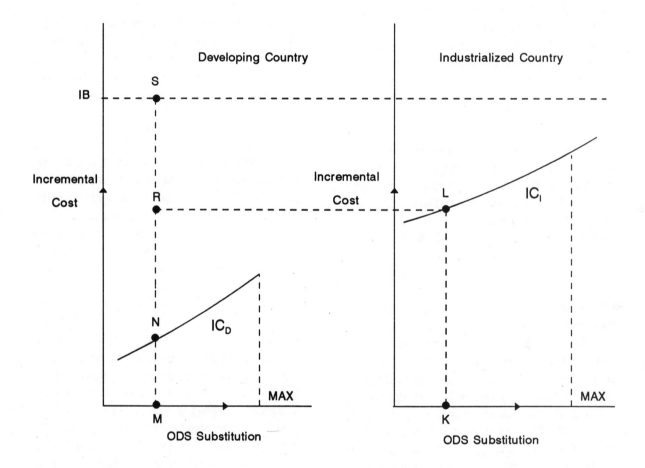

Figure 11-2: Incremental Costs and Benefits of ODS Substitution

aiming for a lower 1996 ODS usage, encourages ramping up consumption (especially when the levels of today are low).

Illustrative growth rates for near-term consumption of ODS are given in Table 11-1. While the actions underway or planned in several countries will actually reduce ODS consumption, the larger nations will expand consumption. The costs of delayed action will be high in countries where ODS use is expanding dramatically (for example, China, India, and Brazil) because the capital stock that ultimately requires modification or replacement will likewise be growing rapidly.

There are two types of delay, each of which imposes costs. First, delaying the target date allows the problem to grow much worse before corrective action is applied. Second, delays in taking action to meet a given target can lead to inefficient adjustment because the action taken is then too abrupt.

The first type of delay is reflected in the ten-year grace period granted to developing countries for the implementation of the phaseout targets. Although this grace period is based on considerations of equity—to reduce the burden on countries least able to afford the phaseout—it may have the perverse effect of increasing their ultimate costs of adjustment. Delays in pursuing ODS reduction in countries with potentially high growth in ODS use will increase the difficulty of ODS elimination. Data presented at a World Bank seminar in October 1990 suggest that if implementation were delayed, overall incremental costs in some countries could increase by about 60 percent, and consumer costs would increase sixfold in about a decade. This results from enormous growth in the domestic market for refrigerators and other CFC-using appliances that may more than offset declining ODS-substitute manufacturing costs resulting from rapid mastery of their production in developed market economies. (In China and India, for instance, it has been a conscious policy to increase the proportion of the population having access to refrigeration.) Not only will the incremental costs be increased, but the relative burden will be shifted more to consumers as refrigerators are purchased.

Information, Administration, and Infrastructure

Costs will be incurred on essential background information, administration, and infrastructure such as: studying the ODS industry within a country; establishing the framework for administering that country's obligations under the Protocol; developing a database on ODS production, trade, and consumption; conducting workshops on the new technologies; training a core group of technical experts in the application of non-ODS technologies; demonstrating new technologies; administering a tradeable ODS permit scheme within a country (if this is part of government policy to phase out ODSs); and designing infrastructure support, such as recovery and recycling facilities, and supply of alternative propellants like deodorized LPG; and ODS recycling and ODS destruction.

Country Incremental Costs

In deciding what "incremental costs" are, one must first distinguish between economic costs (costs to the country as a whole) and financial costs (those incurred by individual agents, such as firms and consumers). Financial costs include various transfer payments (such as interest payments, taxes net of rebates, and duties) that are not economic costs because they do not involve the use of resources or added value. Economic costs, on the other hand, include costs borne by others even if not paid for by the firm whose actions give rise to these costs. Additional unemployment, the external costs caused by pollution and additional infrastructure costs are examples of economic costs that are frequently not "internalized," that is, do not enter the financial calculations of firms.

The overall cost to the country of compliance would be the sum of all the economic costs of all the actions undertaken. The sum of all the financial costs is not a good indicator of country costs, because some significant costs are not included. In fact, there may be large differences between the overall national economic costs and the sum of all the private financial costs (see also Table 11-2).

Table 11-1: Indicative Growth Rates in ODS Consumption

Country	Current usage[1] (thousands of tons)	Expected average annual growth rate (percent)
China[2]	46	12
India[2]	11	15
Brazil[2]	11	8
Mexico[2]	7.9	2
Yugoslavia[3]	7.5	-10
Turkey[3]	4.6	-4
Egypt[3]	2.7	-6
Tunisia[3]	0.73	6

Source: World Bank estimates based on various studies.

1. Consumption in 1990 in terms of CFC-11 equivalent (i.e. ozone depleting potential [ODP]).

2. Based on projected change in ODP to 1996.

3. Based on projected change in ODP to 1993.

Table 11-2: Financial and Economic Incremental Costs:
Hypothetical Modified Plant to Produce ODS Substitutes

	Categories of Cost (millions of rupees)		
Incremental cost component	Private financial	Economic	Public financial
Capital[a]	862	862	---
Taxes and duties[b]	141	---	−141
Additional fuel[c]	71	187	116
Retraining[d]	43	43	---
Labor	---	---	---
Electricity[e]	20	38	18
Industry subsidy[f]	−110	---	110
Road widening and new local government waste disposal method	---	4	4
Pollution damage	---	10	10
Total incremental	1,027	1,144	117[g]

a. All incremental capital expenditure made in a single year.

b. Customs duties on imported components and other taxes paid are financial transfers but do not represent economic value-added.

c. This is an oil exporting country where internal (financial) petroleum product prices are below world (economic) prices, as part of national industrial strategy. In this example, future financial and economic costs are discounted at the same rate.

d. These are one-time worker retraining costs.

e. The financial cost of electricity to the firm is below the (economic) long-run marginal costs of production to the country.

f. The government stimulates investment in manufacturing, by providing a tax credit against income from any source.

g. This "balancing" cost is borne by the government and public at large.

The transition from a development path without constraints on ODS use to one constrained to meet the Protocol targets will impose resource costs on the economy. In principle, one would like to minimize these economic costs by implementing an appropriate "National Ozone Policy" and by judicious selecting of projects. In any case, sharper discussion is needed on the issues involved in practical estimation of incremental costs that are eligible for financing under the Multilateral Fund.

The principle is to minimize the incremental economic costs subject to the constraints defined by the obligation under the Protocol. In essence, the economic problem is the same as developing a least-cost investment program for, say, the power sector. Electric sector plans begin with demand forecasts and a range of technical options that meet the demand. Total capital and operating costs, appropriately discounted, are minimized using an algorithm that determines the selection and timing of feasible investments subject to a variety of imposed constraints. The reasonableness of initial assumptions concerning demand (a function of price) can be tested by extracting estimates of supply cost from the calculation. If necessary, these assumptions can be revised and the whole calculation can be performed iteratively until a desired degree of consistency and convergence is reached.

In the case of ODS phase-out, there are four special technical features to take into account that make the problem more difficult than least-cost programming in other sectors. The first special feature is the nature of the "without" and "with" situations that are being contrasted in order to arrive at an incremental economic cost. These scenarios are not always clearly spelled out, which can lead to confusion. Since there is no obviously right choice, selection will have to be made according to the purpose in hand. In the "without" situation, a choice has to be made whether losses connected to trade with developed countries that have ratified the Protocol are included (say, for compensation purposes). For example, if the desire is to compensate a developing country because

it will lose export markets or incur incremental costs in making its export goods suitable for Protocol signatories, then the "without" scenario should be defined as the one representing what would have been the case if no importing countries had imposed any of the Protocol's restrictions on trade or internal markets. If, on the other hand, trade losses are regarded as noncompensable (since there is no precedent for compensation for trade losses), the "without" scenario must assume that developed countries have ratified the Protocol but that the developing country in question has not done so yet.

In the "with" situation, a major question is whether the cost structure (and hence the price signals and resulting demand patterns) have been in any way affected by assumed levels of compensation by way of government transfer payments or grant finance from the Multilateral Fund. That is, under the assumption that the adjustments are made without compensation by the Fund or the government, incremental costs will be passed on by the producer or manufacturer down to the customer who, in response to higher prices, will consume less of the substitute. If, on the other hand, compensation for incremental costs flows through to the firm, its actual financial costs will be offset. To the extent the market is competitive, its prices will be less than they would have been and projected consumption of demand for ODS services need not be adjusted from what it would have been had no phase-out taken place. Depending on the "without" and the "with" scenario selected, different estimates of incremental cost can be derived.

The second special feature is that the demand for the services of existing ODS must be disaggregated for each one. There are six groups of controlled substances defined by the Protocol, each with its own chemical properties, type of use, and sector of application. In principle, as outlined previously, one should compare total cost and benefit streams obtained in an integrated framework by using the benefits specific to the reduction of each particular substance (for example, by weighing emissions in terms of their ozone-depleting potentials),[1]

---

[1] Because of some scientific uncertainties and data gaps on proposed weights such as ozone- depleting potential (ODP) and chlorine-loading potential, this may not be practical in all cases.

and by discounting future benefits of reduced emissions, which would value more highly the earlier reductions and encourage earlier compliance. In practice, the Protocol stipulates phase-out schedules for the substances and hence the benefits are fixed; only the costs need to be minimized. Furthermore, the phase-out schedules are applicable on a group basis. This means the problem is the sum of six separate reduction strategies with no tradeoffs allowed between substances in different groups. [2] Ideally one should trade off reduction rates among all the ODS until the marginal benefit of a unit reduction in ODS is the same for all. Also, because the Protocol stipulates reduction targets (for example, a 50 percent reduction on baseline consumption for Group II substances by year 2006), the benefit stream in each scenario is implicitly the same with no acknowledgement of any additional discounted benefits resulting from earlier than normal compliance.

The third special aspect concerns data adequacy. In the case of power and water sector development plans, for instance, reasonably accurate demand forecasts and good technoeconomic data for costing alternative supply options at different scales of operation are available. This is not the case for ODS substitution because demand patterns and price elasticities have not been extensively researched, rapid technical change is expected to have a large but unknown impact on supply costs within the planning period, and the cost reductions due to learning and to scaling up of new techniques can only be estimated. Although several alternative technologies are commercially available and have good cost data (such as aqueous cleaning as a substitute for CFC-113 cleaning and CFC-12 recycling system for mobile air conditioners), the cost of emerging technologies (such as HCFC-141b for solvent cleaning and HFC-134a for refrigeration), are less certain.

The fourth special feature is that the costs of ODS phase-out will be highly distributed; they are not borne by one or two utilities or corporations but by a variety of producers, users, and consumers. Additional costs may also be imposed on the government by the need for

administrative measures and infrastructure. And there may be costs on the economy as a whole due, for instance, to consequential unemployment, although these may not be large or easily quantified.

Finally, in determining incremental costs, each cost has to be calculated twice; once for the least-cost Protocol-constrained (or "with") solution, and once for the unconstrained (or "without") case. Incremental cost is the difference between the two.

The analysis requires projections of demand for ODS services, the constraints placed on individual ODS use (that is, the phase-out profiles), a technically feasible program of appropriate substitutions and alternative technologies to meet the demand for ODS services within the constraints set for the ODS themselves, cost data on the current technologies and the alternatives, and the choice of the least-cost approach. (See the box for a summary of these steps.)

Calculating Country Compliance Costs

Step 1: Project demand for ODSs.

Step 2: Ascertain the Protocol's constraints on consumption.

Step 3: Technically assess the most appropriate substitutes and alternative technologies for replacing ODSs.

Step 4: Propose alternative scenarios using these substitutes/alternatives to satisfy the demand for the services of ODSs, but within the constraints for ODS consumption.

Step 5: Calculate the incremental cost of each scenario relative to the without Protocol case.

Step 6: Select the scenario with the minimum incremental cost; this is the compliance cost.

Effect of Country Policy on Country Incremental Costs

Although compliance costs should be minimized, it should be recognized that compliance takes place against a background of a country's policies that are specific to the phase-out as well as those that are general in application

---

[2] Within groups, tradeoffs are implicitly allowed as the consumption subject to control under the Protocol is calculated as the ODP-weighted sum of consumptions in each group.

(but assumed to be fixed). These policies will not only influence the overall level of compliance cost, but also distribute the burden of adjustment differently among various sectors of the economy.

Economic and Industrial Policy

A country's general policies will strongly influence the costs of compliance. An extreme example would be a country that had encouraged small-scale, inefficient domestic production of CFCs behind high trade barriers; in this case compliance with the Protocol would actually remove a distortion and incur a negative incremental cost. More generally, key factors will include the country's development strategy, such as degree of outward orientation; industry strategy, including trade protection and restrictions on ownership and competition; regulatory and incentive structure, including legislation and the tax structure; and institutional capacity to implement regulations.

National Ozone Policy

In addition to the compliance cost (that is, the minimum cost of the phase-out, given the general policies of the country), additional costs will be inevitably introduced by inefficiencies in the adjustment process. One goal of the government adopting a national strategy for protection of the ozone layer would be to minimize these inefficiencies as well.[3] The distinction between compliance costs and inefficiencies in the adjustment process is useful to make, because these costs are related to different policies (the pre-existing industrial policy versus the adopted National Ozone Policy) and can be controlled in different ways.

Incremental Costs to Firms and Individuals

Economic agents (firms of producers and users, and individual consumers) will face incremental costs as the country moves, under the influence of National Ozone Policy, to satisfy the Protocol targets. In many ways the issues and analyses of these private incremental costs parallel those of the compliance costs of countries.

Rational economic agents will minimize their own financial costs—but not necessarily country costs because the policy is often highly distorted. Cost minimization may also entail strategic behavior, especially where the ozone policy provides for compensation and other transfers.

Actual incremental costs need to be evaluated in a dynamic framework—a program with a time dimension. Consumers' incremental costs may be those incurred over the lifetime of new appliances, for example, replacement of a CFC-based refrigerator before the end of its normal economic life, increased energy requirements for operation, and higher recharge expenses, followed by the earlier subsequent replacement of the refrigerator. User firms may experience one-time retooling costs followed by continued higher operating costs. Producers too would need to alter the selection and sequence of investment projects and operations.

As in the case of calculating country compliance costs, certain technical features and imposed characteristics must be recognized. First, there are six groups of controlled substances. Although there is some flexibility of substitution within a group (for instance, reducing relatively more halon-1211 than halon-1301 while still maintaining the overall target reduction for Group II as a whole), substitution between groups is not credited for compliance purposes, even between groups having the same target reduction profile. So economic agents must respond to at least six sets of regulations.

Second, data are scarce. As the elasticities of demand for ODS and related equipment and products are barely known, price effects on demand will be very poorly understood. This will be important for a producer who shifts to a high-cost substitute. Added to the lack of data on elasticities is the uncertainty of supply costs of substitutes from sources outside the country or from domestic producers affiliated with multinational producers. In fact, after the Montreal Protocol, major ODS producers and users in industrialized countries invested substantial

---

[3] A good National Ozone Policy is still required even when compliance costs are negative. For example, scrapping an industry that is CFC-dependent but also uneconomic might result in a certain net gain if handled well. If handled badly, the resulting adjustment inefficiencies might reduce this net economic gain.

financial resources on development of substitute processes. The two large U.S. producers, Du Pont and Allied Signal, have announced plans to have substitutes for ozone-depleting CFC products by the year 2000. The substitute products are likely to have more specialized applications than existing products. For example, industry sources expect about eight chemicals to replace the many applications serve presently by using CFC-11 and CFC-12. Whether the substitutes will be able to benefit from the same economies of scale as the existing ODS is, therefore, uncertain.

Third, there is the issue of passing on the costs between the affected groups. Under normal competitive conditions, incremental producer costs would be partially passed on in the form of higher prices to downstream user groups and ultimately consumers, depending on supply and demand. In this case there are additional complications. One is the extent to which incremental costs might be compensated by the government (or the Fund) and thus not passed on, and the other is the extent to which other aspects of National Ozone Policy might be redistributive.

Economic and Industrial Policy

General economic policy will definitely impact on the incremental private financial costs. (See Table 11-2 for an illustration of the impact of an investment tax credit.) This shows not only that different policies will entail different incremental costs for the economic agents involved in the phase-out, but also that incremental financial and incremental economic costs can differ substantially too as a result of transfer payments inherent in the tax system (and as a result of other costs borne by the government and the public at large shown in the last "balancing" column).

National Ozone Policy

National Ozone Policy seeks to implement the Protocol and, in the process, may redistribute the incremental costs between groups. This will have to be considered in the calculation of the incremental costs actually experienced. For example, ozone tax credits or subsidies will lessen the burden for some, perhaps even affecting the incentive structure and the demand.

One important feature of ozone policy will be in providing a "level playing field," so that those firms undertaking incremental investments for compliance purposes will not be disadvantaged in a competitive market for their goods and services compared with more tardy firms.

Issues and Options for National Ozone Policies in Developing Countries

The standard types of policy instruments for the control of pollution are regulation, pollution taxes, marketable permits, and deposit/refund schemes. These should be viewed in the light of special features of the pollution problem of ozone-depleting substances.

Special Features Affecting Choice of Policy Instruments

First, there is the *incentive framework* provided by the Fund. The Multilateral Fund under the Protocol has been created to reimburse the incremental costs of specified projects within the developing signatory countries. This means that moral persuasion and international pressure are the only incentives for governments in these countries to take difficult domestic policy decisions to minimize these incremental costs. This is likely to be rather difficult politically because the ozone problem is seen as being largely the result of developed country action. Transfers under the Fund are also seen as compensation for the costs borne by developing countries in mitigating a problem that will fall more heavily on developed countries. Furthermore, the incentives within countries may tend to maximize the transfer of resources by ensuring that no eligible project or incremental cost goes unnoticed.

One interpretation of the incremental costs that are eligible for reimbursement by the Fund is that they are only the private financial costs borne by firms. If so, there is still some incentive for the government to ensure that those adjustment costs not included in the financial costs are minimized. For example, it is important for a country to get the long-term industrial structure right to avoid misallocation of investment and other resources. This means among other things that consumer investment in CFC-technologies should be limited to prevent long-term welfare losses due to lack of serviceability.

Second, there is a complex *distributional issue*. Supposing it were decided to speed up the phase-out in order to maximize benefits, as suggested earlier. In that case, restrictions on CFC production and use would be sudden and severe, and might impose heavy losses on entrepreneurs such as owners of production facilities in the developing countries. Thus if ODS bans are implemented immediately, governments will be tempted to provide adequate compensation to firms penalized by these requirements rather than to adopt a "polluter pays principle" whereby the losses are simply absorbed where they fall. However, reimbursement of a producer's incremental costs is a subsidy for a particular new technology (such as HCFCs). It will, therefore, be inefficient since it also subsidizes commercial risk and implicitly penalizes other forms of substitution. For domestic distributional reasons and because of the way the Fund is set up, this efficiency loss may be unavoidable if the phases-out pace is quick.

In fact, developing countries are not under this time pressure and have been granted a ten-year grace period. However, taking full advantage of this grace period may not be in a country's best interests for the reasons mentioned earlier. Also, depending on how competitive the various ODS industries are within the country, the benefits of any grant financing for incremental costs may or may not be passed on to final consumers. Manufacturers may in fact have a windfall gain.

Third, it is generally acknowledged that the benefits of phasing out CFCs (avoided damage due to ozone depletion) far exceed the relatively *modest costs*. See, for example, UNEP (1989). This greatly favors the rise of quantitative instruments (such as bans and percentage reductions) over price instruments. The latter are less certain in their effects, entailing a risk of significant loss of benefits, even if they are less efficient (although efficiency losses are likely to be small in comparison).

Fourth, the *urgency* of the problem makes it unlikely that a new philosophy of environmental pollution control can be established for ozone-depleting substances. Historically, pollution has almost always been the subject of "command-and-control" approaches and this is still generally the case in the United States today. Sophisticated approaches such as marketable permits should be used wherever such systems are used for domestic pollution control. But few developing countries are expected to use them. Given the short time span available, mandated technology standards, bans, reductions, and direct government investments will be more effective.

Fifth, there will be minimal concern over the *dynamic incentives* of the policy instruments. Developing countries are followers in the field of ODS and ODS substitutes, and the most effective way for them to acquire new technology will be through technology transfer from multinational corporations in the developed signatory countries.

Sixth, the problem is a *transitional problem*, not one of constructing an efficient long-run equilibrium. Ozone-depleting substances will have to be phased out completely.

Seventh, the *industry structure* is such that there are very few producers and importers (sometimes only one or two), several user firms (for example, refrigerator manufactures), and vast numbers of consumers. Thus requirements of centralized information and ease of enforceability clearly suggest that direct controls be applied on upstream producers and users, while downstream users should be left to respond to market forces.

Eighth, because of obvious *informational and enforcement problems*, control must be exercised on the production and disposal of the ODS, not on their emissions. It is far easier to monitor and control production, import, recycling, and disposal of CFCs and halons, rather than their direct release to the atmosphere, which occurs from millions of point sources after long lag times.

National Strategies

There are three broad country types insofar as national ozone policies are concerned, distinguished by the degree of *import dependency*:

- Those that import everything, that is, ODS and ODS-using equipment. Most of the smaller developing countries are in this category.

- Those that manufacture some equipment themselves, such as refrigerators, but import ODSs. Several medium-sized developing countries are in this category, such as Egypt, Yugoslavia, and Turkey.

- Those that manufacture at least some ODS (and generally also the equipment). Some larger developing countries are in this category, notably China, India, Brazil, and Mexico.

Several countries are also linked to external markets through exports as well as through imports. The ODS industries in these countries are, therefore, likely to retool and adjust anyway in signatory countries, to protect their markets. For example, Brazil exports refrigerant compressors to the United States, and Tunisia hopes to expand into the European market for domestic refrigerators. The adjustments they make for export markets will service internal markets as well. In this case, the major national policy issue in adjusting to the Protocol is to structure incentives for limiting purely domestic use.

The general policy imperative would be to minimize the domestic (economic) costs of adjustment net of any external transfers of technology (from multinational corporations) and resources (through the Fund) likely to be available.

As a minimum, and whatever category the country falls in, National Ozone Policy will entail the following measures:

- Giving domestic firms and consumers early warning of the future measures and cutbacks required. In this way, adjustment will be less disruptive and costly.

- Administering the compensation payments available under the Fund, that is, identifying eligible projects and assisting in quantification of incremental costs.

- Providing information and possibly technical assistance and retraining. The purpose is to facilitate adoption of cost-effective technologies (such as use of alternative aerosol propellants), or to adjust to changes in export markets.

It is unlikely that the phase-out will cause significant employment or other macroeconomic effects. In most cases, the ODS industries constitute a very small part of total industrial activity.

The general approach suggested in the discussion on policy instruments is one centered on quantities of ODS in circulation, not directly on emissions. This is also in line with the Protocol itself which seeks limitations on total ODS consumption, defined as net imports plus production less destruction. Direct regulation of the amounts available upstream provide the certainty needed to meet phase-out targets, but allowing consequential price rises to flow to downstream users provides some of the efficiency of charge-based policy instruments. Other general interventions would be those that facilitate the adjustment, including market responses where appropriate, such as providing information or technical advice and retraining of servicemen to limit consumer welfare losses associated with existing ODS appliances. Some special attention may be needed if there are general economic distortions that interfere with economic adjustment and if there are any "loopholes" due, for example, to imports of equipment containing ODS or to stockpiling or recycling.

Controls Affecting Consumption

In all three categories of country import dependency previously outlined, the primary policy instrument will be a regulation of the quantity of ODS supplies. Although this will provide sure control over the phase-out, there are some problems.

First, there may be more than one supplier (importers and producers), and the supply quotas will have to be allocated among them. Auctioning marketable permits may suffer from buyer collusion as it is unlikely that there are many importers. This may not matter very much, because the main advantage of these permits is certainty of impact. Allocation could also be done pragmatically either by voluntary industry agreements (as in Mexico) or by grandfathering, that is, by equal percentage reduction for existing importers.

Second, price increases resulting from the quantity controls on ODS are likely to give suppliers a windfall profit until the phase-out is complete. On equity grounds (and perhaps to raise revenue), the government could introduce a windfall profit tax or impose a compensating excise duty on ODS. Note that this fiscal measure is not a primary instrument, it merely corrects for some of the bluntness of the regulatory instrument, which is primary.

Third, although the Protocol stipulates a few target dates for specified reductions, it is otherwise silent on the required reductions in any given year. National Ozone Policy can fill in the targets for the intervening years as well. In fact this would help to minimize overall adjustment costs, since doing nothing until the target date would make the transition abrupt and costly, with steep consequential price changes flowing to downstream users.

Fourth, the broad approach advocated above assumes that the market downstream will allocate restricted supplies of ODS among users and induce switches in a cost-effective manner: rising ODS prices will cause substitution by those users who can switch most cheaply. While this is a reasonable presumption, it does not necessarily assure a cost-effective outcome for the country. Major distortions in the ODS market may affect the outcome and negate its economic cost-effectiveness. For example, taxes and/or subsidies may affect the relative prices of substitutes for various users. If there are large distortions like this, some corrective may be needed. Otherwise they should be ignored, because of the time and cost of information gathering.

Fifth, the control of supplies alone will not ensure that ODS use is reduced. The quota could be partly circumvented by stockpiling ODS in the years before the quotas take effect (not only creating an alternative source of supply but also building up a bigger baseline of imports) or by importing goods with ODS incorporated in them (such as aerosol cans and refrigerators). If these appear to be anything other than minor or temporary flaws, then these sources of ODS should be included in the total sources of supply and subject to the same supply reductions.

For a given consumption target, there are supplementary means by which a government can reduce welfare losses. One is to promote conservation of ODS. For example, large quantities of CFCs are vented during the servicing of domestic refrigerators in developing countries; appropriate training and technical assistance to servicemen can reduce such losses dramatically and help sustain the economic life of existing ODS-dependent appliances. A second approach is for recovery of ODS from old appliances for recycling, as recycled supplies are not part of consumption controlled by the Protocol. Even if it is uneconomic to recycle recovered ODS, it should be destroyed (say, by incineration) because destruction increases the allowable level of imports (the Protocol target is net of destroyed ODS). A third method is to encourage retrofits on large equipment to make it suitable for using alternatives. The costs of training technical assistance, recovery, recycling, destruction and retrofits are "incremental" and eligible for grant financing under the Montreal Protocol.

Ideally, recovery and recycling schemes should be instituted to the extent that they are cost-effective. The benefits are that either a greater amount of ODS remains within the system (given any target of net consumption), thereby reducing adjustment costs, or that ODS consumption undershoots the target. These benefits are difficult to quantify, but clearly some criterion of "reasonable cost" needs to be applied to such schemes.

Other supplementary regulations would be restrictions on the importation of ODS equipment and appliances so as to discourage both the buildup of capital stock that will become prematurely obsolete when ODS is unavailable and the bidding up of the price of the available ODS supply. Alternatively, this might be left to the market, with the government requiring only full disclosure to potential buyers.

Controls Affecting Equipment Manufacturing

In this case, the primary controls over ODS supply are assumed to be in place. There are, however, additional measures for the efficient adjustment of manufacturing industry. Allowing the increased scarcity of ODS to be reflected in prices will encourage those who can minimize ODS use at low cost to do so.

Users (such as refrigerator manufacturers and firms engaged in foam blowing) would receive additional encouragement because they would be eligible for funding under the Montreal Protocol to cover their incremental costs, such as retooling. The higher cost of ODS lessens any advantage that delaying such retooling might have given. The grant financing is also an effective subsidy for the equipment that uses ODS alternatives.

Controls Affecting ODS Production

In those countries that produce ODS, a supply constraint is needed that includes not only imports and stockpiles, but also local production. Supply quotas (whether grandfathered or auctioned, and preferably marketable) could be the primary instrument, with downstream price rises allowed to take effect as before.

Conclusion

Two sets of issues concerning the Fund and the Protocol have been explored: those concerning the design and administration of the Fund as a global policy instrument, and those involved in complying with the stipulations of the Protocol at the national level.

At least in the initial years of the resource transfer, it is preferable to emphasize speed of the phase-out rather than the search for a strictly least-cost solution in each country. Yet, because of the way the Fund is currently set up, much of the effort until now has had to focus on the latter, particularly in defining the incremental costs that currently form the basis for compensation. Yet the incremental cost concept is a difficult one to apply consistently or to use in cost-minimization calculations for the phase-out of ozone depleting substances.

Another factor that must be considered is that national policies to implement the Protocol will be influenced by the Fund's incentive framework and by other special features of the ozone problem. For these reasons, such policies may deviate from what are supposed to be the most economically efficient approaches to phase-out.

Bibliography

King, K., and M. Munasinghe. 1991. *Incremental Costs of Phasing Out Ozone Depleting Substances*, World Bank Environment Working Paper No. 47. Washington, D.C.: September.

United Nations Environment Programme (UNEP). 1989. *Economic Panel Report: Montreal Protocol on Substances that Deplete the Ozone Layer*. Nairobi: UNEP.

World Commission on Environment and Development (WCED). 1987. *Our Common Future*. Oxford, England: Oxford University Press.

Appendix

List of Workshop Participants

1. Hussein Abaza
Assistant Policy Adviser to ED and
CIDIE Coordinator
United Nations Environment Programme

2. Nessim J. Ahmad
Resource Economist, Technical
Advisory Division
International Fund for Agricultural
Development

3. Noreen Beg
Consultant, Environmental Policy and
Research Division
World Bank

4. Jose Cartas
Executive Director for Argentina
Inter-American Development Bank

5. Tim Clarke
Principal Administrator, Directorate
General for Development
Commission of the European Communities

6. U. Dabholkar
Economist, United Nations
Environment Programme

7. Arthur H. Darling
Senior Research Economist, Project
Advisor's Office
Inter-American Development Bank

8. Partha Dasgupta
Professor, University of Cambridge

9. Lual Deng
Division Chief, Environmental and
Social Policy Division
African Development Bank

10. D. French
Senior Programme Adviser
(Natural Resources)
Evaluation and Policy Division,
World Food Programme

11. Christian Gomez
Advisor, Office of the Executive
Vice-President
Inter-American Development Bank

12. Karl Goran-Maler
Director, Beijer Institute

13. I. Higuero
Environmental Economist
Organization of American States

14. Kenneth King
Senior Environmental Specialist
Environmental Policy and Research
Division, World Bank

15. Anil Markandya
Professor, University College London

16. Mohan Munasinghe
Chief, Environmental Policy and
Research Division
World Bank

17. Mario E. Niklitschek
Economist, Sanitation and Urban
Development Division
Inter-American Development Bank

18. F. Petry
Economist, Economic and Social
Policy Department
Food and Agriculture Organization
of the United Nations

19. Roberto Alfredo Recalde
Economist, Department of Regional
Development and Environment
Organization of American States

20. Richard Saunier
Senior Environmentalist
Organization of American States

21. Adelaida A. Schwab
Consultant, Environmental Policy and
Research Division
World Bank